D0987248

# THE IRISH BRIGADE
# AND ITS CAMPAIGNS

Capt. David Power Conyngham, Irish Brigade staff officer
(Courtesy Library of Congress)

# THE IRISH BRIGADE
## and Its Campaigns

*by*

D. P. CONYNGHAM

*Edited, with an Introduction, by*

LAWRENCE FREDERICK KOHL

Fordham University Press
New York

Copyright © 1994 by Fordham University Press
All rights reserved
LC 94-9301
ISBN 0-8232-1578-4
ISSN 1044-5315
Irish in the Civil War, no. 4
Third Printing 1997

Library of Congress Cataloging-in-Publication Data

Conyngham, David Porter, 1840–1883.
    The Irish brigade and its campaigns / by D. P.
Conyngham ; edited with an introduction by Lawrence
Frederick Kohl.
        p.  cm. — (Irish in the Civil War, ISSN 1044-5315 ;
    no. 4)
        Includes bibliographic references and index.
        ISBN 0-8232-1578-4
        1. United States. Army of the Potomac. Irish Brigade.
2. United States—History—Civil War, 1861–1865—
Participation, Irish        American. 3. Irish Americans—
History—19th century. I. Kohl, Lawrence Frederick. II.
Title. III. Series.
E483.I683C66  1994                              94-9301
973.7'41—dc20                                   CIP

PUBLICATION OF THIS BOOK WAS AIDED BY A GRANT
FROM THE HARRY J. SIEVERS, S.J. MEMORIAL PUBLISHING FUND

Printed in the United States of America

# CONTENTS

Illustrations following page 448.

# ACKNOWLEDGMENTS

This new edition of David Power Conyngham's *Irish Brigade and Its Campaigns* is part of a much larger project on the Irish in the Civil War that I have been engaged in for a number of years. During that time I have received the help of numerous people, and I hope one day to acknowledge fully the depth of my gratitude for their assistance. Here, however, I want to give a special thanks to those whose efforts have directly contributed to this volume. Most important was the help of Michael Fitzgerald of Thurles, County Tipperary, Ireland, who shared with me the fruits of his own research on the life of Conyngham. James Jordan of Dublin, in a voluminous correspondence, gave me a great many valuable insights into the Irish contributions in the Civil War. Peter Lysy and Charles Lamb helped me locate important materials in the University of Notre Dame Archives. Kenneth Powers of Westport, Connecticut, and Collin MacDonald of Leesburg, Virginia, gave me their usual great support and provided key illustrations. Danny Lorello of the New York State Archives went above and beyond the call of duty by supplying information at a moment's notice. My colleague Rich Megraw gave the introduction a thorough reading, making my prose more felicitous than it would otherwise be. Finally, my wife Maureen worked many long hours on the index when she was already exhausted from the million and one things she normally does to keep our family functioning. To all of these generous people, I am very grateful.

Research for this volume benefited from financial support furnished by the Research Grants Committee of the University of Alabama, the New York State Archives Research Residency Program, and the National Endowment for the Humanities.

# INTRODUCTION:
## The Irish Brigade, Irish-America, and David Power Conyngham

*Lawrence Frederick Kohl*

Every March seventeenth, New York's 69th Regiment leads the St. Patrick's Day Parade up Fifth Avenue in Manhattan. In December, the faithful still gather in Fredericksburg, Virginia, to lament the destruction more than 130 years ago of the 69th and the other regiments of the Irish Brigade on Marye's Heights. An "Irish Brigade Association" devotes itself both to discovering and celebrating the achievements of this famous unit in the Civil War. Re-enactors use their "living history" techniques to portray the experiences of several Irish Brigade regiments. The Irish Brigade of the Army of the Potomac has not been forgotten. Yet, it has never quite received the attention that its fascinating and illustrious history deserves. Few brigades on either side in the Civil War could boast of so distinguished a military record, and no comparable unit had such a distinctive character and such an unusual perspective on the nation's greatest crisis.

William F. Fox, a nineteenth-century authority on the fighting capacity of Civil War units, declared that the Irish unit was "perhaps the best known of any brigade organization, it having made an unusual reputation for dash and gallantry. The remarkable precision of its evolutions under fire, its desperate attack on the impregnable wall at Marye's Heights; its never failing promptness on every field; and its long continuous service, made for it a name inseparable from the history of the war." Even those who were sometimes critical of the brigade acknowledged the pre-eminence of its military standing. George Alfred Townsend, an English war correspondent who had little use for the Irish, maintained that "when anything absurd, forlorn, or desperate was to be attempted, the Irish Brigade was called upon." This may not have been literally true, though it is remarkable how often the brigade found itself in the hottest fighting of the war. It sustained its martial reputation through nearly every major action in the Eastern Theater, but it distinguished itself most in the Bloody Lane at Antietam, before the stone wall at Fredericksburg, in the wheatfield at Gettysburg, and assaulting the Bloody Angle at Spotsylvania.[1]

Statistics demonstrate that the brigade's fighting reputation was well deserved. It served in the Northern army that sustained the most casualties (Potomac), the corps that suffered the most casualties (2nd), and the division that experienced the greatest losses in that corps (1st). The brigade itself sustained more than 4,000 casualties during the course of the war, despite the fact that it never put as many as 3,000 men in the field at any time. All five of its regiments (63rd, 69th, and 88th New York; 28th Massachusetts; and 116th Pennsylvania) were on Fox's list of the 300 Union regiments that sustained the heaviest losses in battle. And two of them, the 69th New York and the 28th Massachusetts, ranked among the top ten out of more than 2,000 Northern regiments in the number of combat deaths. During the war, two soldiers died of disease or accident for every one who died as a consequence of battle. For the Irish Brigade, however, this ratio was reversed: two died of battle wounds for every one who died of disease or accident. These men knew how to remain healthy in camp and on the march so that they could make their sacrifices where they counted.[2]

One of the reasons for the fighting qualities as well as the health of the brigade was the presence within it of colorful veterans of European armies who were experienced in the ways of war. Captain John Gossen, a staff officer in the brigade, had previously served with the Seventh Hussars of Austria, a dashing Hungarian regiment. W. L. D. O'Grady of the 88th New York had served in Britain's Royal Marines before coming to the United States. He volunteered for the 88th only two hours after landing in New York, giving his address on the enlistment papers as "my regiment." Captain P. F. Clooney, also of the 88th, was a veteran of the Irish Brigade of St. Patrick that defended the Papal States from Garibaldi in 1859–60. The Irish Brigade also profited from the skills of a

distinguished surgeon, Francis Reynolds, who had served on
the medical staff of the British Army in the Crimean War.
Such veterans helped the less experienced men in the brigade
to cope successfully with camp life and they steadied their
ranks when under fire.[3]

For sheer dash and color, however, it would be difficult to
top the exploits of the brigade's commander, Thomas Francis
Meagher. An Irish revolutionary sentenced to be hanged,
drawn, and quartered by the British government, he became
the darling of Irish-America in the Civil War years. His death
sentence was commuted to banishment for life in Tasmania,
but he did not remain there long. After making a bold escape
by sea in 1852, he landed in New York City to the cheers of the
immigrant Irish. Meagher then set about making a new life,
marrying the daughter of a rich New York merchant, editing
an Irish-American newspaper, practicing law, exercising his
justly famous oratorical powers, and involving himself in a
number of Central American adventures. But none of these
roles quite suited him, and, like so many other restless Americans, he found new opportunities in the Civil War. As captain
of a Zouave company in the 69th New York State Militia, he
added to his earlier laurels a martial reputation earned at the
Battle of Bull Run. And, with the regiment's commander,
Michael Corcoran, languishing in a rebel prison after the battle, the way stood open for his own advancement. Meagher
threw himself into recruiting regiments for an all-Irish
brigade that would be offered to the War Department. He was
first given the command of one of the regiments with the understanding that the Irish-born General James Shields would
assume command of the brigade. When Shields turned down
the offer, however, everyone looked to Meagher. His appointment as brigadier general came through in February of 1862
and he took command of the brigade a month later at its camp
in Virginia.[4]

Meagher had much to do with establishing the Irish
Brigade's reputation both for combat ferocity and camp life
frivolity. He not only stood in the thick of the fury, leading the
brigade into its most furious action, he also gathered around
him a staff of spirited young officers with a taste for fun. One
visitor to their camp described them as "fox hunters . . . , a

class of Irish exquisites, they appeared to be,—good for a fight, a card party, or a hurdle jumping,—but entirely too quixotic for the sober requirements of Yankee warfare." The brigade's celebrations of St. Patrick's Day were legendary in the army. Horseraces, athletic contests, dances, theatricals, and recitations marked the day, all well lubricated with whatever spirits came to hand. The brigade was also the center of the Fenian "Officer's Circle" in the Army of the Potomac, the focal point of an Irish revolutionary group bent on the liberation of Ireland from British rule. This circle drew its members from all over the army on the first Sunday of every month, ostensibly to conduct political business, but once serious matters were out of the way, the circle turned its attention to mixing a distinctive milk punch made from whiskey, condensed milk, nutmeg, lemons, and a little hot water. Then, stories of the old sod and poetry from the brigade's resident bard, Surgeon Laurence Reynolds, carried the gathering well into the night.[5]

The Irish Brigade was not, then, just another Civil War unit. Its military reputation alone set it apart from the great mass of Northern brigades. But what made its story particularly distinctive was the Irish and Catholic identity that most of its members shared. Nearly 150,000 Irish-Americans eventually fought in the Union army, but most served in predominantly "American" units where their achievements seldom redounded to the benefit of the Irish-American community. The Irish Brigade was specifically created to preserve this special identity and to advertise the important contributions to the Union cause that Irish Catholics made. Its founders wanted to demonstrate to a skeptical America the devotion Irish-Americans felt for their adopted land. But their motives were mixed, and sorting out their allegiances was not easy. The story of Irish-American attitudes toward the issues of the Civil War is a complex one.[6]

The Irish were not likely candidates to rush to the Union war effort. Most were recent arrivals who had not been welcomed with open arms. The terrible years of the potato famine had pushed more than two million of the Irish overseas, with the

United States becoming the most popular destination. Between 1846 and 1854 well over a million found their way to America. Desperate poverty caused these refugees to crowd into tenements and "shanty towns" in the worst part of the North's urban areas. Willing to accept the poor wages and terrible working conditions, they soon drove blacks out of the most menial employments the North had to offer. By the 1850s Irishmen made up the bulk of the common laborers, dock-workers, coachmen, draymen, waiters, cooks, barbers, and servants in the cities. Elsewhere, Irish workers poured into the mining industry and they dominated canal and railroad construction.[7]

Their poverty alone might have made them outcasts, but the Catholic faith of the Irish also subjected them to the scorn of Protestant America. Anti-Catholicism had its roots deep in Anglo-American history. The earliest settlers of British North America had been steeped in a culture intolerant of Catholics. By the 1820s, an organized "Protestant Crusade" of "No-Popery" began to appear. Throughout the antebellum era this cry was raised, resulting in fierce anti-Catholic riots, the notorious burning of a convent, and the creation of local political parties dedicated to stemming the tide of Catholic immigration. Dread of a Papal conspiracy to undermine republican America combined with economic fear of wage competition from impoverished Irish workers to create a powerful reaction against the massive Irish immigration of the famine years.[8]

The 1850s saw the rise of a national political movement to "war against the immigrant." An "American Party," better known as the "Know-Nothings" for its members' standard answer to questions about their secret rituals, very nearly became the dominant force in American politics by its appeals to anti-immigrant animus. The Know-Nothings attacked the Irish for their poverty, their religion, their Democratic politics, their intemperance, their criminality, their devotion to the old country, and their attempts to sow discord between the United States and Britain. The political tide of anti-slavery eventually submerged the nativist movement of the 1850s, though anti-Irish attitudes and discrimination hardly ceased with the demise of the national political party that had temporarily embodied them.[9]

The Irish had nearly as much reason to reject the new Republican party as they had the nativist party it supplanted. As staunch Democrats, Irish-Americans would have opposed any party contesting their dominance of American politics, but their opposition to the Republicans rested on an even firmer foundation. They were well aware that most of the nativists and temperance reformers who had earlier attacked them from the American party had found a new political home among the Republicans. Moreover, the Republicans had dedicated themselves to the liberation of black Americans from slavery, a development that would threaten the precarious foothold the Irish had on the lower rungs of the social ladder.[10]

The Irish hatred of blacks stemmed largely from the intense economic competition between these two groups in America's unskilled labor market. When the famine Irish flooded into America's cities, it was largely black labor that they pushed out. The black leader Frederick Douglass complained in 1855 that "every hour sees us elbowed out of some employment, to make room perhaps for some newly arrived immigrants, whose hunger and color are thought to give them title to a special favor." In many cases, however, employers found blacks acceptable, but noted in their ads that "Irishmen need not apply." Society's contempt could not have been made more clear than it was in an ad for household help that sought applicants of "any country or color except Irish." The anger and frustration the Irish felt from experiencing such prejudice was often turned against blacks, and observers remarked that the Irish detested them even more than the English or the American whites who looked down on them from a position of social superiority.[11]

When the secession crisis came, then, the Republican party could hardly expect to gain an enthusiastic following among the Irish for its war to subdue the South. Nevertheless, Irish-Americans in the North staunchly supported the Union at the outbreak of war, and they answered the country's call to arms as readily as any group in society.[12]

There were four main reasons for the surprisingly strong Union sentiment among the Irish. The first reason was the intense American nationalism of the Irish. Many of their leaders, despite having opposed Lincoln and his party before the war, felt compelled to defend the constitutional integrity of the country that had provided them with an asylum from tyranny and persecution at home. The New York *Irish-American* called on its readers "by the sacred memories of the past, by your remembrance of the succor extended to your suffering brethren, by the future hope of your native land here taking root . . . to be true to the land of your adoption in this crisis." The Boston *Pilot* was well aware of the prejudice the Irish had encountered in America and it had resolutely rejected the party of Lincoln in the 1850s, but in 1861 it told its Irish-Catholic readers that they must "Stand by the Union; fight for the Union; die by the Union." The feeling was general that, whatever hardships the Irish had met with in America, they owed it a great deal, and allegiance to the government in its hour of need was one way to repay that debt.[13]

A second reason for Irish support focused less on the acknowledgement of a standing debt and more on the expression of a future hope. Many Irish felt that participation in the war offered an opportunity to overcome nativist suspicions. They might prove that "although the Celts be hyphenated Americans in name, they were one hundred percent Americans indeed." The Boston *Pilot* looked toward the day when future generations of Irish-Americans could proudly say that "we too are Americans, and our fathers bled and died to establish this country." They may have been overly optimistic when they believed that Irish valor on the battlefield would erase generations of engrained prejudice, but in 1861, as the government sought to rally every group in society around the flag, anything seemed possible.[14]

Irish hostility to Britain also contributed to their support for the Union. This perspective had several elements. First, the perceived British support for the Confederacy naturally increased Irish support for the North. Second, many believed that the break-up of the Union would only enhance British power in the world and that, in fact, for this reason the British themselves earnestly desired the destruction of their young republican rival. Third, if a war of liberation for Ireland were ever to be launched, America would be its logical base of operations and the Civil War could provide valuable military experience for the men who would obtain Ireland's freedom. One Irish-American poem made the point succinctly:

> When concord and peace to this land are restored,
>     And the union's established forever,
> Brave sons of Hibernia, oh, sheathe not the sword;—
>     You will then have a union *to sever*.[15]

A final reason for the flood of Irish soldiers into the Union army in 1861 can be found in the hard economic times that accompanied the secession crisis. The dislocation of the economy caused by secession hit the working classes hardest. Unemployed Irish laborers and domestic servants often found enlistment in the army to be the only alternative to starvation. Such general economic pressures would ease as the war went on, but economic incentives to enlist, which the government later enhanced with large enlistment bonuses, would always have their greatest impact on impoverished Northerners like the Irish.[16]

Despite all the reasons for Irish support for the Union, their enthusiasm for the war did not last. By 1863 it became very difficult to recruit new members for Irish regiments and most Irish leaders had turned against the war. By then Washington's purposes had come to include black emancipation, a goal that Irish-Americans could not support with the same zeal they had mustered in defense of the Union. Nor did it appear that the war would enhance opportunities for the liberation of Ireland. What was apparent was that too many Irishmen would never have the chance to fight for Ireland because they had spilled their blood in an American war instead. The Boston *Pilot* lamented in 1863 that "We did not cause this war, [but] vast numbers of our people have perished in it." It flatly declared that "the Irish spirit for the war is dead! . . . Our fighters are dead." The New York draft riots of that year brought to a boil the simmering Irish resentment at sacrificing their lives for the advancement of their hated black adversaries. Many Irish-Americans continued to enlist and to fight in the Union army, but neither their numbers nor their spirit matched the early days of the war.[17]

That there was never anything intrinsic about Irish support for the Northern cause is evident from the fact that those who settled in the Southern states had no trouble in accepting the logic of that section on the war. In many ways it was probably a more natural position for them. Being fundamentally conservative rural people whose Catholic faith resisted the kind of abstract idealism that motivated the abolitionists, the Irish could readily defend the Southern way of life. There, too, the cult of white supremacy and the institution of slavery ensured that they would never slip to the lowest rung on the social ladder. Finally, they could see the South's attempt to break from the American union as analogous to Ireland's longing to wrest itself free of its British connection.[18]

Nor did the Irish who remained in the old country show any strong allegiance to the Northern cause. In fact, Irish opinion was overwhelmingly against Lincoln's attempt to preserve the Union by force. A basic conservatism, an abhorrence of the bloodshed, a hostility toward Protestant abolitionists, resentment of Northern recruiting efforts in Ireland, and a horror at the idea of Irishman fighting Irishman on American battlefields all conspired to turn most inhabitants of Ireland against the war.[19]

One of the few exceptions to this rule was the sympathy for the Union cause felt by some extreme Irish nationalists, though they were clearly more interested in the fate of Ireland than in the young republic across the ocean. They thrilled to the exploits of Irish soldiers in the war, believing that the reputation of all Irishmen benefited from the courage demonstrated by such units as the Irish Brigade. "It has restored the somewhat tarnished military prestige of our race," declared the Fenian *Irish People*. "It has restored the Irish people's weakened confidence in the courage of their hearts and the might of their arms." They also had hopes that in tangible ways the war in America might facilitate the liberation of Ireland. A victorious North could supply arms and experienced Irish warriors to throw off the British yoke. Like their countrymen in America, however, the nationalists' hope faded as they watched their best fighters die on American, not Irish, battlefields.[20]

David Power Conyngham had a long career in Ireland and America as a revolutionary leader, novelist, war correspondent, Civil War staff officer, newspaper editor, government bureaucrat, and historian. Despite this fact, remarkably little is known about his life, and the few sources of knowledge about him are often vague and incorrect. Even the precise date of his birth is unknown. While some sources report it as being as late as 1840, it seems almost certain that he was actually born sometime in 1825 in Crohane, County Tipperary, Ireland. He was the eldest son of John Cunningham and his wife, Catherine Power, well-off tenant farmers. Presumably, the young Conyngham received his early education at one of the "hedge schools" in the area and he later attended Queens University Cork, though he left without receiving a degree. His family hoped he would enter the priesthood, but he found himself pulled in another direction.[21]

In the 1840s Conyngham became associated with the "Young Ireland" movement, an Irish nationalist group dedicated to the repeal of the constitutional union of Ireland with England. Young Ireland was born in 1842 with the creation of *The Nation*, a weekly newspaper that catered to a more radical form of Irish nationalism than the popular reformer Daniel O'Connell espoused. After the onset of the famine and the death of O'Connell, Young Irelanders called openly for rebellion. Orators such as Thomas Francis Meagher, Smith O'Brien, Richard O'Gorman, and John Dillon blamed England for causing the famine by its unjust laws and then aiding it to exterminate the Irish population. But while their impassioned speeches called for physical force, they did little to actually prepare for the crisis they were precipitating.[22]

An alarmed British government acted quickly to round up some of the most outspoken leaders, but several managed to lead a brief and relatively bloodless rebellion in the summer of 1848. The lack of arms and food seems to have sapped whatever revolutionary fervor had existed among the people. Large crowds sometimes turned out to hear the rising's leaders castigate British rule, but they melted away quickly when they found that no food was to be provided to potential rebels. The famine may have exacerbated the hatred of the English, but it had placed seemingly impossible hurdles in the way of effectively acting on that hatred. Conyngham served as a local leader in the rising, and was indicted along with many others for his part in it. When the others were arraigned, however, Conyngham was nowhere to be found. He may have gone into hiding or even left the country. In any case, he was never prosecuted and for a number of years he simply disappeared from view.[23]

He resurfaced in the mid-1850s when he began contributing articles to the *Tipperary Free Press*, published in Cashel. He also began his literary career. His first novel, *The Old House at Home* by "A Tipperary Boy," appeared in 1859. This story detailed the suffering of the O'Donnells, a starving Tipperary peasant family during the famine years, under the "heartless evictions of Lord Clearall, the treacherous, unprincipled conduct of his agent, Mr. Ellis, and his sanctimonious protege, the Rev. Mr. Sly." Emigration to America, however, allowed young Frank O'Donnell to make good and return to Ireland to buy back the family home. In 1861 Conyngham republished the novel under a pseudonym, Allen H. Clington, and a new title, *Frank O'Donnell*. When, many years later, he published an American edition, he used his real name and retitled the work *The O'Donnells of Glen Cottage*.[24]

Although the evidence is slight, it appears that Conyngham first came to the United States in 1861, perhaps sent as a war correspondent (or at least acting as one) for *The Dublin Irishman*. Exactly where he spent 1861–62 and what he did is something of a mystery, though it is clear that he made at least one trip back to Ireland during this period. In February of 1862 he married Anne Corcoran in Killenaule, County Tipperary. She was also of a comfortable farming family and a few years younger than Conyngham, who was by then about 37 years old. The marriage did not work out, however, and before the year ended Conyngham was back in America by himself. Over the next decade he made several trips to Ireland, perhaps to heal the rift, but apparently his efforts failed.[25]

The first evidence of Conyngham's contact with the Irish Brigade is his account of visiting its camp during the Christmas holidays after the Battle of Fredericksburg in December of 1862. Reportedly he carried with him letters of introduction from Smith O'Brien and P. J. Smyth, important Irish nationalist leaders. He told the officers who entertained him that he was "enthusiastically attached to the Brigade and to its general" and he expressed a long-held desire to be made an honorary member of the general's staff, a wish that was granted on the spot. That he served the brigade well was evidenced by General Meagher's letter of 1863 thanking him for his "gallantry and other soldierly qualities" while acting as one of his aides at the Battle of Chancellorsville. It is quite possible that Conyngham left the brigade when Meagher resigned after Chancellorsville, as his writings do not suggest that he was an eyewitness to the rest of the brigade's campaigns for 1863.[26]

In August, Conyngham was appointed a war correspondent for the *New York Herald*. The *Herald*, run by James Gordon Bennett, had the largest circulation of any paper in the United States, built primarily by providing the most complete and up-to-date news coverage of the era. Bennett spared no expense in ensuring that his paper beat out all others in bringing war news to an eager public. He hired dozens of correspondents like Conyngham to follow the armies and collect information. As Conyngham himself explained, the *Herald's* correspondents were charged with brief but comprehensive responsibilities: "to obtain the most accurate information, by personal observation, and forward it with the utmost dispatch, regardless of expense, labor, or danger." Conyngham's earlier experience as a correspondent for the *Dublin Irishman*, as well as his service as a staff officer for General Meagher, no doubt provided him with the proper credentials to obtain such a post. Moreover, Conyngham had written a long account of the Battle of Chancellorsville that was carried by the *Herald*. This piece probably brought him to Bennett's attention and gave sufficient evidence of his ability to the *Herald's* demanding owner and editor.[27]

Conyngham accompanied the Army of the Potomac as a war correspondent in the Fall 1863 campaigns, but there is little evidence of his exact whereabouts until March 1864, when he was reassigned to Sherman's army camped outside of Chattanooga. He accompanied Sherman for the rest of the war, watching the fall of Atlanta, making the march through Georgia, and following the army's final campaign into the Carolinas. While traveling with the army he also served on the staff of Brig. Gen. H. M. Judah, and was wounded while carrying dispatches for him at the Battle of Resaca.[28]

When the war ended, Conyngham joined the editorial staff of the *Herald* in New York, but he seems to have spent most of his time in the year after Appomattox writing accounts of his wartime experiences. The first work to appear was *Sherman's March Through the South* (1865), a vivid, first-hand chronicle of his days with the western armies. It was the only book he ever wrote that was completely divorced from his Irish heritage and that had no purpose to preserve or to celebrate Irish history and culture. In *Sherman's March* Conyngham provided the country with an honest and revealing description of the soldiers' behavior during this controversial campaign, sparing neither Northerner nor Southerner in his condemnation of wrongdoing. And fittingly, in a work he dedicated to his *Herald* mentor James Gordon Bennett, he took General Sherman to task for his attempt to censor the press during the campaign.[29]

Upon finishing the Sherman book in September 1865, Conyngham immediately set to work on his history of the Irish Brigade. Such a work had evidently been in his mind from the beginning, as he revealed in his introduction that when he was with the brigade he had collected materials with an eye to communicating "the gallant exploits of that noble little band." The result would be a very different kind of book from his eyewitness account of Sherman's army. Since his own days with the brigade may have been limited to the period from Christmas 1862 to Meagher's resignation in the Spring of 1863, he had to rely on the records of others to draft large sections of the book. He wrote to the New York State Adjutant General's Office to obtain its reports of the first years of the war. He also relied heavily on the letters of "Gallowglass," James B. Turner of Meagher's staff, to the New York *Irish-American* for their rich accounts of life in the brigade. Finally, he made no attempt at all to chronicle the last years of the brigade when he was with Sherman, turning that job over to one of the brigade's learned surgeons (and staunch Irish nationalists), William O'Meagher.[30]

Despite these limitations, *The Irish Brigade and Its Campaigns* remains, well over a century after its publication, the standard work on the subject. It is very uneven in reporting the combat experience of the brigade, but its vivid accounts of particular episodes, its wit and humor, its Irish nationalist perspective, and particularly its diligent attempt to gather biographical data on the men who served in the unit make it an indispensable source for anyone seeking to understand the experience of the Irish in the Civil War.

The clear purpose of the work was to celebrate the accomplishments of Irish arms, "to rescue from oblivion the glorious military record we have earned in America." To remember the feats of Irish soldiers would accomplish two highly desirable goals: to instill a nationalistic pride in Irishmen everywhere and to remind Americans of the debt they owed the immigrant who gave his life to defend the integrity of the Union. Such sacrifice on Civil War battlefields, Conyngham declared, "gives us a stronger claim to the protection and gratitude of the American nation." Further, the book sought to defend the Irish against the charge that they acted as mercenaries in the war. The Irishman, Conyngham maintained, fought because "the safety and welfare of his adopted country and its glorious Constitution were imperilled." He fought not as a mercenary, but as a patriot, defending "the great principles of democracy."[31]

The object of *The Irish Brigade and Its Campaigns* was not, as some readers might be tempted to conclude, the glorification of war. Ethnic pride, political principle, or even Irish nationalism perhaps, but Conyngham had seen too much of war to want to glorify it for its own sake. Elsewhere he revealed his view of war's realities:

> Those who are unacquainted with war cannot realize the fearful sufferings it entails upon mankind. They read of it in papers and books, gilded over with all its false glare and strange fascinations, as a splendid game of glorious battles and triumphs, but close their eyes to its bloody horrors. The battlefield is to them a field of honor, a field of glory, where men resign their lives amidst the joys of conquest, which hallow the soldier's gory couch and light up his death features with a smile. This sounds well in heroic fiction, but how different the reality! Could these fireside heroes but witness a battle-field, with its dead, its dying, and wounded, writhing in agonizing tortures, or witness the poor victims under the scalpel knife,

with the field hospital clodded with human gore, and full of the maimed bodies and dissected limbs of their fellow-creatures, war would lose its false charms for them.[32]

Perhaps to Conyngham it was the very horror of war that made the sacrifices of those who endured it so worth remembering.

During the period Conyngham was working on his Irish Brigade book, he was also trying to obtain a post in the U.S. foreign service. He seems to have had some connections that might have been able to bring this about, perhaps through the *New York Herald*, but for the stumbling block that he was not a U.S. citizen. He discovered that if one were mustered out of a Civil War regiment as a commissioned officer one could qualify for immediate citizenship, so he prevailed upon P. H. Jones, an Irish-born former general who had served under Sherman, to ask the governor of New York to appoint him as an officer in some unit that had not yet been mustered out of the U.S. service. Jones succeeded in getting Conyngham appointed a second lieutenant in the 68th New York Infantry, but the regiment was mustered out of the service before he could reach them. Evidently, this spelled the end of Conyngham's scheme to obtain a consular post.[33]

Instead, Conyngham stayed in the New York newspaper world, where he would remain for most of the rest of his life, taking the helm of a New York Fenian paper, *The Irish People*, in 1866. He edited *The Irish People* for only a little more than a year before founding a new paper in partnership with P. H. Gill, *The Staten Island Leader*. Sometime later he joined the *Sunday Democrat* as part owner, and was functioning as editor of this weekly at least as late as 1873. He apparently left this position to accept an appointment in the New York Post Office Department sometime between 1873 and 1879. A novel of Conyngham's, published in the latter year, was dedicated to the New York Postmaster, Thomas L. James, for being his "esteemed patron" and for his "earnest devotion to the broad principles of civil and religious liberty." At his death in 1883, Conyngham was managing editor and part owner with Michael Kerwin, a prominent Fenian, of still another weekly, the *New York Tablet*. As might be expected, under Conyngham and Kerwin the *Tablet* was a strongly Irish nationalist paper.[34]

Despite his life-long involvement in it, journalism never consumed all of Conyngham's time. During the post-war period Conyngham also poured out a steady stream of historical and literary works on Irish topics. While his history of the Irish Brigade is the best known today, in his own time he was more widely known for his works on the Irish church, *Lives of the Irish Saints* (1870) and *Lives of the Irish Martyrs* (1873). Widely recognized as substantial works of scholarship on Irish religious history, these books were reprinted many times during the nineteenth century, were reissued together as *Lives of the Irish Saints and Martyrs*, and were later incorporated into a larger compilation with Rev. Thomas Walsh, entitled *The Church of Erin: Her History, Her Saints, Her Martyrs, Her Monasteries and Shrines* (1885). In recognition of this service to the Roman Catholic church, the University of Notre Dame conferred an honorary doctor of laws degree on Conyngham in 1873 and Pope Pius IX sent him a special letter of commendation.[35]

Conyngham also returned to his literary pursuits in the post-war period, turning out three more novels using Irish history as a backdrop. *Sarsfield, or the Last Great Struggle for Ireland* (1871) dealt with Patrick Sarsfield, the seventeenth-century Irish military hero, best known for his defense of Limerick from William III in 1690. *O'Mahoney, Chief of the Comeraghs* (1879), was based on stories he heard of his native Tipperary during the Irish rebellion of 1798. The story concerned the fight of the last Gaelic chieftan of the Comeragh Mountains against the fiendish Earl of Kingston who terrorized the peasantry from his Michelstown castle. The novel climaxed with the rising in Wexford. Conyngham's last novel, *Rose Parnell, The Flower of Avondale* (1883), also focused on the events of 1798. In the introduction, Conyngham described its heroine as "the embodiment of all the noble and patriotic qualities which have characterized the Parnell family down to the present day." He also confessed, in an admission that could apply to all his literary works, that "the story was a historical romance, which, under the guise of fiction, tries to infuse a patriotic spirit into the hearts of my readers, as well as to educate them in the duties they owe to their native country."[36]

Conyngham's final work, finished only days before he died, was *Ireland: Past and Present* (1883), a history of Ireland written in collaboration with J. C. Curtin. The work gives ample evidence that, even in his last days, none of the passion that had ignited Conyngham's Irish nationalism in 1848 had cooled. Though the book was touted as a complete history of Ireland "from the earliest settlement of the country down to the present day," it gave disproportionate attention to Ireland's resistance to British rule in the preceding century: the Rebellion of 1798, the agitation to repeal the Act of Union, the events of 1848, the Fenian rising, and the Land League movement. The struggle would never end, for "there never was, nor never shall be, any bonds of affection between the two countries, for wrong, oppression, and coercion on the part of England have driven the iron so deeply into the heart of Ireland, that the sore will continue to fester and rankle even if the barb were removed."[37]

Death came rather suddenly to David Power Conyngham. When he succumbed to pneumonia on April 1, 1883 at his home in New York, even his best friends were caught by surprise, and most learned of his passing from an obituary in the daily papers. His ending, however, seemed to presage the enduring importance of his connection with his Civil War experience. His obituary referred to him as "Major" Conyngham, an honorary title bestowed upon him by the state of New York in 1867 for his "gallant and meritorious services in the late war." The Irish Brigade Association, meeting at the 69th Regiment Armory on Lexington Avenue in New York shortly after his death, passed a series of resolutions praising "our beloved friend, comrade, and historian." William O'Meagher, brigade surgeon and part-author of *The Irish Brigade and its Campaigns*, saw to it that these resolutions were published in the *New York Tablet*, organized his funeral, and served as chief pall bearer as he was laid to rest in New York's Calvary Cemetery.[38]

He left behind one unpublished manuscript, a history of Catholic religious heroism in the Civil War that he had been compiling for nearly a decade. The manuscript, "Soldiers of the Cross: Nuns and Priests on the Battlefield," still lays un-published in the University of Notre Dame Archives, though its fate has been little worse than that of most of his published works. Today they are extremely difficult to find even in major research libraries, and their acidic paper causes them to crumble to dust in the hands of the researcher lucky enough to locate a copy of one of them. Conyngham's life has receded into obscurity along with his works. Even more than 60 years ago when a researcher at Notre Dame sought to dis-cover some traces of the man, his best source lamented that Conyngham "was once a familiar New York figure," but in the "years since his passing his name and fame also have van-ished as far as the present generation is concerned." The chief exception to this dimming of remembrance is Conyngham's work on the Irish Brigade. Reprinted many times in recent years, it serves to keep his memory, along with the Irish Brigade's, green.[39]

## NOTES

1. William F. Fox, *Regimental Losses in the American Civil War* (Albany: Albany Publishing, 1889), p. 118; George Alfred Townsend, *Campaigns of a Non–Combatant* (New York: Blelock, 1866), p. 130.

2. Fox, *Regimental Losses*, pp. 67, 115, 118, 3, 169, 202, 204, 217, 292. On the brigade's reputation of being one of the healthiest units in the Army of the Potomac, see also below, p. 250.

3. See below, p. 555; W. L. D. O'Grady Pension File, National Archives, Washington, D.C.; below, pp. 560, 559.

4. The standard account of Meagher's life is Robert G. Athearn, *Thomas Francis Meagher: An Irish Revolutionary in America* (Boul-der: University of Colorado Press, 1949). See also Michael Ca-vanagh, ed., *Memoirs of Gen. Thomas Francis Meagher* (Worcester, Mass.: Messenger Press, 1892).

5. Townsend, *Campaigns,* p. 130; below, pp. 372–87; Thomas Francis Galwey, *The Valiant Hours* (Harrisburg, Pa.: Stackpole, 1961), pp. 74–75.

6. Ella Lonn put the number of Irish soldiers at 144,221 in her *Foreigners in the Union Army and Navy* (Baton Rouge: Louisiana State University Press, 1951), p. 578, though this figure may be too low. She relies on the calculations of Benjamin A. Gould in *Investi-*

*gations in the Military and Anthropological Statistics of American Soldiers* (New York: U.S. Sanitary Commission, 1869), which are suspect with respect to the Irish. James Jordan to the editor, Feb. 3, 7, 27, 1989, letters in possession of the editor.

7. R. Dudley Edwards and T. Desmond Williams, eds., *The Great Famine: Studies in Irish History*, 1845–52 (Dublin: Browne and Nolan, 1956), p. 328, 388; Kerby A. Miller, *Emigrants and Exiles: Ireland and the Irish Exodus to North America* (New York: Oxford University Press, 1985), pp. 280–344; Leon F. Litwack, *North of Slavery: The Negro in the Free States, 1790–1860* (Chicago: University of Chicago Press, 1961), pp. 162–66.

8. The best account of antebellum anti-Catholicism is still Ray Allen Billington, *The Protestant Crusade*, 1800–1860 (New York: Macmillan, 1938).

9. Ibid., pp. 262–436.

10. Florence E. Gibson, *The Attitudes of the New York Irish Toward State and National Affairs, 1848–1892* (New York: Columbia University Press, 1951), p. 120; Lonn, *Foreigners in the Union Army*, p. 42; Albon P. Man, Jr., "The Irish in New York in the Early Eighteen-Sixties," *Irish Historical Studies* 7(Sept. 1960), pp. 96–100.

11. Litwack, *North of Slavery*, pp. 162–66.

12. Lonn, *Foreigners in the Union Army*, pp. 42–3, 147; Gibson, *Attitudes of the New York Irish*, pp. 121–7, 133, 136; Man, "Irish in New York," pp. 100–108.

13. Lonn, *Foreigners in the Union Army*, pp. 42–43; below, pp. 5–6, 8; Man, "Irish in New York," pp. 101–103; Francis R. Walsh, "The Boston Pilot Reports the Civil War," *Historical Journal of Massachusetts* 4 (June 1981), p. 7.

14. Man, "Irish in New York," p. 103; below, p. 8; Walsh, "Boston Pilot Reports the Civil War," pp. 8–9; Miller, *Emigrants and Exiles*, pp. 324–25.

15. Lonn, *Foreigners in the Union Army*, pp. 74–75; below, p. 6; Man, "Irish in New York," pp. 103–105; Lawrence Frederick Kohl, ed., *Irish Green and Union Blue: The Civil War Letters of Peter Welsh* (New York: Fordham University Press, 1986), pp. 100–104.

16. Miller, *Emigrants and Exiles*, pp. 360–61; Lonn, *Foreigners in the Union Army*, p. 75; Man, "Irish in New York," pp. 105–108.

17. Gibson, *Attitudes of the New York Irish*, pp. 141–44, 169; Miller, *Emigrants and Exiles*, p. 343; Walsh, "Boston Pilot Reports the Civil War," pp. 9–12.

18. Jason H. Silverman, "Stars, Bars, and Foreigners: The Immigrant and the Making of the Confederacy," *Journal of Confederate History* 1 (Fall 1988), pp. 280–83; Ella Lonn, *Foreigners in the*

*Confederacy* (Chapel Hill: University of North Carolina Press, 1940), pp. 53–55; Phillip Thomas Tucker, *Father John Bannon: The Confederacy's Fighting Chaplain* (Tuscaloosa: University of Alabama Press, 1992), p. 13.

19. The best works on the Irish view of the American Civil War are all by Joseph M. Hernon, Jr., "The Irish Nationalists and Southern Secession," *Civil War History* 12 (March 1966), pp. 43–53; "Irish Religious Opinion on the American Civil War," *Catholic Historical Review* 49 (Jan. 1964), pp. 508–23; *Celts, Catholics & Copperheads: Ireland Views the American Civil War* (Columbus: Ohio State University Press, 1968).

20. Even the nationalists were torn by the issues of the American Civil War. Their support for the Union conflicted with their opposition to some of the North's key policies and their desire for Irish military glory eroded as the war took its terrible toll on Irish–American soldiers. Hernon, "Irish Nationalists," pp. 43–53; *Celts, Catholics & Copperheads*, p. 8, 15, 53, 74–75, 121.

21. Michael Fitzgerald, "From Ballingarry to Fredericksburg: David Power Conyngham (1825–1883)," *Tipperary Historical Journal* (1988), p. 192; hedge schools were private schools taught by Catholic schoolmasters (Miller, *Emigrants and Exiles*, p. 76). The change in spelling of Conyngham's name may have been due merely to the error of some immigration officer when he came to America, or it might have been a conscious attempt of Conyngham himself to put on airs. In Ireland, this spelling has a snobbish or aristocratic association, as there are several titled people who use it. Michael Fitzgerald to the editor, June 16, 1988, letter in possession of the editor.

22. Fitzgerald, "David Power Conyngham," p. 193; R. F. Foster, *Modern Ireland, 1600–1972* (New York: Penguin, 1988), pp. 310–17; D. P. Conyngham and J. C. Curtin, *Ireland, Past and Present* (New York: James Sheehy, 1888), pp. 103–106.

23. Fitzgerald, "David Power Conyngham," pp. 193–94; Conyngham and Curtin, *Ireland, Past and Present*, pp. 103–106. The standard work on the Young Irelanders is Richard Davis, *The Young Ireland Movement* (Dublin: Gill and Macmillan, 1987).

24. Fitzgerald, "David Power Conyngham," p. 195. The first American edition was published in New York by D. & J. Sadlier in 1874. It was reissued by the same publisher at least two more times, in 1881 and 1890.

25. Fitzgerald, "David Power Conyngham," pp. 195–96; Conyngham and Curtin, *Ireland, Past and Present*, pp. 9–10; P. H. Jones to Governor Reuben E. Fenton, August 8, 1865, Box 44, New York Ad-

jutant General's Correspondence, New York State Archives, Albany (hereafter NYSA); New York *Irish-American*, Aug. 23, 1863.

26. See below, pp. 360–61, 11; Conyngham and Curtin, *Ireland, Past and Present*, pp. 9–10. The campaigns for the rest of 1863, including the Battle of Gettysburg, are treated in a mere nine pages. There is evidence that Conyngham was with the Army of the Potomac for the Mine Run campaign in the fall, but if he travelled with the Irish Brigade during the campaign he had little to say about it; two pages suffice to tell this story.

27. Conyngham's appointment was announced in the New York *Irish-American* on August 23, 1863. On Bennett and the *Herald* see James Parton, "The *New York Herald*," *North American Review* 102 (April 1866), pp. 373–419, and Douglas Fermer, *James Gordon Bennett and the New York Herald: A Study of Editorial Opinion in the Civil War Era, 1854–1867* (New York: St. Martin's Press, 1986). Conyngham's statement of the correspondent's responsibilities is from his *Sherman's March Through the South* (New York: Sheldon, 1865), p. 6.

28. Ibid., pp. 6, 57–58. Inexplicably, Conyngham refers to General Judah as "J. H. Judah," though he is clearly referring to Gen. Henry Moses Judah, commander of a division of the XXIII corps at the Battle of Resaca. Ezra J. Warner, *Generals in Blue: Lives of the Union Commanders* (Baton Rouge: Louisiana State University Press, 1964), pp. 255–56.

29. P. H. Jones to Governor Reuben E. Fenton, Aug. 8, 1865, Box 44, New York Adjutant General's Correspondence, NYSA; Conyngham, *Sherman's March*, pp. iii, 74–76.

30. See below, p. 9; David P. Conyngham to General William Irvine, Oct. 25, 1865, Box 45, New York Adjutant General's Correspondence, NYSA; Conyngham, *Irish Brigade*, p. 12, 11. In addition to the McSorely edition of Conyngham's *Irish Brigade*, P. Donohoe of Boston printed an identical edition in 1869. There were also three printings done in Glasgow, Scotland, though these were clearly done from different plates, as the book runs to only 302 pages rather than the 599 of the American editions. R. & T. Washbourne published the book there in 1866 and 1868. Cameron & Ferguson also printed it, though without a date of publication.

31. Ibid., pp. 10, 8, 5–6.

32. Conyngham, *Sherman's March*, p. 335.

33. P. H. Jones to Governor Reuben E, Fenton, Aug. 8, 1865, Box 44; P. H. Jones to Governor Reuben E. Fenton, Oct. 22, 1865; David P. Conyngham to General William Irvine, Nov. 27, 1865, Box 45, New York Adjutant General's Correspondence, NYSA; *Annual*

*Report of the Adjutant General of the State of New York For the Year 1901* (Albany: J. B. Lyon, 1902), p. 1149.

34. Fitzgerald, "David Power Conyngham," p. 198; D. P. Conyngham to Rev. Auguste Lemonnier, C.S.C., July 1, 1873, with accompanying newspaper clippings, unidentified scrapbook, University of Notre Dame Archives, Notre Dame, Indiana (hereafter UNDA); D. P. Conyngham, *The O'Mahony, Chief of the Comeraghs: A Tale of the Rebellion of '98* (New York: D. & J. Sadlier, 1879), p. 1.

35. *Lives of the Irish Saints* was first published in New York by D. & J. Sadlier in 1870. P. J. Kenedy (New York) may have published another edition in 1871. Sadlier first published *Lives of the Irish Martyrs* in 1872 or 1873. The two were combined in a one volume edition by P. J. Kenedy in 1885 and again in 1890. They were also included in Kenedy's 1885 edition of *The Church of Erin: Her History, Her Saints, Her Martyrs, Her Monasteries and Shrines*, which lists Conyngham and Rev. Thomas Walsh as co-authors. D. P. Conyngham to Rev. Auguste Lemonnier, C.S.C., July 1, 1873, with accompanying newspaper clippings, unidentified scrapbook, UNDA.

36. D. P. Conyngham, *Sarsfield, or the Last Great Struggle for Ireland* (Boston: P. Donohoe, 1871); *The O'Mahony, Chief of the Comeraghs* (New York: D. & J. Sadlier, 1879); Fitzgerald, "David Power Conyngham," p. 198; *Rose Parnell, The Flower of Avondale* (New York: D. & J. Sadlier, 1883), pp. 3–4; Charles Fanning, *The Irish Voice in America: Irish–American Fiction from the 1760s to the 1980s* (Lexington: University Press of Kentucky, 1990), pp. 75, 80–81.

37. Conyngham and Curtin, *Ireland, Past and Present*, p. 6. During his last years Conyngham also updated James MacGeoghegan's *History of Ireland, Ancient and Modern*. It had earlier been updated to 1852 by John Mitchell, so Conyngham carried the story from that date to 1883. The volume was published in two volumes by D. & J. Sadlier in 1887.

38. Ibid., pp. 9, 11; Fitzgerald, "David Power Conyngham," pp. 197, 199.

39. The University of Notre Dame Archives holds Conyngham's original manuscript of "Soldiers of the Cross" (it is also called "Heroism of the Cross, or Nuns and Priests on the Battlefield") and it has a typescript made from the manuscript. How the manuscript found its way there is explained in the correspondence between Conyngham's brother-in-law, Michael Kerwick, and Rev. Daniel E. Hudson, C.S.C., publisher of *Ave Maria*, in the Hudson Collection at the University of Notre Dame Archives. Thomas F. Meehan to Rev. Thomas McAvoy, C.S.C., Feb. 14, 1932, Conyngham Collection, UNDA.

# THE IRISH BRIGADE
# AND ITS CAMPAIGNS

THE

# IRISH BRIGADE

AND

## ITS CAMPAIGNS:

WITH SOME ACCOUNT OF

THE CORCORAN LEGION, AND SKETCHES OF
THE PRINCIPAL OFFICERS.

BY

## CAPT. D. P. CONYNGHAM, A. D. C.,

AUTHOR OF "FRANK O'DONNELL," "SHERMAN'S MARCH," ETC., ETC.

"Hark from yon stately ranks what laughter rings!
Mingling wild mirth with war's stern minstrelsy;
His jest while each blithe comrade round him flings,
And moves to death with military glee!
Boast, Erin! boast them, tameless, frank, and free,
In kindness warm, and fierce in danger known—
Rough Nature's children, humorous as she;
And he, yon chieftain!—Strike the proudest tone
Of thy bold harp, Green Isle, the HEROES ARE THINE OWN!"

NEW YORK:

## WILLIAM McSORLEY & CO., PUBLISHERS,

3 BARCLAY STREET.

1867.

Entered according to act of Congress, in the year 1866,

By WILLIAM McSORLEY & CO.,

In the Clerk's Office of the District Court of the United States for the Southern
District of New York.

TO

# The Memory

OF THE

## SOLDIERS OF THE IRISH BRIGADE

### Who Fell

SUSTAINING THE CAUSE OF THEIR ADOPTED COUNTRY

AND THE

## COURAGE AND FIDELITY

OF

## THE IRISH RACE,

### This Work

IS REVERENTIALLY DEDICATED BY

THE AUTHOR.

# PREFACE.

THE first shot fired by the Southerners on Fort Sumter blew away all chances of compromise, and the war spirit burst forth.

The Irish people in New York, and throughout the Northern States, were not slow in declaring for the Union and volunteering for its defence.

I believe the second regiment to leave New York for the defence of the National Capital was Colonel Corcoran's Sixty-ninth Irish regiment, which was soon followed by Meagher's Zouaves and other Irish organizations.

The Irish felt that not only was the safety of the great Republic, the home of their exiled race, at stake, but also, that the great principles of democracy were at issue with the aristocratic doctrines of monarchism. Should the latter prevail, there was no longer any hope for the struggling nationalists of the Old World. The Irish soldier did not ask whether the colored race were better off

as bondsmen or freedmen ; he was not going to fight for
an abstract idea. He felt that the safety and welfare of
his adopted country and its glorious Constitution were imperilled ; he, therefore, willingly threw himself into the
breach to sustain the flag that sheltered him when perse-
cuted and exiled from his own country, the laws that
protected him, and the country that, like a loving mother,
poured forth the richness of her bosom to sustain him.

The Irish soldier was, therefore, a patriot, and no mercenary. He had just the same right to fight for America
that the native American had. The Irish, the German, the
Pole, and all other exiles have a vested right in the main-
tenance of the American Union. Several Irishmen gave
up lucrative situations and business to join the army ;
they had sacrificed their interests to their patriotism.
Many a patriotic young Irishman wanted to learn the use
of arms and the science of war, with the hope of one day
turning them to practical use in his own country. A
people like the Irish, deprived of their nationality at home,
and even of the manly right of carrying arms, are always
jealous of their military reputation abroad.

There are few battle-fields in Europe in which the Irish
soldier has not left his footprints.

The flower of the Jacobite army, after the surrender of
Limerick, took service under the *Fleur de Lis* of France,
and their military career is a part of the history of Europe.

When Luxemburg drew his lines around Namur, a

fortress deemed impregnable, it fell before the ringing cheer and dashing charge of Irish valor.

Brilliant were their services under the princely Mount-cashel, whose noble blood dyed the fields of Staffardo. The regiments of Burke and Dillon saved Cremona.

At Blenheim, where Tallard reeled before the superior genius and force of Marlborough, Lord Clare's dragoons bore off two of the enemy's standards.

The services of the brigade at Ramillies and Fontenoy are proudly chronicled in French history. The latter was as decisive, in its way, for the French, as Waterloo was for the English.

"And Fontenoy, famed Fontenoy, had been a Waterloo,
  Were not these exiles ready then, fresh, vehement, and true."

King Louis publicly thanked the brigade, and created Count Lally a general on the field of battle. King George uttered that memorable imprecation on the penal code : "Cursed be the laws that deprive me of such subjects."

Later still, in the desperate struggle for the crown of Ferdinand and Isabella, the young blood of Ireland deluged the olive-groves of Spain.

When the New World rose to disenthral itself from the despotism of the Old, the generous manhood of Ireland flung itself into the contest for liberty.

Even in the republics of Chili, Bolivia, and Venezuela, the praises of O'Brien, Dillon, Devereux, and other Irish patriots are yet sung in the soft Castilian tongue, by the banks of the Orinoco and mountain fastnesses of the Andes.

A new field now opened to Irish valor and Irish gratitude, and the tried heroism of Meagher's Brigade, and several other Irish brigades and regiments, has added a new chaplet to our heroic record, and has given us a stronger claim to the protection and gratitude of the American nation.

The first duty of Irishmen as citizens of America is obedience to the Constitution and laws of the country ; and any attempt to destroy the Government, under which they enjoy the blessings of peace and plenty, is a crime against their indefeasible rights, which they should resent even with their lives.

It is computed that in the Federal armies alone there were about one hundred and seventy-five thousand Irishmen. Most of these were amalgamated with various commands, scattered from the Empire State to sunny Florida, from Rappahannock's tide to the Pacific.

On the bloody fields of Virginia, down amid the cotton-fields of Georgia and the swamps of the Carolinas, lie the bleached bones of many an Irish soldier and chief.

Whether storming the bloody heights of Fredericksburg, or checking the enemy's advance at Fair Oaks and Malvern Hill, or making that fearful dash at Antietam, or rescuing the abandoned cannon at Chancellorsville, or sweeping Early from the Shenandoah, or in planting the Stars and Stripes on the walls of Atlanta and Savannah, the Irish soldier has won a high reputation ; and the greatest detractor of his race, even the London ' Times' itself, has not dared to question his bravery as a soldier or his devotion to the flag under which he fought.

During my connection with the Irish Brigade I fully availed myself of every opportunity to collect all the materials I could relating to what had transpired, and to take notes of what occurred under my own observation, with the intention of writing a history of the gallant exploits of that noble little band. In order to make my work acceptable to the general reader, I give a sketch of the different battles in which the brigade participated, but making the part it took in the strife the leading feature. I have also endeavored to illustrate the elastic vitality of the race by anecdotes, sketches of camp-scenes, and the festivities held on national holidays in the field, and under the guns of the enemy.

I have, too, as far as I was able, collected the names of the officers and men, killed or wounded. I have done my best to give a true and impartial history, and if I have failed in any particular, I trust some other writer will supply the deficiency, that thus we may hand down to posterity a true and correct history of a brigade whose exploits they will rehearse with wondering admiration.

I do not write this work from any mercenary motives,

but with the sole desire of helping to rescue from obscurity the glorious military record we have earned in America.

I hope that the history of every Irish regiment and brigade in the American service will be written, and thus preserve the materials for some future Bancroft of Irish history.

We have given too many Irish regiments and brigades to the American service to let their history sink into obscurity ; besides, their bravery and services are of such a nature as to cause a glow of pride to tingle through every Irishman's heart. I have confined myself to the Irish Brigade ; but we are not to forget that this comprised but a small portion of the Irish element in the American armies. We also have given many distinguished Irish and Irish-American generals to the cause—among them, Phil Sheridan, John Logan, Geary, and Birney ; Sweeny, Lalor, and Doherty, of Illinois ; Gorman, of Minnesota ; Magennis and Sullivan, of Indiana ; Reilly and Mulligan, of Ohio ; Stevenson, from Missouri ; Minty, from Michigan ; the noble Smith, of Delaware ; Meagher, Shields, Corcoran, P. H. Jones, Kiernan, of New York, and several others.

As I have said, I hope other pens will write the histories of other organizations. If I have but contributed a correct account of the Irish Brigade to the general fund, I am satisfied. I devote the first chapter to the gallant Sixty-ninth N. Y. S. M., its services fully entitling it to a place in these pages; besides, it was the nucleus of the Irish Brigade, and supplied it with many able officers and soldiers. I have added an appendix, containing sketches of Generals Meagher and Corcoran, and most of the officers of the Brigade ; and also a roster of the names of the men who were killed or wounded in battle, and have given some of General Meagher's official reports and letters.

To my talented friend, Doctor William O'Meagher, I have left the pleasing task of writing the history of the Brigade for '64 and '65. He was surgeon of the Sixty-ninth during that time ; and, from his literary acquirements and intimate knowledge of its services, is much better qualified for the task than I. As I was then with Sherman in Georgia, I know little personally of its career. He also gives a short sketch, *en passant,* of the gallant Corcoran Legion

As to my own services, both with the Brigade and Sherman's army, I hope it will not be deemed egotism on my part to give the following from several congratulatory notices and letters I have received from the press and from commanding officers with whom I served :

HEADQUARTERS SECOND CORPS,
ARMY OF THE POTOMAC, '63.

I feel very great pleasure in bearing testimony to the gallantry and other soldierly qualities of my friend, Captain D. P. Conyngham, and the efficient services he rendered me at Chancellorsville, where he acted as one of my aids.

THOMAS F. MEAGHER,
Lately commanding the Irish Brigade.

At the battle of Resaca I carried orders under a fierce fire of the enemy, and subsequently led a division into action, getting wounded in the breast. Major-General Schofield thanked me personally on the field, and from the general on whose staff I served I received the following complimentary letter :

CEDAR SPRINGS, GA., May 18, 1864.

CAPTAIN D. P. CONYNGHAM, *Acting A. D. C. :*

CAPTAIN—l cannot disrupt the associations that bind me to my personal staff without thanking you for the many services you have rendered me. The gallant manner in which you have conveyed my orders under a heavy fire, during the fearful ordeal to which my division was subjected on the 14th inst., not only commands my acknowledgment and admiration, but attests my long-confirmed opinion, that the Irish soldier is the nonpareil of a soldier.

With the best wishes of your chief for your future success and welfare,

I am truly yours,

J. H. JUDAH, Brigadier-General U. S. A.

If I have failed in doing justice to the merits of any officer, it is through no spirit of partiality, but from the want of proper information. Among other sources of information, I am much indebted to the admirable letters of the brave, talented, but ill-fated " Galloglass."

THE AUTHOR.

MAPLE COTTAGE, STATEN ISLAND,
May 20, 1866.

# CONTENTS.

## CHAPTER I.

## CHAPTER II.

## CHAPTER III.

## CHAPTER IV.

# CHAPTER V.

# CHAPTER VI.

# CHAPTER VII.

# CHAPTER VIII.

# CHAPTER IX.

# CHAPTER X.

# CHAPTER XI.

# CHAPTER XII.

# CHAPTER XIII.

# CHAPTER XIV.

# CHAPTER XV.

# CHAPTER XVI.

# CHAPTER XVII.

# CHAPTER XVIII.

# CHAPTER XIX.

# CHAPTER XX.

# CHAPTER XXI.

# CHAPTER XXII.

# CHAPTER XXIII.

# CHAPTER XXIV.

# CHAPTER XXV.

# CHAPTER XXVI.

# CHAPTER XXVII.

# CHAPTER XXVIII.

# CHAPTER XXIX.

# CHAPTER XXX.

# CHAPTER XXXI.

# CHAPTER XXXII.

# CHAPTER XXXIII.

# APPENDIX.

# THE IRISH BRIGADE.

## CHAPTER I.

EARLY in the spring of 1861, in response to the call of President Lincoln for the first levy of troops to quell the incipient rebellion, the New York militia promptly and with enthusiastic ardor volunteered their services. Foremost among them, the Sixty-ninth, under the command of Col. Michael Corcoran, threw themselves into the ranks of the national army in defence of their adopted country, its glory, and integrity. The court-martial of Colonel Corcoran for disobedience of orders in refusing to parade his regiment in honor of the Prince of Wales was summarily dissolved, and the charges dismissed, to the intense satisfaction of the community at large, in accordance with the following order :

SPECIAL ORDERS, No. 9.

FIRST DIVISION, N. Y. S. M., }
NEW YORK, April 20, 1861. }

In pursuance of Special Orders, No. 58, from General Headquarters, the Court-martial detailed for the trial of Colonel Corcoran, of the Sixty-ninth Regiment, is dissolved, and the charges dismissed ; and Colonel Corcoran is directed forthwith to resume the command of his regiment.

By order of

MAJOR-GENERAL CHARLES W. SANDFORD.

GEORGE W. MORELL, Div. Eng., Acting Division Inspector.

Colonel Corcoran immediately promulgated the following orders to his regiment, which had already nearly completed its arrangements to start in defence of the national capital :

Colonel Corcoran will embark his regiment to-morrow, viz., between ten and eleven o'clock, on board the James Adger, Pier No. 4 North River, not exceeding one thousand men, all told.

CHARLES W. SANDFORD, Major-General.

NEW YORK, April 22, 1861.

This order provided but for the transportation of one thousand men ; and as the regiment numbered eight hundred more, those who were compelled to remain behind felt bitterly disappointed, but their patriotic zeal was soon fully gratified.

In Colonel Corcoran's general order to the regiment before starting, the following patriotic sentence occurs:

" The commandant feels proud that his first duty, after being relieved from a long arrest, is to have the honor of promulgating an order to the regiment to rally to the support of the Constitution and laws of the United States."

On the day of departure, after the regiment had formed into line in Great Jones street, they were presented with a splendid silk United States flag by the wife of Judge Daly. This appropriate present was received with cheers for the fair donor, and Colonel Corcoran requested Judge Daly to inform his lady that her flag should never suffer a stain of dishonor while a man of the Sixty-ninth remained alive to defend it.

About three o'clock the order of march was given. The regiment moved into Broadway amid deafening cheers; flags and banners streamed from the windows and house-tops; ladies waved their handkerchiefs from the balconies, and flung bouquets on the marching column.

At the head of the procession was a decorated wagon, drawn by four horses, and bearing the inscription, " Sixty-ninth, remember Fontenoy," and " No North, no South, no East, no West, but the whole Union."

The officers of the regiment were as follows:

Colonel, Michael Corcoran.

Lieutenant-Colonel, Robert Nugent.

Major, James Bagley; Adjutant, John McKeon.

Volunteer Aids, C. G. Halpine, John Savage.

Chaplain, Rev. Thomas J. Mooney; succeeded by Rev. B. O'Reilly, S. J.

Engineers, James B. Kirker, John H. McCunn, L. D'Homergue.

Surgeon, Robert Johnson; Assistants, Drs. James L. Kiernan, J. Pascal Smith, P. Nolan.

Quartermaster, Joseph B. Tully.

Paymaster, Matthew Kehoe.

Sergeant-Major, Arthur Tracy; Color-Sergeant, —— Murphy.

Company A, Captain James Haggerty; First-Lieutenant, Theodore Kelly; Second-Lieutenants, Daniel Strayne, Dennis F. Sullivan; Orderly Sergeant, —— Bermingham.  One hundred and twenty men.

Company B, Captain Thomas Lynch; First-Lieutenant, Thomas Leddy; Second-Lieutenant, W. H. Giles; Orderly Sergeant, —— Cahill.  One hundred and fourteen men.

Company C, Captain James Cavanagh; First-Lieutenant, John H. Ryan; Second-Lieutenant, J. Rowan. Eighty-six men.

* See Appendix for sketch of officers.

Company D, Captain Thomas Clarke; First-Lieutenant, Thomas Fay; Second-Lieutenants, James L. Dungan, Michael O'Boyle; Orderly Sergeant, M. Maguire. One hundred and twenty men.

Company E, Captain P. Kelly; First-Lieutenant, John Bagley; Orderly Sergeant, Andrew Reed. One hundred men.

Company F, Captain John Breslin; First-Lieutenant, P. Duffy; Second-Lieutenant, M. P. Breslin; —— D'Alton. One hundred men.

Company G, Captain Felix Duffy; First-Lieutenant, Henry J. McMahon; Orderly Sergeant, Thomas Phibbs. One hundred and twenty men.

Company H, Captain James Kelly; First-Lieutenant, W. Butler; Second-Lieutenants, James Lyons, James Gannon; Orderly Sergeant, F. Welpley. One hundred and twenty-six men.

Company J, Lieutenant John Coonan, commanding; Second-Lieutenant, Thomas M. Canton. One hundred and two men.

During the night the James Adger and the Harriet Lane, with other transports, dropped down the bay, carrying the Sixty-ninth, the Eighth Regiment, and the Thirteenth Brooklyn. After a pleasant voyage, the fleet reached Annapolis, and the Sixty-ninth were placed guarding the line of railroad from Annapolis to Washington. In Virginia it was camped on Arlington

Heights, a beautiful and picturesque situation, forming one of the lovely range of wooded hills stretching
along the southern side of the Potomac River.   From
it was a magnificent view of the river, Georgetown,
and Washington.   The troops were soon busily employed throwing up a fort, which, in honor of their
colonel, was named Fort Corcoran, over which they
raised the first flag of the war hoisted on a Federal fort.
The occasion was a joyous and festive one in camp.
Speeches were made by Colonel Hunter (in whose
brigade the Sixty-ninth was serving), Captain Thomas
F. Meagher, and other officers.   Mr. John Savage, who
was acting on Colonel Corcoran's staff with the rank
of captain, sung to the air of " Dixie's Land" a beautiful and appropriate song, "The Starry Flag," the
whole regiment joining in the refrain.   Mr. Savage first
wrote and sang this on the transport Marion, on her
perilous route up the Potomac, through the masked
batteries of the enemy.   It was suggested by an incident that occurred on the voyage.

In the darkness of the night a rebel boat, with muffled
oars, ran alongside the gunboat, but seeing the troops
on guard, one of them exclaimed, as they shot away,
" D—n the rag ! we cannot pull it down to-night."

Mr. John Savage, in espousing the Union cause,
sacrificed flattering inducements for principle.   While
editing 'The States' in Washington, he had formed the

acquaintance of the leading men in the South; and when war was imminent they offered him the greatest inducements if he would espouse their cause, but nothing could tempt him from the path of principle and honor.

The remainder of the regiment and Meagher's company of Zouaves soon joined them at Arlington Heights. The Fifth and Twenty-eighth New York were also in the same brigade.

While the regiment was thus progressing in drill and efficiency, its patriotic friends at home were exerting themselves to raise funds for the support of the soldiers' families. A committee was formed, of which Judge Daly was Chairman, R. O'Gorman Treasurer, and W. J. Kane Secretary. Among its most energetic members were Messrs. John Hennessy, who labored with unremitting zeal, J. B. Nicholson, Felix E. O'Rourke, and Edw. Hart. Mr. O'Gorman soon visiting Europe, his place was efficiently filled by E. J. Wilson.

At this period McDowell was steadily and cautiously pushing his lines towards Fairfax Courthouse, which place had been occupied by the enemy under General Bonham. Frequent skirmishes occurred between the advanced posts and scouting-parties, and it was quite evident from every indication that a battle was imminent.

General Scott's policy was to raise and organize a sufficient force to crush out the rebellion at one blow. He was unwilling to attack the enemy in their intrenched positions, which he felt should be done at a disadvantage, thereby giving them a probable chance of gaining the first victory, then a matter of vital importance. He was overruled, however, and influenced by the urgent representations of certain influential parties, contrary to his firm conviction and better judgment. Public opinion, also, as expressed in the newspapers, seemed to favor an immediate advance of the Union forces, before the enemy could become more formidable, and thus it was determined to bring on a general engagement.

About the 12th of July, 1861, Colonel Corcoran received orders from General McDowell to hold himself in readiness to march at a moment's notice; and on the 15th the order to march at 2 P. M. next day was read to the regiment while on parade. The ensuing night was, accordingly, spent in various avocations by officers and men. Many went to confession, nearly all wrote home to their friends the exciting news, sending large sums of money which had been just received, while many others gave loose rein to fun and jollification, as numberless empty bottles and kegs could amply testify. Very little sleep was enjoyed by any one.

The morning of the 16th dawned, and the preparations for a general advance of the army were witnessed on all sides; blankets were rolled up, haversacks filled with three days' rations, guns and equipments brightly polished, and cartridge-boxes crammed with buck and ball ammunition. Finally, about twelve o'clock noon, under the full blaze of a scorching sun, the right wing of the army commenced to move. But on this day very little progress was made, owing to a want of proper organization everywhere apparent.

The Sixty-ninth, exclusive of the officers, numbered over a thousand men, and presented as fine an appearance as many regular regiments.

The line of march was taken up about noon. The corps of engineers led the van, under the command of Captain Quinlan, Lieutenants D'Hommergue and M'Quade, followed by an improvised drum-corps, playing the old familiar inspiriting airs. After these came Colonel Corcoran and staff-officers, including Captain T. F. Meagher, acting as major in place of Major Bagley, who had remained in New York; Captain Haggerty, acting as lieutenant-colonel in place of Colonel Nugent, who had been injured some days previously by a fall from his horse; and Captain J. H. Nugent, acting as adjutant. The surgeons, chaplain, quartermasters, and non-commissioned officers, including the color-guard, followed immediately after.

On the march the Sixty-ninth was ordered to join

the brigade commanded by Colonel W. T. Sherman
(who subsequently attained to such enviable distinction), and so continued until after the engagement.
The brigade encamped on the first night near Vienna,
to which place the Sixty-ninth had, in the previous
month, made a midnight excursion to the rescue of the
Ohio troops, which had been surprised by the enemy.

After a comfortless night spent amid the foul exha-
lations of a swamp, the regiment again started on the
march early on the morning of the 17th, and about 10
o'clock A. M. came in sight of Fairfax Courthouse.
Here the regiment made a flank movement for the
purpose of cutting off the retreat of the enemy's
forces, and while executing it were soon confronted
by a force of more than one thousand men, drawn up
in line of battle and apparently prepared to fight.
The order to halt and form was instantly given. The
right wing of the Sixty-ninth was thrown into the
fields to the left, where it joined the Second New York,
and the line moved rapidly down on the enemy. The
latter, however, turned and fled into the village, and
thence towards Centreville, being considerably hastened
in their flight by a few shots from the guns of the
Eighth New York Artillery and Ayres's Battery. In
the village were found the camp equipments, arms,
stores, &c., of General Bonham's division, the sight of
which caused many to think that surely the rebellion

would be soon and easily subdued. Major Sullivan, of the Second Rhode Island, was the first to enter the intrenchments, while Corporal McMahon, of the same regiment, secured the Confederate flag, which had been left flying.

During the march the roads were so much obstructed by felled trees that considerable delay was occasioned by their removal, and several halts had thus to be made. In one of these Captain Breslin was severely wounded in the shoulder by the accidental discharge of a musket that had fallen from the stack. He was placed in an ambulance, in which he was carried to Centreville.

Again the line of march was taken up towards Centreville, and in a short time the news was brought that Germantown also was abandoned by the enemy, which fact added considerably to the previous excitement. Fatigue, hunger, thirst, were all forgotten when the green banner and the National flag were placed on the ramparts of the abandoned fortifications, while between both the Sixty-ninth passed in triumph, "hats and caps waving on the bayonet points, and an Irish cheer, such as never before shook the woods of old Virginia, swelling and rolling far and wide into the gleaming air."

Next morning (18th), Centreville, too, was found evacuated.

The positions of the army at this juncture were as follows: General Tyler's division lay between Germantown and Centreville, Colonel Hunter's at Fairfax, on its line of march to Centreville; Colonel Miles's at Braddock's Cross Roads, and Heintzelman's around Fairfax. In this latter division was the Thirty-seventh New York (Irish Rifles), which, though not actually engaged at the battle of Bull Run, performed good service during the retreat, in guarding the stores and ammunition accumulated at Fairfax Station.

## BULL RUN.

The battle of Bull Run was a series of minor engagements culminating in a general action at Manassas. At first the Federal Army was so far successful that a brilliant victory was anticipated; but Beauregard had made such a judicious disposal of his troops and artillery as to enable him to keep us in check, until the arrival of Jackson's and Johnston's re-enforcements enabled him to take up the offensive at several points, and thus throw our already exhausted army into confusion.

The respective forces under Beauregard and McDowell were nearly equal.

The Federal Army consisted of about forty-three thousand. Of these, several militia regiments from

Massachusetts, Connecticut, Pennsylvania, and one New York regiment, and Captain Varian's light artillery battery, Eighth New York State Militia, left the field of battle and marched home, leaving the enemy in front, their time of service having expired on the the 20th. To the credit of the Sixty-ninth New York and Thirteenth Brooklyn, two Irish regiments, be it said, that they volunteered to remain, though their time had also expired.

Beauregard had only about forty thousand troops around Centreville and Fairfax. He adroitly drew in his outer posts before the Federal advance, and occupied the woods and defiles leading through Bull Run to Manassas. This enabled him to contract his line so as to guard the most important passes and also to cover Manassas Junction, where he hourly expected Johnston's and Jackson's troops from the Shenandoah Valley. Most of these re-enforcements had arrived by the 19th, but Kirby Smith, Cooke, and Longstreet came up at the critical moment, when victory seemed in the hands of the Federals, and by a vigorous assault along the Federal lines soon routed them, their cavalry following up the advantage and throwing them into indescribable confusion. Though the forces were about equal, the Confederates had a decided advantage in artillery, in its commanding position, and the superior manner in which it was served.

Manassas plains are about thirty-five miles from Washington, extending from the foot of Centreville heights across Bull Run to Manassas Junction. Dark, gloomy woods, deep ravines, wood-covered runs, and elevated plateaus afforded excellent covering for the enemy's infantry and artillery.

The first engagement took place on the 18th at Bull Run, midway between Centreville and Manassas, and about three miles from both points. General Tyler, who commanded the right wing of the Union army, ordered Colonel Richardson, commanding the Fourth Brigade, accompanied by Captain Ayres's battery and four companies of cavalry, to reconnoitre along the Run in the direction of Blackburn Ford.

Richardson had advanced about two miles along the Run, and had effected a crossing above Blackburn Ford, and commenced shelling the woods. The enemy's artillery replied, throwing shells among our cavalry, who were drawn up in line. Richardson threw forward heavy lines of skirmishers, who were met with a galling musketry fire from concealed enemies.

The skirmishers on both sides soon fell back, formed, and advanced in line.

The Federal advance was met by the First Virginia Volunteers, who, after a few volleys, retreated in good order, the Federals following pell-mell until their lines were exposed in front of the wood, when the Virginians turned round and poured a volley on them in front and flank. Colonel Richardson, finding that he had got into an ambuscade, hastily fell back. He was re-enforced by Sherman's brigade, the Sixty-ninth in advance, and resumed shelling the enemy's position, while they responding vigorously.

Richardson, finding his force insufficient to dislodge them, fell back towards Centreville. No other movement of importance took place until Sunday, 21st. The sun had risen with more than usual splendor on that fatal Sunday morning, lighting up the varied landscape with pleasing effect. From Centreville heights, Porter's artillery was deliberately shelling Blackburn's and McLean's fords, which were guarded by the enemy's batteries. Eight miles away, too, in the direction of Stone Bridge, smoke ascended from the woods; and the booming of artillery told that the work of death had commenced there.

The sharp sound of musketry came ringing from Blackburn and Mitchell's fords, where Longstreet's and Bonham's brigades were feeling our centre.

Far away to the west rose the dark outlines of the Blue Ridge Mountains, inclosing as it were in an amphitheatre the open plains of Manassas, with its woods and streams, and glittering hosts arrayed in battle strife.

2*

The beautiful and ample woods, with their deep foliage of green, encircled the plains, concealing in their bosom innumerable batteries and columns of deadly enemies.

Such was the morning, and such the stirring scene that inaugurated the first real battle of one of the bloodiest wars on record.

Beauregard's line of battle extended from Union Mills, on the right, which was held by Ewell's brigade, to Stone Bridge, held by Colonel Evans, thus covering a front of nine miles from right to left. The right was much stronger than the left, both in position and numbers.

About two o'clock on Sunday morning, the Federal army broke camp around Centreville, and commenced taking up the different positions assigned them. Richardson moved on the southern road leading to the Run, and Tyler on the northern. Colonel Hunter marched to the right, moving obliquely towards the Run, with the intention of gaining the enemy's flank.

Colonel Miles remained at Centreville, in command of the post and reserves.

The battle opened by an attack on the enemy's left at Stone Bridge, which Colonel Hunter had flanked by crossing higher up at Dudley Ford, driving the rebel general, Evans, before him, while Tyler was fiercely disputing the ford with Wheat's Louisiana troops.

Heintzelman moved towards Red House Ford, and proceeded at right angles with the river towards Stone Bridge, in order to cover the passage of Tyler's division.

Heintzelman crossed the ford, and was confronted by some Alabama troops in line. He cheered on his New York Fire Zouaves to the attack, but they were met by a withering artillery and musketry fire, which made them fall back. The Fourteenth Brooklyn made a better show, but were forced to give way, both suffering severely. Re-enforcements were brought up, and the Alabamians and Mississippians were forced to retreat, and fall back towards Robinson House, suffering severely all the time. We had now secured Stone Bridge, Tyler had crossed and formed a junction with Heintzelman, our artillery was thundering away at the enemy's right and centre, and every thing looked hopeful for the Federals.

Jackson's brigade and Hampton's Legion re-enforced Evans, and were supported by artillery, which unmasked at different openings in the woods, and opened a deadly fire along our lines. The fighting on our right was desperate all the morning; and Beauregard, penetrating McDowell's intention of crushing his left wing, ordered up his reserves and re-enforcements from his right. He also ordered an advance of his right, in order to distract our attention from his left.

Johnston and Beauregard fiercely galloped to the left, to retrieve their disasters there. Jackson sat his horse calmly looking on, while his Virginia brigade lay down near him, waiting to be ordered into action.

Jackson had now formed a new line, which checked Hunter's advance. Keys' and Sherman's brigades were ordered up to support the latter, the Sixty-ninth N. Y. S. M. in advance. The column moved to the right, and drew up in a small open field, separated from Hunter's column by a belt of wood, which was filled with rebel batteries and troops. The rebels were gallantly pushed back by Hunter; but, on reaching their batteries and being re-enforced, they made a fierce stand, meeting our repeated charges with desperate resistance. The incessant roar of artillery came from batteries at close range. Shell and round-shot ploughed through the ranks, and shattered the trees; thick volumes of smoke rose from the woods, and floated along the valleys.

The rebels had repelled charge after charge, regiment after regiment, when the Sixty-ninth was ordered to the assault. Stripped of knapsacks and overcoats, they swept up the hill, across the open field, on towards the wood, delivering fire after fire on their concealed foe. Batteries opened on them right and left, hurling grape into their very faces, while from the shelter of the woods a stream of lead was poured on them. It was a gallant charge, gallantly led and gallantly sustained. After each repulse, the regiment formed and charged right up on the batteries. Meagher's company of Zouaves suffered desperately, their red dress making them a conspicuous mark for the enemy. When Meagher's horse was torn from under him by a rifled cannon ball, he jumped up, waved his sword, and exclaimed, " Boys! look at that flag—remember Ireland and Fontenoy." The regiment bravely but vainly struggled to capture the batteries, and drive the enemy from the shelter of the wood. Colonel Corcoran rallied and charged with them in every assault. Lieutenant-Colonel Haggerty, a native of Glenswilly, County Donegal, and as fine a specimen of a Celt as Ireland could produce, fell shot through the heart; while beside him fell poor Costelloe, a recent arrival from Waterford, and a noble, amiable youth.

The regiment at length was ordered by Colonel Sherman to fall back to shelter. General McDowell, who was a spectator of the charge, rode up to the Sixty-ninth and personally thanked them.

Beauregard was fast pushing infantry, artillery, and cavalry to support his left. Blenker's brigade was ordered from our left to the right.

The fighting was fiercest about Henry's and Robinson's House, where we had Ricketts' and Griffin's batteries. This position was taken and retaken several times during the day.

Despite our repeated repulses and heavy losses on our left, the enemy were so hard pressed that they were about giving way, when troops were seen marching from Manassas Junction. They were the remainder of Johnston's army, under Kirby Smith. That general, with his fresh troops, was ordered to attack our right and rear: which he did, supported by Early's brigade and Johnston's whole line; while Longstreet, Jones, and Ewell pressed our left, and demonstrated on Centreville.

This vigorous assault, supported by a heavy artillery fire, changed the tide of events. Our troops, highly overestimating the strength of the re-enforcements, lost heart, and began to give way at several points. Our reserves seemed not available, or were on their march to support our right wing when the panic began to set in. To add to this confusion, the teamsters, who had moved up too close to the main body and lined the Warrenton road, became terror-stricken. The news spread that the army was retreating, when the teamsters fiercely whipped their animals, soon blocking up the roads: citizens, of whom there were a good many looking on, rushed frantically forward, seizing any animals they could lay hands upon. These were soon joined by the panic-stricken army. To add to the horror of the troops, Jones's rebel brigade had attacked Centreville, and Blenker's reserves were retreating towards Washington. Two masked batteries opened on the retreating masses, blocking up the road with wagons, caissons, artillery, ambulances, sick and wounded soldiers. Artillery horses had their traces cut, and were mounted by officers, privates, and civilians, who made flank movements through the fields. There was a regular mingling and confusion of soldiers without arms, members of Congress and editors without hats or coats, ladies in buggies, wagons, and on horseback; special correspondents, including Bull Run Russell, of the London 'Times,' almost scared to death, while behind all came the rebel cavalry, cutting and slashing.

The disaster of Bull Run, when properly considered, seemed natural and almost inevitable. Raw troops who had never been in a battle were hurled against strongly intrenched positions, well manned and gunned. They had by desperate fighting succeeded in driving the enemy from some of their strongest lines, when fresh troops were hurled against them at all points. As for the panic, it was first commenced by the teamsters and civilians; and the militia, not knowing much more about a battle, became infected, and thus it spread to the whole army. Such a thing could not happen with an army six months in the field. It taught the country a lesson, and made the leaders lay their plans with more judgment in future. It was, after all, but a training-school to open men's eyes to the real necessities and responsibilities of war.

## INCIDENTS OF THE BATTLE.

The standard-bearer of the green flag of the Sixty-ninth was shot down, but the flag was instantly raised again. The second man was shot, and a rebel tore the flag from his grasp. Exerting himself, he shot down the rebel, rescuing the flag, and seized a rebel color; but he was soon overpowered by numbers, and the trophy taken from him, besides being taken prisoner with his own flag. He had a concealed revolver, and shot the two men in charge of him, and captured a captain's sword and a prisoner, which he brought in with him. His name was John D. Keefe, of Meagher's Zouaves.

The Sixty-ninth left the field in good order, with colors flying. Colonel Corcoran formed the remnant of his forces into a kind of square to meet a charge of cavalry, which they repulsed. As they gained the road they were again charged on, and Colonel Corcoran was wounded through the leg. The crowd and pressure of fugitive troops rushing by was so great, and the confusion so general, that his men lost sight of him, and he fell into the enemy's hands along with

Captain James McIvor, Lieutenant Edward Connolly, Color-Sergeant John Murphy, Sergeant William O'Donohue, and about thirty privates.

When lying in front of the enemy's batteries, before the charg, the raised flag was a prominent mark for the enemy. Colonel Corcoran ordered the man to lower it.

"Don't ask me, colonel," he replied; "I'll never lower it," and was instantly killed. Another sprang to it, and met the same fate. Colonel Corcoran was everywhere conspicuous, cheering on and rallying the troops : even when wounded he checked the rebel advance with his little band, and disdained to leave the field until he was captured at his post of honor.

A Southern officer said that, amid the few which held ground, Corcoran's Irish regiment stood "like a rock in the whirlpool rushing past them. . . The Irish fought like heroes," and at the end "did slowly retire."

The losses in the battle were, all told, about two thousand Federals and one thousand five hundred Confederates. The Federals lost most of their artillery, stores, and arms. The Sixty-ninth lost about one hundred and fifty men.

George Wilkes, who witnessed the battle, in his paper, 'The Spirit of the Times,' says:

"The Sixty-ninth, which, with the Scotch regiment of Wisconsin men and the New York Thirteenth, had

been wading through batteries since their arrival on
the field, marched past in splendid order, their banners
flying as if on review, and their faces sternly set.

"They passed down the hill, obliquely to the right,
on their road to support Griffin's battery, which was
within two hundred yards of the artillery of the foe.
Though silent as they passed, a shout rose in a few
seconds afterwards from the direction they had taken,
which every listener could mark for theirs, and the
spiteful one which responded from the rebel battery
was soon quelled by the volume of their musketry.
Most prominent among them was Meagher, the Irish
orator, who frequently, during the contest of that
turbulent day, waved the green banner of his regiment up and down the hottest line of fire."

The Special Correspondent of 'The World,' writing, said:

"It was a brave sght—that rush of the Sixty-ninth
to the death-struggle! With such cheers as those
which won the battles of the Peninsula, with a quick
step at first, and then a double-quick, and at last a run,
they dashed forward along the edge of the extended
forest. Coats and knapsacks were thrown to either
side, that nothing might impede their work; but we
know that no guns would slip from the hands of those
determined fellows, even if dying agonies were needed
to close them with a firmer grasp. As the line swept

along, Meagher galloped towards the head, crying,
'Come on, boys! you have got your chance at last.' I
have not seen him, but heard that he fought magnificently."

The Southerners themselves spoke of the fighting of
the Sixty-ninth in the highest terms. One journal
said :

"No Southerner but feels that the Sixty-ninth maintained the old reputation of Irish valor—on the wrong
side. * * * All honor to the Sixty-ninth, even in
its errors."

Judge Holt, in addressing the volunteers in Kentucky, said: "Leonidas himself, while surveying the
Persian host that like a troubled sea swept onward to
the pass where he stood, would have been proud of
the leadership of Irishmen (Sixty-ninth)."

The following amusing dialogue, which is stated to
have taken place between an Irish United States cav-
alryman and his officer, will show how true was Pat's
allegiance to the flag he had sworn to defend :

*Officer.*—Well, Pat, ain't you going to follow the
General (Twiggs)?

*Pat.*—If Gineral Scott ordhers us to follow him, sir,
begor Toby (Pat's horse) can gallop as well as the best
of 'em.

*O.*—I mean, won't you leave the abolition army,
and join the free South?

*P.*—Begor I never enlisted in the abolition army, and never will. I agreed to sarve Uncle Sam for five years, and the divil a pin-mark was made in the contract, with my consint, ever since. When my time is up, if the army isn't the same as it is now, I won't join it again.

*O.*—Pat, the "Second" (Cavalry) was only eighteen months old when you and I joined. The man who raised our gallant regiment is now the Southern President: the man who so lately commanded it is now a Southern general. Can you remain in it when they are gone?

*P.*—Well, you see the fact of the matter is, Lieutenant C., I aint much of a scholar; I can't argue the question with you; but what would my mother say if I deserted my colors? Oh, the divil a give I'll ever give in, now, that's the ind of it. I tried to run away once, a few weeks after enlistin', but a man wouldn't be missed thin. It's quite different now, lieutenant, and I'm not going to disgrace either iv my countries.

*O.*—Do you know that you will have to fire on green Irish colors, in the Southern ranks?

*P.*—And won't you have to fire on them colors (pointing to the flag at Fort Bliss) that yerself and five of us licked nineteen Injins under? Sure it isn't a greater shame for an Irishman to fire on Irish colors than for an American to fire on American colors.

An' th' oath 'll be on my side, you know, lieutenant.

*O.*—D—n the man that relies on Paddies, I say.

*P.*—The same compliments to desarters, yer honor.

---

General Meagher has paid the following handsome compliment to the memory of Colonel Haggerty:

" On the silent fields which these noble mountains overlook and these deep graves shadow, I see many a strong and gallant soldier of the Sixty-ninth whom I knew and loved; and they lie there in the rich sunshine, discolored and cold in death. All of them were from Ireland, and as the tide of life rushed out, the last thought that left their hearts was for the liberty of Ireland. Prominent among them, strikingly noticeable by reason of his large iron frame and the boldly chiselled features, on which the impress of great strength of will and intellect was softened by a constant play of humor and the goodness and grand simplicity of his heart—wrapped in his rough old overcoat, with his sword crossed upon his breast, his brow boldly uplifted as though he were still in command, and the consciousness of having done his duty sternly to the last animating the Roman face—there lies James Haggerty—a braver soldier than whom the land of Sarsfield and Shields has not produced, and whose name, worked in gold, upon the colors of the Sixty-ninth, should be henceforth guarded with all the jealousy and pride which inspires a regiment whenever its honor is at stake and its standards are in peril."

# CHAPTER II.

Return of the Sixty-ninth.—Its Reception.—Demonstration at Jones's Wood.—Colonel Meagher authorized to raise a new Regiment or Brigade.—Ably assisted by Committee.—Fort Schuyler.—Interesting Ceremony and Speeches at Presentation of Colors.—Departure of Sixty-ninth for Virginia.—The other Regiments follow.—Deputation of Officers waits on the President.

ON their return to New York the men and officers received a regular ovation. Their reception in Washington, Philadelphia, and even Baltimore, which at that time strongly favored secession, was enthusiastic.

In New York the civic and military bodies turned out to receive them. The multitude that crowded Broadway were wild with excitement, and gave vent to their feelings in vociferous cheers. Banners and flags were dipped in salute as the brave fellows marched by, handkerchiefs waved from fair hands, and bouquets of flowers rained down on them. War was novel to the people; it was a splendid game, with its gilded fascination; and the heroes of the occasion were now cheered and fêted, and graced a New York holiday.

There was one drawback to mar the joyous welcome.

The presence of its gallant colonel was missed from the head of the column. His praise was the general theme, yet he was not there to thank the greeting multitude, and reports were so contradictory regarding his fate that he was looked upon as one lost forever. Other familiar faces, too, were missing. Some were pining in dungeons, others had fought the good fight, and now slept as soldiers should.

Soon after the return of the regiment a grand and enthusiastic festival was held at Jones's Wood, under the auspices of the convention of Irish societies, in behalf of the widows and orphans of the members of the regiment slain at Bull Run. It was computed that there were over twenty thousand present on the occasion, which, considering that an entrance fee was charged, was one of the grandest demonstrations which took place in support of the war.

Captain Meagher, who was the orator of the occasion, was introduced in a few appropriate remarks by Judge Connolly, chairman of the committee of arrangements, and a zealous worker in support of the Irish soldier and the wants of their families.

Captain Meagher stepped forward, and was received with a burst of applause. He was fresh from the battle-field, where he had honorably baptized his maiden sword, and his reception was a fit appreciation of his bravery and talent.

His speech on the occasion was truly grand and sublime—a noble tribute to brother-soldiers in battle, a high eulogium on the greatness and justness of the American Constitution, and a powerful appeal to his countrymen to rise in defence of the flag which waved its protecting folds over them, when fleeing from the upas poison of England's supremacy.

He gave a vivid account of the operations of the regiment during its service, and of its noble behavior in the battle.

This able speech had a powerful influence in firing up the spirits of the people and inducing them to join the army.

On the 15th of August Captain Meagher received a telegram from General Fremont, highly complimentary to both parties :

HEADQUARTERS DEPARTMENT OF THE WEST,
St. Louis, Mo., August 15, 1861.

CAPTAIN THOMAS F. MEAGHER :

Will you accept the position of aide-de-camp on my staff, with rank of colonel ? If so, report to me.

JOHN C. FREMONT,
Major-General Commanding.

This handsome offer was gracefully declined by Captain Meagher, as he had been apprised that the Sixty-ninth was about re-enlisting, and he was offered the colonelcy of it.

He at once wrote to the War Department, offering his services, as well as those of his regiment, and soon received the following official reply:

WAR DEPARTMENT, WASHINGTON,
August 30, 1861.

COLONEL THOMAS F. MEAGHER, New York:

SIR—The regiment of infantry known as the Sixty-ninth Infantry, which you offer, is accepted for three years, or during the war, provided you have it ready for marching orders in thirty days. This acceptance is with the distinct understanding that this department will revoke the commissions of all officers who may be found incompetent for the proper discharge of their duties.

Your men will be mustered into the United States service in accordance with General Orders Nos. 58 and 61.

You are further authorized to arrange with the colonels commanding of four other regiments to be raised to form a brigade, the brigadier-general for which will be designated hereafter by the proper authority of Government.

Very respectfully your obedient servant,
THOMAS A. SCOTT,
Assistant Secretary of War.

On receipt of this order, Colonel Meagher, aided by his numerous friends and friends of the cause, decided on forming an Irish Brigade, and offering the command to General Shields, whose arrival from California was soon expected.

He designed raising three regiments in New York, one in Massachusetts, and another in Pennsylvania.

In B. S. Treanor, Esq., of Boston, he found an able supporter and assistant.

In New York, too, he was ably supported by several prominent and patriotic citizens. Foremost among them with their advice, their services, and their purses were Archbishop Hughes, Judge Daly, Daniel Devlin, James T. Brady, Andrew Carrigan, John Savage, Richard O'Gorman, and others. An address was issued and committees formed. The names of the members and their patriotic objects will be seen by the following extract :

" To aid in the formation and dispatch of the Irish Brigade, a committee of citizens who sympathize with the movement has been organized, and now appeals to the public, and particularly to all who claim Irish birth or lineage, for assistance in this most important object.

" The names of the sub-committees will be found below.

" The committee on collections is charged with the organization of collections throughout the city and vicinity, and is proceeding rapidly to the formation of ward collecting-committees, which will be announced in a few days. Pending the organization of the subordinate collection-committees, all persons willing to contribute to this national and patriotic object are invited to hand in their subscriptions, whether large or small, to any member of the committee on collections.

The committees are as follows :

" Joseph Stuart, President ; Richard Bell and Richard O'Gorman, Vice-Presidents ; Eugene Kelly, Treasurer.

"J. T. Doyle, and subsequently John Savage, Secretary.

"EXECUTIVE COMMITTEE.--Daniel Devlin, Richard O'Gorman, Richard Bell, Joseph Stuart, Charles P. Daly, Andrew Carrigan, James O'Grady, Samuel Sloan, William Mitchell, John Savage, Eugene Kelly, John T. Doyle.

"ON FINANCE.—Joseph Stuart, Felix Ingoldsby, Richard Bell, Charles P. Daly, Samuel Sloan, William Watson.

"ON EQUIPMENT.—Walter Magee, Edward C. Donnelly, Andrew Carrigan, Joseph P. Quin, Eugene Kelly.

"ON RELIEF.—Andrew Carrigan, Edward Hart, John Hennessy, Bernard Casserly, Felix E. O'Rourke, Charles P. Daly, James B. Nicholson.

"ON COLLECTIONS.—James O'Grady, Stephen Philbin, Edward C. Donnelly, Richard O'Gorman, Denis Hennessy, Andrew Carrigan, Edmund H. Miller, James Murphy, Henry L. Hoguet, William P. Powers, William L. Cole, of New York.

" Samuel Sloan, Peter Rice, Daniel O'Reilly, Edward Hart, Bernard Casserly, of Brooklyn."

The exertions of Colonel T. F. Meagher were ably assisted by the above committee. Under such combined influence, it is no wonder that the ranks filled up rapidly.

As each company was formed and mustered in it was sent to Fort Schuyler. under command of Colonel Robert Nugent.

At the formation of the Sixty-third, a deputation of officers offered its colonelcy to Felix E. O'Rourke, Esq.

So great was the rush of Irishmen to the ranks of the Brigade, that recruits came from Albany, Utica, Buffalo, Pittsburgh, and other remote towns and places.

The Philadelphia regiment was to be commanded by Captain Robert Emmet Patterson, of the regular army, and son of General Patterson. This was to be accompanied by a squadron of cavalry under Captain Gallagher, for years instructor in cavalry tactics in Carlisle Barracks.

The Boston regiment was to be commanded by Colonel Matthew Murphy.

The patriotic ladies of New York caught up the enthusiasm, and resolved themselves into an effective working committee, for the purpose of getting up an embroidered stand of colors for each of the New York regiments of the Irish Brigade.

On the evening of the 6th of October, Colonel

Meagher delivered one of his most brilliant addresses to a crowded audience in the Academy of Music, taking for his subject, "The Irish Soldier—His History and present Duty to the American Republic—The National Cause, its Justice, Sanctity, and Grandeur—The Memories of the National Flag, and its promised Glory." The gifted speaker seemed almost inspired as he described the many battle-fields in which the Irish soldier had made his mark. Then he depicted in thrilling words the grandeur and greatness of the American nation and its glorious Constitution, and the duty Irishmen owed to a Government which threw open its protecting arms to receive them, exiles, to its maternal bosom. This truly eloquent speech had good effect, and brought many a stalwart recruit to the ranks of the Irish Brigade.

Fort Schuyler, named in honor of General Schuyler, commands a splendid view of Long Island Sound. It has fine casemates, an extensive esplanade, and mounts several guns of large calibre. The interior is roomy and spacious for drill purposes. The situation of the fort, on a jutting neck of land, is delightful.

Here the men spent their time pleasantly enough, reclining on the grass, watching the innumerable sloops and steamers floating by ; or perched along the beach, rod in hand, awaiting a nibble; or, perhaps, watching the declining sun gilding the woods with its golden beams, while around was diffused the purple haze of an Indian summer.

This was the *Alma Mater* of the Brigade, where it learned its A B C of military tactics. Here friendships were formed to be severed only by death. Here they were visited by their wives and children, and many a pleasant day passed over in sweet forgetfulness of the past and hope of the future.

This soon passed away, and the tread of the brave fellows' march echoed on Virginia battle-plains, and their banners soon flaunted defiantly in the face of the foe, and coffinless graves shrouded the manly hearts that now vibrated with love and hope.

After a world of toil and labor, Colonel Meagher succeeded in fairly launching the Irish Brigade.

The Sixty-ninth had its ranks filled, and was ordered to Washington. This gallant regiment was commanded by Colonel Nugent, who served under Colonel Corcoran as lieutenant-colonel of the old Sixty-ninth.

The ladies of New York had prepared their colors, to present to the regiment previous to their departure.

The ceremony was a most imposing one, and was attended by some of the most respectable and fashionable ladies and gentlemen of the city. The flags were six in number, with a corresponding number of guidons, and were of the richest silk, and executed in Tiffany's best style.

The national flags were magnificently embroidered, and fringed with saffron-colored silk; the stars were of white silk on a blue field, and in the centre, in a crimson stripe, was the name of the regiment.

The staffs were surmounted by a globe, with a gilt eagle, with the mounting heavily plated with gold and embellished with two rich crimson tassels pendent from each.

The regimental flags were of a deep rich green, heavily fringed, having in the centre a richly embroidered Irish harp, with a sunburst above it and a wreath of shamrock beneath. Underneath, on a crimson scroll, in Irish characters, was the motto, "They shall never retreat from the charge of lances."

Each flag bore the numerical designation of its respective regiment; namely, Sixty-ninth Regiment New York State Volunteers, First Regiment Irish Brigade, Eighty-eighth and Sixty-third the same, but designated according to their respective numbers.

The staff-mountings were silver-plated; the top being a pike-head, under which was knotted a long bannerol of saffron-colored silk, fringed with bullion, and marked with the number of the regiment.

These flags looked gorgeous, and the needlework, performed by the fair donors themselves, was exquisitely executed.

The guidons were got up with like taste and élegance, and had the State and brigade number of the regiments embroidered on each.

The presentation took place at the residence of his Grace the Most Reverend Archbishop Hughes, in Madison Avenue, on the 18th November.

The streets around the Archbishop's residence were crowded from an early hour. A large number of the *élite* of the city were present.

In the absence of the Archbishop in Europe, the ceremony was performed by the Very Reverend Dr Starrs, Vicar-General.

The steamer Atlas brought the Sixty-ninth from Fort Schuyler, it being the only regiment ready to start, and the officers of the other regiments, who had come to receive the flags and witness the ceremony. The troops landed about eleven o'clock, at the foot of Thirty-fourth street, and formed into column, and were escorted by the First Cavalry and flanked by the batteries of Captains Hogan and McMahon. On arriving at Madison Avenue the column was halted, and faced to the front, amid the cheers of the multitude.

The Very Reverend Dr. Starrs addressed the soldiers as follows :

" Soldiers of the Irish Brigade, officers and men, the Most Reverend Archbishop of New York, previous to his departure for Europe, requested me to attend on this occasion, as his representative, and to open the proceedings by addressing to you a few words. I take great pleasure in complying with his request. I regret that he is not present, because I know that you would be better pleased to see him and hear his voice. However, I know his sentiments in your regard; I know his good wishes are with you; I know he has confidence in your patriotism and your loyalty to the Union and Constitution. I know that he has confidence in the fidelity of the Irish soldiers, for history has told us that the Irish soldier has always done his duty at home and abroad. Wherever his services have been employed he has never been found wanting. He has always been faithful to the trusts confided to him. I regret very much the disturbed state of our country,—to see this great republic, the wonder of the world for many years, so distracted by civil war. I trust, ere long, that the cry of war, which has taken possession of every part of this great nation, will pass away, and that peace will be restored on an honorable and just basis, and all become again united and happy. I will not detain you longer, as colors are to be presented to the Colonel of the regiment by kind and patriotic ladies, and addresses are to be delivered on their behalf by distinguished gentlemen present. I will conclude by exhorting you to be faithful soldiers, faithful in the discharge of all your duties. In the time of trial forget not your God—be Christian

soldiers. And may He who holds in his hands the
issues of life and death, and the destinies of nations,
be with you and direct you in all your actions."

Colonel Nugent then advanced to the front, and Mrs.
Chalfin, the lady deputed to make the presentation to
the Sixty-ninth, was led forward by Judge Daly, the
colors being borne by an orderly. Their appearance
was the signal for a peal of cheers. Judge Daly
said :

" Colonel Nugent, I am requested by this lady
beside me—Mrs. Chalfin—the daughter of an Irishman and the wife of an officer in the regular army of
the United States, and by the ladies associated with
her, to offer to your regiment the accompanying stand
of colors. In committing to your charge these two
flags, I need scarcely remind you that the history of
the one is pregnant with a meaning in the light which
it sheds upon the history of the other. This green
flag, with its ancient harp, its burst of sunlight, and its
motto from Ossian, in the old Irish tongue, recalls
through the long lapse of many centuries the period
when Ireland was a nation, and conveys more elo-
quently than by words how that nationality was lost
through the practical working of that doctrine of
secession for which the rebellious States of the South
have taken up arms. The period of Ireland's greatness was attained when the petty princes who ruled

separate parts of the country, and kept it in unceasing turmoil, were finally subdued, and the spectacle of a united people, under one government, was presented in the wise and beneficent administration of that truly great monarch, Brian Borhoime.  It is that happy period in Ireland's history upon which her bards love to dwell, her historians to dilate, and around which cluster the proudest of her historical recollections.  By what means was that nationality extinguished, and when did Ireland's miseries begin?  When her ambitious leaders, the Jefferson Davises of that period, overthrew the fabric of the national government, and instituted in its stead distinct and separate sovereignties, through whose internal weakness and clashing interests Ireland was finally brought under the power of that stalwart English monarchy which has since held her in its iron grasp.  Does an Irishman, therefore, ask what his duty is in this contest?  Let him learn it in the history of his own country, in the story of that green flag.  Let him, contemplating the sorrows of his mother Erin,

> ' Remember the days of old,
> Ere her faithless sons betrayed her.'

"What is asked of an Irishman in this crisis?  He is asked to preserve that government which Montgomery died to create, and which those Irishmen who signed the Declaration of Independence, George Taylor, James Smith, and Matthew Thornton, meant to transmit, with its manifold blessings, to every Irishman who should make this country the land of his adoption. To the Irish race it has been in every sense a country. A country where their native energy and stimulated industry have met with appropriate rewards, and where they have enjoyed an amount of political consequence and exercised a degree of political influence not found in the land of their nativity Whatever may be the result of our experiment of self-government, the Irish race in America is as responsible for the result as any other. That it has its defects none of us are vain enough to deny; but if, in view of what it has accomplished, any Irish adopted citizen is willing to give it up, let him go and live under the monarchy of Great Britain; but if he still has faith in the teachings of Tone and the example of Lord Edward Fitzgerald, let him stand by that form of government here which they sacrificed their lives to obtain for Irishmen. To preserve that form of government here, it must be sustained as it has hitherto been, in the grandeur, integrity, and power of a nation, and not by a Mexican division into weak and rickety republics. To secure that great end, you are now in arms, and as a part of the military force that has come to the rescue of the Republic, you and the organization of which you form a part, have a weighty and ennobling responsibility.

"You have chosen to be known by the number of a regiment already distinguished in the beginning of this contest, the reputation of which you have assumed to maintain; but more than this, you and the organization to which you belong have designated yourselves by the proudest name in Irish military annals—that of the Irish Brigade. That celebrated corps achieved its historical renown not through the admitted bravery of its members merely, but chiefly by the perfection of its discipline; and it will be precisely in the proportion that you imitate it in this respect, that you will or will not be known hereafter. The selection of such a name only renders the contrast more glaring in the event of inefficiency and incompetency; and it were well, therefore, that the officers and men of the new organization should remember that if any part of the glory which the Irish Brigade achieved upon the plains of Ramilies, the heights of Fontenoy, and at the gate of Cremona, is to descend upon them, it will not be by adopting its name, but by proving hereafter, by their discipline and by their deeds, that they are worthy to bear it.

"You, too, Colonel Nugent, have your own responsibility. You bear the name of that gallant Colonel Nugent who, at the head of the Irish horse, at the battle of Spires, broke the compact infantry of the

Prince of Hesse, and decided the fortune of the day. The Irish soldier has been distinguished by military critics for his recognition of the necessity of implicit military obedience, for the cheerfulness with which he endures the privations and hardships incident to a military life, and for his daring impetuosity in battle. Look to it, that you maintain that character.

" Sir Charles Napier has borne the highest compliment to the merits of a disciplined Irish regiment, in the account which he gives of the one led by him at the battle of Meeanee, in the war of Scinde, and which he calls 'magnificent Tipperary!' With this single corps of but four hundred men and two thousand native troops he encountered and defeated twenty-eight thousand of the warlike Belooches. Of the decisive charge with the bayonet he glowingly tells us how this thoroughly disciplined Irish regiment moved, as on a review, across a plain swept by the fire of the enemy, the men keeping touch and step, and looking steadfastly in the face of their foe. These are examples of Irish valor when regulated by discipline, which, if you may not rival, you can at least try to imitate.

" Again, I commit these colors to your charge, and in view of the obligation imposed upon every officer and soldier by their acceptance, it may not be out of place to mention in that connection, that at the commencement of this war, I had occasion to offer, as the gift of a woman, I think the first flag presented to a regiment departing from this city for the defence of the National Capital. Of that regiment, the old Sixty-ninth, you, sir, were the second in command; and at the head of it was the noble-minded, high-spirited, and gallant officer to whom so much of its after character was due. A descendant by the female line of that illustrious Irish soldier, Patrick Sarsfield, Earl of Lucan, whose name is identified with the siege of Limerick, and who fell fighting at the head of his brigade upon the bloody field of Landen, Colonel Corcoran, in the spirit of his noble ancestor, received that flag with a soldier's promise, and kept that promise with a soldier's faith. It was not brought back from the field of Manassas on that day of disastrous rout and panic, but he at least and the little band who stood around him in its defence went with it into captivity. I need say no more, when presenting this splendid gift with which these ladies have honored your regiment, than to point to this Irish example of the faith and fidelity that is due by a soldier to his flag. Colonel Corcoran is now within the walls of a rebel prison, one of the selected victims for revengeful Southern retaliation; but he has the satisfaction of feeling that he owes his sad, though proud pre-eminence, to having acted as became a descendant of Sarsfield.

" Of this beautiful American standard, illustrative

alike of the munificence of its donors and of the skill
of the hands that wrought it, I would say to you, as a
parting injunction, in the language of John Savage's
song of the Sixty-ninth—

> 'Plant that flag
> On fort and crag,
> With the people's voice of thunder.' "

When the cheers that followed Judge Daly's remarks subsided, Colonel Nugent received the flags
from Mrs. Chalfin, and made a very appropriate reply.

Colonel Baker and the officers of the Eighty-eighth
stepped in front of the archiepiscopal residence, when
Mrs. Thomas F. Meagher was led forward by Malcolm
Campbell, Esq. The appearance of this distinguished
and patriotic lady, to whose exertions the ceremonial
of the day was largely owing, was hailed in the most
exultant manner. Mr. Campbell's address was in a
spirited and patriotic style. He alluded to the past
services of the Irish soldier, and concluded thus :

" With confidence and hope, then, the hands of
beauty commit these standards to the protection of
Irish valor. Guard them well—bear them firmly
through the shock of battle—make the flaunting flag
of sedition trail in the dust before these insignia of
the majesty of the people, and return them, in tattered
shreds if you will, dyed in blood, and begrimed with
the dust and smoke of battle, but free from the

slightest stain or speck of dishonor. Do this, and there is still hope that the wish that lingers on the lips of your dying patriots may yet be gloriously realized,

'That in the days to come the *Green* shall flutter o'er the *Red*.'"

Colonel Baker received the colors from Mrs. Meagher, and, having transferred them to the color-bearer, made a very suitable reply.

Colonel Meagher, as commandant of the proposed fifth regiment of the Brigade, then advanced to the front, the regimental standards were brought forth, and Miss Devlin, who was to present them, was led forward by John T. Doyle, Esq., who addressed Colonel Meagher and his officers in an able and patriotic speech, which he concluded thus:

"Sir, these colors are the gift of fair women to brave men. I need say nothing to you or to your regiment as to the way you are to guard them. You know a soldier's duty, and will discharge it. When the war is over, and peace and Union have been restored, you will bring them back here, stained perhaps with the dust and smoke of battle, reddened with blood, rent into strips by the storm and the wind, and riddled with bullets, so that the stars may be seen through them. But you will bring them back untarnished by defeat or dishonor. So shall they be preserved forever, hung up as sacred relics, which will commemorate to us and to our posterity for all time the deeds, the sufferings, the victories, and the virtues of the Irish Brigade."

Colonel Meagher received the colors from the hands of Miss Devlin. He made a short speech in reply, thanking the noble, patriotic ladies for their handsome present, and assuring them that these flags would be preserved inviolate, and would be guarded by them while a man of the regiment remained. When confronting the foe with those standards before them, he would say to his regiment: "Boys, look on those flags; remember the 18th of November; think of those who presented them to you; *die* if necessary, but never surrender."

At the conclusion of the ceremony three cheers were given for the fair donors, the column was reformed, and proceeded on board the Atlas.

The flag presentation to the Sixty-third, made by W. E. Robinson, Esq., had already taken place on the 7th, at its headquarters, Camp Carrigan, David's Island.

The Sixty-ninth was enthusiastically received in Baltimore and Washington, and the other regiments made rapid preparations to follow. The Sixty-ninth regiment remained a few weeks at Fort Corcoran, but early in December was assigned to Major-General Sumner's division, then encamped near Alexandria. Sumner had lately commanded the Department of

the Pacific, and was a great admirer of Irish soldiers.
The only trouble he had with them, he said, was to
keep up with them in the charge.

In a few weeks the Eighty-eighth and Sixty-third
were ready to follow. They marched through New
York, with Acting Brigadier-General T. F. Meagher
and staff at their head. The strength of the brigade
was as follows :

The Sixty-ninth, about 745 men ; the Eighty-eighth,
about 800 ; and the Sixty-third close on 1,000.

In a few days they joined their old comrades about
two miles from Alexandria, on the road to Springfield
Junction and Fairfax. The camp-ground was on a
dry sloping hill, and commanded a magnificent view.
The batteries of the brigade, under Captains Hogan,
McMahon, Mitchel, and O'Donohue, were under the
command of Major O'Neil.

It was expected that General Shields would take
command of the brigade, which had been tendered to
him. Shields held the rank of major-general in the
Mexican army, and it would be incompatible with his
dignity and services to take a brigadiership with civilian
major-generals over him ; besides, in his reply declining
the offer, he stated that there was no one so well entitled
to the command as Colonel Meagher himself, who had
raised the brigade, and shared the honors and perils of
the first battle of the war with the gallant Sixty-ninth.

Some enemies of Colonel Meagher were intriguing against him, and, in fact, wanted the command to be conferred on an American officer.

When we consider all he did, with pen and tongue, to aid the Union cause, his arduous labors in raising the brigade, we must feel surprised at such petty opposition to a command which he raised himself.

As soon as the officers of the brigade heard of these intrigues they convened a meeting. Resolutions were unanimously adopted in favor of Colonel Meagher's appointment to the command, and the following delegation was appointed to wait on the President, expressing the views of the officers and men of the brigade: Majors Quinlan and O'Neil, Dr. Reynolds, Captains Maxwell O'Sullivan, Butler, Galway, McMahon (Sixty-ninth), Hogan, O'Donaghue, McMahon, Lynch (Sixty-third), and Quartermaster O'Hanlon.

The deputation was accompanied by Colonel Forney, and introduced by the Hon. Preston King, of New York. The views of the deputation were ably seconded by the above gentlemen, and also by Colonel, afterwards Major-General, Frank P. Blair, of Missouri.

The President complimented Colonel Meagher for his patriotism and devotion; also, for his gallant services at Bull Run, and for his services in enrolling such a fine body of men as the Irish Brigade.

He promised to give the subject his earnest consideration.

Next day the name of Acting Brigadier-General Thomas F. Meagher was sent before the Senate by the President, for confirmation as brigadier-general.

# CHAPTER III.

Removal of McDowell.—McClellan assumes command of the army.—
Camp California.—Sketch of General Meagher's quarters.—Christmas
in camp.—Mass in camp.—camp scenes and camp amusements.—
Out on picket.—Brigade drills.—New-Year's Day in camp.

GENERAL McCLELLAN had been ordered to Washington, from Western Virginia, where he was brilliantly successful, to replace General McDowell, who had been relieved after the miserable failure of Bull Run.

On the 25th of July the War Department announced that "The Department of Washington and the Department of Northeastern Virginia will constitute a geographical division, under General McClellan, United States Army—headquarters, Washington." Soon after this the venerable and venerated General Scott resigned command of the United States army, finding that the emergency required a younger and more active man, and was replaced by Major-General McClellan.

McClellan found every thing in confusion. Though there were about fifty thousand troops around Washington, they were badly armed and worse disciplined. He had infantry without guns or camp-equipments; troopers on foot; artillery without horses; the commissariat and quartermaster's departments without wagons, and the medical department without ambulances. Out of such a mass of disorganized elements he had to create an army, and fit it out with all the necessary supplies and equipments, before he could think of taking the field.

He had the fall and winter before him; but, then, the rebels did not mean to let him rest, for Beauregard and Johnston occupied Fairfax, Manassas, and other important points, thus threatening Washington; while a large force had to be detached, under Banks, to occupy Harper's Ferry and the upper lines of the Potomac.

Camp California was so called by the brigade in honor of Major-General Sumner, who commanded the division in which the brigade served. General Sumner, who was also colonel in the regular cavalry, had just returned from California.

The camp commanded a splendid panoramic view of a long stretch of country. It was situated on a rising ground, near the Seminary, between two and three miles from Alexandria. At first it was covered with trees and dense brush; these being cleared away, except some shade-trees, a pretty camp soon sprung up,

like a canvas city. Here the three regiments were
pleasantly encamped, occupying the brows of two hills,
between which lies the road leading from Alexandria
to Fairfax. On the right of the road, as you go from
Alexandria, were the tents of the Sixty-ninth and
Sixty-third, and on the left those of the Eighty-eighth.
From this position there was a very fine view. A perfect amphitheatre of hills girds the plains, looking
picturesque with their waving forests of trees and
innumerable white tents. Some rich valleys of land
lie beneath, and the red brick walls of Alexandria
glow in the distance. There is a slight view of the
waters of the Potomac, while distinctly beyond it rise
the hills of Maryland. About ten miles on the right
is Mount Vernon, the home and grave of the immortal Washington. The encampments were laid out
with the regularity of streets. The tents looked comfortable; some were boarded, their sides lined with
timber slabs, and roofed with canvas; others were built
of light logs, with the interstices plastered with mud.
Inside bright fires crackled and glowed, giving them
a pleasant, cheerful appearance; while outside many of
them, huge piles of burning logs made comfortable
camp-fires. Around these the men were grouped,
some cooking, some furbishing up their arms after
returning from drill, others pitching quoits, or collected
together, listening to some story-teller spinning his

yarns, or to some veteran of the old Sixty-ninth re-
counting for the hundredth time the adventures of that
day—how they fought, and were overpowered—how
every one ran away but themselves, and how at length
they were overslaughed by that awful bugbear, " the
Black-horse Cavalry."

Bull Run was, in the opinion of those engaged in it,
second only to Waterloo, and was a prolific subject
until greater events and greater battles completely
dwarfed it. Throughout the day your ears were assailed with the tramp of marching troops, the clashing
of arms as officers and orderlies dashed by, or as the
many squads drilling on every side came to an " order
arms" or " fix bayonets."

As we are describing the camp of the Irish Brigade,
it is but fair that we drop into headquarters, and
give a pen-sketch of the chief of that gallant little
band, General Thomas F. Meagher, and of his quarters.

On a gentle slope, sheltered by a shady clump of
trees, are pitched the headquarters of the Irish
Brigade. In front of the clean, white rows of tents
are the American colors and the Irish green flag, near
which a sentry with measured pace walks his beat.
In the rear are less pretending tents, grotesquely huddled together.

These are the quarters of the cooks, orderlies, officers'

servants, and provost-guard. Here there is an exciting bustle; some of the men are brushing down the
horses that have just come in; others are preparing
dinner; while one is amusing himself by scratching an
old asthmatic fiddle, and humming some plaintive Irish
ditty about " The girl I left behind me."

We next enter the general's tent. It is small, but
neat and comfortable. The floor is nicely boarded; a
bed, covered with a buffalo robe, lies at one side; a
huge fire of logs glows and crackles in a cavernous
chimney contrived at the rear. In the centre is a
table covered with baize cloth, papers, and writing materials. Near this stands an orderly, cap in hand,
while behind it, on a camp-stool, folding a letter, sits a
man of commanding presence and portly proportions.

His head is round and fair-sized: his hair, which is
a little inclined to gray, is brushed sideways. His
features are strong and distinct, with rather prominent
nose and firmly set lips. His face is shaven, except a
moustache and slight imperial. He is of medium
height, well and finely built, with a great depth of
chest, and fine development of muscle and frame. As
he stands erect, clothed in his rich uniform of a brigadier-general, there is a grandeur and stateliness, and a
sense of intellect and power about him, that make you
almost think you are looking upon one of the old Irish
princes of medieval times.

After the disastrous failure of '48 came the felon's fate and exile. Even when drinking this chalice, the martyr's soul quailed not; for under the shadow of the gallows he spoke words that yet cheer the children of the clubs and the barricades, and are prized by the scholar and patriot.

After this came the convict-ship, with all its loathsome associations—wanderings by sea and land for many a bleak day and weary night—exile and loneliness in the back woods of Australia—the escape, with its many dark and checkered reverses.

America had welcomed him to her bosom: he now stood beside her in her hour of need. His pen of light and his burning words fired many a brave heart to uphold the flag of the Union with its best blood.

His military reputation stands boldly forth from the first Bull Run, through the Peninsula's gloomy campaigns; on Antietam's bloody plains; in that desperate charge on the heights of Fredericksburg; through Chancellorsville, until he sheathed his sword.

Meet him in sociable moments, he is overflowing with wit and humor of the raciest kind; caustic and cutting against intriguers, speculators, and political charlatans, but genial and flowing towards his friends. Full of buoyant vivacity, wit, humor, and historical lore, there is no more genial, instructive, or delightful companion than General Thomas Francis Meagher.

For the most part, the men were kept actively en-gaged during the day by the duties and routine of camp-life. It is only at night that this busy hum of martial life and bustle sank into repose. Then ten thousand camp-fires glowed and sparkled from hill and dale, looking through the darkness of night like the gas-lights of a city.

The imagination can easily picture the scene. The sentinels challenge: the sound of the bugle rings clearly and musically on the night air. Around the immense pine-fires that glow and flame the men were grouped, singing, joking, laughing with a light-hearted ease, as if they never knew "dull care." Most of them were full of practical jokes, light and sparkling as champagne, and had a gay faculty of taking the sunny side of every thing.

Near one of the huge fires a kind of arbor was nicely constructed of the branches of trees, which were so in terwoven on one another as to form a kind of wall. In side this, some were seated on logs, some reclining in true Turkish style.

Seated near the fire was Johnny Flaherty, discours-ing sweet music from his violin. Johnny hailed from Boston; was a musical genius, in his way, and though only fourteen years of age, could play on the bagpipes, piano, and Heaven knows how many other instru-ments: beside him sat his father, fingering the chanters of a bagpipe in elegant style. It is no wonder that most of the regiment were gathered around there, for it was Christmas Eve, and home-thoughts and home-longings were crowding on them; and old scenes and fancies would arise with sad and loving memories, until the heart grew weary, and even the truest and tenderest longed for home associations this blessed Christmas Eve.

No wonder' if, amidst such scenes, the soldier's thought fled back to his home, to his loved wife, to the kisses of his darling child, to the fond Christmas greeting of his parents, brothers, sisters, friends, until his eyes were dimmed with the dews of the heart. The exile feels a longing desire, particularly at Christmas times, for the pleasant, genial firesides and loving hearts of home. How many of that group will, ere another Christmas comes round, sleep in a bloody and nameless grave! Generous and kind hands may smooth the dying soldier's couch; or he may linger for days, tortured by thirst and pain, his festering wounds creeping with maggots, his tongue swollen, and a fierce fever festering up his body as he lies out on that dreary battle-field; or, perhaps, he has dragged himself beneath the shade of some pine to die by inches, where no eye but God's and his pitying angels' shall see him, where no human aid can succor him. Years afterwards, some wayfarer may discover a skeleton with the remains of a knapsack under the skull. This is too often the end of the soldier's dreams of glory, and all

"The pride, pomp, and circumstance of glorious war."

It is but a short transition from love, and hope, and life, to sorrow and death.

Another Christmas, and many a New England cottage, and many a home along the Rhine and the Shannon, will be steeped in affliction for the loving friends who have laid their bones on the battle-fields of Virginia.

If any indulged in such reflections, the lively tones of Johnny O'Flaherty's fiddle, and the noisy squeaks of his father's bagpipes, soon called forth the joyous, frolicksome nature of the Celt.

Groups were dancing, around the fire, jigs, reels, and doubles.

Even the colored servants had collected in a little group by themselves, and while some timed the music by slapping their hands on their knees, others were capering and whirling around in the most grotesque manner, showing their white teeth, as they grinned their delight, or "yah-yahed," at the boisterous fun.

The dance is enlivened by laugh, song, story, and music; and the canteen, filled with wretched "commissary," goes freely around, for the men wish to observe Christmas-times right freely.

"Arrah musha, Johnny O'Flaherty, sthop that fiddle and take a drink, alanna," said a wiry red-haired man, with a strong Kerry accent. "Do, Johnny," said the father, who had taken a long pull at the canteen himself, and now proffered it to his son.

"It is as well to keep up our spirits by pouring spirits down, for sure there's no knowing where we'll be this night twelvemonth," exclaimed another of the group, as with a sigh he comforted himself from his canteen.

"Thrue for you, Bill Dooley; shure myself thinks that our rations will be mighty short again another Christmas comes round," said a little cynic, who was pulling very hard at a dudeen.

"Begor then, Jem, maybe they would be long enough for us."

"Well, boys, long or short we won't disgrace the poor ould dart, any way."

"Bravo, Flannigan, bravo! you said the truth in that."

"Bad scran if I can see what the ould dart (Ireland) has to do with it at all, at all," replied the cynic, as he knocked the ashes out of his pipe against the log.

"Oh, dear me! do ye hear that? and would you disgrace it?" exclaimed an indignant patriot.

"And shure won't they be lookin' at us at home, to see how we'll fight?" said another.

" An' I'd rather be in my grave, any day, than have it said that I was a coward," said a young fellow, slapping his hand forcibly on his thigh.

" Well, that's all very fine," said the cynic, who, seeing the force of evidence against him, was fain to recant; " but, boys, if we were fighting for the poor ould dart, wouldn't it be glorious ?"

" Bad luck to you, Jeff Davis, any way ; only for you we'd be at home, comfortable and happy, with the girls, this blessed Christmas Eve !" exclaimed a lovesick youth.

How often in the lull of battle have I heard the Irish soldier, begrimed with powder, as he grasped his comrades' hands, exclaim, " What harm, if it were for the poor old dart ?"

How is it that the Government of England is blind to the ruin that a people so numerous and powerful in foreign countries, and hating her so intensely, is sure to bring on her in her hour of trouble ?

It might be politic to try conciliation, instead of co- ercion, on such a people.

The dance was followed by songs; and those soft, impassioned Irish airs, " The girl I left behind me," and " Home, Sweet Home," flowed sweetly and softly from hearts that felt their full force; but as the strong political songs of " The Rapparee," and " The Green above the Red," and " Fontenoy," were chorused by a hundred throats, that dark group of soldiers,

3*

scattered around the fire, looked as if ready to grasp their muskets and rush on some hidden foe.

These innocent and exciting revels continued until the tinkle of a small bell from a rustic chapel suddenly hushed the boisterous mirth, and all arose, reverentially doffed their hats, and proceeded to the chapel.

Fathers Willett and Dillon were going to celebrate the midnight Mass. The chapel tents were as well decorated as circumstances would allow. In front of the open tent in which the priest officiated were rude benches of hewn logs, sheltered on each side and overhead by boughs of trees, supported by poles.

The chapel was situated on the brow of a hill, and tall cedars and pines flung their sheltering arms over it.

Father Dillon was chanting a Low Mass, the responses being made by Quartermaster Haverty and Captain O'Sullivan, while the attentive audience crowded the small chapel, and were kneeling outside on the damp ground under the cold night-air.

Father Dillon read the beautiful gospel from Saint Luke, giving an account of the journeyings of Joseph and Mary, and the birth of the infant Saviour in the manger at Bethlehem; after which his hearers quietly retired to their tents.

The weather in camp was fine, almost resembling an Indian-summer. A slight frost at night and a shower of soft snow were the only indications of winter.

In Virginia, the weather at this season is generally mild and balmy, with little of the heavy frost and angry storms that rage at the North.

Such was Christmas morning, 1861, in the camp of the Irish Brigade, where willing hearts piously welcomed this holy festival, laden with the richest freight of happy recollections.

The morning Mass was celebrated in the open air, in order to accommodate the thronging worshippers.

On that hill-side, overlooking the tented valleys, the surpliced clergyman, the attentive congregation, the rude and picturesque chapel, were a rich subject for the pencil of the painter.

Then officers and men returned to their quarters, and tried to pass Christmas day in camp as pleasantly as possible. Hospitable tents were crowded, the "materials" were somehow provided, old friends and old flames at home were toasted, pipes were smoked, conversation became brilliant, and Christmas night was duly honored in camp.

We will accompany a regiment going out on picket, in order to give our readers an idea of how the men got on.

The Sixty-ninth left camp in light marching order, under Lieutenant-Colonel James Kelly and Major Cavanagh; their blankets were thrown over their shoulders, their guns clean and bright. They marched past Clouds' Mills, thence through the woods and heavy roads until they reached Edsall's Hill, some seven miles from camp. Here they halted and established their reserve post, while further on they placed the pickets, with strict orders to keep a sharp lookout.

It was night; the men had to scramble through the brush and trees, through hills and ravines, to gain the different stations.

The position of the advance pickets of a cold winter's night, with the sleet, and snow, and cold wind piercing through them, is not an enviable one. They are not allowed any fire, for in the thick brush beyond, not four hundred yards off, are the rebel pickets, peering out of their lairs, if they catch the blaze of a fire, to reconnoitre, or, perhaps, to send a bullet through some unguarded head.

Thus our pickets in front, quietly and noiselessly, kept their posts. They are relieved every four hours, and then go back to join their comrades, who are grouped around a blazing fire in some ravine, sheltered from the enemy's observation. Here, they are refreshed by a pull at the canteen, and join a game of cards, or listen to those wonderful tales, that, like those of the "Arabian Nights," are got up for the entertainment of the company.

Behind these again, on the side of the hill, are the headquarters of the regiment. Colonel Kelly and

Major Cavanagh enjoy the shelter of a rudely constructed log-house, with an entrance through which you scramble all-fours, and so low inside that you could not stand upright. Yet they are right merry there, and the shanty is crowded with officers, whose companies are in reserve, and who liberally enjoy the colonel's hospitality.

A fine fire blazes in the old log-hut, and the company are frolicsome and jovial, and discuss all sorts of subjects, and many a hearty Irish national song rings on the night air.

The officers of the day, and perhaps the officers of the guard, come to report; and as they are cold, or wet, or dry, as the case may be, the "materials" are again called into requisition, and the crackling logs are poked up to make them throw out more heat and light.

At the other fires around the hill the men are congregated in numbers, enjoying the heat and reclining on rough benches, or couches of cedar and pine boughs. Beside them, and within reach, are their clean muskets. Inexhaustible funds of song and story, jest and joke, are circulated around.

At length some go to sleep, with perhaps the snow or the rain pattering over them; but they are covered by gum-blankets, or their great-coats, with the capes drawn over their heads.

The sentinels walk their beats, and watch for the slightest noise.

Should an alarm be given, or shots fired by the advance pickets, in a moment all are up, under arms, and that hill-side is covered with men ready for any emergency.

Sometimes adventurous officers and men go out beyond the picket lines, particularly when there are farm-houses in view, where some little luxuries could be procured ; or if they chanced to contain the greater attraction of some pretty secesh girls, such attractions were irresistible.

Sometimes the most serious consequences followed these expeditions. The young ladies, in some cases, proved faithless, and betrayed their Yankee admirers ; in other cases, observant bodies of the enemy gobbled up or killed our adventurers.

I knew two officers who were betrayed in this way. Their charmers invited them to a feast on a certain night. On their arrival they found two other ladies present, who were introduced as aunts who had come to them for safety.

The pretended aunts were two rebel officers in disguise, and the betrothed lovers of the girls.

Their servant, suspicious of treachery, wormed the plot out of a colored girl.

Mike pretended to be beastly drunk, tumbled into

the parlor, making all kinds of blunders and apologies, but managed to let his master know how things stood.

The officers seized the pretended ladies, deprived them of their arms, and locked them and their charmers up in the room, and made their escape, though pursued by a small squad of mounted rebels, who were concealed in a large outhouse awaiting the signal from the officers within.

These were more fortunate than another friend of mine, whose servant got killed and himself taken prisoner, under similar circumstances.

Perhaps the men of the Irish Brigade lived on better terms with the rebels than any others. Oftentimes, when the rebel pickets were bitterly firing on our men, they would cease as soon as the Brigade relieved the others, and a most friendly feeling would soon spring up, and a regular barter of coffee, sugar, whiskey, and tobacco take place! An officer on one side would hold up a paper, as a signal that he wanted an exchange. This would be answered on the other side. They would meet between the lines, inquire for mutual friends; would perhaps learn that some cousin or dear friend was on the other side, and send for him. The canteen would be emptied, old times and friends discussed, as the little party seated themselves under shelter of some clump of trees between both lines. In some cases even officers ventured to spend a convivial hour in the enemy's lines. I did it twice, in order to meet an officer who was acquainted with a dear brother, a colonel in the Confederate service. All this is contrary to military orders, and would be severely punished; but men and officers will be sure to select their own time for such escapades.

In front of where the pickets of the Sixty-ninth were stationed lay a long stretch of country, comparatively clear. On the opposite side of this opening the cedars were thick, and the bush dense and tangled. Within these covers the rebel pickets and scouts were concealed. Between the hostile posts were several farm-houses, which were frequented by our adventurous scouts, who were attracted by the fascinations within, and the surroundings, in the way of roosters, pullets, and grunters, without. It was funny to witness the game of cross-purposes between our men and the inmates, who were secret rebels, but pretended Unionists, and who wanted to glean all the information they could for their friends.

"Well, dear me," said a pretty "secesh" to a soldier who was quite soft about her, "what a big army ye have; why, I was upon the top of the hill, and could see all the country covered with tents."

"Faith, in troth, your purty mouth says the truth; shure, though they have all New York making tents for us, we haven't half enough, and every corner of New York is full of men waiting to get tents to join us," replied our gay Celtic Lothario.

" Dear me; I suppose ye'll soon march. Ye cannot remain long here, for want of firewood."

" That's what I'm thinking myself. All the trees around wouldn't make toothpicks for us, let alone cooking and warming; but faix, whenever they go, I know somebody that will leave his heart behind him anyway," and our friend looked most affectionately at the lovely tormentor.

" And can't he stay with his heart ?"

" Troth then that's what he'd like to do, only it is such an ugly thing to be a desarter."

I think I have given my readers a good idea of the pleasures and hardships of picket life, and will now return to camp to witness a brigade drill.

On the 27th of December the Sixty-third, Sixty-ninth, and Eighty-eighth were ordered out for brigade drill by Colonel Nugent. The Sixty-ninth was commanded by Lieutenant-Colonel James Kelly, the Sixty-third by Colonel Enright, and the Eighty-eighth by Colonel Baker.

The drill took place about two miles from the encampment, under shelter of the guns of Fort Ward, one of the innumerable fortifications that command the approaches to Washington.

The day was beautiful and bracing, the wind blew fresh, and the roads and parade-ground were dry and pleasant.

The brigade soon went through the different manœuvres with an alacrity and precision astonishing for such raw material. The Irish soldier has a passion for a military life, and a kind of instinctive perception of its duties, and can, therefore, soon acquire a knowl edge of the most difficult company, regimental, or brigade drill and manœuvres.

Towards evening the troops returned to camp, gay and light-hearted, trudging along the rough Virginia roads, that seemed alternately to run up hill and down hill and into crooked ways, as if seized with a perverse fit of contrariness.

These roads are pleasant enough when not cut into mud sloughs by excessive traffic, or not knee-deep with sticky winter mud, or equally deep with summer dust. There is no firm, clean, macadamized surface, no trim, pleasant hawthorn hedges, with their winter shade and summer fragrance, to shelter and cheer you.

New Year's Day in camp passed over much like Christmas Day. The holidays came round in quick succession, and were duly honored; comrades and companions exchanged sentiment, song, and all those festive hilarities which soldiers can fully appreciate and enjoy.

Father Dillon, too, the chaplain of the Sixty-third,
entered into all the innocent amusements of the
occasion, and established a school and theatricals
for the improvement and amusement of the officers and men. He also gave a party, at which
Johnny O'Flaherty and his violin, accompanied
by his father and bagpipes, figured conspicuously.
The Padre was their patron, and, under his auspices,
Johnny felt himself and fiddle an important acquisi-
tion to the brigade.

Father Dillon had his tent crowded with officers
and amateurs to his concert. The occasion was graced
by the presence of two ladies, who chanced to be in
camp—namely, Mrs. Colonel Baker and Mrs. Captain
Hart. Colonel Baker, Lieutenant-Colonel Kelly, Majors Cavanagh and Quinlan, and several other officers
were present.

Picture to yourself the priest's large hospital tent,
with a pleasant stove in the middle ; the two musicians
at one end ; around them the ladies and gay officers,
with an appreciative audience.

Old Irish tunes, such as your nurse warbled to you
as she carried you through the green fields, or by the
flowing brook where you were born, sweetly flowed
through the tent, and on the still night-air; and their
expression was taken up by the appreciative hearts
around, until scenes and sights and dreams of long,

long ago in the dear old home floated before the fancy in tangible pictures.

Thus passed the Christmas holidays, but days of action, of glory and death, were creeping with the cheerful spring upon the brigade.

# CHAPTER IV.

General Meagher's appointment confirmed by the Senate.—Rejoicing in
camp.—Banquets in camp.—Distinguished guests.—Sketches of Generals Heintzelman, Howard, and Shields.

On the 3d of February the Senate, by a unanimous
vote, confirmed the President's appointment of Thomas
F. Meagher as brigadier-general in command of the
Irish Brigade.

This hearty and unreserved approval of General
Meagher's confirmation, by the highest branch of the
national legislature, was flattering, inasmuch as it was
an exception to almost all other appointments made
during the session. This caused great rejoicing in
camp, and the general rode through the camp, accompanied by General Shields; they were received with
a wild welcome and a burst of cheers: officers and all
joined in the reception, and a general feeling of delight pervaded the brigade.

On the 5th General Meagher formally took command
as brigadier.

The brigade, in full dress, was drawn up in line on
a plateau some distance from the camp. Though a

slight sprinkling of snow covered the ground, still it was a beautiful day, reminding one of balmy April weather in the North. The sun shone out splendidly. The trees around, and away on the distant hills, looked, in their gentle coats of snow and pendent icicles, like so many emeralds set in a zone of white and sparkling diamonds.

General Meagher, accompanied by General Shields, and a numerous and brilliant staff and escort, rode along the line and reviewed the brigade. General Shields addressed a few words to the officers and men. He said that seldom if ever had he looked upon finer fighting material than that presented by the men of the Irish Brigade. He congratulated them and their commander. " You fight," said he, " in a sacred cause, and you must never forget that to you is intrusted the reputation, never yet sullied or stained, of an old military nation. Two worlds are watching you. Courage you have; training, temperance, industry, hard and continued industry, will do the rest."

The occasion called forth a grand banquet from the officers of the brigade to General Meagher and other guests. The affair was one of unmixed gratification to all concerned ; and whether we consider the brilliancy of the company assembled, or the entire success of the festivities—got up as they were under all the difficulties which the isolation and comparative rude ness of camp-life oppose to the obtaining of the many appliances of civilization usually considered indispensable on such occasions—we must equally congratulate the officers to whom the conduct of the affair was committed upon the manner in which they discharged their trust.

Among the invited guests present, in addition to Brigadier-General Meagher, were Generals Heintzelman, Shields, Howard, and Richardson; Colonels Thomas Cass, Ninth Massachusetts Volunteers; Hayman, Thirty-seventh New York; Tucker, Second New Jersey; Terry, Fifth Michigan; Nugent, Sixty-ninth, Baker, Eighty-eighth, and Burke, Sixty-third New York; Lieutenant-Colonels James and Patrick Kelly; Majors Cavanagh and Quinlan; Major Richardson, U. S. A.; Major Riordan, Thirty-seventh New York; Surgeon William O'Meagher Thirty-seventh New York (attached to General Richardson's staff); Lieutenant Buck, Second New Jersey. Besides the military men present, several civilians from New York and elsewhere, attracted by the novelty of such an affair, had accepted invitations.

The banquet was laid out in a spacious marquee, fitted up and decorated for the occasion with much taste. The feast was of the most joyous kind, literally combining the feast of reason and flow of soul. The well-stored tables literally groaned beneath the weight of the tempting viands provided; while the warm welcome that awaited the guests was enhanced by the attention of the stewards of the feast, who left nothing undone to insure the entire comfort of all present.

Captain Felix Duffy, the senior captain of the Sixty-ninth, occupied the chair; Captain John C. Lynch, Sixty-third, acted as secretary; and the following officers ably fulfilled the duties of stewards: Lieutenants Richard L. Ryan, Thomas Touhy, Patrick W. Lyden, of the Sixty-third Regiment, N. Y. S. V.; Lieutenants —— Carr, —— Nagle, —— Donovan, of the Sixty-ninth Regiment, N. Y. S. V.; Quartermaster P. M. Haverty, Lieutenants J. O'Connell Joyce, William M. O'Brien, of the Eighty-eighth Regiment, N. Y. S. V.

*General Committee.*—Captains Felix Duffy, Shanly, Scanlan, Saunders, Sixty ninth Regiment; John C. Lynch, Sixty-third Regiment; Lieutenants George Lynch, Joseph McDonogh, McConnell, Sixty-third Regiment; Captains O'Donoghoe, Nagle, Clooney, Eighty-eighth Regiment; Lieutenant Temple Emmett.

Captain FELIX DUFFY, *Chairman.*

JOHN CHAS. LYNCH, *Secretary.*

General Heintzelman was a good officer, a brave soldier, and courteous gentleman. He was a warm friend of the brigade, and entertained the highest opinion of itself and its gallant commander.

General Howard was a courteous gentleman and good soldier. He lost his right arm at Fair Oaks, and afterwards served at Chancellorsville and Gettysburg. In the West, under Sherman, he won his chief reputation, and rose to the command of the army of the Tennessee. He was a brave soldier and a good, cool general.

General Richardson, subsequently, commanded the division, and was a great admirer and faithful friend of the brigade.

General Shields, being one of those glorious exiles whose brilliant heroism has shed a lustre on his native land—one of those illustrious children of the Gael who

"Fought as they revelled, fast, fiery, and true,"

requires more than a passing notice from my pen.

General James Shields was born in the year 1810, in the village of Altmore, County Tyrone, Ireland. He was cradled under the shadow of the Barlack Mountains, and within five miles of the historic town of Dungannon.

When about sixteen years of age he landed in New York, and soon after manifested his partiality for the army, by joining, as second-lieutenant, in a volunteer force, in the Seminole war in Florida. At the expira-

5

tion of his service he moved to Illinois, and devoted himself to the legal profession. A few years later he was elected to the lower house of the State Legislature, and speedily became a leading man among the Demo- cratic representatives. In 1840 he was appointed Auditor of the State, and in 1843, by a vote of both houses of the Legislature, Associate Justice of the Su- preme Court of Illinois. On the elevation of Jas. K. Polk to the presidency, Shields was made Commis- sioner of the General Land-Office.

At the commencement of hostilities against Mexico, he was commissioned brigadier-general. In the Autumn of 1846 he joined General Wool, in his over- land march to Monclova, and reported to General Taylor, at Camargo, near the Rio Grande. Soon afterwards he was ordered to join General Scott, before Vera Cruz, and actively participated in the capture of that place. Two brigades, led by General Shields and Colonel B. Riley, were ordered to storm the enemy's camp at the pass of Cerro Gordo, on the road to Jalapa.

While leading his brigade over rugged ascents and through dense chapparal, under a severe and continuous flank fire, the intrepid Shields fell, shot right through the lungs by a large copper ball. He was despaired of by the American doctors, but a generous Mexican surgeon saved him, by drawing a silk handkerchief through the wound, thus removing the extravasated blood.

General Twiggs, in his report to General Scott, speaks of him in the most laudatory terms.

He also reported ·favorably of Colonels Riley and Harney, two distinguished Irish-American officers.

General Scott, too, calls Shields a "commander of activity, zeal, and talent;" and takes other occasions to compliment him. "There is," he says, "some hope, I am happy to state, of the recovery of the gallant General Shields." For his gallant and meritorious conduct he was brevetted a major-general of volunteers.

In August, 1847, he is again at the head of his brigade, which is situated at San Augustine, on the main road to the capital, and only nine miles distant. On the 19th of August he again distinguished himself at Contreras and Churubusco. In his report he says:

"In this terrible battle, in which a strongly fortified enemy fought behind his works, under the walls of his capital, our loss was necessarily severe. This loss, I regret, has fallen most severely upon my command. In the two regiments of my own brigade, numbering about six hundred men, in the fight, the loss is reported two hundred and forty killed and wounded. My command captured three hundred and eighty prisoners, including six officers."

General Shields and his command next distinguished

themselves in the attack on Chapultepec and the advance against the city of Mexico. The general-in-chief bears generous testimony, in his official reports, to the great ability and cool, daring courage of General Shields. He makes special and commendatory mention of "Shields badly wounded, before Chapultepec, and refusing to retire !"

Indeed, his services greatly contributed to the decisive results which followed, and placed the Stripes and Stars victorious on the national palace.

Though in Mexico at the breaking out of the late war, he hastened to Washington, to tender his services to the Government, and soon received a division command in Banks's *corps d'armée*.

He served in the Shenandoah Valley, and whipped the redoubtable Stonewall Jackson at Winchester, Charlestown, Martinsburg, and Strasburg, capturing a number of prisoners and two guns. He got slightly wounded, by a piece of a shell. General McClellan makes favorable mention of him in his official report.

Red tapeism and prejudices soon interfered to thwart his military aspirations, and he was removed to a command where his abilities would not interfere with the promotion of less able but more influential officers.

General Shields is a thorough Irishman, in heart and feeling. His warmest love and aspirations are for the land of his birth, and he has often said that he hoped one day to use his sword in her behalf.

The brigade had now settled down to its routine of drilling and picket-duty, enlivened by occasional adventures of scouting parties in the enemy's country. The roads were cut up with the continual traffic of wagons bringing supplies and fuel to camp, and the winter rains had converted them into regular mud-pools and quagmires, so that the men had to wade through slush knee-deep going to drill or picket.

About this time Colonel Enright resigned the command of the Sixty-third, and was succeeded by Colonel Burke, formerly of the Thirty-seventh N. Y. V.

I have said little about the artillery attached to the brigade, and under command of the dashing Major Thomas O'Neil.

It was called the Fifth Regiment (Artillery), Irish Brigade. It was all this time stationed at Camp Meagher, about a mile east of the Capitol, where the men were instructed in their duties. About this time the men of the brigade were paid, and, with true Irish kindness, they sent the money home to their wives and families. Their friends, in return, sent them several articles, both to eat and wear, necessary to add to the comforts of a soldier's life.

While in Camp California, Captain Maxwell O'Sullivan got seriously burned by his tent taking fire at night, from the effects of which he died. He was a son of Captain O'Sullivan, of Cork, and was a young man of fine talents and varied abilities.

# CHAPTER V.

Programme of McClellan's plan of campaign.—The army moves towards
Centreville and Manassas.—Retreat of the Confederate Army across the
Rappahannock.—General Howard harasses their rear-guard — Sixty-
ninth under fire.—Brigade returns to Camp California.—General Kearney escorts them—Brigade embark for the Peninsula.

THE programme laid down by McClellan was to
transport his army to the Peninsula, between the York
and James rivers, keeping Fortress Monroe as a base,
and operating directly on Richmond itself.

This movement would oblige the enemy to abandon
his intrenched position around Manassas and Centreville, in order to cover Richmond and Norfolk. He
should do this, for did they permit us to occupy Richmond, their destruction would soon follow.

Even should McClellan be defeated, he had a secure
retreat down the Peninsula, with the fleet covering
his flanks.

He was very much thwarted, both by the President
and Secretary of War, in the details as well as in the
general plan. Their chief dread appeared to be for
the safety of Washington, which they could not look

upon as secure while so large a rebel force occupied
Manassas and the Shenandoah Valley.

They were even impatient and dissatisfied with
affairs, because McClellan was not ready to move his
army before either the state of the weather or his preparations would permit.

The enemy, having learned McClellan's programme
of action, fell back towards the Rappahannock, so as
to be able to cover Richmond. This was the natural
consequence of McClellan's threatened movement to
the Peninsula.

This relieved the general from the results of the over
anxiety of his superiors, but delayed his contemplated
movement, as it was necessary that he should follow
up the enemy and occupy the important positions they
had held; besides, it was a preparatory school to train
and inure the troops to the march and bivouac previous to the general campaign.

As the transports, too, could not be got ready for
some time, it could not much retard the general plan.

During the night of the 9th of March, the general
issued orders for a regular movement of the army the
next morning towards Centreville and Manassas.

The advance was covered by two regiments of
cavalry under Colonel Averill, with orders to reach
Manassas, if possible, and ascertain the condition of
affairs there, and do whatever they could to retard and

annoy the enemy on his retreat. Our troops reached the abandoned camps around Manassas on the evening of the 10th, and found burning stores and much valuable property.

Having given a summary of the general movement, I will now return to the brigade.

Next morning, General Meagher and his staff were in their saddles at five o'clock, and Colonels Baker, Burke, and Nugent had their regiments formed upon their respective color lines, and soon joined the column.

The Irish Brigade formed a portion of the *corps d'armée* commanded by General Sumner, an accomplished soldier of more than forty years' experience: cool, thoroughly trained, and competent for all the emergencies of war—a firm friend and admirer of the Irish Brigade.

At the head of the column was the advance-guard, comprising cavalry, artillery, and infantry; then came the general commanding and staff; next followed General Howard's brigade, then General French's, and then General Meagher.

That march, the first real march of the grand army, presented a dazzling sight. There they are before you, the columns extending for miles, marching along with their guns and bayonets glittering in the morning sun, and the gay flags and banners flaunting in the

5*

breeze. There they are, cavalry, artillery, and infantry—generals, dressed in gorgeous uniforms, and riding prancing steeds, richly caparisoned; staff-officers, gay and sparkling, full of ambition and the hopes of " winning an honored name."

On they marched, dark Puritans from the New England States; stalwart Yankees, of bone and muscle; men from the West and Northwest; exiles of Erin, from Munster's sunny plains, from Connaught's heights, and Leinster's vales; peasants from the Rhine: all march along through the glorious woods, through forest paths, as if of one race and nation.

On the 15th they reached Union Mills, near Bull Run, finding every thing burned or abandoned on their route. The Junction itself was burned down by Johnston. The rebels had also burned their hospital; and so precipitate was their march, or flight, that they left some unburied bodies in the dead-house, with their hands and feet tied ready for interment. In one of the burned buildings was the charred cinders of a human being. General French had the bodies decently interred.

Of the army, none came up with the rebels except Howard's brigade, which had a skirmish with the rear-guard, near the Rappahannock, and succeeded in driving them across.

The brigade's first lesson in marching and countermarching was rather a hard one, as they were for several days and nights shifted around from Union Mills to Manassas, and Fairfax, and Warrenton Junction. They were not able to enjoy Patrick's Day, which was a source of great annoyance to Irishmen. The brigade reached Fairfax Courthouse, a small village of a few hundred inhabitants, on Sunday evening, the 16th of March, and took up their quarters in an open space outside the village; fires were lighted, water boiled in tin kettles, and coffee, meat, and crackers extracted from the haversacks. The men had just marched ten miles, carrying forty rounds of buck and ball cartridge, a musket, blanket, and rations for a couple of days each; all this through wet and slush, marching over roads almost knee-deep. You will not be surprised, therefore, that they should enjoy their warm coffee and repast. Here they might have made an effort to enjoy Patrick's Day in some shape or other, but the order came for them to return to Centreville, to support French, as the rebels were reported to be marching on him.

The night was dark, with only a few stars in the sky, yet they had to retrace their march, tramping over puddly roads and wading through the creeks. Their way lay along the Centreville route, over roads deserted, almost covered in with overhanging woods, bleak, black, and dismal-looking. About one o'clock in the morning they came to a resting-place, where they found first-rate accommodations in a village of huts lately vacated by the enemy. The sun was up, and looked bright and cheerful on that Patrick's morning. The brigade was placed in line by their respective colonels, and Fathers Ouellet and Dillon, after invoking a blessing upon them, placed them under the protection of the Blessed Virgin and Saint Patrick.

In this bivouac the men picked up several letters, addressed to the Confederate soldiers, some from wives to their husbands. One, after detailing family affairs at home, exclaims in the bitterness of heart:

"Oh that peace could be made on some terms, and families once more be united! Where is our poor son? How is his health? Is he near you? I nightly and daily pray to God that he and you may be spared, that I might rest my eyes upon you once more." Others were from young ladies to their soldier-lovers, full of vows of fidelity and prayers for their safety.

Another, in its bitterness, exclaims:

"It is truly distressing to think of the many hearts widowed and made desolate by the ravages of this cruel war."

Another was from an old invalid lady to her son, stating that all she had was destroyed, and now she must starve unless he could go home to support her.

They were all full of despondency; loving, bitter words, wrung from suffering hearts.

The gushing tenderness of the mother's heart speaks to her child, though far absent, for love is universal, and its language often figurative. The father's pride and longing, though controlled by a sense of duty, breaks through the feeble guise. The wife's love, that clings to the object of its heart's affection through weal or woe; the sister's tenderness, and the brother's manly love, were all here, painted on those strayed leaves so full of the heart's longings.

The army was now divided into regular corps, and Major-General Sumner appointed to the command of the Second Corps; the command of his division devolving on Major-General Dick Richardson, who was an old campaigner in the Mexican war, in the principal battles of which he participated with success. He was in person strong and stalwart, unostentatious in appearance and manner.

Richardson soon became very much attached to the Brigade, which was, in a great measure, owing to the *finesse* of Captain Jack Gosson, of General Meagher's staff. The life and adventures of Captain Jack would throw Charley O'Malley himself into the shade. Full of fun, jokes, and witticism, a thorough soldier both in drill and appearance, he literally kept the camp in roars. He could polish off the most barefaced lie as the gravest truth. He was never at a loss for words or repartees, and was the ruling spirit in every carouse, fun, and battle.

General Richardson was rather of a sociable, easy disposition, and something after Captain Jack's own taste. The captain thought it important, then, to establish the best possible understanding—a regular bond of friendship between the general and the Irish Brigade. He was coming from Washington to take command of his division as the troops were returning to their quarters.

Now was Jack's opportunity, so he ròde along the line and informed the boys that General Richardson was on his way to take command; " and what do you think of the brave old fellow, but he has sent to our camp three barrels of whiskey, a barrel to each regiment, to treat the boys of the brigade; we ought to give him a thundering cheer when he comes along."

The bait took. The general and staff soon after rode along the lines: the captain only took off his cap, it was the signal, and a wild cheer ran through the Brigade that nearly startled the whole army. The general took the compliment paid to the three barrels of whiskey all to himself, and became deeply attached to the brigade, making a special favorite of Captain Jack.

The men were sorely disappointed when they got

into camp and found no whiskey, but with true Celtic humor enjoyed the joke.

The next march of the Brigade was to Warrenton Junction. As all the bridges had been destroyed by the rebels, the troops had to wade through the streams and creeks, oftentimes up to their hips in water; and this in March.

The camp at Warrenton was in a deep wood of lofty pines, which, being stripped of their foliage, afforded little shelter, while the ground was saturated and muddy from the late rains.

The troops had no tents on the expedition, and officers and men had to sleep beside the camp-fires and cover themselves with their blankets as best they could.

The trains, too, had been delayed, which put the men on short rations, yet there was no grumbling or discontent.

The headquarters were in keeping with the other surroundings, yet the time passed pleasantly enough, and General Meagher managed to entertain the other generals; his fascination of manners and rich fund of anecdotes and witticism atoning for the other drawbacks.

In the march from Union Mills to Warrenton the men were dilatory in crossing Cedar Run, which was deep and broad.

"Why not bridge it?" exclaims one.

"Arrah, 'an shure that would give work to the pioneers," exclaims a third.

" Come, forward, march," exclaimed a staff-officer, riding up.

" Easy speak on horseback," muttered another.

"A nice dose of a frosty morning."

Such were the remarks bandied by the men, and certainly the prospect was not very inviting, and one hour's work would bridge it sufficiently for infantry to pass over. A drummer boy, seeing the men hesitate, rushed into the stream, and when he reached the middle commenced playing " Patrick's Day." The men cheered, and dashed in after him.

The first division and Blenker's German Legion, ten thousand strong, all under command of Major General Sumner, were now stationed around Warrenton Junction.

While bivouacking at Warrenton, a portion of Howard's command and the Sixty-ninth went out towards the Rappahannock on a reconnoissance.

Colonel Nugent, Lieutenant-Colonel Kelly, and Major Cavanagh were with the regiment.

When they reached the Rappahannock they found that the enemy had crossed over, except some scouts and pickets, who were compelled to follow. Johnston opened his artillery from the south bank of the river and shelled the Federal forces.

Howard having ascertained the position of the enemy, and that the bridge had been destroyed, returned to camp at Alexandria.

About this time, Doctor Lawrence Reynolds was appointed surgeon to the Sixty-third, and served all through with the Brigade until the close of the war, most of the time as brigade surgeon. He was a man of strong Irish patriotism and considerable practical ability.

Back to Camp California again, but only to bivouac for a night there, for the main part of the army were transported down the Chesapeake, and the Brigade was under orders to follow.

Early next morning the Brigade bade a final adieu to its old camp, which was endeared to them by many pleasant associations, and marched for Alexandria, to embark on board the Columbia and Ocean Queen.

General Kearney's brigade was encamped between them and Alexandria. The general sent his splendid band to escort the Irish Brigade to the place of embarkation, and he himself rode along the lines of the Brigade accompanied by General Meagher and staff. The Brigade received him enthusiastically, while on the other hand the different regiments through which the Brigade marched turned out to receive it.

Kearney was the beau ideal of a grand and dashing

soldier. He sat on his horse like a Centaur. His appearance was stately; his eyes beamed with the fire of enthusiastic ardor. He was the dashing, brilliant Murat of the American army. His military life was one glowing picture of heroic action. At the battle of Williamsburg he swept like a tornado on the rebels. He was called, both by them and when serving in Mexico, the " One-armed Devil."

Of Irish descent, he loved the Irish, and always said there were no better soldiers. He was a great admirer of General Meagher and his brigade, and never lost an opportunity of paying them a compliment.

While serving under Scott in Mexico, he was the terror of the Mexican army. In France, where every man is a soldier by instinct, and where the name of a soldier and bravery are synonymous, Phil Kearney was respected and honored.

The Ocean Queen was a magnificent steamer in size and accommodations; the Columbia was a small river-steamer, used as a transport. What a motley group they carry—generals, officers, privates, horses, and a miscellaneous cargo of sundry things and people; stragglers, who have stayed behind and missed the regular mode of conveyance ; men returning from hospitals to join their commands; chaplains, expounding and expatiating on theology and all things human and divine; doctors of medicine, doling out pills and

lotions; some New England philosophers, filled with
the spirit of the age, and the slang and cant of their
class. They must belong to some sanitary or Christian commission. They cannot claim to be meek
followers of our Saviour; in fact, they think our
Saviour was very wrong in not making more stir and
bustle in the world.

There were sutlers, too, with their stores piled away,
and they calculating on making at least three hundred
per cent. profit. These and the shoddy aristocracy
were the Shylocks of the army, but, like a great many
more evils, had to be tolerated.

The rank and file were huddled together as best
they could, singing, laughing, and cracking their jokes.

"I say, Bill," exclaims one young fellow to his
neighbor, a middle-aged man, who seemed, indeed, lost
in thought, with his head resting on his hands, "what
the deuce are you thinking of; you look as glum as if
you were at your own wake, man alive."

"It is easy for you to speak, Dan; if you left a wife
and children after you, like me, you would feel down-
hearted sometimes; but I'll try and get a furlough
soon."

"That's true, Bill; when the thought of my poor old
mother comes across me, and, and—no matter."

"Yes, Dan; I know who you mean; I expect her
pretty eyes are red crying by this time."

"No, Bill, no; but my poor old mother; what would she do if any thing happened to me? I'd like to see her. I'll try and get home soon, too."

"Won't we have the pleasant times when we go home, Dan?"

Home—alas! poor fellows, how few of ye went home except to your God!

# CHAPTER VI.

THE transports lay off Fortress Monroe for four or five
days, perfectly weather-bound. A dull drizzling rain
and sleet-storm had set in, sweeping across the bay,
and drenching with wet and freezing with cold the
unprotected soldiers on board.

The tossing of the vessels, the nausea caused by the
rocking, knocked all the sentimentalism out of the
love-sick, and even had reduced the twaddling theology
of the chaplains to the dullest possible standard.

Transports crowded the roads, and presented a most
picturesque effect, with their banners flying and bands
playing. Officers visited the various batteries and also
the Monitor, which lay at anchor in the roads, expecting a "killing" visit from the Merrimac.

The weather cleared up after a few days, and the transports steamed up to Ship Point and dropped anchor. It was an intensely cold evening, with a stiff breeze, which prevented the boats from coming close in. The men had to disembark as best they could; some by getting into the small boats; others by jumping into the water, which was up to their breasts, and wading to shore.

A cold, dark, dreary night followed. No preparations had been made for the Brigade; so, wet, wearied, hungry, and tired as they were, their prospect was to bivouac in the woods as best they could. Noticing fires in the distance, General Meagher sent an officer to inquire what command they were, and the chances of getting any assistance from them. Fortunately it was General Howard's brigade, which had arrived three days previous, and occupied a log-hut encampment left by the rebels. Howard generously ordered his command to share their huts, fires, and rations with the Irish Brigade. This the men did with a willing spirit, and emptied many a canteen to warm their visitors.

The headquarters were to be distinguished only by the sentry walking up and down, and the green flag in front.

General Richardson, who commanded the division, had got up a coarse dinner of potatoes and pork, and invited General Meagher to partake of it. To prepare this rough repast, the general had to borrow the only pot in camp from General Howard. General Meagher had taken his leave, and General Richardson sat warming himself over his log fire, with a soldier's overcoat wrapped around him. A servant of General Howard's entered, looking for his pot. Mistaking the general for a servant or orderly, he exclaims, slapping him on the back:

"I say, ould boy, General Howard wants the pot he lent ould Dick Richardson to boil his taters in."

Richardson jumped up, seized a burning brand and aimed it at the intruder's head, who hastily dodged the brand and fled.

Some amusing incidents of this kind are related of General Richardson. He was plain, rather slovenly in dress, generally wearing the blue pants and overcoat of the private, without any insignia of his rank.

On this account he was often mistaken, by those who did not know him, for a private.

On one occasion, he was walking through the camp, when he met an Irish soldier staggering home.

"What do you belong to?" said he to the soldier.

"What do I belong to, is it? Arrah, now, that's a good one, comrade; faïx, and shure I belong to the Irish Brigade: an what, if a body may ax, do you belong to?"

"Oh, I belong to General Richardson's command."

"You do; I don't know the ould fellow; they say he is a rum one; Dirty Dick we call him."

"Indeed: how do ye like him?"

"Oh, very well; I hear the boys saying he is a brave ould fellow; all the boys like Dirty Dick well enough; but wouldn't you have a drink?"

"I thought there was no whiskey to be got in camp now."

"Isn't there, indeed; come along, ould chap," and Pat took the general familiarly by the arm.

It happened that a Mrs. ——, who accompanied the Brigade in the confidential capacity of supernumerary quartermaster or commissary assistant, or something of the kind, always kept on hand a generous supply of bottled commissary, which she retailed on the sly for three dollars per bottle.

She was now doing a decent business on one of the shanties, when Paddy Doran staggered in with his friend.

"I say, Mrs., let me have another bottle of that firewater of yours."

"You have enough, Paddy," said Mrs. —— from the back part of the shanty, where she was putting in a little water to qualify the commissary, for fear it would be too strong and hurt the boys.

"No, I want a bottle; I have a frind wid me."

Mrs. —— was in the act of handing the bottle to Paddy, when she seemed very much taken with the appearance of his friend.

"Paddy Doran, you villain, may my curse light on you ; you have desaved me," and she aimed the bottle at Paddy's head; but he dodged it, and in doing so knocked against his friend, upsetting him.

"Oh, General Richardson dear," exclaimed she, running to raise him up, "don't mind that villain, that—"

Whatever she was going to add remained unsaid, for Paddy Doran, hearing who his friend was, made a dart for the door. It so happened that Mrs. —— was between him and the door, so Paddy, in his fright, knocked against her, completely rolling her over on the general. He did not wait to see the result, but made as straight as a bee-line for camp.

Whether the general thought the affair too ludicrous to make any noise about it, or that he enjoyed it, he let the matter drop, made no noise about it, much to Paddy Doran's relief.

The Brigade was detailed for several days unloading the supplies at Ship Point. This was a very laborious work, as the men were exposed to wet and cold.

The enemy were intrenched and in force at York-town, which is only about seven miles from Ship Point, but separated by an interminable swamp. This had to be corduroyed, at which work the Brigade was also employed.

For the information of the uninitiated, I must tell them that corduroying a road is placing two or three tiers of trees along, like a railroad track; and then across those others are laid, and the interstices filled in with earth. We made hundreds of miles of such roads in our campaigns through Georgia and the Carolinas.

---

Before we enter into a description of the fierce battles fought on the Peninsula, and the important part enacted by the Irish Brigade, it might be well to give a topographical sketch of the scene of operations of the contending armies.

Richmond is situated at the head of the Peninsula, which is formed by the James river on the south side and the York and Pamunkey rivers on the north. Newport News and Hampton Roads are at the foot of the Peninsula, where the James river flows into the Chesapeake Bay.

The Peninsula is something of a parallelogram shape, with Richmond at its Southern head, and McClellan's army at its northern base. Across this flowed the Chickahominy in a diagonal line, running from the northwest, easterly. The Chickahominy was crossed by five roads, leading from Richmond. One

was the Hanover Courthouse pike-road, the Mechanicsville pike, the Nine Mile road, the Williamsburg
road, the Charles City road, and the Darbytown road.

The rebel army covered a front of about seven miles,
strongly defended by field-works of all kinds. As
there is a gentle incline of dry land back towards
Richmond, the rebels had the advantage of occupying
it, while McClellan's army had to encamp in the
Swamps and marshes before Yorktown. The relative
forces engaged during this campaign were nearly
equal.

The Confederates admit an effective force of over
eighty thousand (but might be fairly estimated, when
we include Huger's force, around Norfolk, at ninety
thousand effective troops).

This was a large army, to occupy strong intrenched
positions, such as those around Richmond and through
the Peninsula, and should be a match for twice the
number of an assaulting force. McClellan states that
though he commanded an army of near one hundred
and fifty thousand men, when planning the arrangements of the campaign, over fifty thousand of these
had been withdrawn from him, for the defences of
Washington, and to guard Fort Monroe and other
points; thus leaving him with an army of about ninety-
five thousand effective troops, to capture Richmond,
with its formidable works and superior army.

Magruder held Yorktown with a garrison of about fifteen thousand men, protected by a continuous line of earthworks and strong batteries. McClellan's plan was to turn Yorktown by way of West Point; but his forces being reduced, by order of the President and Secretary of War, he had no choice but to attack it directly in front.

General Wool commanded at Fortress Monroe, and was ordered to act under McClellan, and supply him with ten thousand troops. As McClellan was moving on Yorktown, this order was revoked, and the First Corps assigned to General Wool, thus disarranging all his plans, and considerably weakening his force. Besides, he was promised the co-operation of the navy in his projected attack on the batteries at Yorktown and Gloucester, and in controlling the James River and protecting his flank.

The fleet, including the monitor Galena and other iron-clads, went up the James River, but were not able to force the batteries and swarms of sharpshooters that lined the river towards Drury's Bluff, and had to fall back towards Fort Monroe. Thus stood affairs when McClellan sat down before Yorktown.

Up to this, General Joe Johnston commanded in the field; but General Lee having perfected all his defences around Richmond, assumed the chief command. The works around Richmond swept and covered all the roads and passes leading to the city. Every mound and hillock had its battery.

Redoubts, rifle-pits, casemate-batteries, breastworks, and intrenchments crowned the hills on all sides, mounted with their field-guns and heavy siege-pieces. Despite all this, there was great disaffection and despondency in Richmond. Most of the shopkeepers and merchants had left the city and closed up their places of business, carrying off all they could.

A conscript law had been just enforced, which caused considerable disaffection.

Under these circumstances, any impartial man will come to the conclusion, that had McClellan been left the fifty thousand men of which he had been deprived, there is little doubt but that he would have captured Richmond, and thus spared the country the horrors of wading through near three years more of blood and misery.

Yorktown, memorable in history as the closing scene of the Revolution and the surrender of Lord Cornwallis, is upon the York River, about ten miles from its entrance into the Chesapeake Bay, seventy miles from Richmond, and twelve from Williamsburg.

All the country round is full of thrilling events of the revolutionary times, to which are now added the more fearful scenes enacted in the late war for the

Union.   The old intrenchments cast up by the British remained until covered over by the new works.

In front of Yorktown, which was garrisoned by Cornwallis and about seven thousand troops, the American and French army, of twelve thousand, lay down before the town.   At the same time the French fleet blockaded the river, and the result was a battle, which resulted in the surrender of Cornwallis and his army, on the morning of the 19th of October, 1781.

Troops were hurrying to the front as rapidly as possible, and by the 10th of April the army occupied the following position:

Heintzelman's corps, composed of Porter's, Hooker's, and Hamilton's divisions, lay in front of Yorktown, extending from the mouth of Wormly's Creek to the Warwick Road, opposite Winn's Mills; Sedgwick's division of Sumner's corps, being the only one up, opposite Winn's Mills on the Warwick Road.

Keys's corps, including Smith's, Couch's, and Casey's divisions, was on the left of Sedgwick, facing Lee's Mills, on the west bank of Warwick.

Thus, instead of four corps, McClellan had but three, the first corps and Blenker's division of the second being withdrawn from him at the critical moment of commencing operations; besides, he was informed that the navy was not in a position to render him much assistance.

The four corps under McClellan were commanded by Generals McDowell, Sumner, Heintzelman, and Keys. McDowell commanded the first corps, which was withdrawn. While lying before Yorktown, the left wing under Sumner was engaged in ascertaining the practicability of crossing the Warwick and forcing the enemy's lines on the other side, thus gaining possession of the Williamsburg road and cutting off Yorktown from its supplies. Heintzelman was similarly engaged between Winn's Mills and Yorktown. The fact was soon demonstrated that the Warwick was not passable except by a narrow dam, which was swept by several batteries and intrenchments. Heavy and continuous firing was kept up, and thus went on the siege, without much progress on either side.

We will now return to the brigade, which is held in reserve. The men have been supplied with shelter-tents, which weigh only ten pounds each and are in two parts. Each soldier has but five pounds to carry, and when they halt they can button them together and fix them up in a few minutes. The Brigade was now encamped in a dry, pleasant spot, well shaded by dwarf cedar-trees, as green and lovely as the choicest shrubs. The men took a pleasure in decorating their officers' quarters and their own.

In this temporary encampment the men made an effort to celebrate the 1st of May, by decorating their rustic chapel with wild-flowers, which here bloomed even at that early period, and attending divine service. The priest's confessional tent was crowded. The camp was surrounded by swamps, musical with toads and reptiles.

In the rear, under the shade of some magnificent trees, and interwoven with beautiful evergreen cedars, were General Meagher's headquarters, comprising one large tent, and four smaller ones for his staff.

Here the Berdan sharpshooters began to show that unerring aim that sent many a man to his long account. One of these fellows, who was a dead-shot, was also remarkable for his cruel disposition. He carried a stick, and whenever he shot a man he made a notch in it. He would sit for hours behind a stump or clump of earth until he got sight of a rebel's head, when bang went the rifle, and down dropped the rebel, and out came the stick to receive its notch. The rebels often tried the ruse of holding up a stuffed figure, but this soon proved fatal to themselves, for as soon as our men got up to the dodge, one would fire at the figure when the man holding it would examine it just to see how it fared; when thus exposed, another was sure to hit him.

While encamped here one of the men was killed by the falling of a tree. In his pocket was found the following note; it shows how men are not insensible to the uncertainty of life at such a time.

"My name is Patrick Casey, Co. B, Sixty-ninth Regiment N. Y. S. V. Any one finding this note on my person when killed will please write a note to my wife, and direct it as follows: 'Mrs. Mary Casey, No. 188 Rivington-street, New York.'"

The poor fellow was decently buried, and his last wish fulfilled.

---

A good story was told of an African cook belonging to one of the officers.

Where Sam was engaged at his culinary operations was often visited by a round-shot and an occasional shell. It was getting too hot for him, so he removed to, as he thought, a safer place, when a shell comes right bang near him. Sam jumped like an acrobat and grinned like a gorilla.

"Eh, Sam! are you scared?" asked an officer who was calmly looking on.

"Golly, massa, I can put up wid dem black fellows," meaning round-shots, "but dem d—n rotten fellows, dat burst so, dey play de bery debil; you don't know where dey strike you," said Sam, alluding to the shells.

---

This encampment of the Brigade was called "Camp Winfield Scott."

The roads around were in a delightful mucilage condition. The late rains and the continual beating of wagons disturbed the rails, and the swampy foundations were moved to their very depths, causing holes and quagmires and miniature lakes of almost fathomless depth. If an unlucky wagon, or mule, or man chanced to get into one, they would sink almost out of sight. Such are the terrible tracks over which an army of ninety thousand men and their immense supplies had to pass. After a short ride towards the front you strike upon General McClellan's headquarters, simple and unpretending. Every thing was quiet and orderly about them. Only for the large flag floating from the staff in front and the extra number of tents, you might fancy you had got into some brigadier's quarters. There was a fine view from them. You could see the enemy's intrenched works and lines, and also the waters of the York River, with the transports and gunboats quietly floating on its surface.

McClellan was pushing forward his left, which, after some hard skirmishing, was threatening the Williamsburg road. This compelled the enemy to evacuate Yorktown, which they did on the 4th of May, falling back to their strong lines of works in that locality. The cavalry, under General Stoneman, was ordered to harass their retreat with Hooker's division, moving on the Williamsburg road to support him, while the divisions of Kearney, Couch, and Casey followed them on the Yorktown road. Some heavy skirmishing took place, but the enemy succeeded in reaching their intrenched works at Williamsburg, leaving several guns behind.

Early in the morning the Brigade was under arms and on their march for Yorktown, where they arrived in the evening. Heavy cannonading was heard in the direction of Williamsburg.

Rain was pouring in torrents, and the men hastily put up their little tents, consoling themselves with the hope that they were under shelter for the night. Scarcely were they pitched, when orders came to get under arms and march immediately. A battle was raging in front of Williamsburg, our advance was heavily pressed, and re-enforcements were hurrying up. In double-quick time they were under way.

The ground around Yorktown was full of torpedoes, several of which exploded, inflicting ghastly wounds. Some were thrown on the surface, and as the men marched by they could not cease joking even at these dangerous missiles.

"Arrah, Bill, isn't that a pretty ham of bacon! It looks to be well cured," says one. A torpedo is a metal or copper vessel, something of the shape of a ham.

"Yes, a pretty chap to cure one's bacon: faix, I

think it would cure yours if you only tried it," was
the reply. " Begor, boys, they'd be pleasant things to
have at home against the winter."

" Yes, if you had a scolding wife and bad neighbors,
they would be an excellent receipt to get rid of them.
Faix, I wish I had the fellow full of whiskey instead
of powder, then I'd like to see him go off."

The rain continued to fall, the night was chill and
dreary, the roads knee-deep with mud, oftentimes holding the men fast, who, in their struggles, left their
boots behind, or fell into some hole, out of which they
were dragged coated over like a pie-crust.

The artillery, which was hurried to the front, got
stuck in the mud, and the men had to drag it out.
A brigade of lancers were also rushing to the front,
and sometimes rider and horse would roll into the
deep ruts. They were up again, the man and horse
looking like some strange animals covered with a coat
of mud-mail, rushing to the contest.

At two o'clock in the morning General Meagher
received orders to halt and bivouac in the woods. Here
the general and staff took up their quarters before a
blazing fire under a luxuriant tree. While there, the
Duke de Chartres, who was on his way from the front
to Yorktown, hearing that it was the Irish Brigade,
rode up to General Meagher's quarters, had a friendly
conversation with him, and informed him that Wil-

liamsburg was ours. This was pleasing news, and lightened the fatigue of the wearied troops.

The woods around were full of stragglers, while artillery and wagons had blocked up the roads. Some had switched off for the night, and others were whipping, lashing, and cursing their jaded animals.

Perhaps the whole annals of the campaign did not present such another scene of misery and confusion.

The general, officers, and men lay down in their damp clothes on the wet ground, to snatch a few hours' hasty sleep.

Williamsburg is the oldest incorporated town of Virginia, and was the capital of the State and seat of Colonial Government previous to the Revolution. It is built on a plain midway between the York and James rivers, and about six miles from each. Among the numerous antique remains of the past are the statue of Lord Botetourt, the palace of Lord Dunmore, the last of the royal governors of Virginia, Benton Church, the old Magazine, the old Capitol, where Patrick Henry exclaimed, " Cæsar had his Brutus, Charles the First his Cromwell, and George the Third——," and many other fine old buildings and reminiscences of Virginia's days of pride and glory.

## BATTLE OF WILLIAMSBURG.

The battle of Williamsburg was opened by Hooker's

division attacking Fort Magruder, which he continued to assault for several hours, under a most destructive fire from the fort and rebel infantry ; but being exhausted, and overpowered by numbers, he was giving way, and had lost a battery, when Kearney's division came to his support. Kearney at once renewed the attack with desperate vigor, while Hancock's brigade crossed on the right, occupying the enemy's redoubts, which commanded Fort Magruder, while Heintzelman was engaged on the left, but cut off from the other command by a thick belt of forest. Smith and Naglee were ordered to Hancock's support, but before they could reach him he had to fall back, but again took up a more favorable position, and turning on the enemy, charged them with the bayonet, routing and dispersing them. Meantime, the gallant Kearney was contending against desperate odds; but his success soon decided the day, for we now commanded the forts, and the enemy retreated during the night.

Our loss in this stubborn conflict was : killed, four hundred and fifty-six ; wounded, one thousand four hundred ; missing, three hundred and seventy-two ; total, two thousand two hundred and twenty-eight.

The enemy left several guns and colors, and a large number of wounded, in our hands.

The divisions of Franklin and Sedgwick, Porter

and Richardson, including the Irish Brigade, were sent from Yorktown, by water, to the right bank of the Pamunkey, in the vicinity of West Point. The remaining divisions, trains, and artillery moved by land.

A clear, bright morning rose on the Brigade, after that dismal night, in their cold, wet bivouac. They still continued to advance towards Williamsburg, and encamped the following evening and night in its vicinity.

The next morning they were ordered to return to Yorktown. It was a beautiful day; the sun shone brilliantly, the sky was clear and bright, the men were cheerful, with the favorable change in the weather and the news of the victory at Williamsburg. The Brigade returned by a new road through the forest, and marched by once pleasant homesteads, already desolated by war; green fields, and orchards in full bloom, despite the desolation and ruin around them. Their march lay through a pleasant valley, bordered on each side by the green forest-trees, while beside them flowed a clear, babbling stream, that merrily sang and foamed as it tumbled from rock to rock. The sunbeams glistened on the burnished arms, and glittered through the forest-trees. At length they reached Yorktown, where they at once embarked.

On the 19th of May, McClellan had his headquarters at the White House, where a permanent depot was established. On the 20th the headquarters and Porter's and Franklin's corps moved to Tunstall Station, five miles from the White House.

On the 21st of May, the position of the troops was as follows:

Stoneman's cavalry, advance-guard, one mile from New Bridge.

Franklin's corps, three miles from New Bridge; Porter's corps, in its rear.

Sumner's corps, on the railroad, about three miles from the Chickahominy, connecting the right wing with the left.

Keyes's corps, near Bottom Bridge, and Heintzelman's corps at supporting distance in its rear.

On the 22d of May headquarters moved to Cold Harbor. On the 26th the railroad was in operation as far as the Chickahominy, and the railroad-bridge across that stream nearly completed.

About this time Porter's and Sykes's divisions, and the reserve artillery, were organized into the Fifth Corps, under Fitz John Porter, and Franklin and Smith's divisions into the Sixth Corps, under General W. B. Franklin.

# CHAPTER VII.

Sketch of the White House.—Brigade at Cumberland Landing.—The Chickahominy and Pocahontas.—Brigade encamped on Tyler's farm. —Battle of Mechanicsville.—Battle of Hanover Courthouse.—Interrupted racing amusements.—Battle of Fair Oaks.—March of the Brigade.—The Brigade in battle.—Its gallant conduct.—What General Sumner thought of it.—What others thought of it.—Incidents and sketches of the battle and the battle-field.

> " The cannon now resounds ; the hurrying drum
> Loud beats to arms, and tells the foeman's come :
> Quick forms in line and marches our brigade,
> As gay as if they mustered on parade."

HAVING reached Yorktown on Sunday, the 11th of May, the Brigade was embarked on three large transports, and, accompanied by two other brigades of the division, proceeded up the York River to the White House, and disembarked at Cumberland Landing, near which they encamped for a few days.

On the 19th they reached a place called St. Peter's Church, and encamped on an elevated ground near, called Tyler's farm. The Richmond and York Railroad crosses the Pamunkey River at the White House.

The latter place is memorable as being the residence

of Mrs. Custis, who became the wife of Washington.
The house itself was a two-and-a-half-story frame
building, containing but six rooms, and surrounded by
out-offices and a handsome, well-kept garden. McClellan placed a guard on the house, and ordered it to be
protected from intrusion or injury. It belonged to the
Lee family, who were descended from the Custis
family. The mother of General R. E. Lee was a Miss
Custis.

The river at this point is pretty wide, deep, and
muddy. Its banks were now crowned with a busy
crowd, unloading transports and supplies, while over a
thousand vessels floated on its waters, laden with
troops, horses, mules, artillery, railroad-cars, corn, and
commissary stores in general.

The landing of such heterogeneous cargoes of men,
animals, and materials presented the most noisy and
ludicrous scenes imaginable. A mule or horse would
sometimes fall into the water, and the poor animal's
struggles to gain land afforded the greatest fun to the
crowds of idle soldiers who lined the shore. Soldiers
were disembarked, formed into line, and marched for
their respective camps. Commissary stores, sutlers'
shanties, and shops sprung up like mushrooms, and
one could not but feel the contrast with the quiet and
repose of the place in the days when Washington
tarried here to woo and win the pretty widow Custis.

The White House is no more ; even the stately pines along the river's banks, and the graceful cedars beneath which he whispered his love and spent a few elysian days of love and happiness, are swept away by the cruel hand of war.

About a mile beyond the White House were pitched a large number of hospital tents, in which were treated the sick and wounded sent down from the advance.

While McClellan was hurrying up his troops and preparing for the advance, the enemy were concentrating near the Chickahominy River.

The Chickahominy in this vicinity is about forty feet wide, fringed with a dense growth of heavy forest-trees, and bordered by low, deep marshes, varying from half a mile to a mile in width. McClellan's operations embraced the part of the river between Bottom and Meadow bridges, which covered the principal approaches to Richmond from the east. The bridges had all been destroyed, and it was necessary to reconstruct them, and also to build new ones.

Casey's division effected a crossing at Bottom Bridge on the 20th, thus covering our left flank in an advantageous position while building the bridge. At the same time our right and centre advanced to the river, and on the 24th of May we carried the village of Mechanicsville, after a heavy artillery fire. General

Naglee at the same time dislodged a force of the enemy from " Seven Pines," on the Bottom Bridge road, thus strengthening the position of our left flank. Owing to the swampy nature of the ground along the Chickahominy eleven new bridges had to be built, and all their approaches corduroyed.

It was up this same Chickahominy, which is now made even more memorable by the bloody scenes of the late war, that the celebrated Captain John Smith sailed when captured by the Indians in the early days of the settlement, when the white and the red men warred for the possession of its rich hunting-grounds. Here were the pleasant retreats of the gentle Pocahontas, and not far the Indian encampment where Smith was going to be sacrificed to the Great Spirit, when the tender maiden, at the risk of her life, saved him.

Around here were the scenes of many of the struggles and deadly encounters of the adventurous white men who first trod the wilds of Virginia.

While McClellan was preparing roads and bridges for the passage of his army across the Chickahominy swamp, McDowell was operating along the lines of the Rappahannock; Jackson fell back towards Richmond from Fredericksburg; General Fitz John Porter encountered a force of the enemy at Hanover Courthouse, and defeated them on the 28th.

The enemy were now concentrating every thing on Richmond, with the intention of hurling them on McClellan.

## Battle of Fair Oaks.

On the 30th of May, McClellan's army on the south side of the Chickahominy occupied the following position:

Casey's division held the right of the Williamsburg road and the centre at Fair Oaks Station; Couch's division, at Seven Pines; Kearney's division, on the railroad from Savage Station to the bridge; Hooker's division reached to the edge of White Oak Swamp. This was the position occupied by the advance of our army, when, on the night of the 30th, a very heavy rain-storm set in, swelling the river and swamps, and destroying some of the bridges. The enemy, perceiving the advance of our army, placed in such an unfavorable position, endeavored to cut it off from the main body.

On the morning of the 31st of May, Johnston, who still commanded in the field, massed a large force on his right in order to crush in our left, thinking that, on account of the roads and broken bridges, McClellan would not be able to re-enforce it in time.

Accordingly, about six o'clock in the morning, the grand divisions of D. H. Hill, Huger, Longstreet, and

J. W. Smith were formed into line of battle, and commenced moving down on the position occupied by Casey's division.

About twelve o'clock the advancing columns struck Casey's pickets, sweeping them before them, and were moving down in force along the Williamsburg road.

General Keyes, commanding the corps, ordered General Couch to move General Peck's brigade to support Casey's left.

The enemy now attacked General Casey simultaneously in front and on both flanks. General Naglee's brigade received the first shock of the enemy, and made a gallant resistance against the overwhelming numbers that pressed them on all sides. Casey's artillery was doing excellent execution, while the rebels were not yet able to bring up their artillery, owing to the nature of the ground. Casey's division had no fewer than eight new regiments in it, and some of these, seeing themselves in danger of being cut off, broke and fell back in confusion.

The rebels had now occupied Casey's first line of works on Basker's farm, and were still pressing on. Some of our guns had already fallen into their hands, and they made a dash on Regan's battery; the fire of the battery was redoubled, and four infantry regiments hurried up to save it. The fighting about it was deadly, and it had nearly fallen into their hands, when Casey ordered a bayonet charge. This drove back the rebel torrent.

Casey was now driven back; Bates' and Fitch's batteries next opened on the enemy, tearing lanes through their columns, while a regular fusilade was kept up along the infantry lines. The rebel batteries replied with good effect, while under their cover their infantry dashed up, stormed the redoubts and rifle-pits, capturing Bates' and Sprat's guns. Casey's division was now completely broken and routed: his artillery was in the enemy's hands and turned on him. They next bore down on Couch's division, which was supporting Casey. A little after four the enemy's columns struck Couch, D. H. Hill on the right, Anderson on the left.

Once more a livid flame of lead and fire was belching from the woods, as these solid columns swept down on our lines. Couch's division bravely stood the shock, charged the enemy, repulsing them, but on they came again, driving Couch's advance lines. At the same time a column was sweeping down the Tenth Massachusetts on our extreme left. McCarty's and Miller's batteries were vainly striving to keep them in check. The regiment broke, and the enemy pressed in the left flank, doubling it on the centre. General Couch was driven back half a mile towards Grapevine Bridge, when he re-formed, facing Fair Oaks station.

General Keyes had sent to Heintzelman for re en

forcements. Kearney and Hooker did not receive their orders to advance until near three o'clock, and it was near five when their advance arrived on the field.

Sumner's corps, consisting of Richardson's and Sedgwick's divisions, was also ordered up. At three o'clock Sumner moved rapidly to Heintzelman's support.

General Berry's and Jamieson's brigades, Kearney's division, arrived in time at Seven Pines to check the enemy by a flank fire. Berry's brigade pushed far enough to sweep the camp occupied by Casey in the morning, and now in the enemy's hands. They gallantly held this ground until darkness set in, and enabled Casey to fall back to the main body. The advance of Sumner's corps arrived in time to support Couch. Sumner ordered five regiments to charge with the bayonet, which they did in admirable style, checking the further advance of the rebels. Thus ended the first day's battle, the enemy having gained a decided advantage, capturing some of our camps, and many prisoners. But they were unexpectedly and effectively repulsed by the sturdy gallantry of Berry's brigade, which consisted of the Thirty-seventh N. Y. (Irish Rifles) and three Michigan regiments.

The brigade-officers, feeling the *ennui* of camp-life on Tyler's farm rather oppressive for their restless, mercurial natures, subscribed a purse, and resolved to have a race. Unfortunately, the day appointed for the affair to come off was that on which the battle was raging in front of Fair Oaks. Not expecting such an episode to wind up the day's entertainment, the races came off as announced.

General Meagher had given as a prize the skin of a tiger which he had shot himself in South America. The riders were to come to the post in jockey-dress. This was the difficulty. The nearest approach a certain captain could make to a uniform was a pair of yellow drawers and red shirt, surmounted by a cap, with a tassel furiously bobbing about. He had to get into a pair of top-boots borrowed from the general, and, being a very small and light-limbed man, his feet looked laughably ludicrous in them.

Captain Jack Gosson looked conspicuous in a pair of pants, made out of flaming red window-curtain, borrowed from some rebel house for the occasion, and a general officer's jacket, turned inside out, crowned by a huge smoking-cap, bedizzened with beads and gold fringes. Hurdles were built, flat-jumps sunk.

It was a May morning—a beautiful morning, calm and soothing as the impassioned visions of early love. The rich amber clouds floated through the deep blue sky, and the dim shadowy woods near you looked such as our druidical ancestors peopled with all kinds of strange beings. Cheers and shouts and laughter came from the plain, where the men were engaged in a friendly contest at football. Near the centre of the field was a stand, something like those you might have seen on county courses at home; while staffs, with small flags attached, marked the course.

As troops were ordered to the front in anticipation of a battle, the course was not crowded with martial sportsmen; however, the horses came to the post in the most approved racing style, and the following is an account of the affair:

THE CHICKAHOMINY STEEPLE-CHASE.

*Judges*—Generals Richardson and French.

*Stewards*—Captain McMahon, Lieutenant-Colonel Fowler, Dr. Smith, Quartermaster P. M. Haverty, Captain W. H. Hogan.

*Clerk of the Course*—Quartermaster O'Sullivan.

### FIRST RACE.

A steeple-chase, open to all horses, the property of and ridden by officers of the Irish Brigade, over a course to be decided upon by a committee of three, appointed for that purpose. The best of three heats of once round the course to decide the winner.

Entrance, $3; the second horse to save his stake.

First Prize—A magnificent tiger-skin, presented by General Meagher, the spoil of his own gun in Central America. The skin is similar to those worn by the officers of the Eighth Royal Irish Hussars.

Lieutenant-Colonel Kelly's b. g. "Faig-a-Bealac," ridden by owner; blue jacket, black cap.

Lieutenant Turner's b. m. "Katie Darling," ridden by Major Cavanagh; green jacket, tricolor cap.

Colonel Nugent's (Sixty-ninth Regiment) b. g. "Mourne Boy," ridden by Captain Gosson; scarlet jacket, scarlet cap.

Captain McCoy's b. m. "Molly," ridden by owner; white jacket, white cap.

Major Quinlan's (Eighty-eighth Regiment) b. g. "Tipperary Joe," ridden by Lieutenant Joyce.

Brigade-Surgeon Taylor's b. g. "Rapid," ridden by owner; gray jacket, red and black cap.

Major Warrington's b. g. "Rasper," ridden by owner; white jacket, ermine cap.

Quartermaster O'Hanlon's (Sixty-third Regiment) b. g. "Little George," ridden by Lieutenant McCormack; gray jacket, black cap.

Quartermaster O'Hanlon's (Sixty-third Regiment) b. m. "Neighbor Nelly," ridden by owner; lavender jacket, black cap.

Dr. Reynolds' (Eighty-eighth Regiment) b. g. "Bully for You," ridden by owner.

Lieutenant-Colonel Kelly's (Sixty-ninth Regiment) b. g. "Honest John," ridden by Captain Saunders; blue jacket, red sleeves, and red cap.

Lieutenant-Colonel Kelly's (Sixty-ninth Regiment) b. g., ridden by owner; yellow jacket, red cap.

Major Cavanagh, riding " Katie Darling," let the others lead, all topping the first hurdles, and from thence round the house, over a ploughed field, through a stretch of stumps, into and through a heavy bottom, and then the home-stretch, where the little mare, beautiful as her name, ridden by Major Cavanagh, did herself honor. On the first heat " Molly" was held up in the stretch of stumps; the b. g. " Bully for You" spilled his owner in a fine manner; " Faig-a-Bealac" and " Rasper" followed the mare up well over the leaps on the bottom; but, once on the home-stretch, the speed of " Katie Darling" told, and, distancing the most of the thirteen, she came in an easy winner.

This was followed by another race, and then came the great event of the day, a mule race, for thirty dollars, mules to be ridden by drummer-boys. If the other races were amusing, this was doubly so, from the obstinacy of the animals and the shouting and lashing and witty sayings of the riders. A theatre was built for the evening's enjoyment. Parts were studied, dresses prepared, for the characters were to appear in costume on the sylvan stage. Glowing handbills were out; a grand evening's entertainment was expected, but all were doomed to disappointment. The actors had to appear on another stage, and take their parts in a more thrilling scene. The theatre was abandoned, the call to arms sounded, accoutrements hastily donned, for the wild din of battle came along, borne on the evening breeze.

---

The booming of the cannon from the front was the first intimation the Brigade had that a fierce conflict was going on.

General Meagher ordered the Brigade under arms, and to be in readiness.

Soon the order came for them to march. On the road an aid of General McClellan rode up, ordering General Richardson to hurry up. The command quick-marched as rapidly as the nature of the ground would permit, and crossed the Chickahominy at Grapevine Bridge.

The route of the Brigade was now through a swamp, deep, dark, and dismal, as desolate and dreary as the imagination could picture. Just conceive a waste of stagnant waters, full of snags, fallen trees, and brush, and highly musical with croaking frogs and reptiles of every kind and species, and you have some idea of the ground. It was difficult for the infantry to march over this, but when it came to the artillery and cavalry, there ensued a scene of horses plunging up to their bellies in water and sending their riders sprawling into the mud, of caissons stuck up to the axletrees, and teamsters whipping, swearing, and flogging the helpless animals. About twelve o'clock at night the Brigade halted and bivouacked in the forest. Here they prepared a hasty cup of coffee, and then resumed their march.

It would shame a lazy cook to see with what expedition the soldiers prepare their meals.

The moment they stacked arms, fires were lit of rails or branches, the knapsack heaved off, a cup of water clapped on the fire: they threw their coffee and sugar into this, and in a few minutes they had it fit to drink. Then they took a slice of pork and roasted it before the fire on the point of a stick. In this way, a soldier cooked and consumed his hasty meal in about fifteen minutes. They soon reached a part of the battle-field of the previous day, near Fair Oaks.

Even through the intense darkness and gloom of the night you could perceive the sad indications of the desperate struggle of the previous day.

The shifting lights of the lamps as the doctors passed from sufferer to sufferer, the stifled cries and groans, the shriek of agony and despair that burst from the lips of some, smote sadly on the heart; and as the morning broke, the trees shattered with shot and shell, broken caissons and guns, the dead and dying men and animals around, were sad traces of war.

But two regiments of the Brigade, Sixty-ninth and Eighty-eighth, were sent to the front. By order of

General Richardson, the Sixty-third was detailed to extricate the artillery and guard the bridge.

## SECOND DAY'S FIGHT, (JUNE 1ST).

During the night Couch's division, and what could be collected of Casey's, with Kearney's, occupied the rifle-pits near Seven Pines. General Hooker's division took up position to the rear and right of the rifle-pits. General Sedgwick's division and Couch's division held about the same positions they did the evening previous. Richardson connected with Kearney, with French's brigade posted along the railroad, and Howard's and Meagher's in second and third lines. On account of the state of the roads, he was not able to get up his batteries until morning. There was a wide gap between Richardson and Kearney's lines; to close this, Richardson's line had to be extended to the left, and his first line moved over the railroad.

About five o'clock in the morning the enemy was rapidly approaching in columns of attack, with flanking columns on both sides. They had no skirmishers, as if determined to sweep all before them by one crushing blow. They first burst on French's brigade, which held the first line, and withstood the desperate shock for near an hour, when, being desperately pressed, Howard, with his brigade, was ordered to his assistance. French's fine brigade comprised the Fifty-third Pennsylvania, Sixty-first, Sixty-fourth, and Sixty-sixth N. Y. V., and made a noble, bitter, and bloody stand against the enemy. Howard's brigade moved forward, dashed into the woods, and the ringing, defiant cheers and roll of musketry told the desperate nature of the conflict. General Howard, while leading his men, was shot through the arm; but declining to leave the field, the surgeon was dressing it, when another shot shattered the bone, compelling him to go to the rear. The arm was subsequently amputated.

As soon as Howard's brigade had advanced upon the enemy, Col. Nugent formed his regiment (Sixty-ninth), into line of battle along the edge of the wood. The regiment moved in the direction of the enemy with a bold defiant cheer. As they reached the open out of the woods, the fire of the enemy told on them, striking the head of the column. Here they were ordered to halt for further orders.

The Eighty-eighth advanced in line of battle through the woods to an open plain which was swept by the shot and shell of the enemy. On this plain was a small house which it was important to occupy. Two companies, Captain Egan's and Captain William Hogan's, under command of Col. Pat. Kelly, gained this point under a most withering fire.

Capt. McMahon, of the Sixty-ninth, one of Gen. Meagher's aids, who was to conduct the Eighty-eighth, rode ahead and discovered a first-rate place where the regiment could be posted with effect.

The regiment soon occupied this position, and were able to pour in a withering fire on the enemy's flank, compelling them to fall back : the fire swept along the line, checking the rebel advance.

Meantime, General Hooker made a bayonet charge with the Fifth and Sixth New Jersey, Third Maine, Thirty-eighth and Fortieth New York, driving back the enemy in confusion. Couch and Heintzelman were engaged on the left, while Sickles, with his Excelsior Brigade, dashed into the timber and put the enemy to flight at the point of the bayonet.

The enemy were checked on all sides, but resolved to make one desperate effort. They again massed in front of Richardson, and strove in vain to break his line. French still stubbornly held his position, supported by Howard's brigade, while the Irish Brigade met them with fixed bayonets and a sweeping fire, hurling their lines before them. At length, baffled, broken, and beaten, the enemy retired in considerable disorder. Fair Oaks was fought, lost, and won ; and all honored the Irish Brigade, from the commander-in-chief down to the humblest private, for their noble conduct.

The incidents of a battle are often more interesting than the general details. As the Eighty-eighth was

7*

about charging across the open plain, through which ran the railroad, beyond which the enemy were in force, General Sumner, seeing the importance of the position called out—

" Boys, I am your general. I know the Irish Brigade will not retreat. I stake my position on you." A Sergeant McCabe of Company K replied : " General, we have never run yet, and we are not going to do it now." " I know it, I know it," replied Sumner, as he rode off.

General Meagher and staff were indefatigable, riding from line to line, cheering on the men. The general was all the time under fire. Among his staff I will mention Captain McMahon, who guided in the Eighty-eighth; the brave, talented, and brilliant Lieut. Turner; the noble and chivalric young Emmet; the quaint and erratic Jack Gosson ; the cool, gray veteran, Captain Hogan. The officers and men of the Eighty-eighth nobly did their duty. It seemed a laudable rivalry between themselves and their companions of the Sixty-ninth. The brave Timothy King fell mortally wounded ; also Patrick E. O'Connor, who was wounded while waving his sword and cheering on his company. Among the heroes of the day, one of the drummer-boys of the Eighty-eighth figured conspicuously.

George Funk was out skirmishing on his own hook. One of Howard's regiments was falling back, when the lad, from shelter of a big tree, saw a rebel sharpshooter rise from behind a log and fire after them. George at once covered him and took him prisoner. It was rather an amusing sight to see the little lad manly marching at a charge-bayonet, escorting his big prisoner to the rear. General Meagher rode a beautiful mare during the engagement, and his groom, who insisted on keeping near him, got shot through the legs. When the general went next morning to the hospital, to see him, the first question Moore asked him was, " General, has Dolly got her oats yet ?"

The noble conduct of the Brigade was admitted on all sides. Dr. Thomas Ellis, in his work entitled, " Leaves from the Diary of an Army Surgeon," says: " Soon the fire became general, and spread along the lines of the Irish Brigade, French's brigade, and Howard's brigade. There was the Irish Brigade in all the glory of a fair, free fight. Other men go into fights finely, sternly, or indifferently, but the only man that really loves it, after all, is the green, immortal Irishman. So, there, the brave lads from the old sod, with the chosen Meagher at their head, laughed, and fought, and joked, as if it were the finest fun in the world. We saw one sitting on the edge of a ditch, wounded, with his feet in the water, and both the sun and water, too, very hot. As we rode by, he called out to know if we had ever seen 'a boiled Irishman!' "

A corporal of the Eighty-eighth pressed ahead of his company and shot a sergeant of the Eleventh Mississippi, and then sheltering himself behind a tree, loaded and shot another. By this time his regiment had reached him.

The same sergeant's officer being struck by a bullet, he lifted him on his shoulders, and while bearing him to the rear got shot through the ribs. After a tedious delay of many hours, himself and his captain, whom he attended all through, though badly wounded, were carried to the rear. Brave fellow! he died from his wound.

Headley, in his history of the war, speaking of Fair Oaks, says:

" Meagher's gallant brigade was then brought up to relieve the hard-pressed regiment.

" Advancing with their well-known war-shout, they closed with fearful ferocity on the foe, and for an hour mowed them down almost by companies."

The field-hospitals of each regiment were points of sad attraction. Dr. Taylor, the eminent brigade-surgeon, and brother to Bayard Taylor, the distinguished traveller and writer, had his quarters part of the day on the field.

The general hospital was a farm-house, at the end of the plain. Here was the hospital of the Sixty-ninth, under care of Dr. Smith.

Dr. Frank Reynolds, of the Eighty-eighth, had his quarters behind a barn, near the railroad track; here he was busily engaged, treating not only his own men, but those of the enemy who were brought in.

"Yes, it is rather an ugly wound," said the doctor, in reply to a bright young rebel, whose fractured thigh he was examining.

"Well, I may thank myself for that, doctor. I heard that whoever would shoot that one-handed devil, Phil Kearney, would be promoted. So I set out on my own hook to have a crack at him, and got this for my pains."

After the amputation of the leg, when he recovered from the influence of chloroform, he turned to the doctor and said: "Well, doctor, Phil Kearney is better off than I am now, after all!"

Too much praise cannot be bestowed upon the chaplains of the Brigade, Fathers Ouellet, Dillon, and Corby, for the care and kindness they bestowed on the dying and wounded.

They spent the previous night with their lamps, going through the battle-field, shriving the dying, and attending those who might recover. Oh, what a boon is even a drink of water to the maimed soldier, lying on the battle-field, tortured with pain and thirst! How gladly would I, betimes, have drank the veriest sink that could flow.

If any of my readers have ever been in a battle, and many of them have, they will recall all the horrors of that sad scene;—the blood and carnage of the fight; the wild shouts of victory and vengeance; the ghastliness of the dead, piled in all shapes and forms; the groans of the wounded, who call on you in mercy to shoot them, and put them out of pain;—and they will agree with me, that a visit to the field-hospital is about the most painful thing of all.

It looks like a perfect butcher's shambles, with maimed and bloody men lying on all sides; some with their arms off; some with their legs off; some awaiting their turn; while the doctors, with upturned cuffs and bloody hands, are flourishing their fearful knives and saws around, and piles of raw, bloody-looking limbs are strewn around them: while some who have died on the dissecting-table, add to the ghastly picture.

The first time I witnessed such a scene was after a hard day's battle. Tired, and wearied, and slightly hurt, I rode to inquire for a dear friend at the field-hospital.

I stayed a few moments, looking on, but the ghastly picture affected me more than the roar and din of battle. I felt faint, and had to get stimulants to revive me.

The sufferings of the wounded were fearful, owing

to the wretched state of the roads and limited transportation. Proper hospitals could not be established on the field, so they had to be carried down to the railroad, thence to the White House, West Point, or North. Transportation was so limited that several lay on the battle-field for days. Dr. Ellis, who had charge of them, and whose Christian kindness and attention will be long remembered by many a poor soldier, says in his book:

" The rebels having destroyed the railroad-bridge across the river, the cars were run down to the riverside, filled with the wounded, after the battle of Fair Oaks. It was here, lying around on the track as they had been taken out of the freight-cars, I found over three hundred wounded, many of them in a dying condition, and all of them more or less mutilated, and still enveloped in their filthy and blood-stained clothing as they were found on the battle-field. In many instances maggots were creeping out of their festering wounds."

After the battle, General Meagher's headquarters were near the railroad, close to where the locomotive stopped to take up the wounded.

Numbers of them were brought to this point from the field-hospitals, and laid on the embankment until the train arrived. Dr. Dougherty was in charge, and indefatigable in his attentions.

A rain-storm set in ; the doctor at once ordered details to cover the wounded with huts made of lumber, rails, and branches. When tenderly helping the men into the cars, a fine-looking young Southern officer takes him by the hand, and says:

" Doctor, I have experienced much kindness from you—more than I expected ; I wish to learn your name before I go; I may yet have it in my power to thank you."

" I have only done my duty. My name is Dougherty."

" Oh ! Dougherty, indeed !  Of what descent ?"

" My grandfather was Irish."

" And so was mine; I am a son to Judge Dougherty, of Alabama."

Thus the pride of Irish ancestry was a bond between the kind doctor and the dashing soldier.  I have found this in the highest circles in America, North and South ; they feel a pride in tracing their progenitors to some old Celtic stock.  It is only those who have " left their country for their country's good" that are low and snobbish enough to deny their native country. No true man denies his country.

Dr. Laurence Reynolds was also in attendance, and after kindly treating one of the secesh who had been wounded in the leg, the poor fellow remarks:

" You're an Irishman, doctor ?"

" Yes."

" Well, you Irish fight like devils, but you are very kind when the battle is over."

So it is; but officers and men forget that the wounded and captured were their enemies. They treat them then as they would their friends. Chaplains and doctors know no distinction between rebel or Federal. Their mission is to console the mind and heal the body, and in this they know no distinction.

The battle of Fair Oaks, though not considered one of our great battles, was of vital importance; for, had the rebels driven us back on the second day's fight, from the swollen state of the Chickahominy and the bridges being swept away, a retreat would have been disastrous to the Federal army.

The losses on both sides were pretty fairly balanced. Johnston reports his loss, all told:

In Longstreet's and Smith's divisions... .......... 4,283
Hill's division.................................... 2,500
                                                   ------
                                                    6,783

McClellan sets down his loss:

General Sumner's Corps......................... 1,223
    "     Heintzelman's Corps.................... 1,394
    "     Keyes'      "    ..................... 3,120
                                                   ------
                                                    5,737

The loss in the Irish Brigade was about one hundred, in all.

We lost few superior officers—Colonel Riker, Anderson Zouaves, and General Howard, badly wounded.

The rebels had, in general officers, General J. Johnston, commanding, badly wounded; Brigadier-General Pettigrew, wounded and captured; Brigadier-General A. C. Davis, killed.

## CHAPTER VIII.

The army intrenched before Richmond.—Views of Richmond.—McClellan rides along the lines.—His reception.—Visit of the Spanish General Prim.—Out on picket.—A brisk skirmish.—Ominous signs.—Our right threatened by Jackson.—Danger of communications being cut off.—Retreat from before Richmond.

" In countless thousands, on the rebels came,
  With cries of vengeance and with hearts of flame :
  They came to hurl destruction on our rear,
  But you—Green Erin's bold Brigade—were there."
                                        DR. REYNOLDS.

AFTER the battle of Fair Oaks, McClellan should march the troops from Mechanicsville and other points over the left bank of the Chickahominy by Bottom Bridge, for the Williamsburg road, a distance of twenty-three miles, in order to concentrate and follow up the rebels. As this move would take two days, the enemy would have time to get into their intrenchments around Richmond; therefore he ordered the army to hold the position already gained, and intrench themselves. An advance in two columns, with the Chickahominy between them, would have exposed each to defeat in detail.

After a few days, the left was enabled to advance considerably beyond the battle-field. They fortified themselves by strong intrenchments, redoubts, forts, and abatis.

Richmond was only about five miles from our advance posts, and could be plainly seen from the tops of some of the tall pine-trees. Flushed with victory and full of hope, the army sat down before the city with the full assurance that its fall would be only a matter of time, a few weeks at most. The consternation in Richmond itself showed their insecurity. Civilians and the families of officers fled the city, taking with them all their valuables. They thought that re-enforcements would be sent to McClellan, and that Richmond would fall. McClellan was not re-enforced, and Jackson soon left the Shenandoah and hurried up his forces to the rescue of Richmond.

The following pleasant incident is worthy of record in this place:

The Spanish General Prim, while visiting the Army of the Potomac in company with General Heintzelman, rode by the Sixty-third and Eighty-eighth, drawn up in line, with General Meagher and some members of his staff in front.

Struck by the stalwart appearance and martial bearing of the men, the Castilian inquired: " What troops are these ?"

General Meagher replied : " A portion of the Irish Brigade."

The marshal's eye brightened at sight of such fighting material. In a dignified manner he complimented the Brigade and its commander, Meagher replying :

" Spain had reason to appreciate Irish valor. Spain and Ireland were old friends from ancient times, and their soldiers had often stood side by side together on many a hard-fought field." As the generals and their brilliant staffs and escort of cavalry galloped off, the boys gave Prim one ringing cheer. The general turned to an officer, remarking : " I don't wonder the Irish fight so well ; their cheers are as good as the bullets of other men."

General McClellan, accompanied by his staff, among whom was the Duc de Chartres, paid a visit to Sumner's *corps d'armée.*

On reaching the Brigade, they were met by General Meagher and staff. General McClellan spoke of the men and officers in complimentary terms, and charged General Meagher to return them thanks on his behalf for their steady and gallant conduct at the battle of Fair Oaks.

General Meagher addressed the brigade thus :—
" Officers and men of the Brigade ! It is my pleasing duty to announce to you that General McClellan has desired me to express to you the gratification he feels

at your steady valor and conduct at the battle of Fair Oaks, June 1st.

" He has also desired me to say, that when he calls upon you again, which he will do in the hour of need, he has the fullest confidence in you, and feels assured you will emulate the brave efforts of that day."

General McClellan was very popular with the army : his presence was always hailed with the wildest enthusiasm, by both officers and men. The soldiers felt and knew that he was their friend, and that any shortcomings in the way of their rations or attendance were not owing to him.

The Brigade occupied the front line of the division, and was kept incessantly engaged, either building intrenchments or on picket duty. General Meagher was so indefatigable, that one of the colonels wanted to know did he ever go to bed.

All this vigilance was now necessary, for a cautious, determined foe was only a short distance in front. Continual skirmishing and artillery firing were kept up on either side along the line, and shells often fell into camp.

The nights about this time were lovely, with a full, clear moon floating in the heavens. Johnny Fleming was again exercising his musical faculties, and had around him several officers. As a specimen of the gayety of the Brigade, we will give the following incidents of an evening's enjoyment in camp:

"Take care," said Captain Jack, "don't hit your heads against the roof—particularly you, Captain Donovan; you'd want to make yourself two inches short, for accommodation sake."

"Don't mind, Jack, but give us a pull at that bottle; you're wonderfully affectionate towards it."

"That's a mistake; see how rapidly I am trying to get rid of it," cried Captain Jack, suiting the action to the words.

"Let him alone," said Doctor Reynolds, "we'll soon have him in one of his moods."

"Very good, doctor; but tell me, is it true that you were so scared at the battle of Fair Oaks that you cut the sound leg of a man instead of the shattered one?"

"Not exactly, Jack; but if you should come in my way, look out: I have some scores to settle with you."

"Faith, I'm glad of that; I hope you'll clear them up; I'm living on tick since we came to this cursed place."

"Nothing new, Jack, nothing new; I have never known you to live on any thing else."

"Do you know, doctor, what Jack said to me the day of the battle, when the shells were coming around a little too fast to be pleasant?"

" No, let us hear."

" In the heat of the thing Jack turns to me and says, 'Blake, this is hot; I expect we have had our last toddy together. Wouldn't it be pleasant to be knobbing it down Broadway this blessed morning ?' "

" Yes," said Jack, who was a thoroughly brave officer, "I must confess I have a decided objection to be peppered with powder, and then served up on the half-shell, as if I were some huge *molluscus*."

" That is childish," said a young lieutenant, who had not been in action yet; "I tell you, gentlemen, I would not be one bit afraid of them; a man has to die but once, and—"

" Stop, for heaven's sake," said the captain. "Here, take a pull; I'm afraid that puff let all the spirits out of you."

" Do you mean to intimate that I'd be afraid ?" said the other, with offended dignity.

" By no means, my dear fellow, I know you'll show them something: no matter, have a drink ?"

As the lieutenant had the bottle to his mouth, a shell came right through the tree over the tent, cutting off its branches. As these fell on the tent, the hero of the bottle let it fall, and threw himself on his face and hands.

" By jingo, the bottle is broken," said Captain Jack; "pick it up."

"Is he badly hurt," said the doctor, running over to the lieutenant.

It so happened that one of the limbs struck him, and he, taking it for a piece of shell, faintly replied:

"Not much, doctor, not much."

"Where did it hit you?"

"Just behind the shoulder."

The doctor examined it, but not seeing any wound he winked at the other officers.

"Serious case this; no wound, increased extravasation, danger of congestion."

"You don't say so, doctor," groaned the patient. "What harm if a man were struck down in battle? but this—O Lord!"

"Does it pain you very much?" inquired the doctor.

"Well, not so bad, doctor."

"Worse again: fatal wounds never pain much; mortification deadens the nerves."

"Oh, heaven! is it so bad as that, doctor?"

"I didn't say it was, but one never knows what things come to."

"Oh, dear! if I were at my quarters."

"Easily done, my dear fellow; we'll have a stretcher here in a minute," exclaimed the captain.

The officer did not belong to the Brigade, but was on a visit; he was a bore about his bravery, so they resolved to carry out the joke.

8

The stretcher was procured ; he was tenderly placed on it, and a procession formed, with Johnny Fleming at the head of it, playing the dead-march. After going a little distance they met the officers of his regiment, who had heard of the affair, coming to convey him to hospital, where the regimental surgeon examined him. Of course he could discover no wound.

He was never seen inside the camp of the Irish Brigade after that.

As I said before, the Brigade held an advanced position ; the pickets of the two armies were in sight of each other. So near were they at some points of the line, that they occasionally exchanged newspapers, tobacco, coffee, and the like.

Perhaps picket duty is more full of scenes and incidents than any other of the numerous duties of the soldier. The hostile pickets are most likely separated by some open valley. The men sit at the foot of tall trees, or sheltered behind a clump of wood, gazing intently, trying to see their enemy through the dense forest branches. Only a few hundred yards off are the Confederate pickets, watching just as intently. The least little indiscretion, the least noise, and you attract the keen gaze of your enemy, and quick as lightning a bullet is aimed at you.

If it has struck you, you quietly tumble over beside the log: if not, you try your chance in return.

When the men are spiteful on both sides, picket duty is the most dangerous and least cheering part of the service.

It has not the excitement of battle—the presence of comrades, the charge, the cheer, the wild huzzah of victory and triumph; it has no such stimulating influences. No matter how cold the weather may be, even in the depth of winter the advance pickets are not allowed fires, and they dare not walk about to warm themselves.

On the 15th of June the Brigade heard reports of musketry on the left and front of their pickets, as if they were attacked. An officer was sent forward to ascertain the cause of the firing. He soon learned that a force of the enemy, taking advantage of a by-road, attacked our pickets, but were repulsed, with a loss of one man killed and two wounded, belonging to the Brigade.

Lieutenant Emmet and a comrade found the body of Lieutenant Palmer, of Sickles' staff, lying stiff and lifeless, on the road. He had been out on a similar mission with themselves, but was shot by the rebels.

While lying here the Brigade was re-enforced by the Twenty-ninth Massachusetts, under Colonel Ebenezer Pierce, formerly Brigadier-General Pierce, of Big Bethel fame. This was a very fine regiment, and did good service in connection with the Brigade, participating in all the trials, privations, and glories of the Irish Brigade, while in connection with it.

It served with distinction at Gaines' Mills, Savage Station, White Oak Swamp, Nelson's Farm, Malvern Hill, Antietam, &c.

At Malvern Hill, Colonel Pierce lost his arm, and the command devolved on Lieutenant-Colonel Joseph H. Barnes.

This regiment became a part of the Brigade June 9, 1862, by virtue of the following order:

HEADQUARTERS RICHARDSON'S DIVISION, CAMP AT FAIR OAKS, VA., June 9, 1862.

[Special Order.]

The Twenty-ninth Regiment Massachusetts Volunteers is hereby assigned to the brigade of General Meagher.

By command of

BRIGADIER-GENERAL RICHARDSON.

JOHN M. NORVELL, A. A. G.

It had been doing camp duty at different places before this, but had now taken the field in conjunction with the Irish Brigade.

At four o'clock on June 19th General Hooker sent out a regiment on a reconnoissance, and the Brigade was ordered under arms to support it.

General Sumner dashed by with his staff. Seeing General Meagher, he calls out, "General Meagher, are the green flags ready?"

"Always ready when wanted, general," was the reply.

A few scattered shots were exchanged on both sides. Then came a volley, followed by a fusilade of musketry. Our big guns opened their brazen throats, and commenced vomiting shot and shell on the enemy. Every shell burst over in the woods, where the enemy was in force. Some burst high in air, leaving a balloon-shaped cloud of smoke after them, and hurling their deadly missiles down on the men; others tore and ploughed through the woods. The roll of musketry increased; the enemy's pickets were falling back—ours pressing on them. General Meagher and his staff were on an eminence looking on, and waiting their time to dash in.

A young officer of fair complexion and slender figure rode up to the general. A mutual recognition and friendly shake of hands ensued. He asks:

"General, where may I find General Sumner?"

On being informed, he gallops off. He was one of the most active aids on General McClellan's staff. He was always about, ever busy, never resting; one would think that he had his quarters in the saddle.

He was a fine, noble-looking young soldier. He has royal blood in his veins, for he is no other than the Duc de Chartres, a prince of the house of Orleans. He was born in a palace; reared in sumptuous luxury; yet he cheerfully submitted to all the privations and hardships of the humblest officer of the staff. He dashed about like a dragoon, taking his full share, like a man and a soldier, of all the discomforts of his position. Should time, in its varying changes, restore to him his princely honors—and who knows? we have seen stranger things even in our time—he has not only faithfully won his citizenship in the great republic, but has learned a lesson in the rough school of warfare that must have prepared him to act a noble part, whether on the battle-field or in the senate chamber. Princes seldom learn such lessons of usefulness.

The reconnoissance passed over with only the loss of a few men, and towards evening the troops returned to their quarters.

The heaviest loss was in the Sixty-ninth Pennsylvania—a kindred regiment, carrying the green flag.

Things continued in this state for some time, the *ennui* being enlivened by an occasional skirmish and heavy picket duty.

About this time, the rebel General J. E. B. Stuart made rather a successful raid around our lines. He had under him Colonel Fitzhugh Lee, son to General Lee, and Fitzhugh Lee, his nephew. With him he had four pieces of flying artillery and about fifteen hundred cavalry. They had several brushes with our cavalry, but succeeded in completely sweeping around our rear, and destroying considerable stores and Government property, besides clearing out several sutlers' establishments. A squad of them made an attempt to cut off the communications between the White House and Fair Oaks, and made a dash on the train, which they captured and emptied of every thing valuable. A paymaster's safe on one of the freight-cars, containing $30,000, escaped their search.

McClellan's position was now becoming critical; Jackson's column was moving towards Hanover Courthouse, threatening his right and rear. Lee's army, which, since Johnston was wounded, had been under the command of Longstreet in the field, was largely reinforced from the troops operating in the Valley.

The forces of Milroy, Shields, Banks, Fremont, and McDowell were concentrating in the Valley to crush Jackson, while he gives them the slip, and, by a rapid march, throws his forces on McClellan's flank and rear, in order to co-operate with an attack in front, and thus crush McClellan before re-enforcements could arrive. On Wednesday, June 25, Jackson had reached Hanover Courthouse, within fifteen miles of McClellan's right, and next day moved to the rear of Mechanicsville. Longstreet's and D. H. Hill's divisions suddenly marched from the Williamsburg road the same day and bivouacked on the Mechanicsville road, while Huger's command held the right.

General Ambrose Hill's division held Meadow

Bridge road, to the left of Longstreet, and General Branch's brigade occupied the extreme left on the Hanover Courthouse road.

It was evident that Lee's intention was to crush in McClellan's right wing, and cut off his line of retreat across the Chickahominy.

McClellan was fully aware of all this movement, and though he could not prevent the impending danger, he did his best to meet it. Fitz John Porter held the right of his line, Sumner the centre, and Heintzelman the left. Blind policy had detained a splendid army along the line of the Potomac and in the Shenandoah Valley, which was now powerless to render any service. A handful of intrenched troops decoyed them, while Lee was hurling the whole weight of his army on McClellan. Beauregard had also joined Lee with large re-enforcements.

McClellan telegraphed to Secretary Stanton on the 25th:

"I incline to think that Jackson will attack my right and rear. The rebel force is stated at two hundred thousand, including Jackson and Beauregard. I shall probably be attacked to-morrow, and I now go to the other side of the Chickahominy to arrange for the defence on that side. I feel that there is no use in my again asking for re-enforcements."

On the 25th, General McClellan, having completed

his bridges and intrenchments, ordered an advance of the picket lines on the left. In front of his most advanced redoubts on the Williamsburg road was a large open field, with a belt of woods and a swamp. Beyond this was another open field, commanded by the enemy's guns. It was decided to push the lines to the edge of this wood. Between eight and nine o'clock A. M. Heintzelman's corps advanced and skirmished sharply with the enemy, but finally succeeded in gaining their point.

McClellan intended a general advance on the 26th, but learning that Jackson, with an overwhelming force, threatened his right, he had to give up this project and turn his attention to the protection of his communications and depots of supply.

Porter held the left bank of the Chickahominy. On the 26th Jackson felt Porter's lines driving in his advance pickets. Jackson's move not only threatened McClellan's right, but also his base of supplies at the White House, compelling him to make an immediate change of base across the Peninsula, on the James River.

Such a movement in the face of a powerful enemy is one of the most dangerous undertakings in war; but he had no choice. It was too evident that the White House would fall into the enemy's hands should McClellan meet a repulse.

Orders were also issued to have all the subsistence and stores at the White House, that possibly could be transported, sent to Savage Station by way of Bottom Bridge; and if the White House should be abandoned, to have what could not be removed destroyed. All these commands were obeyed, and almost every thing was saved.

At noon on the 26th the enemy's pickets crossed above Meadow bridge.

Three brigades were moved forward and deployed towards Shady Grove, to cover the flank.

The left of McClellan's line extended along the left bank of Beaver Dam Creek, the extreme left resting on the Chickahominy, and the right in the thick woods beyond the upper road from Mechanicsville to Coal Harbor. Timber had been felled, rifle-pits dug, and the position well strengthened.

About three o'clock the enemy's skirmishers rapidly advanced, supported by a strong line of battle.

Their heaviest effort was to force the passage of the upper road, which was successfully defended by General Reynolds.

A rapid artillery fire, with desultory skirmishing, was maintained along the whole line. They made another effort on the lower road, but were repulsed by General Seymour. They were simply feeling our lines, and fell back about nine o'clock.

General McClellan, finding that his position on Beaver Dam Creek was too weak to hold out against a heavy force, ordered all the heavy guns over the Chickahominy. He determined to resist Jackson with the Fifth Corps (Fitz-John Porter's), supported by all the disposable troops he could possibly spare, in order to cover the withdrawal of the trains and heavy guns, and to give him time to secure the James River as a base of supplies in lieu of the Pamunkey. This could not be effected without giving a stubborn resistance to Jackson. Otherwise, Jackson could cross the Chickahominy in the vicinity of Jones' Bridge, and interrupt us, by falling on the rear and flank of our army, and thus place us between two fires, and head us off before we could reach Malvern Hill with the army and trains.

Such were the positions of the contending armies on the night of the 26th of June.

A stillness reigned around, broken now and then by the occasional boom from the guns. It was well known throughout the camp that Jackson had re-enforced Lee, and was but waiting for the morning's light to hurl his masses upon us, and that every thing was being removed from the White House preparatory to a retreat; yet, under such desponding circumstances, the Irish Brigade was as cheerful as ever. The men lay grouped around the camp-fires, some seated on logs, others reclining on the green pine-boughs that served them for a couch. Around the blazing fire was a wall of pine-tops, giving the place a most comfortable appearance, and defining more strongly the dark figures grouped inside.

A slight drizzling rain was falling, tempering the sultry air of the night, and crackling with a pleasant splurge on the burning brands.

The lone sentry paced to and fro in the clear full blaze of innumerable fires; and the Stars and Stripes, with their brother flag of green, damp with the night dews and the mist, lazily hung around their staffs.

Though they feared that this was to be their last night in camp, perhaps their last on earth, though the hearts of the different groups were laden with sad memories and hopes, sacred to the homes and the loved ones that were left forlorn and sorrowful to mourn in solitude, or, should death strike down their protectors, to pine in want and anguish, they were gay.

As such dark pictures saddened the heart, many a soldier "wiped away a tear." And yet, soon after, their voices, gay, cheerful, and musical, with all the proverbial elasticity and spirit of the Irish soldier, recklessly joined in the snatches of patriotic songs—chiefly from Davis—that wildly rose from those darkened groups. Their love songs were soft and sympathetic as their own genial clime, while their war-songs were fierce and defiant.

Men's voices were turned to maiden sweetness as they sang "The Colleen Bawn," "Cathleen Mavourneen," or "O'Connor's Bride;" while knitted brows and a dark scowl marred their features, and their hands involuntarily grasped their muskets, as some powerful voice sang of the penal days and English oppression towards Ireland.

Such groups, now soft with love, now surged with passion, as the bright fires lit up their features, might look no bad representative of a camp of Italian bandits, did not the white tents that dotted the plain amidst the innumerable fires that glistened and glowed through hill and vale, and the sentinels on their beats, and the stacked arms and dark groups beneath the swaying pines, and then the Stripes and Stars that fluttered so proudly in front of headquarters, all tell you that you were in the camp of the Irish-American army.

## CHAPTER IX.

Battle of Gaines' Mill.—Capt. O'Shea's flying artillery.—The wounded
soldier.—Battle of Savage Station.—Battle of White Oak Swamp.—
Of Glendale.—Gallant conduct of the Brigade in the different actions.

> "Here Scots and Poles, Italians, Gauls,
>     With native emblems trickt ;
>     There, Teuton Corps, who fought before,
>     *Für Freiheit und für Licht ;*
> While round the flag the Irish, like a human rampart, go :
> They found *Cead Mille failthe here*—they'll give it to the foe."
>                                        SAVAGE.

FRIDAY morning, 26th of June, 1862, opened bright
and beautiful ; the rising sun sparkled through the
forest-trees, glancing its red beams along the bright
bayonets of hosts of men who were already moving into
position. Various and disheartening rumors were
current. All the indications showed that McClellan
dreaded the result of the coming conflict, for vast preparations were making on all sides to cover a retreat.

The new position of the Fifth Corps was something
in the shape of an arc of a circle, covering the
approaches to the bridges, which connected the right
wing with the troops on the other side of the river.

Merrell's division held the front line ; McCall's division, having been engaged the previous day, held the second line. In rear of these was General S. G. Cooke, with five companies of the Fifth Regular Cavalry, two squadrons of the First Regulars, and three squadrons of the First Pennsylvania Lancers, in order to watch the left flank and defend the advances to the river.

Shortly after noon the enemy approached in force.

Heavy lines of skirmishers covered the advance, and the forces of Pryor, Wilcox, and Featherston vigorously attacked on the left, and Ambrose Hill in the centre.

The battle at these points was desperately sustained by both parties. The rebels frequently charged upon our works and lines, but were every time met by sweeping volleys of canister and musketry. This desperate struggle continued with varying success.

Meantime, Jackson moved down in massed column on our right, near Cold Harbor. About three P. M. the battle had become so severe, and the enemy's overpowering numbers so telling, that our entire second line and our reserves were moved forward to sustain the front, which was threatened with destruction.

Slocum's division reached the field soon after, and immediately went into the action, strengthening the weak points along the line. Though they increased Porter's command to near thirty-five thousand, still they were only able to stem the irresistible current of Jackson's force.

Porter reported his position critical, and the enemy had gained the woods held by him.

Five companies of the Fifth Cavalry tried to regain the position, and unsuccessfully charged on them. The rebels followed them up, breaking our lines and out-flanking them, which caused a general retreat to a hill in the rear, with the rebels yelling and firing fiercely after them.

McClellan, in despair, "ordered up his last reserve, his latest chance to try," and soon French's and Meagher's brigades were seen steadily moving forward in double-quick time.

As they swept on the enemy, high above the roar of musketry might be heard their ringing cheers and the welcoming shouts of their comrades. The green flags are proudly unfurled. Clouds of smoke obscure the view, and the woods smoke on all sides. The rattling of musketry-fire, the deafening roar of artillery resound on every side, as they sweep over the plain, driving be-fore them, at the point of the bayonet, the fugitives who were rushing for the bridge.

The enemy quailed before the charge of these fresh, vehement troops, and fell back.

In the words of McClellan, "This gave an oppor-tunity to rally our men behind the brigades of French and Meagher, and they again marched up the hill, ready to repulse another attack."

The artillery, protected by the Irish Brigade, took positions on the hills near, and swept the enemy's lines in front. The stragglers, who were breaking over the battle-field on all sides, took heart and rallied into some kind of line behind the batteries. The enemy now having fallen back, at this point the Brigade was ordered to change front and double-quick to support Sykes' regulars, who were badly pressed.

Steadily up the hill, wheeling to the right, the four regiments marched, greeted by a fierce fire of shot and shell from the enemy, killing a lieutenant of the Twenty-ninth, and wounding some men.

That friend of the defeated, darkness, had now set in, and the regulars, wearied by a hard day's fighting, fell back, in the rear of the Brigade, which held the ground, right in view of the enemy.

The battle was over. The rebels had gained a decided advantage, and had captured several pieces of artillery, stores, caissons, and camp-equipage. Had they succeeded in breaking through our lines, or wedging between us and the James River, McClellan could not have saved his army.

The Brigade lay on their arms all night, wearied and hungry; the enemy's lights and fires gleamed and blazed before them, while they lay at their posts, screened by the darkness, and silent as shadows.

During the charge of the Brigade an incident occurred too thrilling to be omitted.

The first regiment thrown into the fight to stem Jackson's force of over twenty thousand was the Ninth Massachusetts, an Irish regiment, then commanded by the brave Colonel Cass. This noble regiment dashed on the enemy, hurling back their advance lines. The enemy, seeing the green flag, thought it was the advance of the Irish Brigade, and Jackson ordered up his reserves to sweep away "that d—d Brigade." This brave little regiment stood the shock of the whole of Jackson's force, but, being fearfully mowed down, they had to fall back to some temporary intrenchment, still fighting like so many tigers at bay. Just then the Irish Brigade was gallantly dashing in, as the Times correspondent said, "breathing fire and dirt." Colonel Cass, seeing himself reinforced, sallied forth again with his handful of men. General Meagher was at the head of his Brigade : when he saw the colonel in his shirt, all covered with blood and dirt, he called out, " Colonel Cass, is this you?"

" Hallo, General Meagher, is this the Irish Brigade? Thank God, we are saved."

Soon after, the noble Cass fell on the battle-field of Malvern Hill.

As the men rested on their arms, they could hear the rumble of artillery and the tramp of troops moving over the hill, down the slope across the bridge; infantry, cavalry, and artillery rapidly but quietly filed and marched along. They knew that the army was retreating. They could plainly hear the groans and death-shrieks of our own men and the rebels in front, yet they were powerless to assist them.

All the other troops and trains had safely crossed the Chickahominy, while the Brigade held the hills, guarding the passages to the bridges.

General Meagher and staff lay all night under the shelter of some trees. It was near day when all had passed by, and they got the order to march. The bridge was already much torn up, so they had to temporarily fix it, and after passing blew it up, rendering it unfit for friend or foe. They marched on, leaving the scene of yesterday's battle, with all its horrors, its dead and wounded, and debris behind.

Soon they perceived the rebel cavalry sweeping down on their rear, but the Eighty-eighth was drawn up to receive them, and soon made them fall back. The picket lines were so close to the enemy's at night, that two Georgia officers strayed into our lines instead of their own, and felt highly surprised when they learned their mistake.

Major Thomas O'Neil, of the Brigade Artillery, got

captured in a similar manner, for he rode into the enemy's pickets, thinking they were his own.

Captain O'Shea, of the Tammany regiment, was ordered with his company to repair one of the broken bridges across the swollen Chickahominy. One of McClellan's aids rode up in a great hurry, and asked:

"Who commands here?"

The captain stuttered considerably, and replied:

"I—I—d-o."

"I want to know, sir, can artillery pass over?"

"Yes, yes, by jabers, if they are fly—flying ar—artillery," replied O'Shea, casting a look at the broken bridge.

Poor O'Shea, there was no truer Irishman or braver soldier. A patriot in his own country, being one of the Phœnix prisoners, he was full of national hope and aspiration, and readily volunteered to support the flag of his adopted country. Kerry has given some good men to the cause, but none truer or braver than O'Shea. The last time I met him alive, I was starting on Sherman's great campaign, he to join his regiment with the army of the Potomac. About a year afterwards, when marching through the Wilderness on our triumphal return, his unburied skeleton lay on that bloody battle-field. When parting, I jokingly told him that I would write his obituary; alas! that I have to perform the task. Peace to his ashes.

The battle-field of Gaines' Mill was rich in spoils for the enemy. Cannon, brass and bronzed field-pieces, caissons, horses, camps, clothing, small-arms, banners, and other insignia of war fell into their hands. The woods and plains were covered with rebel and Union dead and wounded.

The rebel accounts confess that they stripped our dead and wounded for the clothing. The writer of the " Battle-fields of the South" apologizes for it by saying : " I could not blame the poor fellows for securing clothing of some kind ; the greater number of them were ragged and dirty, and wearing-apparel could not be obtained at any price in Richmond."

The rebel army bivouacked upon the battle-field. Generals, colonels, officers, and men were scattered through the timber, cooking their suppers or sleeping on piles of branches, while ambulances and carriages were busy all night carrying off the wounded. In the darkness, these rolled over the inanimate bodies of some and bumped against the writhing forms of others.

The rebels had removed the dead bodies to clear a space for their camp-fires, and in many cases the living were piled with the dead, or flung with them into a common grave. I heard the following story from a soldier who was shot through the head, and lay for dead :

" Though I was suffering fearfully from my wounds,

for one bullet had gone through my shoulder and another passed in through my jaw, coming out through my neck, still I was fully conscious, but could not speak.

"There were plenty of dead around me, both Union and rebel, and one stalwart rebel rolled right across me in his death-agonies. I was powerless to throw him off. Soon the rebel line advanced over us and formed just in front. This revived my spirits, for now, I thought, some humane person will see me. Strange, how strong the desire of life, even in such moments! Darkness soon set in, the men stacked their arms, and commenced to light fires and cook their suppers. In removing the dead bodies out of their way, they piled a number of them on top of us. I thought to cry out; but no, I couldn't, my tongue was swollen and my mouth was full of blood. I heard ambulances moving around, and the sound of spades as they interred their dead. Now, thought I, they will come to bury those around, and will assuredly see me.

"I lay there, I don't know how long, and must have fainted, for the next thing I recollect was, feeling myself being dragged out of an ambulance, and the subject of the following conversation:

"'By ——, Simon, this fellow has a splendid pair of boots. I guess he won't grudge them to a fellow: he'll be warm enough without them.'

"So off go my boots. Simon then took a fancy to my coat, which was a new one, and fell at tugging it off.

"I was all this time like a man in a nightmare, striving to waken from some fearful danger, but couldn't. The writhing pain, caused by twisting my shattered arm, broke the spell, and I groaned.

"'By —l, the fellow is not dead yet; what will we do with him?' exclaimed the ruffian who had taken off my boots.

"'Well, you see,' said the other rebel, who had finished with my coat, and let me fall back heavily, 'if he ain't dead, he soon will; so shove him in.'

I turned around, tried to rise up, and held out my good hand towards them.

"'No, Simon, no; I'm b—d if I bury any poor devil alive; let him have his chance; we'll leave him here.'

"'Wall, as you choose; it would be only putting him out of pain to cover him in, or give him a crack in the sconce.'

"They soon covered up the pit and left me, forgetting to return the boots or coat.

"I lay there in the most fearful agony under the scorching sun all the following day; towards evening, fortunately, a kind doctor, going over the field, stood to examine my wounds, and then sent me to the hospital. It took me some time to come around, but you see I did; and with the exception of this hollow in my jaw and the loss of some teeth, I am not much the worse of being twice shot and nearly buried alive."

———

The 28th June passed over with some heavy artillery firing, our guns preventing the enemy repairing the bridges across the river.

Early in the morning the baggage-trains of the whole army were started; Keyes moved his command to White Oak Swamp, with Porter somewhat to his rear.

A large complement of stores, which could not be carried, were heaped up at Savage Station for burning.

We had about one thousand wounded there, and it was feeling to see the poor fellows, as soon as they found the place was to be abandoned, and that they could not be carried along. Some got up from their beds, weak and bleeding, and hobbled along after the wagons. Some of them sank down, weak and exhausted, to perish by the wayside; others managed, with the help of their comrades, to crawl along.

Those who were too sick to move were left behind. A number of surgeons volunteered to remain with them: Dr. Page, of Heintzelman's division, in charge.

It was generally known among the troops on Saturday morning that the army was evacuating its line of intrenchments on the north bank of the Chickahominy, and falling back to the James River, as a new source of supplies and base of operations. The wounded, who lay on the battle-field and in the hospitals, were told nothing; but the ominous silence and the hurried preparations on all sides convinced them that they were to be left in the hands of the enemy.

As I have said, it was a heart-rending sight, but retreating soldiers become so absorbed in their own safety, and are so apt to magnify the danger, that the finest feelings become blunted, and every one looks out for himself. At no other time is the apothegm, " Self-preservation is the first law of nature," so fully carried out as in war. All looked forward now to the coveted James River and the shelter of the gunboats. The most absurd rumors circulated through the army: some said that the enemy were pushing a large column between us and the river; others, that Beauregard was there with a hundred thousand men to prevent our reaching the gunboats. Full of such evil forebodings the army moved on, insensible to the sufferings of the long and straggling lines of wounded at their sides, whose dripping blood was saturating the sands and dyeing the streams a crimson hue.

Some hobbled on through the first day on crutches; and one poor fellow, who had received a ball in the hip, and had the ankle of the other leg broken, kept up with the ambulances for eleven hours.

The ambulances were so crowded that many of them broke down; some poor fellows sat on the tails of the wagons, their blood-dripping feet dangling behind.

The scene of confusion and bewilderment all through the camp among the troops, and particularly at the station, on that Saturday morning, has seldom been equalled, scarcely even by the rout and disaster of Bull Run.

As I have said, Saturday passed over in comparative quiet, except an assault made by Magruder on one of our batteries in the left-centre of our works, which was repulsed with considerable loss.

With the exception of this assault and partial skirmishing among the pickets, the day passed over in quiet. General M'Clellan's headquarters were at Savage Station on Saturday night, about seven miles from the battle-field of Gaines' Mill. Thither the Brigade was ordered to report. At the time, the Sixty-ninth was picketing in front of Sumner's corps, and had to occupy the ground until all had retired.

Next morning it joined the other three regiments at Meadow Station, about two miles below Savage Station. All day the troops were marching past this point, *en route* for the James River, Sumner's corps alone remaining to cover their rear.

Thus two mighty armies were within about a mile of each other, one manœuvring to reach a base and secure a position, the other, to entrap and destroy it.

Lee's army was moving in a kind of semicircle, its points closing in around McClellan's forces. Fortunately, the nature of the country was such, the swamps of the Chickahominy so deep and impassable, the dense woods almost impenetrable, that, though the Confederate army followed up our columns with fearful dispatch, they were not able to bring McClellan to bay until he turned on them at Malvern Hill.

## BATTLE OF SAVAGE STATION.

About four o'clock on Sunday evening, June 29, the whole army had passed, and Sumner's corps was preparing to follow, when the rebel guns, from the neighboring hills, opened upon us. Frank's, Hazzard's, and Pettit's batteries replied with good effect, and a spendid artillery duel followed. The rebels were moving in force along the Williamsburg road, having hastily repaired one of the bridges across the Chickahominy.

It was Magruder's force which was in pursuit, assisted by a railroad iron-clad with a thirty-two pounder in her front, which vigorously threw shells on both sides of the railroad, as she came along.

In order to understand our position, I will give a short *resumé* of the movements of the enemy after we

had crossed over to the south side of the Chickahominy.

Jackson tried to follow up after us, but we gallantly
held the bridge, compelling him to build bridges further up ; this detained him until Sunday afternoon,
when he commenced advancing on our right flank.
Huger was in advance and in our rear, Longstreet,
Magruder and the Hills on our right flank, while General Holmes was endeavoring to make a circuit around
our left flank, and cut us off from the James River.

The whole region of country traversed by these vast
armies was full of swamps and sand-hills, brooks, heavy
timber and chapparel, so that such large bodies had to
move slowly and with caution.

McClellan's masterly manœuvres had even deceived
the enemy ; they were undecided whether he was striking for the mouth of the Chickahominy or the James
River.

However, Huger's advance struck Sumner's pickets
on Sunday forenoon, on the Williamsburg road.

Heintzelman and his corps were ordered to hold the
Williamsburg road, but from some misapprehension of
orders, he fell back about a mile to the rear, to the
intrenched lines. This left a space of nearly a mile
between Sumner's right and Smith's division of Franklin's corps.

The rebels wedged in here, taking possession of Dr.

Trent's house. This movement compelled Sumner to fall back from Peach Orchard to Savage Station, where he formed into line of battle in conjunction with Smith's division.

Brooks' brigade held the wood to the left, and Hancock's brigade was thrown out into the woods on the right and front, both doing excellent service.

About five the enemy commenced the attack, which was gallantly met by Burns' brigade, supported by two reserve lines, and the Eighty-eighth and Sixty-ninth, Irish Brigade. The Eighty-eighth was commanded by Major Quinlan, in the absence of his superior officer from sickness, and led the charge, supported by the Sixty-ninth. A desperate conflict ensued, which lasted for about two hours, being at times a regular hand-to-hand *melée*. Our batteries were all the time doing excellent service, throwing shell and canister among the enemy's lines. They nobly sustained their position, but finally give way before the steadiness of our fire and the points of our bayonets. I will here quote Dr. Ellis's description of the part the Brigade took in this fight, as he must be looked upon as a disinterested party:

"In the mean time, a rebel brigade was observed stealing down to the right, as if with the design of flanking our troops, by reaching a position on the Williamsburg road. Captain Pettit at once placed two guns on the railroad, and swept the column with grape and canister until it went back to the woods on a run. Some of the sharpest infantry fighting of the war ensued, in which parts of Sedgwick's, Richardson's, Hooker's, Kearney's, and Smith's divisions engaged, with various success.

" The rebels came determinedly across the fields, firing as they advanced, until General Sumner ordered our troops up at double-quick to charge. About four thousand of them went off at once with a roar that might have drowned the musketry. The rebels kept their position for a moment, and then fell back to the rear of their batteries. Meagher's brigade, however, succeeded in charging right up to the guns of a Virginia battery, two of which they hauled off, spiked, and chopped the carriages to pieces. The Eighty-eighth, Sixty-third, and Sixty-ninth participated in this gallant act. It was here that the brave Colonel Pierce, of the Twenty-ninth Massachusetts, formerly General Pierce of Big Bethel fame, lost an arm; it was taken off by a solid shot. Night came on and put an end to the carnage."

It was near midnight when the wearied and hungry soldiers were ordered to fall back rapidly beyond White Oak Swamp.

Bear in mind that since Friday morning the army had been fighting by day and marching by night, no time to prepare food or to eat it. Many of the men had thrown off their knapsacks and haversacks in the hurry and dash of the fight, and could not again recover them, and thus lost their stinted rations. Men and animals went for days without any thing to eat.

The enemy was making desperate attempts to gain the high ground beyond the swamp. Should they succeed in placing the swamp between ourselves and them, our retreat would be cut off, and nothing could save the army. In this fearful emergency, there was no flinching nor murmuring, nothing but the subdued talk of soldiers, the gritting of teeth, the rolling of the trains and artillery, and the steady tramp of the troops. All the supplies at Savage Station were burned, and our dead and wounded left behind.

The loss of the Brigade was not heavy, considering the desperate nature of the conflict. All our officers, from the general down, as well as the men, behaved with the cool bravery of veteran soldiers. Major Quinlan, who commanded the regiment, with Captain O'Donohoe, and Captain William Horgan, as lieutenant-colonel and major, distinguished themselves leading on their men.

Of the line officers, the gallantry of Captains Clooney, Smith, Neagle; Lieutenants Joyce, Burke, Egan, Gallagher, Murphy, and others, was commendable.

## White Oak Swamp.

Next morning the Brigade took up a position on Nelson's farm, after marching all night in line of battle; for the enemy was striving to turn our flanks, and sweep down upon our large train of supplies, baggage, and artillery. The last wagon and cannon had crossed the creek, and the weary soldiers, having torn up the bridge, threw themselves down on the ground and into the creek, to cool their parched limbs and lap up the stagnant water.

Many of the men were hungry, many of them were wounded, with their faces and dresses grimed with blood and powder.

White Oak Creek, like the Chickahominy, flows through swampy woods and morasses. It was only from four to six feet deep, and was crossed by a good corduroy bridge.

On the north side was a sloping hill, crowned with a farm-house. This hill was encircled by a line of rifle-pits, intrenchments, and abatis stretching down to the river.

Hancock held the right of the line, resting on a small creek; Brooks and Davidson lay next to him; Sumner, Heintzelman, and Porter extended in line of battle bordering the swamp, with their batteries ranged on a very commanding hill. A strong picket was sent out to Charles City Cross-roads, where it was expected the enemy would attack in force. The railroad bridge had been burned, and all superfluous ammunition and baggage run on the trains into the Chickahominy on the day previous.

The enemy opened on Hancock's position, which was a very strong one. Their batteries opened with fearful violence, causing a regular stampede amongst teamsters, wagoners, and some artillerymen, in which some of the troops also joined.

Our batteries soon recovered from the panic, and our infantry gallantly repulsed all attempts made by the enemy to cross the creek. The firing was intense, and extended along the whole line. Soon the enemy were found to be moving in force along the Charles City Cross-roads which lie about four miles from the swamp, and near two miles from the James River, at Turkey Bend.

Eight brigades, coming direct from Richmond, under General Henry A. Wise, were thus trying to get between us and the river.

Porter and Keyes were ordered up to meet them, and were received with a well-directed, steady fire.

It was now about five o'clock, the enemy were pressing us badly, when the gunboats Galena, Aroostook, and Jacob Bell opened from Turkey Bend with shot and shell from their immense rifled guns. These

9*

monsters seemed to drown the roar of the battle, and to hurl death and dismay into the rebel lines.

Heintzelman, seeing the rebels wavering, ordered a charge along the line.

The Galena was signalled to cease firing. Soon that mass of poor, jaded, but brave, unflinching heroes, was seen moving like a huge serpent, belching fire and flame before it. Dr. Ellis says:

"The fiery brigade of Meagher dashed up gallantly on the right, using the musket quite soldierly; and General Sickles' Excelsior Brigade, already fearfully cut up, went into the action like a battalion of fresh veterans. The brigade of Hooker was ably led by that distinguished officer, and the general seemed ubiquitous, as he screamed his orders here and there, always urging his men on to the foe." All efforts of the enemy to check or turn this human avalanche proved unavailing, and they broke in confusion through the swamp. We lost heavily in men and materials. Mott's and Randall's batteries, and one of Ayres' guns, fell into the enemy's hands in the beginning of the engagement.

Our average losses here were about the same as at Gaines' Mill.

Perhaps the following graphic account from the pen of Lieutenant Turner, who gallantly participated in the charge, and afterwards fell in Grant's campaign

before Richmond, is more forcible than any description of mine. What soldiers, patriots, and scholars
composed that little Irish Brigade !

"All was as peaceable as paradise, as still as summer
noon could be—the shade of the trees was much
affected, and the lawn and piazza of an old and rather
respectable farm-house was patronized by some of the
officers of the Brigade. The owner was quite affable
and hospitable, when all at once the serene air was
disturbed and startled by the discharge of a couple of
batteries of the enemy's guns; and having our range
they kept it up, the projectiles literally raining down
upon us, and almost at the first discharge breaking
the leg of the old farmer, a sort of equitable proceeding, for I have a suspicion that the enemy received
from him, or from some of his folks, our precise situation.

"We were aroused ; but the Brigade is never
startled, never alarmed, always as cool as courage and
danger demand. Some of our comrades on the hills
on the other side do not stand quite so well. They
leave their ranks, they move from their position at a
rate of speed not recognized by any of the books of
tactics. A famous fancy regiment, quite eminent in
drill and decorum throughout the country and the
army, scatters on the first fire and goes to the rear ' to
the sound of the enemy's cannon.'

"The baggage train of the Brigade happened to be in the rear, and with it are our quartermasters, as in duty bound. They formed themselves into a body, and endeavored to stop the stampede; but soon shot and shell began to fall among them, and their animals became frightened and restive, compelling them to retire to a more secure locality. Under the first fire they were grouped waiting the movement of their trains. Close to them, on a fine gray horse, rode Brigade Quartermaster Martin's man, Ben—a strong, tall, gigantic, and powerfully built specimen of the African. A shell burst, the leg of Ben's gray charger was taken off, and it is affirmed that his bright, strong face became of a very light color while he was extricating himself from the wounded animal.

"Towards the front, towards the point of the first attack, where the shrewd enemy concentrated his fire, let us return. Hazzard's battery takes a position on the hill commanding the position which the enemy have occupied, and from which they are pitching into us with such effect. Our brigade was formed so as to support the battery—the four regiments in line—and then they lie down flat upon the ground, in order that the effect of the enemy's shell may be as ineffectual as possible. Up there, on the hill to our right, goes a tremendous explosion. One of the caissons of Ayres' battery has exploded; the fire is thick and heavy, horses are disabled, men fall; many fly, horse and man, over the hills in the direction of the trees and the cover of the woods. Hazzard's battery opens in splendid style; the captain and Lieutenant King work like heroes. It is curious and trying work supporting a battery in this position. Nothing can be done by us unless the enemy appear, and until that time it is a beautiful artillery fire under which we are—shell burst, round shot ricochet.

"Major Quinlan is in command of the Eighty-eighth, Colonel Nugent in command of the Sixty-ninth. But the latter officer reported sick, and the command devolved upon Lieutenant-Colonel James Kelly.

"Each part of the field and each portion of the day has its incidents. A round-shot ricochets, strikes with a dull, heavy sound the body of a fine brave fellow in the front rank, and bounds over him. He is stone dead; the two men on each side of him, touching him as they lay, rise up, lift the stiff corpse, lay it down under a tree in the rear, cover his face with his blanket, come back to the old place, lie down on the same old fatal spot, grasp the musket again without saying a word. How brave, how cool, how dauntless these men are! A hundred thousand of these Celts would—but no matter: what is speculation here? That shell came very near—scattered

—a portion of it strikes Lieutenant Foley, of. the Eighty-eighth, stuns him for a time; he recovers, will recover. Captain Whitty, of the Sixty-ninth, is just borne by, badly wounded; then Lieutenant Burns, of the same regiment. It is getting serious, you perceive, and they are keeping it up. The escapes are wonderful. Poor, brave Captain O'Donohoe, of the Eighty-eighth—mortally wounded next day at Malvern—acting lieutenant-colonel, is reclining in his position; a ball comes, buries itself in the ground not six inches from him, ploughing a hole deep enough and wide enough to put an infant into. He does not stir, he does not shift: he is not shocked at all. He smiles—a brave, cool, deliberate, assured smile. Lieutenant Emmet suggests that two shots never strike in the same spot; therefore if the captain changes his place so as to cover the ground just touched, he will be safe all day. The captain does not move; under fire, in the battle, he never moves except forward. It was just as well; he had another day's life, for immediately after another ball plunges into the same spot, buries itself deeper than the first, but still the captain keeps his place, and kept it.

"In this position the Brigade remains during the day, holding and sustaining the bridge at White Oak Swamp, supporting Hazzard's and Pettit's batteries. Captain Hazzard had his leg shot off, after which Lieutenant King worked the battery superbly, silencing the batteries of the enemy, and dealing desperate destruction upon them. All this time there is a terrible battle raging on our left, in the direction of what are called the Charles City Cross-roads.

"Towards night, when the crisis of the day came, and Heintzelman and Sumner were pressed by superior numbers, we were sent for. It is our fate to march into the battle-field under the most—to other men—depressing circumstances. We are the reserve—our corps is the reserve of the army; and it is only when the black need comes that we press forward to the work. The dead, the wounded, the beaten, the broken and disheartened line our path—but our cheers reanimate —our *élan* gives them hope. I pledge you my word that when the Irish Brigade approaches the turning point of the battles, the hearts of that portion of the army that see them are moved within them, the most graceful and glad cheers greet us all the way, the wounded take heart, and the beaten and broken, reassured, join in our sturdy ranks and go along with renewed courage to the battle front. 'That is the Irish Brigade'—'that is General Meagher,' uttered in tones of hope, are the words you hear as you march along. 'I wish I had twenty thousand men like yours,' said one who is second to none in command, to our general the other day. And one of the most gallant generals of the army of the Potomac—the chief of the favorite *corps d'armée*—looking at their steady front, as they marched up the Malvern Hills, under a crushing fire, the sound of which our cheers almost drowned, said to our general, 'I envy you the command of that brigade.' The speaker of the first eulogium was General McClellan; the speaker of the second was General Fitz-John Porter. As for General Sumner's opinion, you know that of old.

"When our rear position was taken up near the cross-roads, night fell and the fight was ended—the enemy repulsed; and unmolested, at one o'clock in the morning, the troops took up the line of march for Malvern, which was reached about five A. M. on Tuesday, the 1st of July.

"On this day again the proper dispositions of the troops for battle were made, and magnificent they were. From an eminence the eye could discern, wherever it turned, column after column of infantry, cavalry in abundance, and artillery without end. Our front was semi-circular; one flank, it was said, resting on the river—the other protected by the gunboats. Early in the day the enemy opened his fire upon us from the right, and kept it up with precision and force. From the commencement the Brigade was in range of their artillery, to the sound and effects of which they have now become familiar. They remained there for hours, when the new position was taken up in a ravine, and the fire at this point ceased. During the day the firing was sustained by the Confederates at intervals and at different points of our position."

## CHAPTER X.

Battle of Malvern Hill.—Desperate fighting on both sides.—The Brigade engaged.—The army falls back to Harrison's Landing.—Feeling incidents of the battle.—Death of Captain O'Donohoe and others.—Captain Donovan's reply to the rebel general.—General Meagher's account of the seven days' fighting.

In the dead of night, after its fierce conflict with the enemy, the army fell back to Malvern Hill, and took up the following position, awaiting the morning's dawn and the enemy :

The left and centre of our lines rested on Malvern Hill, while the right curved back to the James River.

Malvern Hill is an elevated plateau, free from timber, and traversed by several roads. It was well capable of defence, for several ravines protected the front; the ground is sloping, and presenting clear, open ranges for artillery.

Another sheltered ravine extends on the northwest to the James River.

Owing to the position and circumstances, it was reasonable to expect the heaviest attack from the direction of Richmond and White Oak Swamp. Here the troops were massed, and several batteries put into position. Porter's corps held the left of the line, Couch's division the right of Porter; next came Kearney and Hooker, next Sedgwick and Richardson, next Smith and Slocum, with the remainder of Keyes' corps, extending in a curve back to the river. The timber on the right was slashed and the roads barricaded.

Commodore Rogers, commanding the flotilla on the James River, placed his gunboats so as to protect our flanks and cover the approaches from Richmond.

About ten o'clock, Tuesday, 1st July, the enemy felt our lines, and some sharp firing took place among the skirmishers. This was followed up by a column of the enemy, moving on our right, in front of Heintzelman's corps, but it did not develop itself in action. About 3 P. M. a heavy fire opened on Kearney's left, followed by a brisk attack on Couch's position.

Couch's men lay under cover until the enemy closed on them, when they sprang up, and poured a deadly volley into their faces, which drove them back on their supports.

A lull followed, broken only by the rapid artillery firing. About six the enemy again opened on Couch and Porter with his artillery, followed by an attack from his infantry columns; but the sweeping fire of our guns, with the steady fire of the infantry, drove them back to shelter, followed by our columns charging at the point of the bayonet. About seven o'clock they were massing fresh troops in front of Porter, with the intention of overpowering him, when Meagher's and Sickles' brigades were sent to re-enforce him.

These fresh troops charged with their usual vehemence, repulsing the enemy in their front.

The enemy repeatedly attempted to take the position by assault, but were each time met by a ringing cheer and charge of the Irish Brigade, that drove them back to their lines, until night, the friend of the vanquished, put an end to the carnage.

After the above general outline of the battle, I will now go back and follow the fortunes of the Brigade on that eventful day.

The Irish Brigade was consoling itself with the hope that it was going to enjoy one day's rest at least: it was evening, and "the boys" had not yet been ordered to the attack. They had ordered supper, and some stray sheep they had captured were being cooked, and they were enjoying in anticipation what they had not had for a week, at least—a good supper—when about seven o'clock an order came that Couch and Porter were hard pressed, and to double-quick to their support.

"Ah," said poor Captain Joseph O'Donohoe, "I think some of the twenty-five who engaged supper will not be on hand when it is ready," little thinking that he would be one of the absent himself.

The four regiments, Sixty-third, Colonel Burke; Sixty-ninth, Colonel Kelly; Eighty-eighth, Major Quinlan; and Twenty-ninth Massachusetts, Lieutenant-Colonel Burnes, formed in quick time and marched rapidly for the heavy firing. On, over the plain, at a double-quick, and cheering, the four regiments dash. They are greeted with congratulatory cheers.

Stragglers, wounded, and retreating lines cheer on the Irish Brigade, as it proudly and defiantly dashes forward. They gain the hill-top amidst showers of shot and shell, and defiantly reply to it with a continual musketry fire. As they advanced they met the remnant of the brave Ninth Massachusetts, bearing their dying colonel to the rear, who greeted them with hearty cheers. The Sixty-ninth first dashed in with a vengeance: the Eighty-eighth is immediately behind them, with the Sixty-third and Twenty-ninth in the rear. General Meagher and his staff rode along the lines, cheering and encouraging his men.

The cannon and musketry of the enemy were sweeping this hill. It was one sheet of molten lead, round-shot and shell ricocheting over it.

The Sixty-ninth is sending murderous volley after volley into the enemy, moving on slowly but steadily as they fire. The guns in the men's hands become hot and clogged, when onward dashes the Eighty-eighth to the front, and the Sixty-ninth coolly and steadily moves out by the flank.

The men are inspired by their brave, gallant officers, including Lieutenant-Colonel James Kelly, and the fiery Major Cavanagh. Their captains, too, Duffy, Leddy, Benson, Scanlon, and all the other officers, bravely cheer them on. The color-sergeant flaunts the flags at the rebels and falls; another grasps them and falls, and they are then borne by the corporals. On comes the Eighty-eighth, its dashing acting-colonel, Major Quinlan, ably seconded by the brave O'Donohoe as lieutenant-colonel, and Horgan as major, supported by the chivalric Captain Clooney, guarding the colors, all working, fighting, and cheering on their men like brave officers, as they were. The fight still goes on, men fall on every side, dead and wounded comrades are strewn around, but still on they press.

The Eighty-eighth is exhausted, and the Sixty-ninth dashes in again to relieve them, and it moves out by the flank, the men begrimed with blood and powder. Comrades grasp each other's hands, in mute thanks for their deliverance.

Some exclaim, "Thank God we have escaped." Others, "Ah, what harm if it were for the poor ould dart we were fighting?"

Even at such a moment that grand emotion, love of country, is uppermost in the Irish soldier's heart.

Sometimes, when the guns get foul, they fling them away, and coolly take up the nearest dead man's.

The fire of the enemy increases; it is awful. He is gathering all his strength for one final struggle. Shells, canister, and bullets are falling around like a hail-storm. The enemy is now sweeping on the Sixty-ninth; they grandly hold their ground.

Lieutenant Emmet dashes up to Major Quinlan with orders from General Meagher, who rides along the line encouraging his troops. The Eighty-eighth in a moment dashes in with the Sixty-ninth, under a fierce fire from the enemy, who are concealed in the woods and a neighboring house; still, there is no faltering, but wild cheers, and on they press for the hill-top, where a hand-to-hand conflict ensues. Men brain and bayonet one another. The enemy make a bold stand to hold the hill, but in vain. They sullenly retire, but the darkness prevents our brave fellows from following them up. They send a parting good-night after them. Malvern Hill is fought. McClellan's army is saved, but that hill-side is covered with the dying and the dead of the Irish Brigade.

The Sixty-third and Twenty-ninth were ordered to support some batteries, and therefore escaped the fiery ordeal through which their brother regiments had passed. Colonel Burke got wounded, and the senior captain, O'Neil, took the command. He and his brother officers, Captains John C. Lynch and Warren, and the gallant Captain Condon, only regretted that they were not allowed to lead their men to support their friends.

After a few hours' rest they had to turn their backs upon their dead and wounded comrades, and march, tired, wearied, hungry, and bloody, in the dead of night, for the James River, which was reached early on Wednesday. Some threw themselves exhausted on the ground, others rushed to the river to lap up the water. Tents, camp equipage, and provisions were all abandoned or destroyed. No matter, all was soon right. The river was floating with barges laden with provisions, tents, and stores. A soldier seldom grumbles.

The retreat, for retreat it was, was ably conducted in the face of vastly superior numbers of men, brave and desperate as ourselves, men who followed us with a bull-dog pertinacity, hoping to annihilate us.

Besides, they had the advantage of personally knowing the country, and found every one ready to befriend them and give them all the information they could, while we had to wade through swamps and dense forest, ignorant of the way, with every one our enemy and ready to set us astray or betray us.

The losses on both sides, in this battle, were very heavy. General Lee in his official report of the seven days' fighting, admits a heavy loss, and that his army was almost demoralized, which was proved by the fact that he did not follow McClellan to Harrison's Landing, though his army was drawn round him in a semicircle.

McClellan sets down his loss of killed, wounded, and missing for the seven days' fighting, at 15,249. This certainly is not under the mark. The rebel loss was something more, as they were in most cases the assaulting party. Both armies were desperately cut up. The loss of the Brigade during these fearful seven days was large, both in officers and men, amounting in all to about seven hundred.

At Malvern Hill, General Meagher and his staff were conspicuous during the day. Among the officers, Lieutenant Turner, of his staff, had his horse killed. Lieutenant Emmet, who, though in delicate health, greatly distinguished himself, was wounded.

Captain Joseph O'Donohoe was acting Lieut.-Colonel when killed. Lieutenant Frank Hacket was also killed, and Captain Egan wounded. Lieutenant Foley had been wounded the previous day.

In the Sixty-ninth, Lieutenant Reynolds killed, and Captains Whitty and Leddy wounded.

Lieutenants Cahil, Donovan, Carr, Burns and Maroney were all wounded. Several other officers were wounded, and Major Cavanagh had his horse shot under him.

Sergeant Haggerty, brother to the late Colonel Haggerty, was mortally wounded.

Our troops held Malvern Hill all through the night, while the main army was on its route for Harrison's Landing, a position in which the enemy dare not attack them.

The men were wearied out with the fatigue of fighting and marching, and many sank down from exhaustion on that night's retreat.

Our dead and most of our wounded were left behind, while the line of march was flanked with abandoned wagons, stores, guns, caissons, and other military paraphernalia. In the darkness of the night and the confusion, regiments got intermixed, and wagons and teams hurried on through the marching columns; and when they reached Harrison's Landing, some threw themselves down on the ground, others into the river to quench their thirst.

---

Captain Joseph O'Donohoe, who was perhaps one of the bravest and most promising officers of the Brigade, was a native of Bantry, County Cork, and was about twenty-two years of age at the time of his death. He was a fine, soldierly-looking young man, full of a laudable ambition, and a great desire to distinguish himself in his profession. He had had so many escapes that he had almost a Turkish belief in his good fortune, and looked upon himself as one of the fortunate, who were fated to pass scathless through the fiery ordeal of war. At the breaking out of the Rebellion, he joined Meagher's company of Zouaves, and greatly distinguished himself at Manassas, where he received three bullet-holes through his clothes. On the formation of the Irish Brigade, General Meagher proffered him a captaincy, and he served in all the battles of the campaign, always distinguishing himself at the head of his command. He was a brave, devoted soldier, and met a soldier's death; but had he lived, he would have made his mark and attained a high position in his profession.

A battle-field is full of thrilling interest, and the incidents and adventures of individuals would make an interesting volume.

Lieutenant John H. Donovan, of Company D, Sixty-ninth Regiment, afterwards captain, while in the act of charging with his company, was shot through the right eye, the bullet going out through the ear just under the brain, and was left for dead. Next morning Generals Hill and Magruder went round to the several officers and demanded their side-arms and revolvers. On coming to young Donovan, Hill demanded his. Donovan replied that he had sent them to his regiment by his servant after falling. " I think," said the general, " from the apparent nature of your wound, you won't have much need of them in future."

"I think differently, general," replied the other, indignantly : "I think I have one good eye left yet, and will risk that in the cause of the Union. Should I ever lose that, I'll go it blind !"

"What command do you belong to ?"

"Meagher's Irish Brigade."

"Oh, indeed !" said the other, passing on.

When Lieutenant Frank Hacket was shot, his brother, a lieutenant in the same regiment, raised him in his arms for a moment; but finding that he was dead, gently laid him down, and then pressed on with his regiment into the middle of the fight, under a most terrific fire. After the fight was over, he at once returned to the body of his younger brother. It was then dark, yet he picked out the body, and sat down beside it, remaining there all night, with none but the dead and badly wounded around him. When day broke, with a strength and depth of affection that neither death nor danger could weaken, he scooped out a grave with a broken bayonet, his sabre, and his hands, for he could find neither spade nor pick. Then with boards, taken from an old house near, he constructed a sort of rough coffin, placed the body of his brother, wrapped up in his overcoat, in it, printed a last kiss on the cold lips as a few honest tears streamed from his eyes, and then covered it up.

What grander spectacle than this young soldier burying his dead brother, threatened by the advancing enemy, the rear of his own column having long since disappeared?

What a strong evidence of the true affection of the old Celtic stock is this love that follows to the grave, and beyond it, all that is near and dear of their friends!

I have seen this strong love displayed in many ways. After the paymaster's visit the chaplains' tents were usually crowded with men sending remittances to their wives and families. I was one day present when a man handed in seventy-five dollars.

"Why, Jem," said the chaplain, "that's all your pay."

"So it is, your reverence; but, as I don't smoke, I don't want any of it, and shure they might want it at home."

Such is the spirit of remitting money to their friends, to bring them out, that after a few years more, if things go on as they are, all the strong bone and manly sinew of the Irish peasantry will be turning the wilderness of America into a garden; building up the railways and the commerce of the Great Republic; leaving their own native land to the sleek oxen and south-downs of the Saxon.

A rebel colonel at the battle of Malvern Hill seeing the Irish Brigade sweeping down on them, cried out: "Steady, boys, here comes that d—d green flag again."

Well, the boys were so steady that few of them left where they were; and those that did, turned their backs to the green flag.

The night after the battle of Malvern Hill, the Eighty-eighth was again so close upon the enemy that some rebel officers walked into their lines, and were astonished to find themselves prisoners.

A soldier whose cheek was laid open with a bullet apologized to the surgeon while dressing it:

"Sure, doctor, I wouldn't come to you with that little scratch, only the blood was blinding me, an' as soon as you have it all right, I'll go back again and have another shlap at the rebels."

"Is it badly hurt, doctor?" said another, as the doctor was examining his arm, which was shattered by a bullet.

"Yes, indeed; it must be amputated."

"Don't say so, doctor! ·Wasn't it the luck it wasn't my right arm?"

An Irish color-bearer of a Massachusetts regiment, named Sullivan, finding the regiment hard pressed, and the colors in danger of falling into the enemy's hands, tore it from the staff and wrapped it around his body inside his overcoat.

He was badly wounded, and fell, but managed at night to creep into camp with the saved colors around him.

Our men showed the greatest fortitude and patience under the most fearful sufferings.

"Halloo, captain!" said one poor fellow, who was having his arm amputated, to his captain, who was being carried by on a stretcher. "Sorry to see you; hope you're not badly hit."

"Are the boys pitching into them?" exclaims another, to a new arrival for amputation.

"Begor, that cheer revives me; sure I'd know it in a hundred; it's our boys are at it now, and faix I can't give them a hand either!" exclaimed a prostrate Irishman, as the ringing cheer of the Brigade saluted his ears.

"Begor, Jem, they have all the fun to themselves!"

"Sure, then, we got enough of it," replied his comrade.

"Bedad, and that's true, Jem; but I'm thinking a good many of them will come to visit us soon."

"Maybe so, but faix some of them will get the shortness of breath before then."

Patrick Dargan, Company E, who was killed at Savage Station, was nephew to Dargan the great Irish contractor.

Poor Dargan was a brave young fellow, and had

previously served in the Papal Brigade. He belonged
to the rank and file—those unknown demigods whose
names seldom or never find their way into print.

The bodies of the Brigade color-sergeants were
found with their hands closed, as if trying to retain
the colors even in death. But their comrades had
relieved them, ere they had gone on the long march—
true to the last to their trust—for no flag of the Irish
Brigade has ever yet emblazoned a rebel display,
though they captured more than twenty of the
enemy's.

The screaming and tearing of the dreadful missiles
—bars of iron about eighteen inches long and six
inches diameter—from the Monitors, struck terror into
the enemy's lines. It seemed as if a mountain could
not hide one from such dreadful engines of death.
They mowed down trees, cut the bodies of their
victims in two, and added not a little to the confusion
of the enemy, by their deep volcanic shocks.

In a few days the troops were all encamped in comfortable quarters, with abundant supplies of provisions
and clothing. They soon forgot their late labors and
fallen companions, and began to enjoy themselves, as
when in the old camp near Washington, before ever
they had witnessed the horrors of a battle-field. Sutlers, speculators, and peddlers, who had been frightened away during the late campaign, had now re-

turned, prepared to reap a golden harvest, and a stirring scene of bustle, traffic, and speculation soon followed.

Your New England soldiers, true to their instincts of making "the almighty dollar," hawked and traded about camp, realizing large profits out of small sales.

The Irish soldier seldom joined this Shylock class; and if one did, he was sure to be treated with scorn, as if a disgrace to the name of soldier and the country he came from.

A person rather seedy in uniform, with a strong Irish accent, and well laden with "Yankee notions," newspapers, and the like, was passing the sentry of the Sixty-ninth, crying out his wares.

"Arrah, an' are you a soldier?" asked the sentry, looking at him.

"Yes," replied the other, looking rather sheepish.

"Then why the hell do ye be seen peddlin'? Sure, an' you ought to take off them soldier's clothes, any way, and not be disgracing the uniform."

"Well, you see, I had a little time to spare, an' a little money, an' I thought I might turn an honest penny like the rest, you see—"

"Git out of this quick, or, by jabers, I'll make a target of you. Hell blow you! can't you leave the peddling to the Yankees—an Irish soldier disgracing himself peddling like any Yank! Oh!"—and the indignant sentry went his rounds, in order to cool down his boiling indignation.

Fathers Scully and Ouellet, who remained with the wounded, near Savage Station, until taken by the rebels, returned to the army while here. They were treated with courtesy and consideration by their captors.

"What a fine lot of Yanks we have got to-day!" said a Confederate officer to Father Scully, taking him for one of his own.

On finding out his mistake, he heartily regretted his levity, and apologized in the most handsome manner.

They reported Major O'Neil, who was captured at Allen's farm, and about whose fate so much uncertainty existed, in good health and spirits, and expecting to be exchanged soon.

Speaking of our chaplains, I must state that the Catholic chaplain, and, in most cases, the doctors, never left the field while they had a duty to perform, but cheerfully allowed themselves to fall into the enemy's hands sooner than neglect the spiritual or temporal welfare of our brave sufferers.

After the army reached Harrison's Landing, McClellan rode through the lines, and was everywhere received with the wildest demonstrations. One would think it was a victorious army, resting after the success of their campaigns, and not a beaten one, fleeing to a place of safety.

The army had faith in McClellan ; they believed that he and themselves and the country were all sacrificed at the shrine of politics.

## CHAPTER XI.

The army retreats to Harrison's Landing.—Its encampments there.—Life
in camp.—Soirée in camp.—The Major's Story, or " The Dying
Friend."—A review.—General Meagher goes to New York to recruit
the Brigade.—His reception at a public meeting.—His speech.—Death
of Temple Emmet.—Brigade out on a reconnoissance near Malvern
Hill.—The Brigade on the march.—Brigade gets a new band.

" Most disastrous chances :
Of moving accidents by flood and field ;
Of hair-breadth 'scapes i' the imminent deadly breach ;
Of being taken by the insolent foe."

McClellan's position was now a strong one, protected
by the gunboats on one hand, and his intrenchments and the nature of the ground at other points.
The bluffs at Berkley were peculiarly well adapted for
defence.   This had been proved during the Revolution
of 1776, and in the year 1812, when British forces
occupied the same place.

Lee did not seem inclined to press the Federal troops
here, but disposed his army so as to watch their movements.

Finding the position impregnable and the troops
well prepared to defend it, the enemy fell back, and

commenced the erection of a fort on the opposite side
of the river, from which they could open on McClellan's camp. This attempt was foiled by the gunboats.

The encampment about Harrison's Landing was
both picturesque and pleasant. The men were all
provided with tents and a change of clothing; and
other luxuries and comforts were supplied for the well-
being of the soldiers.

The men looked clean and well cared for, and every
thing was soon restored to the order of a well-regu-
lated camp. Parades and company drill, regimental
and battalion, were again the order of the day. The
canvas castles of the officers were erected in the shade
of the leafy woods, and in the cedar slopes of the
hills.

It was an imposing sight to see a long stretch of
country, rich and beautiful as the sun ever shone
upon; lowlands and meadows, fruitful as a mother's
love; the deep pine and cedar forests; belts of woods
whose dark-green foliage contrasted strongly with the
white tents; fields lately luscious with vines, or droop-
ing with amber-colored corn, all now covered over
with innumerable white tents, laid out with street-like
precision, with regiments, squadrons, or battalions on
parade or review, with martial music echoing along
the hills from splendid bands. Add to this the James
River, flowing on in majestic grandeur; on its bosom

innumerable transports and steamers, rushing up and down, with the gunboats grimly and protectingly looking on. Such was the encampment at Harrison's Landing.

The nights were surpassingly fine. No fairy tales of magic wonder, nor genii power of Aladdin's wonderful lamp could produce any thing more sublimely grand.

Here, in this eastern clime, the nights are superb; the moon floats grandly through a clear, azure sky of the deepest blue. The white tents glow, and the bright arms glimmer in the moonshine, while the river looks like a sea of molten silver, quivering under the soft moonbeams.

The camp-fires glimmer like so many lamps, the bands are playing, and soft, sweet music floats from camp to camp, while song and mirth and laughter resound from many a tent and camp-fire.

In this fair and fertile land, marred by man, but blessed by God, the nights and days passed merrily. At night the tents resounded with laughter, music, and fun; by day, the leisure hours were spent riding about, or visiting, or taking a cool bath in the river.

The Irish Brigade was not backward in enjoying its full share of the fun and merriment.

We will introdnce our readers to a tent full of

officers, who are enjoying themselves with songs, jokes, and drink.

"Why," asked Captain Gosson, "are love and war so closely allied? I cannot see the analogy between them at all, unless it be that one leads to a future being, the other to a future world."

"Bravo, Jack! now you have given and solved a conundrum in the same breath. It is always said and sung that

'None but the brave deserve the fair,'"

exclaimed the jolly Blake from a corner of the tent.

"That may be very well," replied Captain Jack, "but you find the dear creatures seldom trouble their heads much about a fellow if he gets an ounce of lead in his stomach; they generally bear the thing with Christian resignation, and console themselves by picking up some sensible man who stayed at home to look after them."

"A plague on such cowards!" said another. "Jack, you are losing your gallantry; didn't you see how they literally buried us in flowers? As for handkerchiefs, I have got so many Marys and Seraphinas, that I would have a larger harem than the Grand Turk, could I but marry them all."

"All very fine; it reminds me of a hungry man snuffing at a delicious feast, while some sensible fellows walk in and enjoy the banquet. But shove that bottle around: it is a long time between drinks."

"Wait, Jack, until I drink your good health first; by Jove, it is getting near the bottom: here, my dear fellow."

"Blake, how did you feel at Malvern Hill? I saw you ducking and dodging bullets as if you had the ague."

"No, Jack; only I feel you are joking, I think I would order supper for one and pistols for two. In truth, I must confess when those cursed things were whistling around my ear I felt like Maurice Quill, and wished that my greatest enemy was kicking me down Broadway."

"My greatest adventure there," said Captain Jack, "was with one of our worthy sutlers. I don't mean our generous, portly friend here, O'Donoghue, but Claffan. I heard he had a load of wines, and brandies, and Bourbon, and other delightful luxuries, so agreeable to the tastes of soldiers in general, and mine in particular, and that he was selling them at exorbitant prices in the rear. I went to the general and told him, 'It's too bad, general; he won't have a drop when he comes here.'

" 'Go, captain, and order the villain up.'

"Off I rode, and sure enough, there he was with a crowd about him, selling his vile rot-gut whiskey at five dollars a bottle.

" ' Claffan,' I exclaimed, 'bring up that wagon, and don't sell another drop here: the general has sent me for you.'

" ' O Lord ! Captain Jack, sure you would not ask me: the shells are flying about there like hail.'

" ' Why, you rascal, I have nothing to do with that; I'm only delivering the general's orders, and you know he will have you discharged if you don't go up at once.'

" ' Oh, dear! Oh, dear! Captain, if you take the wagon yourself, you can drink what you please.'

" ' Come on, you ruffian ; wouldn't it be very becoming for me in my regimentals to mount your old wagon, and a battle going on !'

" ' Oh, dear! Oh, dear ! Captain, stay near me, any way.'

" He lashed his team for the hill, where the troops were drawn up ; and as we went along, shells came whistling about. When one would burst near he'd exclaim, ' Oh, captain darling, look at that fellow: for certain, we'll be killed.'

" ' Drive on, man ; don't be frightened : you are not the first man killed to-day.'

" ' O Lord ! O Lord ! If I were out of this—'

" We had got just to the rear of the Brigade, when a round-shot tears through the top of the wagon. Off falls Claffan like an acrobat, and rolls in under the wagon, stretched all-fours, with his face to the ground. Every shot and shell that would come round he'd kick spasmodically, hug the ground, and cry out:

"'O Lord! I'm killed, I'm killed! Oh, Captain Jack! my death be on your hands. Oh, there is another. Oh, dear! Oh, dear! Good Lord, deliver me!'

"I at once sent word to the officers, and all that could took a run down and a run back with a bottle, while those that had more time drank and feasted on cakes, canned fruits, cheese, and other delicacies.

"All this time our friend was keeping up the kicking under the wagon, as if he were galvanized; and in order to keep him in proper ecstasies, after every volley, if any shot or shell was not obliging enough to come near, we were sure to supply the deficiency by rolling a round-shot against the wagon, or near, which sent him off into another fit. I became quite generous; invited all the officers, not only of our brigade, but of the whole division; gave out that I had got up the whole thing myself, and I declare to you, there is scarcely an officer's tent I go into but he will thank me for the manner in which I stood to him that day.

"Why, I have been tight ever since, on the strength of the sutler's store."

"What became of Claffan?"

"We moved off and left him there. The rascal after-

wards had the impudence to come to me to know what
had become of his load of stuff."

"What did you tell him?"

"Why, I told him, the villain, that I was no sutler's
clerk to take care of them, and to get out with himself,
or else I'd run my sword through him. This payment
seemed to satisfy him, for he never troubled me since."

"Do you know," said Major Cavanagh, "I feel worse
after a fight than while engaged in it. Whilst actually
engaged, I am carried away by the excitement and a
sense of duty, so I forget all its dangers and horrors.
After Malvern Hill, when we were falling back, I
came across a young officer. He was lying up against
a tree, with the pallor of death on his brow. I at
once saw that he was a Confederate officer. Something in his appearance struck me. So I alit, gave
him a drink from my flask. It revived him a little,
and he muttered—

"'I think I know you; aren't you James Cavanagh?'

"'I am, and your face is familiar to me.'

"'Don't you remember Arthur Scanlon, that went
South some years ago?'

"'Scanlon, Scanlon, my dear friend, is this you? Oh,
in God's name, what brought you here?'

"'You know, Cavanagh, I went to live with an
uncle in Charleston, some eight years ago. He was a

bitter rebel; so was every one I associated with, and it is no wonder that I became one. I joined the ranks; was commissioned for my bravery; was in that desperate charge in the morning. But, Cavanagh, when I saw the dear old green flag, my heart failed me. I was almost glad to have us driven back. I knew it was the Irish Brigade did it; but as we retreated ye followed with a vengeance, and I was shot through the breast, and here I am.'

"'Alas! alas! dear old friend! it is too bad that we Irishmen should be killing one another, and we so much wanted at home. But can I do any thing for you? Let me bandage your wounds.'

"'No, Cavanagh, it's no use. I have but a few minutes to live, and if you remain long here, you'll fall into the hands of our men.'

"'No, my dear fellow, I'll not leave you!'

"He took my hand and squeezed it, and I thought a tear stole down his pale cheeks.

"'Go, dear Cavanagh, go. But whisper, when did you see Kate —— ?'

"'Before I left New York.'

"'You know we were to be married when the war broke out?'

"'I know all—all!'

"'Is she still true, Cavanagh?'

"'Faithful, as a true woman should be.'

"'God bless her!' he murmured.

"'Cavanagh, will you give her these, and tell her, that with my last breath I blessed her?'

"I took the locket, containing a curl of his dark hair and a photograph likeness of himself, and promised to do so.

"Her hair and photograph were pressed on his breast; he kissed them, and then lay back. I was holding up his head.

"'Go, Cavanagh, they're coming. God bless her! Don't forget!' he whispered, and his eyes closed.

"I laid him back gently on the grass, closed his eyes, kissed his cold lips, and jumped on my horse, for I heard the enemy's cavalry dashing up the road, within a few hundred yards of me. I have sent the locket and photograph to Kate ——, and when I go to New York I will tell her how her brave but misguided lover died."

" That was a sad case," said another, but scarcely as bad as one that occurred in my company. I had a Sergeant Driscoll, a brave man, and one of the best shots in the Brigade. When charging at Malvern Hill, a company was posted in a clump of trees, who kept up a fierce fire on us, and actually charged out on our advance. Their officer seemed to be a daring, reckless boy, and I said to Driscoll, 'If that officer is not taken down, many of us will fall before we pass that clump.'"

"Leave that to me," said Driscoll; so he raised his rifle, and the moment the officer exposed himself again bang went Driscoll, and over went the officer, his company at once breaking away.

"As we passed the place I said, 'Driscoll, see if that officer is dead—he was a brave fellow.'

"I stood looking on. Driscoll turned him over on his back. He opened his eyes for a moment, and faintly murmured 'Father,' and closed them forever.

"I will forever recollect the frantic grief of Driscoll; it was harrowing to witness it. He was his son, who had gone South before the war."

"And what became of Driscoll afterwards?"

"Well, we were ordered to charge, and I left him there; but, as we were closing in on the enemy, he rushed up, with his coat off, and, clutching his musket, charged right up at the enemy, calling on the men to follow. He soon fell, but jumped up again. We knew he was wounded. On he dashed, but he soon rolled over like a top. When we came up he was dead, riddled with bullets."

Thus the days and nights passed over as we enjoyed ourselves as none but soldiers can. The monotony of camp-life was broken by a review. McClellan was received with the same wild cheers and deep devotion that has always characterized the soldiers' love for their idolized general.

On the 22d of July the *corps d'armée* of General Sumner was paraded early in the morning on the plain, a little above the landing, and reviewed by General Sumner on the same place at a later hour of the forenoon. General McClellan and a portion of his staff were present. In the absence of General Richardson, who was enjoying the breeze of Old Point Comfort, General French commanded the division; and in the absence of General Meagher, in New York on special service, at the request of Generals McClellan and Sumner, Colonel Nugent being still confined to his hut, Lieutenant-Colonel James Kelly commanded the Irish Brigade. The Sixty-ninth, under command of Major Cavanagh; the Twenty-ninth, Lieutenant-Colonel Burnes; the Sixty-third, Captain O'Neill; and the Eighty-eighth, under command of Major Quinlan, were out at an early hour. Shortly after six o'clock the regiments were in line and under arms on their own parade-ground, from whence they marched to and forward upon the plain aforesaid, and were in position between seven and eight o'clock. The ground selected was quite extensive, and very well suited for the formation and inspection of troops. This was followed by a review of the whole army by the President, which admits of very little difference, excepting in the number of troops reviewed. It was painful and sad, indeed, to survey the scant lines and the great gaps made by time and death, by pestilence and the bullet, when one remembers how buoyant and full of hope they were on leaving, in the month of March, the banks of the river from which the army takes its name. One could not help recalling to mind the labors, the marches, the battles of these brave battalions. And the eye, with a kind of rapt wonder, followed them from Camp California across the multitudinous and magnificent beauties of the Potomac River to Manassas and Bull Run—the everlasting mountains now in sight, and looming, like the clouds from their eminence, down upon us—onward to Warrenton and the Rappahannock. Then the weary march back again to Alexandria, the embarkation, the journey down the Potomac, the delay at Fortress Monroe, the landing at Ship Point, the capture of Yorktown: more fighting and more marching into the interior of the land; many days spent in the vicinity of the Chickahominy; the battle of the 1st of June; their picket duty, skirmishing and exploiting for six-and-twenty days; then the brilliant week of battles, and the last march.

When it became evident that the troops would remain inactive some time at Harrison's Landing, General Meagher solicited leave from Generals Sumner and McClellan to go to New York in order to recruit the Brigade. This was granted. His reception there was a perfect ovation. I think I cannot give a better idea of the unanimity and harmony that seemed to actuate all classes to recruit the Brigade than by giving the particulars, with a synopsis of General Meagher's speech on the occasion.

Previous to the adjournment, Charles Kirkland, Esq., presented General Meagher with a check for one hundred pounds to aid the recruiting of the Brigade.

On the evening of July 25, pursuant to a call issued by the Irish Brigade Committee, a mass meeting of citizens of Irish birth and extraction was held in the armory of the Seventh Regiment, N. Y. S. M., over Tompkins Market, the use of which was given specially for the purpose by Colonel Stephens. Eight o'clock was the hour fixed for the organization of the meeting, but long before that time the vast room (the largest in the city, capable of holding about five thousand persons) was crowded to such a degree that large numbers, unable to bear the excessive heat, were compelled to go away. Their places, however, were as quickly supplied by new-comers; so that up to the termination of the proceedings, the room was crowded to its utmost capacity.

Shortly after eight o'clock General Meagher entered the room, and was conducted to the platform amid the wildest outbursts of popular enthusiasm. The cheering and waving of hats and handkerchiefs continued

11

for several minutes, and was gracefully acknowledged by the distinguished object of this genuine Irish ovation. General Meagher was in uniform, and was accompanied by Lieutenant-Colonel Patrick Kelly, Major Warrington, Captain Jasper Whitty; Lieutenants Egan, Burns, and O'Connor; John Savage, Esq.; Judge Mitchell, Honorable Samuel Sloan, John Bryan, Esq.; Daniel Devlin, Esq., and others.

The meeting was called to order by Daniel Devlin, Esq., one of the committee, who proposed that the chair be taken by the Honorable Samuel Sloan, which was carried by acclamation. John Savage, Esq., was appointed secretary.

The chairman then briefly explained the object of the meeting, which was to second the appeal made for re-enforcements on behalf of the Irish Brigade, who had so nobly sustained the credit of their race in the Army of the Republic.

He said that letters of apology had been received from Honorable James T. Brady, William and John O'Brien, Esq's, and other gentlemen, who were prevented from being present; but as he knew how impatient they were to hear their distinguished countryman, he would not detain them, but would now introduce Brigadier-General Thomas Francis Meagher. When silence was at length restored, General Meagher spoke as follows:

" Fellow-countrymen and fellow-citizens.—The cordial and energetic spirit displayed by this great meeting gratifies me beyond expression. Would to Heaven
that the cheers which have leaped exultingly from so
many Irish hearts to-night were heard in a certain
camp on the James River, where, at this hour, the three
green flags that were proudly borne down Broadway
seven months ago are furled, in all their torn beauty,
over the brave fellows who held them aloft in the
fierce storms that have lately made this, to thousands,
a fatal summer in Virginia. Deep and glowing, indeed, would be the gratitude, the pride, the exultation,
with which such cheers would overflow that camp;
and many are the little privations, many the severe
duties, great the fatigue, and great the exhaustion,
which would be forgotten in the conviction they would
bring, that the soldiers of the Irish Brigade, fighting
beyond the Potomac to maintain the authority of the
American Government, were the favorites and idols of
every Irish home in this vast city. This meeting has
been called for the transaction of business—called to
adopt the speediest measures to fill up the exhausted
ranks of the Irish Brigade; and it would be out of
place for me to relate the story which justifies me in
accepting for the Irish Brigade, as a just reward, and
nothing more, the praises and applause you have bestowed. Time will not permit me to do so, neither will

the urgent demands and necessities of the public service, the national cause, and growing boldness of the enemy. Hereafter I may have an opportunity to speak of the patient and vigorous endurance, the cheerful activity, the order on the march, the vigilance on picket, the alacrity to push on and re-enforce, the grandeur of the line of battle, the unwavering steadiness of the advance, the precision and rapidity with which volley after volley was poured in upon the foe, the impetuosity and desperation of the charge—which was a dazzling defiance of death itself, where death was most supreme. Of these traits and features, of these high qualities and doings of the Irish Brigade I may hereafter speak, when, as I fervently pray, the colors of the Sixty-ninth, the Eighty-eighth, and the Sixty-third, suspended in some public edifice—revered objects of interest and pride to every patriotic citizen—shall, in their solemn repose, announce that peace has once again possessed the land, and that the golden sheaf of plenty has replaced the lightnings of devastation in the talons of the eagle.

" The Sixty-ninth, commanded by Colonel Robert Nugent—than whom a more accomplished or gallant officer the volunteer service does not possess—is reduced to two hundred and ninety-five men. This noble regiment went into the battle of Fair Oaks, on the 1st of June, seven hundred and fifty strong. Since that day, the day on which it won its first laurels, it has lost four hundred and ten brave fellows. The Eighty-eighth—of which the command, in the absence of my friend, Lieutenant-Colonel Patrick Kelly, whom the swamp-fever struck down upon the field of battle—was most intelligently and gallantly maintained by Major Quinlan all through the tempestuous march from Fair Oaks to Malvern Hill; and who still maintains it with a spirit that does credit to himself, whilst it contributes to the efficiency and reputation of the regiment—the Eighty-eighth has just four hundred men fit for duty. It has lost more than two hundred splendid fellows, and among them I grieve in my heart to think there were such brilliant, handsome, chivalrous young Irishmen as Captain Joseph O'Donoghue and Lieutenants Donovan and Cahill—well-bred, high-toned, talented, fearless young Irishmen—of whose services the most martial and imperial nation might well feel proud. By the way, I should state that the first of the two last named has just turned up—come back to life, in fact—as I learned by a letter I received a few hours since, and which I shall read for you as an evidence of the unfaltering spirit that animates every soldier of the Irish Brigade, even in the very jaws of death."

General Meagher then read the following letter, during the perusal of which he was frequently interrupted by the applause which it elicited:

BELLEVUE HOSPITAL, NEW YORK CITY,
July 26, 1862.

BELOVED GENERAL :—I cannot describe to you the pride and contentment I experienced on ascertaining through the newspapers the news of your arrival in this city, as I then felt assured that you had escaped the storm of July 1st unharmed, notwithstanding your exposed and conspicuous position, while leading your gallant band to the contest. I came here on the *Vanderbilt*. I was a prisoner in Richmond for eighteen days, during which time I suffered intensely from my wounds, the humiliation of being in rebel hands, and a scorching fever; but when delivered from the contagion of their despotic atmosphere, and placed once more under the "Old Flag," I became revived and refreshed, and have been on the gain ever since.

I received a very severe wound during our second engagement with the enemy, while in the act, with other officers, of rallying our left wing, which was being hard pressed, and on the point of being outflanked by a numerous force of the enemy. The ball carried away a part of the right ear, entering the skull and passing through the right eye, totally destroying it. When taken to the hospital, the doctors pronounced it fatal, but I was determined not to "give up the ship." Next morning, the 2d July, I found myself totally eclipsed, and remained so for four days. Generals Hill and Magruder visited the wounded the morning after the battle. General Hill went round to the several officers, and demanded their side-arms and revolvers, which they delivered up with reluctance. The general demanded mine. I told him I had taken occasion to have them sent to my regiment the night previous. He replied that, from the apparent nature of my wounds, I wouldn't have much need of them in the future. I told him that I had one good eye left, and that I would still risk it in the cause of the old Union ; and that, should fate deprive me of that, I would "go it blind," until rebellion was put down, and the supremacy of the Federal Government established. He asked me the name of my regiment. I told him the name of my regiment and brigade with the greatest pride, when the general quietly passed away. I was told at Richmond, that had they known the precise whereabouts of the Irish Brigade on the field, they would have sent a whole division to take itself and General Meagher prisoners, and hang the "exiled traitor" from the highest tree in Richmond. I told them that they would need several divisions to accomplish that job, and that even then they couldn't do it.

I am pleased to tell you that Major O'Neill is unharmed, with the exception of a slight bruise in the arm, from a piece of shell. He is a prisoner in Richmond, in company with Generals McCall, Reynolds, and numerous other officers. The major visited me under a guard as an escort. He felt rather indisposed, and as uneasy as a caged tiger. I am much grieved at our heavy losses, but heartily proud that we have maintained the honor of the two flags which we so proudly and jealously bore, as well as the military *prestige* of our noble old race. In conclusion, I have the honor to be, most esteemed general, your odedient servant,

JOHN H. DONOVAN, Lieutenant,

Company D, 69th Regiment, Irish Brigade.

To Brigadier-General T. F. MEAGHER.

" The Sixty-third requires at least two hundred recruits to give it an effective strength of seven hundred and fifty men—the minimum strength required of an infantry regiment. Even partially, then, to re-enforce these three regiments of the Irish Brigade—to give to each of them merely the minimum strength of seven hundred and fifty men—we stand in need of one thousand men at the very least.

" I have heard it said, however, that the Irish Brigade was overworked. I emphatically deny it. It had no more marching to do than other brigades—no more, for instance, than that commanded by General French,

one of the perfect gentlemen and accomplished officers
of the army, and which brigade I here particularly
mention; for we had the honor and satisfaction of
being associated with it in many hardships, in many
dangers, and in more than one bold enterprise and
bright success. The Irish Brigade, in the way of
marching, did no more than this Brigade did; nor did
it do any more duty in the trenches or on picket than
the brigades of Caldwell and Sickles ; nor was it more
exposed to the unhealthiness of the climate—to the
dampness, to the miasma, to the drenching rain, or the
deadening sun of the foul lowlands in front of Richmond—than any other brigade along the line. Ah!
but it did more fighting, and it is that which reduced
its ranks. Well, whose fault is that? If Irishmen
had not long ago established for themselves a reputation for fighting, with a consummate address and a
superlative ability ; if it had not long ago been accepted, the world over, as a gospel truth, that Galway
beats Bannagher, and Bannagher beats the devil; and
if the boys of the Irish Brigade had not, with an un-
toward innocence, shown themselves, the first chance
they had, as trustworthy as their blessed old sires, and
just as eager and ravenous for a fight as that magnificent old heathen from Connaught, the last unbaptized
monarch of Ireland, who ran wild about Europe, daring every son of a Goth or Frank to tread on his coat-

tails, until he came slap up against the Alps, where he went off in a flash; if it was not for this, you may depend on it, the Irish Brigade would not have had any more fighting to do than any one else. Had the boys wavered a bit at Fair Oaks; had they made a copy of the battle-field, and written 'skedaddle' inside and outside the lines on the largest scale, followed up by the invigorating assurance that 'he who runs away lives to run another day;' had the boys of the Irish Brigade just done this, you may depend on it the heroic old Sumner would never have asked us, as he rode along the front, 'Are the Green Flags ready?' Nor would the gallant Fitz-John Porter have kindled into rapture, as he did on Malvern Hill, as the 'Irish hurrah' came sweeping through the flame and roar of the battle from the rear; nor would the Mississippian colonel have exclaimed, as the Eighty-eighth burst to the front, 'Here's that damned green flag again.' Nor would General McClellan, the indomitable young chief and glory of the Army of the Potomac, have thanked the soldiers of the Irish Brigade, as he did on the 4th of July, for 'their superb conduct in the field'—those are the very words he used; nor would he have expressed the wish, as he ardently did on the same occasion, that he had twenty thousand more of them. There's not a doubt or question of it, it was the fighting did all the mischief to us, and nothing else.

11*

"Somebody, however, asks me if sickness won't account for some of it? I resent the imputation. The Irish Brigade maintains the character of being the healthiest as well as the quietest brigade in the Army of the Potomac. Dr. Hammond, the Medical Director of Sumner's corps, congratulated me on the fact. I am not a whit healthier or stronger than hundreds and hundreds of men in the Brigade, nor have I had one whit more ease or comfort than most of them. Oftentimes, indeed, I have been worse off; for oftentimes I have been puzzled as to where I could get a morsel of breakfast or dinner, the brigade commissary being compelled to supply the men with sound and sufficient rations, while it is optional with him to accommodate the officers or leave it alone. The latter is generally considered the less hazardous and inconvenient alternative for our intrepid dispensers of molasses and beans to adopt. The sutlers, on the other hand, who, in the more tranquil and confident scenes of a campaign, drive a brisk and fearless trade, abruptly vanish the moment the first gun intimates a change in the performance; and the most ponderous of them, taking to himself the wings of the morning, or it may be the wings of the night, placidly alights on the *trottoirs* of Baltimore, where he remains in luxurious security until, the tempest being over, he pounces once more on his prey. Now, it is on these fountains of plenty that

we officers, from the highest to the lowest, have to
depend; and if the liberality of the one and the heroism of the other should suddenly fail, you can easily
imagine into what a desolate vacuity some of us may
sometimes be pitched, in a country destitute of hen-
coops and dairies, and all the other little essential
accessories to the felicity of an Arcadian pic-nic under
arms. If, however, notwithstanding all we have suffered in this way, the bloom of health is still richly
imprinted on our cheeks, it is but reasonable to infer
that the health of others, equally as well built and full-
blooded, who have not been compelled to undergo
such privations and trials of appetite, is not less
exuberant.

"Irishmen, since neither insufficient nor unsound
food, nor insufficient clothing, nor excess of work, nor
disease, nor any injustice, blunder, or neglect has been
the cause of those red gaps in the ranks of the Brigade
which this day, on the battle-fields of the New World,
transmits the military reputation of our race, and so
redeems, by a page of honest valor, the contemporary
history of a people from whose political sceptre, in the
ancient palace, the pride and power seem to have
passed away—since to their own fidelity, their own courage, their own utter disregard of life in the discharge
of their duties, the declination is owing, which I have
come here to endeavor to repair, and since it should

be the vehement desire and the intense ambition of every Irishman, who has one chord within him that vibrates to the traditions of that old lyric and martial land of his, not to permit its flag, so vividly emblematic of the verdure of its soil, and the immortality of its faith, to be compromised in any just struggle in which it is displayed—since these things are so, I here this night call upon my countrymen in this city to throw themselves forward, and pledging themselves in life and death to it, to stand to the last by that noble little brigade which has been true to its military oath, true to the Republic, against the enemies of which it strikes, true to the promises of its unfaltering friends, and true to the memories, the pride and hopes of Ireland.    Come, my countrymen, fling yourselves with a generous passion into the armed lines over which waves, with achieved and admitted honor, the flag that was once borne in wrath and triumph by the O'Neill beyond the mountains and the fords of Ulster against the stateliest and most stalworth foes of the Irish race—the flag which flew in defiance from the walls of Limerick, until neither towers of granite nor hearts of oak could avail for life and freedom—the flag which Robert Emmet—the last of the consecrated martyrs of our race, lavished his wealth, his genius, his life, and, above all, denied himself eternally the promised happiness of a home radiant with the light

and love of a wife in harmony with his own grand
nature, so that he might plant it high above the
stronghold of the enemy of his country, and from that
eminence announce to the world, through the flashings
of its emerald folds, the redemption of what in history
may be one of the oldest, but which in resources, in
hope, in faith, in heart, in all that infuses and perpetu-
ates a national vitality, will ever be the youngest nation
of the world. Come, my countrymen, one more effort,
magnanimous and chivalrous, for the Republic, which
to thousands and thousands and hundreds of thousands
of you has been a shelter, a home, a tower of impregnable security, a pedestal of renown and a palace of
prosperity, after the worrying, the scandals, and the
shipwreck that, for the most part, have been for many
generations the implacable destiny of our race. Come,
my countrymen, in the name of Richard Montgomery,
who died to assert the liberty, and in the name of
Andrew Jackson, who swore by the Eternal to uphold
the authority of the nation. As you exult in the gallantry of James Shields—and as you point with the
highest pride to the staunch loyalty, the patient
courage, and stern nerve of Michael Corcoran—and as
each and all of you should emulate their example,
as you are inspired by it, follow me to the James
River, and there cast your fortunes with that Brigade
which, to the credit and glory of Ireland, has already,

on seven battle-fields, proved its devotion to this Republic, under the command and chieftainship of the fearless, the gifted, the indomitable young general of the Army of the Potomac—General George B. McClellan—to whom that army is thoroughly and unanimously devoted, and whose great and good heart has been its inspiration, as his splendid genius has been its salvation in the most critical of times."

Brigadier-General Meagher detailed the following officers on the recruiting service in New York, for the Irish Brigade: Major Richard Wm. Warrington; Captain P. K. Horgan, Eighty-eighth New York Volunteers; Captain Leddy, Sixty-ninth New York Volunteers; Captain Shanley, Sixty-ninth New York Volunteers; Captain Whitty, Sixty-ninth New York Volunteers; Lieutenant Egan, Eighty-eighth New York Volunteers; Lieutenant Patrick O'Connor, Eighty-eighth New York Volunteers; Lieutenant Burns, Sixty-ninth New York Volunteers. Most of these officers being severely wounded, but happily recovering their health and strength.

We have now to record the death of one of the noblest and bravest officers of the Brigade, Lieutenant Temple Emmet, grand-nephew of Robert Emmet, which took place in the twenty-sixth year of his age, at the residence of his father in Astoria, Long Island. Lieutenant Emmet was attached to the staff of Gene-

*r*al Meagher, and during the memorable "week of battles" was distinguished by his coolness and gallantry in every engagement. His conduct on several trying occasions elicited the warmest praise from General Meagher, who wrote a most complimentary letter to the father of the gallant youth, expressing in flattering terms his satisfaction at the bravery of this scion of a patriotic Irish house.

The following is a reply from Lieutenant Emmet's father to a letter of General Meagher, complimenting his son. This has a melancholy interest, when we recollect that a few days after this gallant young officer was in his grave:

NEW YORK, August 2, 1862.

My DEAR SIR :—On my return home, a few days since, I had the unexpected and utmost pleasure of reading your letter in relation to my son, Temple, and should have acknowledged its receipt before this, but press of business prevented me.

The ordeal through which you have just passed, with so much brilliancy to yourself and those under you, has indeed been a most severe one ; and had my son fallen, or been severely wounded, your letter might have been regarded as simply the effusion of friendship, tendering its consolation in the hour of misfortune ; but under the present circumstances it is so complimentary to him, and expressed in such a kind, generous, and feeling manner, that I feel unable to express to you how fully and sincerely both Mrs. Emmet and myself appreciate it.

I trust he will continue by your side to emulate the good example you have set him ; and may the same kind Providence, which has thus far attended you both, continue to watch over you, and carrying you on to a successful and speedy termination of your most righteous efforts, restore you to your home in safety, and that "*tam Marte quam*

*Mercurio* " you may enjoy through a long life the rewards of a well-earned distinction among your fellow-men.

With the sincerest esteem and respect,

I am yours, most truly,

THOMAS ADDIS EMMET.

To THOMAS FRANCIS MEAGHER,
Brigadier-General, commanding the Irish Brigade.

Lieutenant Emmet had returned to New York with General Meagher, for the purpose of assisting to recruit the ranks of the Brigade. However, he was attacked by typhoid remittent fever, the seeds of which he brought with him from the camp, and after a short struggle sank under the influence of the disease, aggravated, no doubt, by the hardships of the latter days of the campaign through which he had passed.

The funeral was attended by all the convalescent officers of the Brigade in New York. Of the estimation in which the deceased was held by all his companions in arms, we need offer no better evidence than the annexed letter, written previous to his departure for the army, by General Meagher, on learning the sad news of the death of Lieutenant Emmet:

NEW YORK, August 10, 1862.

MY DEAR COLONEL NUGENT :—The news has just reached me that our gentle, gallant, noble young friend and comrade, Temple Emmet, of the Eighty-eighth, died last night at his father's residence in Astoria. I am grieved to the heart to hear this ; for I esteemed, trusted, loved him as a favorite brother. His spotless integrity ; the sweetness of his manner ; the innate refinement and delicacy he betrayed in every word and look ; the high, proud character of his mind ; his perfect self-possession and utter fearlessness in battle, made us all admire and love him. Beautifully and bravely has he, in his short career as a soldier, upheld the historic honor of his family, discharging, at the peril of his life, the grateful duty to the country in which no name is more revered than that of Thomas Addis Emmet. Ever since our expedition to the Rappahannock, in March last, he was a member of my staff, and as such I have especial reasons to speak of him with the warmest and brightest remembrance. In him I lose a companion, affectionate and devoted, whose society brightened whilst it softened many of those ruder associations which all of us have to submit to in active military life. Returning to the camp of the Brigade, I shall miss him more keenly far, perhaps, than I do even now, the morning of his death. So far as it will be agreeable to the wishes of his sorely afflicted father, I beg you will see that the officers of the Irish Brigade at present in New York will pay the remains of their noble young comrade the respect due to the memory of his character and military service.

Believe me, my dear colonel, your attached friend,

THOMAS F. MEAGHER,
Brigadier-General commanding Irish Brigade.

The Brigade had to picket towards Malvern Hill, and was sent out on several reconnoissances, as the following summary of events, published at the time, will show :

### MALVERN AGAIN.

About the 5th of August information was current that an expedition proceeded to Malvern Hill, had a slight encounter with the enemy, chased him, and held the ground in the vicinity of the battle-fields of the 1st of June. That evening our division was drawn out by General French on the fine plain be-

tween our encampment and the banks of the river.
It was dark when we were dismissed, and on our
arrival at our quarters, orders met us to march immediately with two days' rations. In half an hour the
division, under the command of General French, was
under way. Our brigade was commanded by Lieutenant-Colonel James Kelly, Colonel Nugent being
still confined to his tent, and General Meagher not yet
returned from New York. The Sixty-ninth was led
by Major Cavanagh, the Sixty-third by Major Bently,
the Twenty-ninth by Lieutenant-Colonel Barnes, and
the Eighty-eighth by Captain William Horgan.

The long, weary tedium of the camp was at length
at an end, and the blood began to thrill at the near
approach of active operations on the field once more;
and there were very few who did not wish the line of
march to take the direction of Richmond again, in
order that the Army of the Potomac might have
another chance to reach the goal for which many
long months ago it started on a clear March morning
from Alexandria, and from the heights of Arlington.
We passed by the outworks, and recognized the road
by which we were proceeding to be the same one on
which we had marched from the Malvern Hills to
Harrison's Landing on the 2d of July. After marching till about midnight, the division halted, and took
up a position to the left of the road, on a fine rolling

space. The Brigade was posted, the left nearly resting upon the road, and the four regiments in column
of division, extending up the hill on the brow of
which was the Sixty-ninth.

The semi-tropic nights of this region are full of
wonder and delight; the sky is as clear and cloudless
as the face of happy, healthy innocence; the lonely
moon, majestic and mournful, sails along in silence
and solitude; the stars, notwithstanding her brilliancy,
are sparkling and bright in their companionship; the
dark woods bound our view; around us lie the sleepy
columns.

The day-dawn found the division on the alert, and
shortly after one of General French's aids rode over
to Colonel Kelly with orders to proceed about two
miles further up the road with the Brigade, and report
to General Pleasanton, who was in command there.
In a very few moments we are off again, and are
halted near a little old ruin on the roadside.

The colonel reports, the regiments of the Brigade
take up their positions in the woods on the right of
the road, the Sixty-third and Twenty-ninth about half
a mile in front of the little ruin aforesaid, and in front
of the cavalry and artillery; the Sixty-ninth and
Eighty-eighth about midway between the other two
regiments, and the guns in position.

Up the river-road they march. The day is now

somewhat advanced, the sun pours down upon our devoted heads with a terrible and torrid intensity. The
dust *will* fly in clouds, that choke and blind. The
advanced guard, composed of one company of the
Eighty-eighth and one of the Sixty-ninth, under the
command of Captain Hart, of the former regiment,
leads the way. The cavalry pickets are left behind;
we give the last vidette a parting look, and with
keen glances face towards the creek, and the broken
bridge at the foot of the hill. A few mounted men
advance to the stream, and there, on the other side,
sure enough, are our friends, the enemy. They have
arrived since Lieutenant O'Hanlon and his troop were
here before. The two regiments halt, take up a better
position, Captain Hart deploys his company as skirmishers, and some movements are made on our part,
simply to draw the enemy from his cover, but he is
cautious, wary, and will not be tempted from his position. Glimpses of his forces are had at intervals,
sufficient to indicate his strength. A courier is sent
in with word, our object has been gained, the skirmishers called in, we form the rear-guard on the
journey home.

It was about seven o'clock in the morning when the
two regiments were formed and marched to the place
at which they were to separate. The Twenty-ninth,
under the command of Lieutenant-Colonel Barnes,

and a squadron of the Eighth Regiment Pennsylvania Cavalry, advanced up the river-road, following the route of the day before, until their skirmishers found the enemy in some force near Malvern. The Sixty-third, commanded by Captain O'Neil, marched to the right of the road referred to above, Lieutenant-Colonel Kelly and Captain Duffy, of the Sixty-ninth, heading the column with a squadron of cavalry. After proceeding about two miles, a negro, who knew all the localities in the vicinity, was pressed into the service as a guide.

The tall corn, green and luxuriant, hides from sight the loftiest of the troopers riding between the rows. Nothing stays their progress, however. Up quiet lanes, where one would think it, in ordinary times, a privilege to ride, the troopers go. At length they reach a homestead, suggestive of all the comforts and of many of the luxuries of life. The outhouses, such as barns, stables, &c., are roomy, capacious, well stored; the cottage, white-walled and exceedingly neat, is a treasure in its way. There is a vine, a lawn, shade-trees antique and innumerable; above all, a bright young matron on the stoop, and two wondering little ones holding on to and half hiding behind the folds of her skirt. The proprietor of this little paradise is an invalid, reclining upon a mat at the foot of one of the leafiest of the trees—a brown-faced, dark-haired, black-

eyed, bilious-looking man he is, with not a little of
the stripe and manners of a country gentleman of very
fair standing in the community. While he is talking
with the colonel, the mounted lookouts discover in the
trees, and on the hills beyond, the enemy. The recognition is mutual and simultaneous. There is evidently
a stir on the hill beyond. The dust rises in cloudy
columns, sufficient to indicate the presence of a respectable force. If they recognize the paucity of our numbers there will be a grand chase. They make a
movement—so do we. The infantry is soon reached
and under way—the cavalry falls back leisurely. A
company of the Sixty-third, under Lieutenant O'Connell, deploy as skirmishers across the stream and along
the bank, waiting their opportunity, march coolly and
deliberately, the men of the regiment waiting for
orders. Captain O'Neil is ahead; Captains Lynch,
Warren, and Condon, and others, are at the head of
their companies. There is a volley—the skirmishers
are in front. Their comrades pass over to support
them. It looks like warm work. The pickets of the
enemy, mounted and standing like statues, are posted
along the skirt of the woods—an open field between
us and them. They do not fire; we do not either, but
we are ready. From this point the party retired leisurely, and returned to quarters pretty well wearied
with a long march on a very hot day.

This picketing at the front is full of pleasant reminiscence; there were duties enough of an exciting nature to keep one on the *qui vive* and relieve one of the tedium of mere camp-life.

About eight o'clock on the morning of 16th August, the last of Sumner's corps marched from Harrison's Landing towards the bank of the James River, and evidently intending a journey towards the other end of the Peninsula. The weather was most favorable for the movement of the troops and for the transportation of the material, which is of so much importance to an army. Half a day's march, with a fresh breeze blowing towards the river, cleared away from us those horrible plagues of camps, the flies, and gave some rest and release from persecution to the poor horses. As the column advanced through noble, fertile, and beautiful lands, one was forcibly reminded of the contrast of these regions and those which border the banks of the brook, and witnessed the earlier scenes of the campaign. Of a certainty, this is a garden-spot of Virginia; and indeed this opinion was coincided in by all. That night we halted and bivouacked not far from Charles City Courthouse. In the morning the march was resumed, the Chickahominy was crossed during the night, the immense trains, the artillery, the infantry passing over a pontoon-bridge. After having reached the other bank and proceeded a little distance further on, the halt for the night was ordered and obeyed, the men having marched since morning about seventeen miles. From this point, in marches varying in length and interest, the journey was made by Williamsburg, Yorktown, and Warwick Courthouse to Newport News, from whence the Brigade embarked for the Potomac.

## CHAPTER XII.

McClellan's views thwarted.—Pope's great preparations on the Rappahannock.—Jackson defeats Banks at Slaughter Hill.—Jackson's grand flank movement.—Captures Manassas Station.—The second battle of Bull Run.—Total defeat of Pope's army.—The rout and scenes on the battle-field.—Battle of Chantilly.—Death of Major-General Phil Kearney.

It soon became evident that McClellan's plans for the capture of Richmond were about being frustrated, and the Peninsula abandoned. Pope had forty thousand men on the Rappahannock, and McClellan's failure gave him a chance of impressing his views and importance on the Administration.

Pope, who was vain-glorious, boasted, had he McClellan's army, he would have marched right into Richmond. He had strong political influence, and was the pet of the New England legislators.

Banks, too, who was justly styled Jackson's commissary of subsistence, had his powerful political clique at his back, and McClellan was sacrificed to make room for such imbeciles.

With such powerful party and political influence operating against him, McClellan was powerless to

12

carry out his able programme of operations, which subsequent events fully justified.

Whatever may be McClellan's failings or defects as a military leader, he was always actuated by the purest military feelings and regard for the general welfare of the country, while his enemies were willing to sacrifice all to private ambition and self-aggrandizement.

Burnside, instead of being sent to re-enforce McClellan, as he expected, was ordered round to assist Pope. McClellan, seeing that he was to be sacrificed to party spirit, and finding the Peninsula untenable unless re-enforced, prepared to evacuate, and withdrew his troops from the south side of the river.

General Lee, seeing that all available troops were sent forward to Pope, at once perceived that the theatre of action was shifting to the Rappahannock.

Banks, with a strong force, held Culpepper Courthouse, and some of Pope's cavalry had penetrated as far as Gordonsville. This was an important position, as the only two routes to Richmond united there, and could Pope hold it, it would cripple Lee's movements.

Soon after the opening of the campaign Pope was re-enforced by McDowell and part of Sigel's forces. This gave him command of a very fine army.

Pope was inflated with conceit and vanity, and entered on his campaign issuing the most vain-glorious orders. He, too, was as cruel as he was vain, and suffered his army to practise all kinds of plunder and depredations on the unfortunate inhabitants.

His campaign was such as might have been expected from such a braggart—one scene of disasters and panic.

Jackson's command was the first to leave the Peninsula, and by rapid marches soon reached Gordonsville, where a sharp cavalry fight took place, Pope falling back beyond the Rapidan River.

Jackson soon came up, but found the railroad and other bridges destroyed. The river was deep and unfordable, but Jackson made a feint at this point and safely crossed his main army higher up the river, moving down on Banks's flank; for his old commissary friend had massed his troops at the foot of Cedar Mountain, or, more properly, Slaughter Mountain.

Jackson now rapidly swung round on Banks's flank, with the intention of cutting him off before Pope could re-enforce him. Pope's army held the following positions :

Sigel, with his corps, was at Sperryville, watching the roads and lines of communication with Mount Washington, Warrenton, and Manassas Junction. A heavy force was guarding the line of the Rappahannock, while McDowell's corps lay to Pope's rear, in reserve.

During the night of August 8th, Jackson took pos-

session of Slaughter Hill, a prominent position, which
no one of any military brains would have left slightly
guarded, and established his batteries on it,

Desultory picket firing followed next morning, while
Jackson was quietly but expeditiously moving his
columns into position. This continued until evening,
when Banks sent forward a heavy column to capture
the few guns that had opened on the hill. The rebels
slackened fire as if falling back, which encouraged the
others, who, with a shout, charged up the steep hill.
All of a sudden, several batteries opened from the
dense wood, and Jackson's concealed columns poured
one sheet of lead down the hill.

Banks ordered up brigade after brigade, which
literally melted away before the terrific fire of the
enemy. Fortunately, Banks had not the whole army
there, or he would have thrown them into the
slaughter-pen.

Banks's centre was now broken, and, to complete his
discomfiture, Jackson hurled down a strong column on
his left wing, making it give way. Banks was completely whipped. Pope was concentrating all his
forces to fall upon Jackson, but the latter fell back
behind the Rapidan to await Lee's main army, which
was rapidly marching to join him.

When Jackson was re-enforced by Lee's army, Pope
fell back on the 17th August, closely harassed by

Stuart's cavalry and flying artillery, and succeeded in crossing over men and materials by the 20th.

Though Lee did not attempt to cross the river for some time, Stuart's cavalry was raiding on our rear, and succeeded in capturing Pope's headquarters at Catlett's Station, with all his clothes, papers, and docu ments.

Lee, finding Sigel's position on the Rappahannock too strong to attempt a crossing, contented himself by making heavy demonstrations along our front, while Jackson proceeded with some twenty-five thousand men for the head-waters of the Rappahannock, with the intention of getting in Pope's rear or flanking him, and thus cut him off from his supplies and stores. Jackson swept around Mount Washington, Salem, and Gainesville, until he struck the railroad connecting with Pope's rear, at Bristow Station, where he captured large quantities of stores, includ ing provisions of all kinds—bacon, pork, bread, flour, tea, coffee; also, several pieces of cannon, ten locomotives, sutlers' stores, wines, Bourbon, and other useful things.

They compelled the telegraphic operator to tele graph to Alexandria, calling for an immediate supply of artillery, and other things. A train was immedi ately dispatched with the supplies, which were at once confiscated, and what could not be removed burned.

Pope broke up his encampment around Warrenton, and marched out to meet Jackson.

The latter drew his corps together, and took up a strong position of defence. His case looked critical, for Pope's army was apparently bearing round him on all sides. Jackson, when laying his plans, had established means of carrying them out. Hill moved up in time to save Jackson's right from being outflanked, which Pope vainly tried to do.

The engagement all day was pretty brisk. Lines of men, advancing in column, or wheeling into line or deploying, were moving in all directions across the plains. The two armies were trying to outmanœuvre each other.

Though Jackson kept his troops well in hand, and Ambrose Hill had succored him just in time, still he was hard pressed, and had to fall back, and would have to give way had not Longstreet succeeded in forcing a passage through Thoroughfare Gap and formed on his right on that eventful night.

Next day Pope endeavored to open his road by Centreville, and some hard fighting ensued, in which Longstreet was driven back a considerable distance.

### Second Battle of Bull Run.

The position occupied by both armies was nearly the same as at the first Bull Run. Heintzelman's corps held the right of our line, and McDowell the left, with Fitz-John Porter, Sigel, and Reno's divisions in the centre.

Early on the morning of the 29th of August a portion of Longstreet's corps moved as if to take up position on our left flank; sharp skirmishing followed this movement, and soon extended along the whole line. This continued without intermission, at times getting brisker and again slackening, until about noon. It appeared as if both sides were watching for some advantage to commence the engagement.

McDowell, being harassed by the enemy's right, advanced in line of battle, with reserves supporting. He did not throw forward any skirmishers. The rebel skirmishers gave way, and their column soon advanced, and both fired volley after volley into each other. This was soon followed by a general advance, which presented a most magnificent and imposing appearance.

Across Manassas plain, along the hillside, down in the valley, as far as the eye could scan, two parallel lines of glittering bayonets were flashing in the sun, and columns of troops extended like dark lines on every side. Generals, aids, officers, and orderlies were riding around, guiding these steady lines that are so solemnly moving to death and slaughter. As the contending columns came in sight, cheers and yells arose.

Then of a sudden a flash of fire burst from the lines, followed by curling smoke and the rattling of musketry. The battle had fairly commenced. The cannonading was terrific, particularly between Fitz-John Porter and Longstreet.

About four o'clock the whole of Pope's army, except Banks's troops, were desperately engaged. The rebels rushed forward in massed columns, actually sweeping down every thing before them.

Longstreet gallantly precipitated his forces against McDowell, and being rapidly re-enforced by reserves, he compelled McDowell to fall back, and followed up the advantage, driving the column almost in on our centre, creating considerable panic. Lee's main army now pushed on our centre, and a fierce, almost savage conflict ensued. Our centre maintained itself with obstinacy, but being in danger of getting outflanked on the left, had also to fall back. "Old Stonewall," with Ambrose Hill and Ewell, were desperately trying to force our right. Jackson was, as usual, the master-spirit, hurling himself and troops amidst showers of shot, and blood, and dirt, and holding on, like grim death, to every inch of ground he gained.

Lee hurled all his reserves upon our right, and massed his batteries, actually blasting away the head of our column. The right gave way, and our whole army, beaten and dispirited, fell back beyond Bull

Run, to the protection of the forts around Centreville, where General Pope (or, as the army called him, "Granny Pope") established his headquarters, leaving about ten thousand of his army in killed, wounded, and missing on the battle-field, several batteries, and most of his supplies.

His whole army was dispirited and demoralized, and nothing saved him from total destruction but that the heavy rain of Saturday night prevented the enemy from following up their advantage on Sunday.

This second battle of Bull Run, if not the most terrible, was at least the most disastrous of the war. Though McClellan was beaten in the battles before Richmond, still he always covered his flanks, and never allowed the enemy to surprise him. His retreat was orderly and well conducted. Pope, on the other hand. entered on his campaign with great flourish of trumpets grandiloquent orders, and flattering telegrams, but the moment he met the enemy nothing but defeat, rout, and disasters followed. Outflanked and outgeneralled on every side, he did not know what to do with himself or his troops. The battle-field, as described by the wounded, and the doctors who remained behind, was fearful.

The temporary hospitals were full of maimed and wounded men, with surgeons, in blood-stained garments, busily plying the knife.

Moans, groans, and death-cries arose on every side.

Headless and limbless bodies strewed the ground, which was furrowed and ploughed by shot and shell.

Riderless horses, foaming and affrighted, rushed here and there, or, exhausted from their wounds, dropped down to die.

The streams around were clogged with dead bodies. Some had fallen into them, some had dragged themselves there to quench their burning thirst, and rolled in.

Friends and foes, dead and wounded, were piled on every side. The grass and shrubs were trodden down, and were wet and bloody; the streams were discolored with human gore. Hundreds of bodies had been ridden over and crushed by artillery, wagons, and cavalry; there they lay, their blood and entrails scattered about, presenting a disgusting and sickening sight. Near the batteries the ground was covered with the debris of caissons, guns, dead men, and horses: trees, fences, and houses all riddled and torn down. Nothing but death, ruin, and disaster on every side.

Such was the second battle of Bull Run, fought on the 29th and 30th of August, 1862.

## CHANTILLY.

Monday morning the scene of bustle around the heights of Centreville was enlivening.

The weather was clear and balmy, and the soft southern atmosphere was full of invigorating life.

Columns of troops were changing places, or moving into position, for it was feared that Lee would cut off our retreat to Washington.

A battery occasionally opened, and you would see the flashes bursting through the woods; and then came the boom of the gun, and the whirring, hurtling shell.

Lee followed up his advantage on Monday morning, September 2d. Jackson wheeled to our right, with the intention of wedging in between us and Washington, at Fairfax Courthouse, while Lee rapidly pushed on our rear. Several minor skirmishes ensued, in which Lee had the advantage.

Pope's army retreated as fast as possible, with Jackson close on his flank. A perfect panic ensued. Stevens and Kearney faced about with their divisions, to check Jackson, in order to save the army, and a sharp battle ensued at Chantilly, in which both Stevens and Kearney and several other officers were killed.

This forlorn effort checked Jackson, and Pope was enabled to bring the remnant of his army into the defences of Washington.

## CHAPTER XIII.

Evacuation of the Peninsula by McClellan's army.—Scenes on the march.
—Sufferings of the people of Virginia.—The Brigade reaches Aquia
Creek.--Sent to support Pope.--Its marches.

FOR some days there were strong indications that the
army would evacuate Harrison's Landing. Heavy
ordnance and loads of ammunition had been shipped
down the river ; also the contrabands, who had flocked
to our camp, were sent away by water, and the gunboats were all ordered up to cover our movements.

The movement created a good deal of surprise in
camp, for the majority of men and officers thought
that now would be the time to move on Richmond, as
the main portion of Lee's army had been drawn off to
attack Pope.

Had an advance been made on Richmond, Lee
could not have re-enforced Jackson to the extent he
did, or could never have ventured into Maryland,
and consequently no Antietam could follow.

The Administration thought otherwise, and ordered
McClellan to evacuate the Peninsula; not only that,
but the War Department issued the following order,

virtually relieving him from the command, as all available troops were now transferred to the Army of Virginia:

The following are the commanders of the armies operating in Virginia:

General Burnside commands his own corps, except those that have been temporarily detached and assigned to General Pope.

General McClellan commands the portion of the Army of the Potomac that has not been sent forward to General Pope's command.

General Pope commands the army of Virginia, and all the forces temporarily attached to it.

All the forces are under the command of Major-General Halleck, General-in-Chief.                E. D. TOWNSEND,
Assistant Adjutant-General.

McClellan's army had to march down the Peninsula from Harrison's Landing to Yorktown. When the army first commenced moving, the general impression among the officers and troops was that it was for Richmond. They could not realize the fact that the proud Army of the Potomac was retracing its steps, after such a sacrifice of life and treasure, without accomplishing its purpose. Though worsted in some of the battles, the soldiers had fought well, kept a superior enemy in check, inflicting on him severe chastisement, and covering themselves until they had secured a strong position. They had also stood by their general, through thick and thin, and had full confidence and reliance in his skill and judgment.

They could not understand why all was to be abandoned, and a retrograde movement made.  So it was, and the brave veterans of the Peninsula were soon turning their backs on the James River and Richmond.

Sykes' division led the advance on the line of march, followed by McCall's.

The incidents and descriptions of the scenes connected with the march of an army are stirring and interesting.  Though the army under McClellan was kept in more order, and less depredations were committed on the inhabitants than under any other general during the war, still he could not control the actions of stragglers and bummers ; and these liberally helped themselves to chickens, poultry of all kinds, bacon, and whatever other little luxuries they could find along their line of march, leaving wretched families to starve for want of the common necessaries of life.  The suffering in Virginia has been fearful.  The men all joined the army, while the negroes fled to us, leaving unfortunate women and children to shift for themselves.

Our troops soon deprived them of almost every thing they had to eat, and when the rebel troops took our place, they took whatever we left.

No crops were cultivated, as rival armies occupied the country by turns, and there was no one but delicate women and children to attend to them even if they had been planted.

Villages and houses were burned down, thus driving

their starving inmates to seek shelter in the woods. On every side were ruin, desolation, and starvation. I have seen children crying with hunger, with their starving mothers striving to quiet their cravings with the milk from their breasts, while themselves were suffering all the pangs of hunger. I have met children dead, their little bodies emaciated skeletons, as they lay in their cold cots, waiting to have some soldier pass the way that might take and consign them to some grave, for the starving mother and women around were not able to perform that sad rite. I have seen emaciated dogs feeding on the unburied dead bodies. It reminded me of the famine years in Ireland.

It was a fearful state of things. One would think it cruel of their husbands and natural protectors to leave them : but what could they do? had they remained, we would have taken them, and most likely sent them to luxuriate in the Old Capitol. Then they could not, or would not, be allowed to take them into the rebel lines. The officers and quartermasters in our army relieved many cases coming under their notice, but they were few when compared with the many that suffered.

The portion of country over which the army was marching is remarkably fertile, and is justly called the garden of Virginia. The most of it now was lying waste, without hedges or fences, with briers and weeds and young trees encumbering the rich soil, in place of the golden grain and rich harvests of corn. In addition to want, there was deep mourning in every house we passed, for dear ones who had bravely laid down their lives in an unfortunate and unnatural war.

It was evident that Lee was either aware of our movements, or had sent off his main army to oppose Pope, otherwise he would not suffer us to cross the Chickahominy without opposition, which we did on a magnificent pontoon-bridge, near half a mile in length, on the evening of the first day's march.

The march was without interruption, and the different corps had arrived at Yorktown, Newport News, and Hampton, awaiting transportation to join the Army of Virginia, under Pope. The Irish Brigade took shipping, at Newport News under orders for Aquia Creek, to report to General Burnside, at Falmouth, where it was encamped but two days when ordered to Alexandria.

At Alexandria, the Brigade was hailed with enthusiasm, both by the people and the army. They halted and stacked arms near their old camp-ground at Camp California, but had scarcely lit fires to cook their coffee, when ordered to "fall in" and proceed to Arlington Heights, and had scarcely arrived there, when they were ordered forward to the support of General Pope.

The division was under French's command, Richardson being in Washington, but he overtook the column at Falls Church, and was received with unbounded enthusiasm by the Brigade.

We passed at midnight through Fairfax Courthouse, and reached Centreville after the disastrous battle of Bull Run.

Pope's army was in the most disheartened, demoralized condition, and only that the re-enforcements coming from McClellan's army gave them heart, they could scarcely be kept from rushing pell-mell into Washington. As it was, the roads and woods were crowded with them.

Sumner's Corps now covered the retreat of Pope's army, and the Brigade had had some skirmishing with Stewart's Cavalry. General Howard, who had returned to his command, having recovered from the loss of his arm at Fair Oaks, commanded the rear-guard. The Brigade next encamped at Tenallytown.

The following extracts from letters written at the time, will give a correct account of the proceedings of the Brigade since their embarkation at Newport News, down to their arrival at Rockville.

" The four regiments of the Brigade—the Sixty-ninth, Lieut.-Col. James Kelly; the Twenty-ninth, Lieut.-Col. Barnes; the Sixty-third, Col. John Burke; and the Eighty-eighth, Lieut.-Col. Patrick Kelley, went on board the transports and proceeded to Aquia Creek, landed there, and from thence travelled by rail to Fredericksburg. Events, you will bear in mind, were progressing under Pope. Jackson was not bagged, neither was Lee repulsed. On the contrary, flushed with success and full of hope, they were pushing the Army of Virginia and its leader back in the direction of the Potomac, and bearing down upon the Capital. Of the bitter and bloody fighting of those days I have nothing to say. The result tells the story. The Confederates occupy the same lines they did last winter; and there is every prospect, if not immediately driven back, of their planting their colors on the soil of Maryland. All this is deplorable enough, depressing enough.

"Well, in consequence of these repeated defeats, the Brigade did not remain any time near Fredericksburg —from that place by rail back to Aquia Creek, once more on board the transports, and this time they landed at Alexandria. The cry of these generals is like the daughter of the horse-leech. They, too, exclaim give! give! and when only a few minutes ashore they were under marching orders and off to Pope. The familiar roads about Alexandria, about Fairfax, about Bull Run, knew and rung with their heavy, steady footsteps once more. Within sight of the battle-fields of the few days before, within reach of the scattering shells of the vic-

torious enemy, and then back to the banks of the Potomac.

" For the few days succeeding the fight of Gen. Pope
with the Confederates in the vicinity of Washington,
those portions of the troops which had been most hotly
engaged and most vigorously pressed, and it may be
broken, were reorganizing and reconstructing themselves. Battles in which there are great reverses scatter regiments, brigades, divisions to an extent scarcely
comprehensible to those who never witnessed retreats
or defeats ; and of course these disasters are intensified
and increased under the supervision of a general who
lacks breadth and strength of vision to comprehend the
vastness and variety of the situation. At the end of a
few days, however, the troops were either reorganized
on the Virginian side of the Potomac, or having crossed
the river were attended to within the District, where,
after some hours of doubt, all hearts were gladdened
by the announcement of McClellan's resumption of his
command. In consequence of the new situation of
affairs, and of the necessity of new plans and projects
in conformity therewith, many of the troops hitherto
campaigning in Virginia have changed their localities,
crossed the Potomac, and are now encamped in Maryland, along the line of the river, waiting and watching
the advent of Jackson and his confederates. Very
early after the defeat of Pope, Sumner's corps was

posted in the vicinity of Washington. The Brigade was encamped in a very pleasant locality at Tenally-town, a few miles only from Washington. While remaining here, of course, various rumors were heard, and various surmises made, as to the destination and designs of the successful rebels. That they had occupied Leesburg, that their scouts had appeared in the vicinity of the Chain Bridge, were facts pretty well settled and ascertained; the line of the Potomac, at what point, if any, the enemy would cross over; those have been the points and themes of interest and inspection. The lower portion of the river we knew to be well protected by the gunboats stationed there. To attempt a passage through the fortifications in front of Washington, now strengthened by the mortar fleet, was certainly never dreamed of thus far. There remained, then, only the narrow upper portion of the stream, with its numerous fords, now increased by the lowness of the water, and with all of which the foe were intimately acquainted. Here, then, was to be the scene of their operations, and from those places information was eagerly and anxiously looked for.

After remaining a few days at Tenallytown, the corps received marching orders, and proceeded in the direction of Rockville, Montgomery County, marching on the first day about eight miles before halting for the night. They were next day on the road again, and marched past the town and beyond it, without meeting with any thing other than the usual stoppages of the march. When a little over two miles from Rockville, a halt was called, lines of battle formed, the men ordered to load. Information had reached General Sumner that a column of the enemy, thirty thousand strong, was bearing down in the direction of where we were halted, while another force, still stronger, was going round to reach Baltimore by another route. Acting upon this news, the dispositions above described were made.

# CHAPTER XIV

Great excitement in Washington.—McClellan restored to the command of
the army.—Movements of the rebel army.—Surrender of Harper's
Ferry.—Battle of South Mountain.—Battle of Antietam.—Dreadful loss
of the Brigade in men and officers.—Meagher's horse killed under him.
—Magee rescues the colors.—What McClellan and Doctor Ellis say
about the Brigade.

" The ebbing blood of Ireland is shed by foreign streams,
  Where our kinsmen wake lamenting, when they see her in their
       dreams ;
    Oh ! happy are the peaceful dead—it is not for these we weep,
    Whose troubled spirits rest at length in balmy laurelled sleep."

AFTER the defeat of Pope's army the excitement in
Washington and throughout the country was intense.
The scene about the hotels, newspaper offices, and in
the streets, beggars description. All kinds of reports
were current, and even bad as the defeat had been, it
was much exaggerated. Some accounts stated that
Pope's army was totally destroyed, and that Jackson
was moving on Alexandria. Citizens, senators, members of Congress, President, old women and all were
excited and in trepidation, for all telegraphic communication with Pope was cut off, and nothing definite

was known except that he was whipped and falling back as fast as he possibly could.

In this dilemma several citizens left Washington for the benefit of their health, and the President sent for McClellan, and besought him to resume command of the army, or rather of the disorganized masses now rushing into Washington.

That the major part of the blame of this unhappy state of things must be laid at the door of the War Department is too evident to be denied. General McClellan's army was not only withdrawn from the Peninsula against his advice, thereby giving up what had cost us so much blood and treasure, and affording the rebels an opportunity to mass their forces on the other side of Richmond, and overwhelm the troops under Pope and McDowell; but, on their arrival at Aquia Creek, they were sent piecemeal to re-enforce Pope, leaving to McClellan the barren command of the mud forts around Washington, instead of allowing him to lead the Army of Virginia to the victory which his skill and generalship would have secured. Pope and McDowell were beaten in the field, and at their own request were relieved from command after sacrificing an army, with four of our bravest generals, Kearney, Taylor, Stevens, and Bochlen.

On resuming command, General McClellan proceeded to inspect the troops and fortifications on the south side of the Potomac. His reception, both by officers and men, was most enthusiastic, and a new spirit seemed to actuate the troops; for his presence seemed to act magically on the desponding army.

He spared no toil or exertion in reorganizing the army and placing it in an effective state.

McClellan was left somewhat in doubt as to the real intention of the enemy, for Longstreet still held Centreville with a strong force. However, he hurried on preparations. On the 13th September all doubts were set aside by the following order, which fell into his hands:

SPECIAL ORDERS, No. 191.

HEADQUARTERS ARMY OF NORTHERN VIRGINIA, \
September 9, 1862.

The army will resume its march to-morrow, taking the Hagerstown road. General Jackson's command will form the advance, and after passing Middletown, with such portion as he may select, will take the route towards Sharpsburg, cross the Potomac at the most convenient point, and by Friday night take possession of the Baltimore and Ohio Railroad, capture such of the enemy as may be at Martinsburg, and intercept such as may attempt to escape from Harper's Ferry.

General Longstreet's command will pursue the same road as far as Boonsboro', where it will halt with the reserve supply and baggage trains of the army.

General McLaws, with his own division and that of General R. H. Anderson, will follow General Longstreet. On reaching Middletown he will take the route to Harper's Ferry, and by Friday morning possess himself of the Maryland Heights, and endeavor to capture the enemy at Harper's Ferry.

General Walker, with his division, after accomplishing the object in which he is now engaged, will cross the Potomac at Cheek's Ford, ascend its right bank to Lovattsville, take possession of Loudon Heights, if practicable, by Friday morning, Key's Ford on his left, and the road between the end of the mountain and the Potomac on his right. He will, as far as practicable, co-operate with General McLaws and General Jackson in intercepting the retreat of the enemy.

General D. H. Hill's division will form the rear-guard of the army, pursuing the road taken by the main body. The reserve artillery, ordnance, and supply-trains, etc., will precede General Hill. General Stuart will dispatch a squadron of cavalry to accompany the commands of Generals Longstreet, Jackson, and McLaws, and with the main body of the cavalry will cover the route of the army and bring up all stragglers that may have been left behind.

The command of Generals Jackson, McLaws, and Walker, after accomplishing the objects for which they have been detached, will join the main body of the army at Boonsboro' or Hagerstown.

Each regiment, on the march, will habitually carry its axes in the regimental ordnance wagons, for the use of the men at their encampments, to procure wood, etc.

By command of General R. E. Lee,

R. H. CHILTON, Assistant Adjutant-General.
MAJOR-GENERAL D. H. HILL, commanding division.

Lee and his generals were not idle at this time. They didn't content themselves with Pope's defeat, but resolved to follow up the blow. Lee did not intend to attack Washington by way of Alexandria or Arlington Heights; for no one knew better than he the strong nature of the intrenched positions held by the Federal army at those points. He resolved to invade Maryland, making the line of the Upper Potomac the next field of operations. Jackson proceeded by the Drainsville road for Leesburg, with a parallel line

13

moving on the Gum Spring road. Thence Jackson crossed to Point of Rocks, tearing up the Baltimore and Ohio Railroad—thus cutting off Harper's Ferry from Washington; and then struck for Frederick, the State capital of Maryland; having crossed the Potomac, without opposition, at White's Ford, Coon's Ford, and Ball's Bluff.

Jackson was now in his element. He was in the midst of a fertile country, where he could feed his starved men and animals. The army was all excited, and the bands never stopped playing " My Maryland." The reception of the rebel army in Maryland was cold and restrained. The majority had wished to remain neutral in the strife; and now they had seen war brought to their doors, which would be sure to bring destruction on their properties. Those who sympathized with the rebels felt afraid to join them, feeling certain that they would be soon expelled. Had Lee gained Antietam, he had Maryland with him, for such a victory would confirm his friends and gain over the doubting.

## Capture of Harper's Ferry.

Lee had also sent forces to occupy Berlin and Loudon Heights, which would give him command of the Federal position around Harper's Ferry and the Shenandoah Valley.

Colonel Miles, with a large force, commanded there, and remained inactive while all these preparations were going on.

On the 11th September Jackson moved towards Hagerstown, and Ambrose Hill towards Jefferson, as if going to Harper's Ferry.

Lee was concentrating in front of South Mountain, which opposed a natural barrier to McClellan's advance. Through this ran several gaps, which could be held by a very small force. D. H. Hill occupied these gaps. Hood held Boonsboro', and Hill himself Turner's Gap, on McClellan's main line. All these passes were fortified and well defended, both by Hill and Hood.

It was their object to check McClellan's advance here, while Jackson and his generals were attacking Harper's Ferry.

On the afternoon of the 12th, Jackson occupied a position in sight of Bolivar Heights. Colonel Miles held the Bolivar, Maryland, and Loudon Heights, with a strong force. Jackson did not attack them in front, but sent forces to attack from the rear of Maryland Heights.

On Friday evening Jackson had closed in on the enemy's works. On Saturday, at sunrise, he opened fire, and a fierce struggle of infantry commenced for the possession of the heights, which Jackson succeeded in taking, after a terrific resistance. This gave him command of Miles's position with his artillery, which poured down such a shower of shot and cannister on the devoted troops beneath that nothing could live under it ; yet Miles was fighting against time, for he knew that McClellan was not thirty miles distant. Next morning, Monday 15th, Jackson opened a fearful fire from every hill in his possession on our troops, now cooped up in the valley. About noon Colonel Miles unconditionally surrendered.

Just as the white flag of surrender was run up, Colonel Miles was killed ; some state by a cannon-ball, fired by the enemy ; others that he was killed by his own troops for surrendering.

McClellan has been censured very much for not re-enforcing Miles, while others blame General Miles for not holding out longer. I believe General Miles allowed himself needlessly to be cooped up in the valley, and then fought while he could.

McClellan's army was now rapidly advancing, and on the night of the 13th, occupied the following positions :

Reno's corps at Middletown ; Hooker's corps on the Monocacy road, two miles from Frederick ; Sumner's and Banks' corps and Sykes' division near Frederick ; Couch's division at Leeksville ; Franklin's corps at Buckeystown, with the following marching orders for

the morning : Hooker to march at daylight to Middletown; Sykes to move after Hooker; Sumner to take
the Shookstown road; Couch to move to Jefferson
with his whole division; artillery reserve to follow
Sykes closely.

The line of march lay through a pleasant country,
with the fields waving with grain and corn, and the
new-mown hay sending forth a fragrant perfume.

The Irish Brigade bivouacked that night in an open
field, near to a meadow, full of stacks of hay. Our
irrepressible friend, Captain Jack Gosson, climbed to
the top of one of these, and buried himself in the hay,
where he slept comfortably till roused by the sound of
reveille. He rubbed his eyes, and slid down the side
of the stack, alighting heavily on some one's ribs beneath.

" Oh, dear !—my ribs are broken, you scoundrel;
who the devil are you ?" exclaimed the injured party,
trying to extricate himself from the hay.

" And who the h—l are you ? Get up out of that,"
and Jack gave him an application of his boot to ac-
celerate his movements.

He did get up in a rage, using very strong language,
and faced Captain Jack. The latter fell back a pace
or two, and exclaimed : " Bless my soul, General
Richardson, who the h—l could think I was kicking
you ; I assure you I am sorry for it, general, an' I have

a small drop, it's good, here in my flask, and the morning air is a little bitter."

" Captain Jack, my dear fellow! Oh, dear, my ribs pain me; but I know you couldn't help it, or you didn't know who was in it. That's good, Captain Jack—I feel better; I'll have another pull."

Between them they emptied the flask, and walked off to headquarters together to have breakfast.

### The Battle of South Mountain.

The strong positions occupied by Hill in the mountain passes were formidable, and sufficient to keep a large army at bay for some time.

On the 13th the advance of McClellan's army encountered Hill's position. A portion of Cox's division went forward as skirmishers, covered by our artillery. In the evening Scammon's Ohio brigade deployed to the right of the road, while the Forty-fifth and Forty-eighth Pennsylvania formed on the left. The rebels were screened behind rocks and stone walls, and from their cover they opened a fierce fire on our men as they advanced. After a stubborn resistance and heavy loss, we carried the position. Next day Slocum's division, of Franklin's corps, engaged the rebels under McLaws, at Clayton Pass, driving the enemy through the pass and town of Burkettsville. The enemy had a strong position here, occupying the slopes and sides of a steep mountain pass, which was swept by their artillery. Our troops had to climb the high rocks and slopes of hills as they pressed back the enemy. We captured a large number of prisoners, and nearly all the Cobb Legion, with their colors inscribed " Cobb Legion—in the name of the Lord."

Hill's position at Turner's Gap was well selected, and protected by all the natural advantages of the place. The dense woods and rock on each side were well calculated to conceal troops and masked batteries. The road ascending the side of the mountain was steep and narrow, and filled with barricades of large stones. The fight, properly speaking, began on Sunday forenoon, by our troops assaulting the South, or Seared Mountain. The fighting continued all day until nine o'clock at night, when we had driven the enemy from the different passes. Perhaps the heaviest fighting of the day fell on the Ninth Corps, under General Reno, who was shot dead. Cox's division made a splendid charge on the rebel works, routing them at the point of the bayonet.

Towards evening the Federal army charged at different points. Reno, with his troops, driving the enemy from cover to cover, from rock to rock, until they had cleared the passes. Hooker had engaged Hill in person at Turner's Gap, and repelled him after some hard fighting. Sumner was in reserve and did not come on the field until evening, and was therefore but partially engaged. This saved the Irish Brigade from participating much in the battle of South Mountain. They reached Mount Tabor Church, in a position to support the right, should Hill renew the fight in the morning.

Hill was driven from all his strong posts along the mountain, and had to fall back on the main army, closely followed by the Federal army, which was now pouring through the gaps.

Lee, finding a general engagement unavoidable, withdrew his forces towards Sharpsburg, and, crossing the Antietam River, arranged his line of battle on the west bank. On the evening of the same day the advance of McClellan's army reached Keadysville, but a few miles east of the river.

### BATTLE OF ANTIETAM.

The Antietam River joins the Potomac almost at right angles, and is spanned by three bridges, the centre one being on the direct road to Sharpsburg, The second was about two miles lower down, and commanded a road leading to the Potomac; and the third, about two miles above, commanded a road leading direct to Hagerstown.

The stream is fordable in many places above the upper bridge. The land in the neighborhood is rather hilly and full of bluffs, which afforded shelter to the defending force, and were favorable positions for artillery. As I have said, at the upper part of the line the river was fordable, and afforded free access to an army.

McClellan's army followed up the retreat from South Mountain. General Richardson's division of the Second Corps, pressing the rear-guard with vigor, passed Boonsboro' and Keadysville, and came upon the main body of the enemy, occupying a strong position a few miles beyond the latter place. The Irish Brigade had the advance of Sumner's corps, and, consequently, of the whole army.

Richardson, close on the heels of the foe, halted and deployed near Antietam River, on the right of the Sharpsburg road.

The other corps had not yet got into position; besides, it was too late in the day to commence the battle: so the evening was spent in getting into line and exchanging artillery salutes with the enemy.

The enemy's artillery was posted on all favorable points, and their reserves concealed behind the hills and bluffs.

All the approaches to the bridges were guarded with sharpshooters and artillery. Lee's flanks and rear were protected by the Antietam and Potomac, while his line of battle formed a kind of arc, connecting the two streams.

13*

Sumner and Hooker's corps occupied the right, near Keadysville, on the Sharpsburg turnpike. Richardson's division was in advance, and just up to the Antietam River. General Sykes' division of Porter's corps was on the left of the turnpike, and in line with General Richardson, protecting the bridge over the Antietam. General Burnside's corps held the left of the line. General Mansfield's corps was massed in the rear of Sumner and Hooker. General Franklin's corps and Couch's division held a position in front of Brownsville. General Merrill's division of Porter's corps was *en route* from Boonsboro', and General Humphrey's division of new troops was marching from Frederick, Maryland.

Our artillery was judiciously posted on all the hills commanding the turnpikes and accesses to the river.

Some heavy firing took place early on the 16th, which continued with more or less intensity until towards noon. All the morning was spent in examining ground, in finding fords, clearing their approaches, and reconnoitring the enemy's positions.

About four in the afternoon of Tuesday, Hooker was ordered to cross Antietam Creek at the upper ford on the right, with his whole corps, attack the enemy's left, and occupy a position on their flank. He crossed without opposition, sent forward cavalry as skirmishers, who were speedily driven back, and then advancing with his whole force about six, took possession of strong ground, close to the rebels' left, and immediately became engaged with artillery and infantry. Darkness ended the fight, with slight loss on either side, Hooker carrying and holding the woods from which the enemy's fire first came.

During the night, Mansfield's corps, consisting of Williams and Green's divisions, crossed the Antietam at the same ford and bridge as Hooker.

At daylight next morning, the 17th, the action was commenced by the skirmishing of the Pennsylvania Reserves, and soon after the fight was renewed suddenly and vehemently, both sides opening fire together. The number and position of the rebel batteries the evening before, had disclosed that they were in great force on the right.

McClellan's plan of battle was briefly as follows : Hooker was to cross the creek on the right, as before stated ; Sumner, Franklin, and Mansfield to co-operate with and sustain his attack. In front, the batteries were to push forward with infantry supports, and an effort to be made to carry the heights on the left. Burnside was to cross the creek by the bridge, and attack the rebel right, moving on Sharpsburg also, which was in their rear, and thus cut off their retreat. Porter and Sykes were held in reserve. The plan, if successful, must result not merely in the defeat, but the destruction or surrender of the rebel army.

The rebel line was formed on a crescent-shaped ridge, which in front slopes down into an undulating valley, irregularly broken by connecting ranges of hills. Behind the crest the rebel forces lay in uneven and strong positions, sheltered by ridges and hills, and especially strong on the flanks. Antietam Creek, a stream too deep to be forded, except in very few places, sweeps by the base of their position, and protected it from assault.

McClellan's forces were first formed in front, afterwards thrown to the right and left. There was little or no ground on our side equal in height to the rebel position.

Hooker sustained, unaided, the attack on the rebel left for nearly four hours. His line had been formed the night before, and fought in the same order. Ricketts' division was on the left, Meade's Pennsylvania Reserves in the centre, Doubleday's division on the right. Meade gained ground in his first attack. Ricketts also went forward through the woods in his front, and Doubleday, with his guns, held front against a heavy cannonade. Meade advancing, finally met a heavy body of fresh troops thrown suddenly and vigorously against him, and was driven back over part of the ground he had just won. Ricketts' line was at the same time hard pressed, and became disordered. Mansfield, who had come over the creek the night before, was ordered into the woods to Ricketts' support ; and Hartsuff's brigade, part of Doubleday's command, was sent to sustain Meade. Mansfield took the greatest part of his troops to Ricketts' help, but they were unable to extend their line, and, in the effort to push forward his men, General Mansfield was mortally wounded. General Hartsuff advanced to the relief of Meade with the Twelfth and Thirteenth Massachusetts, and another regiment. The Pennsylvania troops were retiring in haste and some confusion. Hartsuff seized a bridge in front of the field, over which the rebels were pressing, and held it in splendid style for more than half an hour against a greatly superior force. His men behaved most gallantly, standing on this exposed ground, firing steadily, and never wavering once. General Hartsuff was very soon severely wounded. His troops retained their position, and finally, by the precision and rapidity of their fire, compelling the enemy to retreat, instantly advanced in pursuit. While they had been engaged, Hooker ordered up Crawford's and Gordon's brigades to their support. Hartsuff retained the advance, and Crawford and Gordon followed them up. A rebel battery on the right, which had been most annoying by an enfilading fire, was about the same time silenced by Doubleday's guns, and Hooker ordered his whole line forward.

The rebels were driven through the cornfield again into the woods beyond. At this time the fearless and indomitable Hooker received a shot in the foot and was carried from the field. The fighting in Hooker's front was of the most desperate nature, and his losses were very heavy; but the punishment he inflicted on the enemy was fearful. Had the enemy succeeded in crushing his lines, disaster should follow. He knew that, and desperately sustained his ground against all odds.

The enemy's lines were screened by the woods, behind which his movements were concealed, and his batteries on the hill, and rifle-works, covered by the fire of our artillery in front.

For about two hours the battle raged with varied success, the enemy endeavoring to force back our lines, and we, on the other hand, trying to take possession of the line in our front.

At about 3 o'clock Sedgwick's division of Sumner's corps arrived. Crossing the ford, this division marched in three columns, and on reaching the scene of action were halted, and changed front, forming three parallel lines by brigade, Gorman's brigade in the front, Dana's second, and Howard's third.

The division then moved forward, under a heavy

fire of musketry and artillery from the enemy's lines on the hill. The firing here was terrible, and the column—unable to withstand it—broke in considerable confusion.

General Williams was ordered in to support them, but finding Sedgwick's left giving way, they had to fall back to the second line of works. About this time Sedgwick, Dana, and Hooker were seriously wounded, and affairs began to look critical.

While this contest was obstinately raging on the right, Sumner ordered French's division to attack vigorously, in order to make a diversion in favor of the right. French's division swept on the enemy, driving them back for some time; but his new troops got into some confusion. These he rallied as a reserve, and ordered Kimball to the front. The enemy occupied a strong position here, and opened a galling fire on Kimball, and a terrific slaughter ensued.

Richardson's division came up on the left of French. It had formed line in a valley or ravine, behind the high grounds, in the following order:

Meagher's Irish Brigade on the right, Caldwell's brigade on his left, with Colonel Brooke's brigade in reserve. As the troops debouched on the open plain, the enemy turned their artillery against them.

General Meagher rode at the head of the Irish Brigade, which dashed forward, in the following order:

The Sixty-ninth Regiment, under Lieutenant-Colonel James Kelly, occupied the right of the Irish Brigade; next to them were the Twenty-ninth Massachusetts; then the Sixty-third New York, Colonel Burke; the Eighty-eighth, under Lieutenant-Colonel Patrick Kelly, forming the left wing.

They marched up to the brow of the hill, cheering as they went, led by General Meagher in person, and were welcomed with cheers by French's brigade. The musketry firing at this point was the severest and most deadly ever witnessed before—so acknowledged by veterans in the service. Men on both sides fell in large numbers every moment, and those who were eye-witnesses of the struggle did not suppose it possible for a single man to escape. The enemy here at first were concealed behind a knoll, so that only their heads were exposed. The Brigade advanced up the slope with a cheer, when a most deadly fire was poured in by a second line of the enemy concealed in the Sharpsburg road, which at this place is several feet lower than the surrounding surface, forming a complete rifle-pit, and also from a force partially concealed still further to the rear.

At this time the color-bearer in the right wing advanced several paces to the front, and defiantly waved his flag in the faces of the enemy: as if by a miracle, he escaped without serious injury.

The line of the Brigade, in its advance up the hill, was broken in the centre temporarily by an obstruction, the right wing having advanced to keep up with the colors, and fell back a short distance, when General Meagher directed that a rail fence, which the enemy a few minutes before had been fighting behind, should be torn down. His men, in face of a galling fire, obeyed the order, when the whole Brigade advanced to the brow of the hill, cheering as they went, and causing the enemy to fall back to their second line—the Strasburg road, which is some three feet lower than the surrounding surface.

In this road were massed a large force of infantry, and here was the most hotly contested point of the day.

The fight here was terrific. The rebels were intrenched and screened in the sunken road, all the time pouring a deadly fire into the advancing column of the Brigade. The green flag was completely riddled, and it appeared certain death to any one to bear it, for eight color-bearers had already fallen. The last had fallen, and the Irish green lay trailing in the dust. Meagher cried out—

"Boys, raise the colors, and follow me!"

Captain James McGee, of the Sixty-ninth, rushed forward, and crying, "I'll follow you!"—seized the flag.

As he raised it, a bullet cut the standard in two in his hand; and, as he again stooped down, another bullet tore through his cap. Still, he jumped up, waved the flag, shook it at the rebels, and cheered on the troops, almost miraculously escaping.

McClellan viewed the battle from a hill, and anxiously watched the charge of the Irish Brigade.

Seeing the colors fall so often, and the line in temporary confusion, an aid cried out—

"The day is lost, general—the Irish fly!"

McClellan looked on for a moment, and smilingly replied—

"No, no! their flags are up—they are charging!"

The muskets were become red-hot in the men's hands, for they were three hours engaged. The men had often to fling away their muskets, and pick others up.

Another wild cheer, and on they dash, the rebel lines breaking in their front. The Brigade was nearly cut away; it could not hold out much longer.

General Meagher's clothes were perforated with bullets; his horse was shot under him, and he being stunned by the fall, had to be carried to the rear; while Lieutenant Mackey, of his staff, received his death-wound when carrying out an order of the general's. Lieutenant Gosson's horse was shot under him, and a second shot through the nose. The poor animal had covered himself and rider with flecks of blood, and some called out—

"Gosson, are you badly wounded ?"

"Not touched at all, my dear fellow ; its only this fellow's snuffers that are injured."

Lieutenant Colonel James Kelly, of the Sixty-ninth, who gallantly led the charge of his regiment, and Lieutenant-Colonel Fowler, of the Sixty-third, and Captain Shanley were wounded, while the brave Captain Cavanagh, the gallant Clooney, Duffy, and Joyce lay dead on the field, and the hill-side was covered with the dead and dying. No matter, the Irish Brigade was victorious.

Doctor Ellis in his excellent work, speaking of the charge, says :

"As the Irish Brigade, led by the gallant Meagher himself, charged the enemy's lines, their cheers rose in one great surge of sound over the noise of battle, over the roar of a multitude of artillery, and was heard far down the lines to the left, where Burnside's boys were just getting at it. Thus met, the rebel advance was checked and broken, and they were driven with awful slaughter."

McClellan in his report bears the following testimony to their bravery :

"Meagher's Brigade, advancing steadily, soon became engaged with the enemy, posted to the left, and in front of Roulette's house. It continued to advance under a heavy fire nearly to the crest of the hill over-looking Piper's house, the enemy being posted in a continuation of the sunken road and cornfield before referred to. Here the brave Irish Brigade opened upon the enemy a terrific musketry fire. All of General Sumner's corps was now engaged,—General Sedgwick on the right, General French in the centre, and General Richardson on the left.

" The Irish Brigade sustained its well-earned repu-tation. After suffering terribly in officers and men, and strewing the ground with their enemies as they drove them back, their ammunition nearly expended, and their commander, General Meagher, disabled by a fall from his horse, shot under him, this Brigade was ordered to give place to General Caldwell's brigade, which advanced to a short distance in its rear.

" The lines were passed by the Irish Brigade break-ing by company to the rear, and General Caldwell's by company to the front, as steady as on drill."

Did a commanding general ever bear higher testi-mony to the service of any brigade than this? About one hundred and twenty recruits had joined the Bri-gade the day previous to the battle, and were assigned to provost-duty, but requested to be allowed to partici-pate in the engagement; fully seventy-five of them were either killed or wounded.

## CHAPTER XV.

The battle of Antietam continued.—Total route of the rebel army.—The battle-field at night.—Heavy losses on both sides.—Fearful loss in the Brigade.—General Richardson mortally wounded.—Brigade encamped on Bolivar Heights.—Review by the President.—Army again on the march.—Promotions in the Brigade.

AFTER the Irish Brigade gave place to Caldwell's, the latter continued with determined gallantry to push the enemy, and, supported by the Fifty-seventh and Sixty-sixth New York, of Brookes' brigade, Fifth New Hampshire, and Eighty-first Pennsylvania, succeeded in completely routing them.

Having gained the left, the enemy re-enforced the front in order to recover their position, but were met by Richardson's division, driving them back until we gained possession of Piper's house, which was an important point

General Richardson was conspicuous at the head of his division, and, while directing the fire of Graham's battery from the hill, was struck by a piece of a shell, and mortally wounded. Hancock now took command of the division. Meagher's brigade was again ordered forward, and took position in the centre of the line, which was now close up on the enemy. The Fourteenth Connecticut and One Hundred and Eighth New York came up to their support. Richardson had to hold so strong and extended a line, he was able to form but one line of battle. Jackson seeing this, oftentimes tried to outflank them, but was met by changing front. The enemy again came on in line, but by this time our artillery had got into position, and several batteries opened on them with such effect as to break their lines, and drive them back in confusion. This closed the fighting at this part of the field, which was by far the heaviest of the day.

Franklin reached the field of battle about one o'clock, and was at once sent to the support of Hooker and Sumner, and Colonels Irwin's and Brookes' brigades took up position on the right of French, and soon became engaged, and prevented the enemy from wedging between Sedgwick's and French's divisions.

Porter's corps, consisting of Sykes' division of regulars and Morrell's division of volunteers, held a position on the east side of Antietam creek, filling the interval between the right wing and Burnside's command. Six battalions of the regulars were thrown across the Antietam bridge to drive in the sharpshooters who were annoying our batteries. Warren's brigade, of Porter's corps, was detached to hold a position on Burnside's right. Slocum's division replaced a portion of Sumner's exhausted troops. Burnside's corps, consisting of Generals Cox, Willcox, Rodman, and Sturgis' divisions, held the left of the line, and was to support the attack on the right by a simultaneous movement, with instructions to take the bridge at all hazards. This was accomplished by a brilliant charge of the Fifty-first New York and Fifty-first Pennsylvania Volunteers. It was followed by a gallant advance of Burnside's corps upon a steep hill on which Longstreet's troops were intrenched, but were dislodged, with considerable slaughter on both sides. The enemy were re-enforced, and again retook the hill. The fighting here for a time was very severe, being one series of assaults and counter-assaults—batteries captured and recaptured—fierce hand-to-hand conflicts. It was near dark, and Burnside was hard pressed, when Sturgis' division moved forward with spirit, checking the enemy. A fierce war of artillery echoed from both sides along the field of battle.

About one hundred and seventy thousand men, and four hundred pieces of artillery were for fourteen hours engaged in this desperate battle, which saved the capital and the nation.

The hardest fighting of the day was undoubtedly in front of Sumner's, Hooker's, and Mansfield's Corps, and their losses were fearful.

Sumner's loss was five thousand two hundred and nine, near or about half its effective force. Hooker's, two thousand six hundred and nineteen. Porter's, one hundred and thirty. Franklin's, four hundred and thirty-eight. Burnside's, two thousand two hundred and ninety-three. Banks' corps, one thousand seven hundred and forty-three. Making a grand total of twelve thousand four hundred and sixty-nine. The enemy officially acknowledge a loss of about nine thousand; Sumner's corps lost in officers alone forty-one killed, and eighty-nine, including four general officers, wounded, and eight hundred and nineteen enlisted men killed. The loss of the Irish Brigade was out of proportion high, but then we must consider that it stood the fiercest tempest of the battle for nearly four hours, keeping several thousand men at bay.

The Sixty-ninth regiment had killed, Captain Felix Duffy, Lieutenants Charles Williams and Patrick Kelly; and Lieut.-Col. James Kelly, Lieutenant Richard A. Kelly, Captain Jasper R. Whitty, Lieutenant Garret Neagley, severely wounded, and Capt. T. L. Shanly, mortally.

Sixty-third. Killed :—Lieutenants Patrick Lydon, George Lynch, Cadwallader Smith, and acting Major John Kavanagh, and Lieutenant J. H. McConnell. Wounded :—Lieutenant-Colonel Henry Fowler, Major Richard Bently, Lieutenant James Mackey, aid to

General Meagher, mortally. Captain Michael O'Sullivan, Captain P. J. Condon, in the thigh, Lieutennat Thomas W. Cartwright.

Eighty-eighth. Killed :—Captain P. F. Clooney ; Captain J. O'C. Joyce. Wounded :—Adjutant Turner, Lieutenant M. Egan.

Twenty-ninth Massachusetts had no officers killed or wounded, as they had the fortune to be held in reserve.

The casualties among the non-commissioned officers and enlisted men amounted to about four hundred in all.

McClellan sets down the respective forces engaged, as follows :

His own army, First Corps, fourteen thousand eight hundred and fifty-six; Second Corps, eighteen thousand eight hundred and thirteen; Fifth Corps, twelve thousand nine hundred and thirty; Sixth Corps, twelve thousand three hundred ; Ninth Corps, thirteen thousand, eight hundred and nineteen ; Twelfth Corps, ten thousand one hundred and twenty-six ; Cavalry, four thousand three hundred and twenty : grand aggregate, eighty-seven thousand one hundred and sixty-four.

He then makes the following estimate of the rebel forces engaged. General T. J. Jackson's corps, twenty-four thousand seven hundred and seventy-eight. Longstreet's corps, twenty-three thousand three hundred and forty-two. D. H. Hill's two divisions, fifteen thousand five hundred and twenty-five. J. E. B. Stuart's cavalry, six thousand four hundred. Ransom's and Jenkin's brigades, three thousand. Forty-six regiments not included in the above, eighteen thousand four hundred. Artillery, estimated at four hundred guns, six thousand. Grand total, ninety-seven thousand four hundred and forty-five.

Of generals, we had Mansfield, Richardson, and Hartsuff killed, and Hooker, Duryea, Dana, Rodman, and Ricketts wounded.

The rebels had: Stark and Branch, killed—and Anderson, Wright, Lancton, Armstead, Ripley, Ransom, and Jones, wounded.

The troops lay beside their stacked arms on the battle-field all night. The mournful cry of the whippoor-will, and the croaking of the frogs in the marshes, mingled with the groans of the dying and wounded, broke the solemn stillness that reigned over the field of carnage.

The chaplains were quietly moving over the field with lamps in their hands, shriving the penitent, and binding up the wounds of the suffering. The doctors too, were moving among the groups of the dead and wounded, stanching their wounds, or easing their sufferings.

The dead lay piled around in all kinds of manner.

Here are two men, a Federal and rebel soldier, with their bayonets driven through each other's breasts; both of them are dead, and their features wear all the fierce expressions of the hate and passion of the conflict.

Near them is a little drummer-boy, of about fourteen; a piece of shell has gone through his drum and himself together. Poor child! he has beaten his last tattoo.

Some bodies are disfigured; they have been either torn in pieces by shells or scattered about by the horses and wheels of the artillery. Their clothes only keep the shattered remains together. The streams are full of bodies: the wounded dragged themselves there to drink, fell in, and were drowned, while several were killed in crossing.

Dead and maimed horses lie about. Some still plunging and trying to drag their broken limbs after them. The poor animals look at you most reproachfully, as much as to say:

"I had nothing to do with all this carnage; I was brought here against my will, and why should I suffer?"

After all, the physical sufferings here are not greater than the moral sufferings of dear ones at home, whose friends have been engaged in the battle. They hear that a great battle has been fought, a great victory won. This is joyful news, indeed; but the heart yearns to learn the fate of friends. Many a parent, wife, and sweetheart tremblingly open the papers and cast their eyes along the list of killed and wounded. Alas! that cry and stifled groan tells the fearful news. There is mourning in that house, mourning in many a house, North and South, for the soldiers that will never return. There are broken hearts, gray hairs, desolate homes, widows and orphans, as the price of victory.

There are some whose names appear on the paper among the missing, and yet they have not been heard from. Friends hope that they have been taken prisoner. Comrades return from the war, but can tell nothing about them. Hope grows into suspense, the heart is sick of this uncertainty. The green leaves have become brown, the winter's frosts have passed away, and the beautiful spring is smiling again, yet they have heard nothing from the long absent, but not forgotten soldier.

No, they will never hear from him until that great accounting day, when all mankind shall be summoned together, for he dragged himself to die beneath the shade of a tree, where his flesh was picked by the birds of the air, and his bones have long since mouldered into dust.

The Army of the Potomac was victorious, and Mc-

Clellan gravely weighed the chances of following up the victory, and renewing the attack on the following morning. After anxious deliberation and a careful revision of the diminished numbers of our army, and the strong position held by the enemy, he decided on not risking any more. When we consider the demoralized state of the army after Pope's campaign, and the short time McClellan had to reorganize it and fit it out with the necessary supplies, we must feel grateful for his signal victory. Besides, his army was severely handled, and the chances of whipping the enemy again on their own ground were not too certain.

Did he succeed, he would certainly break up Lee's army; did he fail and get repulsed, Washington was at the mercy of Lee, and would certainly fall.

Antietam, though not the bloodiest, was certainly the most important battle of the war, for the fall of the national capital was sure to follow a defeat; therefore the national cause could suffer no risk of defeat. Lee fell back to the Virginia bank of the Potomac, where he intrenched himself in a position sufficiently strong to resist any further attacks.

Stuart's cavalry had wheeled round to Williamsport, and the infantry was marching to join him by way of Winchester. General Couch's division, and some cavalry, were sent to attack them, which they did, driving them across the river.

The rebel army did not retreat from the battle-field until about dusk on the evening of the 18th. They removed most of their wounded, but left large numbers of both dead and wounded on the field.

Jackson covered the retreat, and on the 19th the whole army had crossed the Potomac.

The retreat was managed skilfully.

On the 20th McClellan began to move. Jackson had placed a few batteries to cover the river. After a few discharges the guns were abandoned. Our forces pressed on, but Hill opened on them from the shelter of the woods, inflicting severe loss on a Pennsylvania brigade.

The rebel forces withdrew, and took up position on the Opequan, with their left extending towards the Potomac.

While here, Stuart made a bold dash on McClellan's rear, so as to draw his attention from the retreating army.

After crossing the Potomac at Harper's Ferry, the Brigade was encamped on Bolivar Heights. General Meagher had his headquarters on a beautiful rising ground, a little above the junction of the Shenandoah and the Potomac. Trees and shrubs were planted around, giving it a most exquisite appearance, while in front lay a panoramic view of surpassing grandeur. Behind lay the Blue Ridge Mountains, and near by rushed the Shenandoah to embrace the Potomac. The rich Shenandoah Valley, the garden of Virginia, extended far away in the distance.

While encamped here, the One Hundred and Sixteenth Pennsylvania, under the command of Colonel Heenan, arrived, and was assigned to the Brigade under General Meagher.

In this lovely region, surrounded by all that could delight the imagination—a lovely picturesque country with unrivalled scenery, a sky of Italian blue—the men soon forgot their losses, and began to enjoy themselves.

Soldiers are so accustomed to encounter death in every shape and form, and hold their lives by so slender a thread, that they soon forget their dearest friends who have fallen. Racing, evening parties, and amusements were the order of the day.

While here, the army was reviewed by the President, accompanied by his staff, General Gorman of Illinois, General Sully of Minnesota, and other distinguished parties.

The President, accompanied by General McClellan, and other generals, rode along the lines, and was received with cheers.

They next rode over the battle-field of Antietam.

General Sumner had gone home on sick-leave, and was presented with an address by the general and officers of the Brigade, to which he replied in a most complimentary style.

Major-General Couch took command of the corps in his absence, and Hancock of the division.

The Brigade was sent out on a reconnoissance as far as Charleston, but met no opposition, and again returned to Bolivar Heights.

About the 5th of November the army broke camp around Harper's Ferry, and commenced marching through the gaps of the Blue Ridge.

While at Bolivar Heights the following promotions were made in the Brigade:

HEADQUARTERS IRISH BRIGADE, SECOND CORPS,
HANCOCK'S DIVISION, ARMY OF THE POTOMAC,
IN CAMP ON BOLIVAR HEIGHTS, HARPER'S FERRY, VA.

(General and Special Orders No. 1.)

The brigadier-general, commanding this Brigade, feels truly gratified in officially announcing that Lieutenant-Colonel Patrick Kelly, of the Eighty-eighth N. Y. V., the fourth regiment of the Irish Brigade, has been appointed and commissioned as the colonel of that regiment.

Major James Quinlan has been promoted to the Lieutenant-Colonelcy of the Eighty-eighth N. Y. V., and has received his commission as second highest officer of the same regiment.

Captain William Horgan has been commissioned as major of the Eighty-eighth N. Y. V.

The brigadier-general, in promulgating these appointments, takes the opportunity of congratulating the gallant Eighty-eighth in having permanently, in superior command, officers of proved capacity and courage—officers who have never, in any instance, failed in the discharge of their duty, and who, under the most exacting and desperate circumstances, have been true to the honor of their regiment, the reputation of the Brigade, and the hopes and pride of the Irish race.

The brigadier-general feels most happy in the assurance given to him in these appointments, that soldiers discharging their duties with fidelity and spirit, with promptitude, cheerfulness, enthusiasm, and courage, will meet with the recognition they deserve; and it will be the earnest and zealous endeavor of the brigadier-general to see that all such soldiers under his command, from the humblest to the highest in rank, shall have the honorable reward which their services and devotion shall entitle them to receive.

By order of     T. F. MEAGHER,

Brigadier-General.

THOMAS O'NEIL, Major and Acting Adjutant-General.

---

HEADQUARTERS SIXTY–THIRD REGIMENT N. Y. V.,
CAMP ON BOLIVAR HEIGHTS, VA., October 27, 1862.

(Regimental Order No. 10.)

The following named officers and non-commissioned officers having been recommended by their commanding officer, Captain Joseph O'Neil, for bravery on the battle-field, are commissioned by his Excellency, Governor Morgan, and assigned to duty as follows:

First-Lieutenant Jeremiah McDonough, to be captain Company E, vice Prendergast, with rank from September 17, 1862.

First-Lieutenant John H. Gleeson, to be captain Company B, vice Warren, with rank from September 17, 1862.

First-Lieutenant Thomas W. Cartwright, to be captain Company D, vice Tobin, resigned, with rank from September 17, 1862.

Second-Lieutenant Thomas Tuohy, to be captain Company I, vice Kavanagh, killed in action, with rank from September 17, 1862.

Second-Lieutenant Richard P. Moore, to be first-lieutenant Company H, vice Gleeson, promoted, with rank from September 17, 1862.

Second-Lieutenant James J. McCormack, to be first-lieutenant Company I, vice Meehan, with rank from September 17, 1862.

Second-Lieutenant P. Gormley, Jr., to be first-lieutenant Company A, vice McDonough, promoted, with rank from September 17, 1862.

14*

Sergeant-Major William Quirk, to be first-lieutenant Company G, vice Cartwright, promoted, with rank from September 17, 1862.

First-Sergeant William Taylor, to be first-lieutenant Company C, vice Ryan, with rank from September 17, 1862.

First-Sergeant Timothy Murray, to be second-lieutenant Company A, vice Tuohy, promoted, with rank from September 17, 1862.

First-Sergeant William Higgins, to be second-lieutenant Company C, vice Russell, declined reappointment, with rank from July, 1862.

First-Sergeant Laurence Daidy, to be second-lieutenant Company D, vice McCormack, promoted, with rank from September 16, 1862.

Sergeant Miles McDonald, to be second-lieutenant Company F, vice Leyden, killed in action, with rank from September 17, 1862.

Sergeant Patrick H. Riordan, to be second-lieutenant Company C, vice Moore, promoted, with rank from September 17, 1862.

First-Sergeant Michael Grogan, to be second-lieutenant Company K, vice McConnell, killed in action, with rank from September 17, 1862.

Sergeant William Daley, to be second-lieutenant Company I, vice Gormley, promoted, with rank from September 17, 1862.

By order of          JOSEPH O'NEIL,
          Captain Commanding Sixty-third N. Y. V.

Approved :

THOMAS FRANCIS MEAGHER,
          Brigadier-General, Commanding Irish Brigade.

# CHAPTER XVI.

The Brigade at Warrenton.—General McClellan relieved from command.—Burnside supersedes him.—McClellan's departure from the army.—The old flags consigned to Daniel Devlin.—Presentation of new colors.—The Brigade at Falmouth.—Battle of Fredericksburg.—Desperate assault, and fearful loss of the Brigade.—Banquet in Fredericksburg.—Brigade returns to their old camp.

> They fight, and fall, and bleed,
> And mingle blood with blood ;
> A prayer ascends to heaven—a sigh—
> God, our flag, Ireland, liberty !—they die.

GREAT excitement was created throughout the army by the announcement that McClellan was again relieved from command, and replaced by General Burnside. The feeling was so intensely bitter at this change that several officers tendered their resignations. " Little Mac " was a great favorite with the army—his very name was a talisman. After saving the capital—after Pope's disastrous campaign—the Administration and War Department now threw him aside. He was the only general in whom the army of the Potomac had confidence, until Grant turned up; and old veteran officers and soldiers ought to be better judges in military matters than politicians.

The reason adduced for relieving General McClellan was, that he would not advance into Virginia. Since the battle of Antietam scarcely a day passed that some important movement was not taking place. Besides, General McClellan allowed his weary troops time to recruit, while he was getting forward supplies and making preparations for the next campaign.

On receipt of the official order relieving him from command, General McClellan issued an address to his soldiers, informing them that the command now devolved on General Burnside, and taking an affectionate leave of them.

The generals of the army waited on him to pay their parting respects, and the day he left the army lined the roads to show their respect and bid him farewell.

The feeling ran so high that several officers resigned. In the Irish Brigade some had tendered their resignations, which General Meagher promptly declined, and issued an official order denouncing such a course.*

While at Warrenton the Twenty-eighth Massachusetts was added to the Brigade, thus giving General Meagher the command of six veteran regiments, namely: the Sixty-third, Sixty-ninth, and Eighty-eighth New York; the Twenty-eighth and Twenty-

* See Appendix.

ninth Massachusetts, and the One Hundred and Sixteenth Pennsylvania.

About the middle of November the Brigade moved to Falmouth, and was joined by a number of recruits.

The winter had set in; cold and bleak winds whistled over the fields of Virginia, and the soldiers, imagining that they had gone into winter-quarters, prepared comfortable huts. Of this pleasing hope they were soon disabused.

The Press and the War Department had loudly called on McClellan to move forward and crush the rebel army. Because he did not do so he was relieved by Burnside. Burnside should now do something to please his friends. He resolved to make some movement—no matter how desperate—no matter though an army should be sacrificed. In fact, Burnside was hounded on to it, and readily became a willing tool in order to wear the brief honors of commander-in-chief. Burnside moved his army to the lower Rappahannock. This, perhaps, was a wise move, for it gave him two modes of transportation, one by water to Aquia Creek, the other by railway.

On the march from Warrenton to Falmouth, General Hancock had issued orders to respect all private property.

This was all very good, but hungry men did not relish it. A certain regiment of the Brigade, passing by a fine field of turnips, helped themselves liberally, both the colonel and chaplain setting the example. Hancock chanced to pass at the time, and there were the men with the green stalks of turnips in their hands and the roots in their mouths, most comfortably craunching away at them, while their pockets and haversacks were loaded with them, giving the regiment the appearance of one huge moving evergreen.

Hancock stormed, and swore, and rode up to the colonel. It happened that the colonel and chaplain were flanked on each side with turnips, while they hung like garlands from the saddles, and they were actually in the act of eating them at the time.

" Are you colonel of this regiment, sir ?"

" Yes," muttered the other, with a huge piece of turnip in his mouth.

" Did you know my orders to respect private property ?"

" Yes, general, but the men were hungry, and we thought it no harm to take a few turnips."

" A few, indeed! and your worthy chaplain has joined in helping himself to his neighbor's property. Colonel, I place you under arrest. Send your sword to my quarters."

The colonel did send the sword, but retained the scabbard, as there was nothing said about it, and marched about with it dangling at his side. The general returned the sword after a few days.

When nearing Hartwood Church, the Irish Brigade was ordered by Sumner to advance up the road towards Falmouth, to see if any of the enemy should be there. As they did so, the enemy revealed a battery beyond the river. Sumner ordered them to charge upon it. They plunged into the Rappahannock, dashed across it, flung themselves on a battery of the enemy, capturing two guns. As they dashed at it, they gave one Irish cheer, kicked over kettles, frying-pans, coffee-pots, and every thing in their way. The enemy fled without firing a shot. Hancock cried out, " General Meagher, I have never seen any thing so splendid."

On the 17th of November General Sumner appeared before Fredericksburg, and demanded a surrender of the place. This was followed by Burnside himself demanding a surrender on the 21st, and, after this heroic display, did nothing more. The enemy were all the time strongly fortifying the hill, building forts and establishing batteries.

Burnside gave them near a month's notice before he began the slaughter of the 13th December; and they were consequently well prepared.

Had he attacked the place when he first appeared before it, there was little force there to oppose him, as the left wing of Lee's army, under Jackson, had not

yet arrived, and the enemy had not thrown up fortifications.

Both sides picketed the Rappahannock, the men
being separated only by the river. Amusing scenes
and conversations occurred between the men on both
sides; and they often passed over to one another in
canoes or by wading the river, in order to carry on a
little traffic.

" How are you to-day, Yank?" was the usual morning salute.

"I reckon I feel rather cold, Johnny; I'd like a nip."

"Any coffee, Yank?" and the reb would hold up a
canteen of the ardent.

" Plenty; and tobacco, too."

Thus a trade was established, and either party would
manage to cross over.

It often happened that old friends and relatives met
this way.

I heard of a case where a rebel picket crossed over
to traffic. One of our pickets chanced to be an old
enemy of his.

As soon as he saw him, he jumped up from the fire,
his eyes glaring, and exclaimed:

" Ha, Ned Haskin, you cowardly bastard, I have
you now. You know me—aye, Ned! you know how
you treated me in Norfolk, when you thought to take
my life, you worthless spawn, you!"

The infuriated man drew his bayonet; the other did the same; and before those around could interfere, they were stabbing and cutting one another savagely. Soon Haskin fell; the other rolled over him, burying his bayonet in his breast. Haskin's friends on the other side looked on for a moment, and, seeing their comrade fall, took deliberate aim and fired, killing or wounding every man around.

This is the worst feature though, for often *badinage* and jokes were freely exchanged.

" What's the news to-day, Yank?" was the inquiry by a rebel picket one morning.

Stirring news, Johnny reb; there is a great oreaking out in New York."

" You don't say so; the people all up in arms?" queried the delighted reb.

" Oh, not at all," exclaimed Paddy; " it's only a breaking out of the measles."

Paddy hadn't the joke always on his side, as the following story testifies:

" How are ye, rebs, this blessed cowld morning?" asked an Irishman, good-naturedly.

" Oh, we don't feel good to-day," was the reply, " we have suffered an awful loss: Jackson has re-signed!"

"Arrah, whist! is that true? An' what the deuce made him resign?" asked Paddy, highly delighted at the news, for there was no general in the Confederacy more dreaded than Stonewall Jackson.

"Oh, yes; he resigned because they removed his commissary-general, and he would not stand it."

"His commissary-general, eh! then who was he?"

"General Banks," was the sarcastic reply.

On the second of December took place the interesting ceremony of confiding the tattered battle-stained flags, under which the Brigade won such universal applause in Virginia and Maryland, to the custody of Daniel Devlin, Esq., City Chamberlain and Chairman of the Executive Committee of the Irish Brigade. Mr. Devlin's unwavering attention to the interests of the Brigade rendered him the most fitting person to be their temporary custodian. The trust could not be confided to a more deserving gentleman or a truer friend. Captain James E. McGee, who had honorably distinguished himself in their defence, was deputed by General Meagher to bring the flags to New York, and deliver them to Mr. Devlin.

The flags were delivered to Mr. Devlin at his country seat, Manhattanville, where a committee of American gentlemen were to present, in return, a new set of colors. These were to be purely the gift of Americans, in appreciation of the Irish Brigade. Mr. Spalding was the promoter of this very handsome token of American gratitude for Irish valor in defence of the republic.

A number of distinguished gentlemen were invited on the occasion, among whom were his Grace Archbishop Hughes, and his secretary, Rev. Mr. McNeirny; George Law, Esq.; Hon. Judges C. P. Daly and H. Hilton, of the Common Pleas; James T. Brady, Esq.; John Savage, Esq.; Hon. James Brooks; Hon. August Belmont, Minister to the Netherlands under President Pierce; John E. Develin, Esq.; Bartholomew O'Connor, Esq.; Stephen Massett, Esq.; H. F. Spaulding, Esq.; Shepherd Knapp, Esq.; J. B. Nicholson, Esq.; Dr. Ives, John Bryan, Esq.; E. C. Donnelly, Esq.; J. Devlin, Esq.; H. L. Hoguet, Esq.; Samuel Babcock, Esq; Rev. Michael McKenna, of Derry, Ireland; C. Lamont, Esq.; and others.

The following were the officers present, some of whom were home on sick-leave, and some on recruiting duty:

Lieutenant-Colonel James Kelly, Captains Leddy, Whitty, McGee, Nagle, Carr, Moroney, Lieutenant J. Gosson, Adjutant Smith, of the Sixty-ninth; Captains Egan, O'Brien, and Lieutenants Gallagher, Emmet, and Wall, of the Eighty-eighth; and Captains John C. Lynch, Gleeson, and Tracy, of the Sixty-third; and Lieutenant Giles, of the old Sixty-ninth.

The presentation of the old flags to Mr. Devlin was

made by Captain McGee on the part of General Meagher. In the delivery of them he made a most effective address, direct and soldierly, referring to the injunctions given to those who carried them away; but leaving to others to say how they had been defended. He paid a worthy tribute to Mr. Devlin, who, on receiving the colors, said:

"Captain McGee and officers of the deputation from the Irish Brigade—You will excuse me for saying that I feel a peculiar pride in being made the custodian, however temporarily, of these immortal flags. I saw them when in their maiden beauty they first floated upon the breeze and were presented to the several regiments of the Brigade, some twelve short months ago. It was with pride and hope, and an anxiety almost akin to apprehension. that I beheld them borne by your standard-bearers through our great thoroughfares, amid the cheers and blessings of countless multitudes. At Castle Garden they and the brave hearts that surrounded them disappeared from my view; but I have followed them with the anxious though confident eyes of my heart in their every movement, in the camp, the siege, and the battle-field, from that day to this. To this most glorious day, when they are restored to us, and stand before us, as does the remnant of the Grand Army of the Potomac before the nation —without a single stain of defeat, dishonor, or re-

proach—immortal. Oh, could these war-worn flags
but tell us what they have witnessed on the hard-
contested, hard-won fields over which they were borne
triumphant ; could they but tell us how the boys, with
buoyant heart and ready hand, by day and night, in
cold and storm, applied themselves to the exhausting
labors of the siege ; how when death had thinned their
ranks and quenched their joyous spirits, the remnant
few were still prepared, at the word of their gallant
leader, to rush with unfaltering step upon the assail-
ing foe! Oh, could these tattered flags but tell us how
often, when the storm of battle raged to its very height
—when comrades had fallen in frightful heaps on
every side, and other flags had been stricken down or
had disappeared in the grasp of a hostile hand, and
hope seemed .fast receding on the swelling tide of
blood, they were still borne aloft, as it were with new-
born strength, were seen far and wide to beckon on
and on to the point of deadliest encounter; and could
they tell us how, as the tumult of the onset ceased and
the smoke of the battle swept from the plain, they
still were seen aloft waving in triumph, amid the
shouts of victory, then would not every Irish and
every patriotic heart swell with honest pride, and be
eager to offer on the altar of his country's welfare a
new tribute in honor of the Irish Brigade? Oh, gentlemen, I cannot express to you in words the feelings

of pride and gratitude that fill my heart for the service you have rendered to the cause of our country, and the lustre and the glory you have shed upon our native land and race. And now the old flags are here before us to inspire anew our patriotism, and receive our grateful thanks. Let us never forget the brave fellows who are still exposed to the perils and hardships of the field. And it would be a pleasing duty could I place them in some Chapel of the Invalides—as at Paris—where the worshippers, as they cast an eye there, might, in the spirit of our Church, utter a prayer to the Throne of Mercy for the happy repose of the brave spirits who, with short shrift, fell beneath them. I beg you, gentlemen, to convey to your gallant general and his Brigade the assurance that I shall guard these mute witnesses of your glorious deeds as a sacred trust. These, gentlemen, as I have already intimated, were your maiden flags. They have fulfilled their destiny, and now you are to receive from other friendly hands, and in presence of the illustrious chief under whose guidance your honors have been won, flags which are new indeed, but which will be endeared to you by the record within their folds, of all the noble achievements that were witnessed by those which you have now committed to our keeping. When, in the contest which to all human view must again be renewed, your eye shall catch a glimpse of the thrilling names of Fair Oaks, Malvern Hill, and above all, Antietam, let them serve as so many trumpet tongues to stir your souls to final victory. And let your watchword and battle-cry be: 'The Union, our Nation, and Ireland forever!'"

At the conclusion of Mr. Devlin's speech, Henry F. Spaulding, Esq., proceeded to present the new flags in the following language:

"Lieutenant-Colonel Kelly and Officers of the Irish Brigade—We are delegated (and are glad to avail ourselves of this occasion) to present new colors to the Sixty-ninth, Eighty-eighth, and Sixty-third regiments, New York Volunteers, of the Irish Brigade, with the names of the battles in which they have won distinction inscribed upon them. Here are your green flags and the Stars and Stripes. Allow us, American-born citizens, to present them in grateful commemoration of the gallant deeds of your Brigade in the army of the Potomac, on the battle-fields of Virginia and Maryland, in the war to maintain the national domain and the honor and integrity of the American Union. They are intended to replace the old flags which you have borne so long with honor, and which you have just returned to the donors all battle-torn and riddled. When you unfurl these new banners to General Meagher, say to him, for us, that his brilliant and heroic conduct, and that of the Irish Brigade under his

command, wins the unqualified praise of all. Tell his
brave soldiers that they would be yet prouder could
they see with what enthusiasm their services are
appreciated. On the soil of their adoption they have
added fresh and enduring pages to the chivalric history
of their native land. Take, then, these standards. We
intrust them to you, as did your fellow-countrymen the
first, knowing that so long as any of you are left to
guard them, they will defy captivity and dishonor; and
may the 'sunburst' on the flag of Erin prove prophetic
of that peace which shall soon break gloriously through
the storm of war which now desolates our beloved
country. Then shall old Erin's harp be tuned afresh
to the proud song of 'The Land of the Free and the
Home of the Brave.' Then shall we represent 'one
country, one constitution, one destiny.'"

Mr. Spaulding's remarks, delivered as they were
with feeling and earnestness, were enthusiastically
received by the officers. The wound in Lieutenant-
Colonel Kelly's jaw preventing him from responding,
Captain McGee was appointed to that duty, of which
he acquitted himself most happily. Captain McGee
said in his remarks:

"General Meagher never asks his men to share any
dangers which he himself is not the first to brave. He
never says, 'There's something to be done—go do it,'
but, 'Come on, boys, follow me!'"

A banquet of the most magnificent description was provided by the bounteous hospitality of Mr. Devlin, and round his board many dear reminiscences and patriotic sentiments were evoked in toasts and speeches by the host, Judge O'Connor, John Bryan, John Savage, and others.

## BATTLE OF FREDERICKSBURG.

Fredericksburg is situated in a basin, with a range of hills girding it on the side occupied by the rebels. Lee had thrown up very strong intrenchments, which, added to the natural strength of the place, rendered it almost impregnable to an assault. The Confederate army was posted in the following order:

Longstreet, with Ransom's, McLaws', and Picket's divisions, held the left of the line. Anderson's division held Marye's Hill, against which the Brigade charged. Unfortunately, there were several Irish regiments in this division, and were thus pitted against their countrymen. Hood extended to the railroad and connecting with the right, which was held by Ambrose Hill and Early, with Stuart's mounted division, light artillery and infantry, protecting the extreme right and left.

D. H. Hill was held in reserve.

The Washington Artillery corps held position on Marye's and Lee's Heights.

Burnside's plan of battle was to throw his right, comprising Sumner's command, across the river at Fredericksburg and United States Ford, to attack Marye's Heights, Hooker to demonstrate heavily on the centre, while Franklin would cross down the river, and try to flank the enemy's left.

The movement commenced on the night of the 10th December. During that night the pontoons were conveyed to the river, and one hundred and forty-three pieces of artillery were placed in position opposite the city. At five o'clock next morning, the pontoon-train, in charge of the Seventeenth and Fiftieth New York Engineers, and under command of General Woodbury, proceeded to the river-bank, where, with infantry supports, an attempt was made to throw three bridges across the river—one at the point where the railroad bridge formerly crossed, and two more opposite the city, but nearer Falmouth. The pontooniers had succeeded in partially constructing the bridges, when the rebels suddenly opened a very brisk and deadly fire of musketry from along the banks of the river and the windows of the houses, compelling a cessation of the work. The planks and boats were riddled by every volley. Once more they were compelled to withdraw, and they fell back to the cover of the ridge of hills running parallel with the river.

Our artillery opened with terrific effect upon the

houses in which the rebel sharpshooters were concealed. After the first fire they became untenable by the rebel riflemen, who retreated to the rear of the town, where they took shelter behind the as yet unharmed buildings.

It soon became evident that the bridges could not be built till a party could be thrown over to clean out the rebels and cover the bridge-head. For this mission General Burnside called for volunteers, and Colonel Hall, of Fort Sumter fame, immediately responded. The Seventh Michigan and Nineteenth Massachusetts, two small regiments, numbering in all about four hundred men, were selected for the purpose.

Nothing could be more admirable or more gallant than the execution of this daring feat. A landing was soon effected, and then a vigorous bayonet-charge drove out the rebel riflemen, not, however, before a number of them were killed and about one hundred made prisoners. The loss of the gallant volunteers was trifling. In less than half an hour after the bridge was completed, and the head of the column of the right grand division, consisting of General Howard's command, was moving upon it over the Rappahannock. A feeble attempt from the rebel batteries was made to shell the troops in crossing, but it failed to inflict any material damage.

On Friday morning a dense fog hid every thing

from view. The troops commenced moving at an early hour, Major-General Sumner's grand division leading the way over in front of the city, followed by Major-General Hooker's division.

At a quarter past nine the first gun was fired.

At a quarter past two the rebels opened with all the guns posted on the first ridge of hills. Their main fire was directed upon the city, which was filled with our troops. Those guns which were posted on the left of the ridge were opened on the large body of troops which crossed on the two lower bridges, and had formed in line of battle, and were moving obliquely down the river, fronting the Massaponax.

The general engagement, to which the operations thus detailed led, commenced on the morning of Saturday, the 13th.

Skirmishing commenced on the left about daylight. Soon after a rebel battery opened on our lines, and the Ninth New York Militia was ordered to charge it, but after a fierce struggle was compelled to retire. The remainder of the brigade, under General Tyler, then charged the enemy's guns, when the fight became general on the extreme left. General Meade's and General Gibbon's divisions encountered the right of General A. P. Hill's command. The cannonading was terrific, though our troops suffered but little from the enemy's artillery. Gradually the fight extended around to the right. General Howe's division went in, and then General Brooks' division.

At ten o'clock A. M. General Sumner's troops advanced to engage the enemy on the right. General Sumner had selected French's division of General Couch's corps for the advance of the attacking column.

Early in the morning the Irish Brigade was drawn up in line of battle at " order arms" and a " parade rest." A green sprig was ordered by General Meagher to be placed in the caps of both officers and men, himself first setting the example. At about half-past nine o'clock they were marched up to the centre of the city, nearer the enemy, and formed in line of battle on a street running nearly east and west. Here brigade and regimental hospitals were established. General Meagher, accompanied by General Hancock and the members of his staff, now addressed his " little Brigade," each regiment separately, briefly in his eloquent style, and in words of real inspiration. Each man was made aware of the great and terrible work before him, and each man measured in his mind the part he had to perform. The general's remarks were responded to by the men with great spirit and acclamation. Colonel Nugent gave instructions to his "boys" in his usual calm and earnest manner, when every man stood in his place, with set lip and flashing eye, awaiting the word to advance. French's division was first to attack the enemy, supported by Zooke, Meagher, and Cald-well's brigades of Richardson's division in succession. General French made the attack at about twelve o'clock M., when the battle became general. Zooke's brigade moved up, followed by Meagher's. The aspect was already terrible. Noonday was turned to dusk by the smoke and storm of battle. A ravine in rear of the town, through the centre of which runs a mill-stream seven or eight feet wide, over which they were obliged to cross on a rude bridge, was swept by a raking fire from the enemy's batteries. Having crossed this, the Brigade halted in line of battle, the men relieved them-selves of their blankets and haversacks, and awaited the order to advance. French's division fire, fall, lie down, scatter, rally ; but in vain—it is already placed *hors de combat.* Zooke's brigade advanced in fine style, but rapidly fell ; and though its ranks were thinned, still on they went! "Irish Brigade, advance," is heard in bold, distinct accents above the clamor of battle—"For-ward, double-quick, guide centre;" and on it dashes through the cornfield, in the face of the most invul-nerable point of the enemy's works. They are greeted by a murderous fire of grape and canister and minie balls. Gaps are opened in the ranks, but they close again and move still onward. The first fence is gained and passed. The enemy now falls back from his first behind his second line of breastworks. They gain the

second fence, within sixty yards of the enemy's batteries, and are met by a most disastrous enfilade and
direct fire from the rebel artillery and infantry. They
had not a single piece of artillery to support them,
and yet they stood against shot and shell, grape and
canister, minie and conical balls, to fight a formidable
enemy, artillery and infantry, posted behind stone
walls and fortifications.

The rebel position was unassailable, it was a perfect
slaughter-pen, and column after column was broken
against it.

Our artillery did so little injury to the enemy, that
they were able to concentrate all their fire on the
advancing columns of troops. Besides, an oblique flank
fire swept us, so that whole regiments melted away
before it. Some broke for the rear, others lay down
among the dead. The advance of the Brigade was
actually impeded by the bodies piled upon one another.
Brave fellows! their own bodies were soon to be added
to the number. But foremost in the ranks of the honored
dead were the boys with the green sprigs in their caps.

It was not a battle—it was a wholesale slaughter of
human beings—sacrificed to the blind ambition and
incapacity of some parties.

Franklin and Hooker's advance had not been a bit
more successful. They, too, were hurled against
intrenched positions, and driven back with consider-

able slaughter; but nothing like that on Marye's Heights, where the battle was carried on with more desperation, and the troops more exposed. But to return to the Irish Brigade, which was madly striving to gain the crest of that bloody hill.

Two-thirds of the officers and men of the Brigade are lying on that bloody field. Let us take a look along the shattered ranks—an awful sight. See that number of brave fellows now stretched in their gore, who but an hour ago were the personification of life, and strength, and manliness; who had marched up with stout hearts to the fray—a march only from earth to eternity. They will never march again. The clouds grew darker—the casualties increase. Colonel Nugent was wounded and gone to the rear. The command devolved on Major Cavanagh, acting lieutenant-colonel.

"Blaze away and stand it, boys!" cried the "little major."

Captain Thomas Leddy, acting major, who had arrived only the day before the battle from Washington, was wounded severely in the left arm. He had just recovered from the effects of a wound received at Malvern Hill.

Lieutenant Callaghan, first-lieutenant of another company, who had been detailed to command Company H, was wounded in four different places. He was an "old veteran." Fredericksburg, according to his own statement, was his fortieth battle, and nobly did he fight it.

Second-Lieutenant David Burke, while bravely performing his duty, received rather a severe wound in the left shoulder.

First-Lieutenant Bernard O'Neill, commanding Company D, was severely wounded while in the act of discharging a musket at the enemy.

The greatest coolness and bravery were displayed by General Meagher. General Hancock was also on the field, mounted, but only to witness the wholesale slaughter of his fine division in a reckless engagement not of his choice or style of fighting.

Captain O'Donovan, who lost his eye at Fair Oaks, was struck with a piece of spent shell on the left breast, rendering him insensible.

The sun went down that fearful evening behind the rebel breastworks upon no pleasing shouts of victory, no flank of the enemy turned by Sigel, no Banks— nor, from the firing on the left, no ground gained by Franklin—nothing of any good obtained ; while night was soon to cast its shadows upon a field of carnage and slaughter, the most frightful and terrible ever experienced.

Who are these lines of men that lie stretched along the right and left, as if asleep on their arms? They are the dead and wounded soldiers and officers of the Irish Brigade !

15*

A cold, bitter, bleak December night closed upon that field of blood and carnage. Thousands lay along that hill-side, and in the valleys, whose oozing wounds were frozen, and whose cold limbs were stiffened, for they had no blankets; they had flung them away going into the fight. Masses of dead and dying were huddled together; some convulsed in the last throes of death; others gasping for water—delirious, writhing in agony, and stiffened with the cold frost. The living tried to shelter themselves behind the bodies of the dead.

Cries, moans, groans, and shrieks of agony rang over that sad battle-field. There was no one to tend them; no one to bring them a drop of cold water to moisten their swollen tongues; for that field was still swept with shot and shell, and in the hands of the enemy.

And this was war—" glorious war "—with all its pomp and parade—all its glittering attractions. If we could see it in its true colors, it is the most horrible curse that God could inflict upon mankind. Never glorious, unless when an oppressed people are contending for the great boon and birthright of liberty.

The heroism displayed by some of our men in trying to rescue their wounded officers and comrades. was no less noble than that which actuated them during the battle. Several were shot in this laudable effort, and sacrificed their lives for their fellow-man.

The following letter from an officer gives a graphic picture of the whole proceedings:

"Never since the war began have the Union forces met with such a disaster as that we have just suffered. As for the Brigade, may the Lord pity and protect the widows and orphans of nearly all those belonging to it! It will be a sad, sad Christmas by many an Irish hearthstone in New York, Pennsylvania, and Massachusetts.

"In order that you may have a succinct account of what has occurred, I will commence at the beginning. On last Thursday the ball was opened at daybreak. A detail of men had been all the previous day arranging and decorating the green-house (some one hundred and twenty-five by thirty feet) for the proposed banquet on the following Saturday, on the arrival and presentation of the flags. At midnight the orders were issued to the troops, and the next morning the enemy opened the engagement by firing two signal-guns on the right, and after a short while two answered on their extreme left—showing, as usual, that they are as well posted on all our *secret* movements as ourselves. The same cannonading was kept up all day by both sides, and at evening we were enabled to cross.

"On Saturday, however, both armies seemed to concentrate all their energies. Our corps and the Ninth having all crossed over the evening before, and the enemy having been driven literally from house to house out of the town, French's division was ordered to advance and storm the enemy's earthworks. They went on a piece until they came to a sort of rise in the ground, when they all lay down after delivering their fire.

"At two o'clock the Irish Brigade was ordered up to a position mentioned to them, which French's division was supposed to have reached, but which, in consequence of the dense smoke and fog, could not be seen. On they came in *their* usual style, and took up line of battle in the position they were told, and held it all day, even after they had fired every round, and had to collect ammunition out of the dead and wounded men's pouches in order to prevent the enemy's learning they were out of ammunition. They charged the enemy, who were well protected behind a stone wall, and received a murderous fire from both musketry and artillery; and, what was worse than all, they were caught between two fires. The musketry fire began at half-past nine o'clock, and continued without an instant's cessation until a quarter to seven in the evening—the longest and at the same time the heaviest fire of musketry on record.

"The most harrowing part to relate is the fact that almost all our most serious casualties lay all night on the battle-field, not alone of our Brigade, but the whole grand division. Captain Eagan went out with a party to try and bring in some, and one man and two horses were shot. Lieutenant McCormick, of Company F, got shot in a like laudable effort. Lieutenant Murphy was killed, and his brother, a sergeant in Company A, wounded alongside of him ; he lay there in a dying state, without a drop to wet his lips. Lieutenant Young was shot in three places; others in the same state lay there, dying of thirst and exposure. The Eighty-eighth mustered, after the fight, seventy-three muskets. Dr. Powell had never taken a minute to himself since the first wounded man was brought to him. Colonel Kelly was as coolly courageous as usual, walking along his line. A bullet cut his coat and pants at the end of his vertebral column. Colonel Quinlan was not with the men, having had an attack of scurvy. Major Horgan was shot through the mouth ; the ball must have passed upwards into the brain, as he died instantly. He lay out with Murphy and Young, near the stone wall. No regiment ever had a more gallant, unassuming, and better loved officer. Although this battle has been the most disastrous to the Union cause of any yet fought, yet it is an extraordinary fact that the proportion of wounded to killed is greater than on any other occasion. The Sixty-ninth had every man wounded, except forty that Captain Saunders had out skirmishing, all of whom escaped. The Sixty-third had forty-three by their report, and was commanded by Captain Condon. Major Cavanagh was shot in the hip, not dangerously. Lieutenant Bermingham had both thighs broken. Lieutenants Buckley and Burke both wounded. The One Hundred and Sixteenth had all their field and staff, and almost every line officer, wounded ; this was their first battle, and they behaved like veterans. The Twenty-eighth Massachusetts numbered about one hundred and fifty muskets, being the largest regiment of the Brigade. The five regiments numbered but two hundred and sixty-three after the battle.

"I have never seen the army so dejected after any engagement. As for the remnant of the Brigade, they were the most dejected set of Irishmen you ever saw or heard of."

---

The correspondent of the London "Times," who was present, and who cannot be suspected of partiality, speaking of the Irish Brigade, says :

"The battle, which had dashed furiously against the lines of Generals Hood, A. P. Hill, and Early, was little more than child's play, as compared with the on-slaught directed by the Federals in the immediate neighborhood of Fredericksburg. The impression that the Confederate batteries would not fire heavily upon the Federals advancing in this quarter, for fear of in-

juring the town of Fredericksburg, is believed to have
prevailed among the Northern generals. How bitterly
they deceived themselves subsequent events served to
show. To the Irish division, commanded by General
Meagher, was principally committed the desperate
task of bursting out of the town of Fredericksburg,
and forming, under the withering fire of the Confederate batteries, to attack Marye's Heights, towering
immediately in their front. Never at Fontenoy, Al-
buera, or at Waterloo, was more undaunted courage
displayed by the sons of Erin than during those six
frantic dashes which they directed against the almost
impregnable position of their foe. There are stories
that General Meagher harangued his troops in impassioned language on the morning of the 13th, and plied
them well with whiskey found in the cellars of Fredericksburg. After witnessing the gallantry and devotion exhibited by his troops, and viewing the hill-sides
for acres strewn with their corpses thick as autumnal
leaves, the spectator can remember nothing but their
desperate courage, and regret that it was not exhibited
in a holier cause. That any mortal men could have
carried the position before which they were wantonly
sacrificed, defended as it was, it seems to me idle for a
moment to believe. But the bodies which lie in dense
masses within forty yards of the muzzles of Colonel
Walton's guns are the best evidence what manner of

men they were who pressed on to death with the daunt-
lessness of a race which has gained glory on a thousand battle-fields, and never more richly deserved it
than at the foot of Marye's Heights on the 13th day
of December, 1862."

The flag of the Sixty-ninth was lost during the fight,
and the men felt very uneasy about it, for it was their
proud boast that they had never lost a flag.

Next day the color-sergeant was discovered sitting
up against a tree, dead, and his hands clasped on his
breast, as if protecting something. Near him was
the staff of the missing flag. When removing the
body, the men found the flag wrapped around it, with
a bullet hole right through it and his heart.

Though the Brigade had suffered fearfully, never
had they displayed more desperate bravery than in
this fight. Not more dashing courage, not more desperate daring were displayed by our countrymen of
the last centuries at Cremona, at Fontenoy, than by
their compatriots of this generation at the Malvern
Hills and at Fredericksburg. Is there any thing in the
records of the greatest efforts of human fortitude and
endurance finer than the placing, by the men and officers of the Irish Brigade, those sprigs of evergreen in
their hats, and the fact reported by the officer in command of the details for burying the dead under the

flag of truce, that nearest to the enemy's breastworks, nearest to that terrible stone wall, from behind which such frightful volleys of death were hurled, nearest to the foe and to his strongholds, were found the men of the Irish Brigade, the men with the green emblem in their hats. This Brigade was composed of five regiments, and numbered in all not more than twelve hundred men, of which it lost about two-thirds in the fight. If these regiments had been at all full, if they had been even respectable skeleton regiments, the works of the enemy might have been successfully stormed: their work would have been effectually done. "If we had two Irish Brigades," said a brave young officer who was wounded there, "we would have carried the works, and won the battle."

Men who know nothing of war, or the imperative duty of a general to go where he is ordered, blame General Meagher for making this forlorn desperate assault. Do these men forget that several brigades went in besides the Irish Brigade? and if they had not suffered so badly, it is because they did not so long or so desperately sustain their position.

On the contrary, as the general himself expressed it, in words of pathetic eloquence on the morning of the battle of Fredericksburg, within the hearing of every man of his brigade, he never sent them to any place where he had not received orders to send them;

and that he never had nor never would send them to any place where he was not willing and ready to lend them aid, and share with them in all their dangers.

But the history of this storming party, of this forlorn hope, is not the only Irish event of the day. The new green colors had arrived from New York : while the battle was raging, Captain Martin arrived from Washington with supplies to celebrate their reception. The little theatre of the city was appropriated, tables and seats arranged, guests invited, among whom were Generals Couch, Sturgis, Wilcox, and Hancock, and the feast opened. The shot and shell of the enemy played about the building, the walls shook and trembled with the roar of the artillery. Some houses were toppling down in the vicinity, and others were in flames, set on fire by the combustibles showered upon them. Inside the theatre the tables were set, the wines placed, the guests enjoying themselves, the wit and the oratory of the general-host flashed and sparkled around the board. General Hancock, a thorough, gay, dashing, splendid soldier, had seen the Brigade in battle, on the charge, in the hot strife ; he knew their dauntless courage, their pluck, the calmness, the serenity, the enthusiasm with which they went into battle. Looking at the banquet, he exclaimed, " Only Irishmen could enjoy themselves thus."

## CHAPTER XVIII.

Despondent feeling throughout the country.—Requiem Mass in New York for the dead of the Irish Brigade.—General Meagher in New York.—Sketches about camp.—General Meagher in camp.—Patrick's day.—Horse-racing, and other amusements.

BURNSIDE'S failure, and the disastrous battle of Fredericksburg, had a depressing effect on the country. The Confederate cause seemed to gain strength and influence on every side. Successful in the field, they readily found foreign aid and sympathy, as it was the policy of both England and France to crush the spread and power of the Democratic institutions of America. Burnside followed up his defeat by a ridiculous campaign, justly designated "Burnside's mud campaign," in which one half the army had to be employed to dig the other half out of the mud.

Soon after, he was superseded by Major-General Hooker.

The Christmas of 1863 was a sad one in many a home throughout the North, and full of despondency for the Union cause.

The Brigade returned to its former quarters near

Falmouth, and General Meagher went to New York on leave of absence.

Christmas festivities were kept up in the camp in the usual light-hearted manner.

The Corcoran Legion, too, which, after its organization, had been sent to the Peninsula, and were now at Newport News, were keeping Christmas time like Irishmen.

After his release from prison, Colonel Corcoran was promoted to a generalship, and authorized to raise a legion. With this fine body of men he was guarding some posts on the Peninsula.

As I have said, they were enjoying Christmas time with horse-racing, theatricals, and other amusements, in a style such only as Irishmen can.

The remnant of the Brigade was too small to get up amusements on a large scale, but still they enjoyed themselves.

On the 16th of January a grand Requiem Mass was held in Saint Patrick's Cathedral, New York, for the repose of the souls of all the dead of the Irish Brigade since the beginning of the war.

The spacious Cathedral was densely thronged, long before the commencement of the ceremonies, by a congregation among whom were some of the highest citizens of New York, connected with Ireland by birth or descent. Preceding the officers of the Irish Brigade, as they came up the centre aisle to the pews reserved for them, immediately in front of the high altar, appeared General Thomas Francis Meagher, accompanied by Mrs. Meagher, and attended by his staff. Colonel Nugent, of the Sixty-ninth N. Y. V., was also present, as well as a large number of the officers of the Sixty-ninth Regiment N. Y. S. M.

The *coup d'œil* inside the cathedral at the commencement of the services was very striking, and at once marked this as one of the most impressive and solemn religious ceremonies that had taken place here for many years. The dark bier, surrounded by its military escort, the sable vestments of the officiating clergy, the vast congregation uniting their prayers with the service of the altar, and the solemn tones of the organ pealing the *Dies Iræ*—all combined to produce a sensation of awe and devotion to which no heart susceptible of the finer emotions of our nature could be indifferent.

The High Mass selected was Mozart's Requiem, a composition well adapted for the occasion, and admirably rendered by the highly efficient choir of the cathedral. The orchestral arrangements were also much enhanced by the excellent performance of the band. Their rendering of Rossini's beautiful *Cujus Animam* was one of the finest pieces of concerted instrumentation we have ever heard.

The Rev. Father Ouellet, Chaplain of the New York Sixty-ninth Volunteers, sang the Mass, Father Maguire was the deacon, and Father Wood sub-deacon. The Very Rev. Dr. Starrs, V. G. (in the unavoidable absence of Archbishop Hughes), performed the absolution, and Rev. Mr. McNeirney was Master of Ceremonies. Among the assistant clergy were the Rev. Messrs. Lafont, Curran, Donnelly, Farrell, Neligan, Malone, Killeen, Cauvin, Concilio, and others.

Immediately after the conclusion of the High Mass, the Rev. Father O'Reilly, S. J., ascended the pulpit, and, taking his text from the forty-fourth chapter of Ecclesiasticus, as follow,—*Laudemus viros gloriosos, et parentes nostros in generatione sua* : " Let us praise men of renown, and our fathers in their generation"— delivered a talented and feeling oration, paying a just tribute to the memories of the brave men whose obsequies they had met to celebrate.

The following requiem was written for the occasion by our talented countryman, John Savage:

> Come, let the solemn, soothing Mass be said,
> For the soldier-souls of the patriot dead.
>
> Let the organ swell, and the incense burn,
> For the hero-men who will ne'er return.
>
> Men who had pledged to this land their troth,
> And died to defend her, ere break their oath.
>
> But if high the praise, be as deep the wail
> O'er the exiled sons of the warlike Gael.

From their acts true men may examples reap;
And women bless them, and glorying, weep.

Proud beats the heart while it sorrowing melts
O'er the death-won fame of these truthful Celts.

For the scattered graves over which we pray
Will shine like stars on their race alway.

Oh, what doth ennoble the Christian man,
If not dying for truth, in freedom's van!

What takes from death all its terrors and gloom?
Conscience to feel justice blesses the tomb!

And oh! what doth build up a nation's weal,
But courage to fight for the truths we feel!

And thus did these braves, on whose graves we wait,
Do all that make nations and races great.

OREMUS.

Ye living, your hearts combine
In praise and prayer, to the heavenly shrine;
Ye widowed and stricken,
Your trustfulness quicken,
With faith in the Almighty Giver;
And may blessed repose
Be the guerdon of those
Who fell at Antietam and James's River;
By the Rappahannock and Chickahominy;
*Requiem æternam dona eis, Domine!*
May their souls on the Judgment-Day arise,
*Et lux perpetua luceat eis.*

————

Though the Brigade had but few officers in the
field, they nevertheless fully enjoyed Christmas fes-

tivities, and fun, and frolic of the most exuberant
kind.

During the Christmas holidays, a civilian who was
enthusiastically attached to the Brigade and to its general, paid a visit to the headquarters of the Brigade
during the absence of the brigadier in New York.
The visitor was, therefore, deprived of half the pleasure
of his trip ; however, he fell into good, genial, hospitable hands.   Messrs. Gosson, Blake, and others of the
staff made his stay as agreeable as circumstances
would permit.   Our civilian visitor thought the
cheerful hut, and its log fires, and the gay companions
around, pleasant enough ; the more so, when certain
materials of a spirituous description were produced, hot
water procured, and a huge bowl of the most palatable
punch brewed by scientific hands.   The civilian was
convivial.   Under the influence of congenial spirits
his heart warmed, his soul expanded, the dearest wish
of his life was confided to his gallant young friends.
Since the Brigade had taken the field, he had sighed
for a position on the general's staff.   A commission
was nothing, rank was nothing, pay was nothing—he
longed for the honor only.

Although it is an honor limited to a very few, yet,
the officers agreed, as their friend was so enthusiastic
and so good an Irishman, that he be nominated,
appointed, and elected their civic comrade and an

honorary member of the staff of the brigadier-general.
He was delighted—his gratification knew no bounds.
He returned thanks in a neat, eloquent, and appropriate speech. Healths were proposed; the new member
drank them with all the honors. His campaigning
experiences were, of course, limited; he could not bear
up so well against the continued conviviality as his
older and more hardened associates.

As I have said, it was Christmas, and the huts were
decorated with evergreens. Among the decorations of
the hut in which the ceremony of the election had
been celebrated, was a harp formed of the green
twigs. Potations began to tell on the new member,
his speech grew incoherent, he sank upon a rustic
couch near by, his eyes still open, resting on the
harp aforesaid and the swords about the apartment.
He was heard to utter, as he dozed into unconscious-
ness—

"Place a sword by my side, and the harp, the
emblem of Erin, at my head. I die happy—a member of the staff of the Irish Brigade."

He soon fell off, was laid on a cot-bed, and decently
waked.

I will here give a few incidents of rather an
amusing nature.

After the terrible disaster at Fredericksburg, the
chaplain of one of the regiments of French's division

16

was conversing after service with one of his hearers, a line officer. Their conversation naturally turned on the horrible incidents of the late fight.

*Chaplain*—"It must have been a consolatory reflec-. tion, my dear young friend, in the midst of the perils and dangers encompassing you, that you were supported, in the day of trouble, by the divine grace."

*Officer* (unguardedly)—Why, d—n it, no ! I thought I told you we were supported by the Irish Brigade."

Speaking of Fredericksburg recalls another, not indeed, like the above, inciting to gladness and mirth, but rather the contrary, as showing how much our race suffered that day, and how dreadfully our poor fellows were cut up. Some short time after the battle General Hancock was inspecting the Brigade. After getting through with some of the other regiments he came to the Eighty-eighth. My informant did not say what formation the battalion was in, but, at all events, one of the companies was represented by only three men. The commandant of it had to go to his quarters for something or another. However, he was absent when General Hancock rode up. The general has an emphatic way of speaking, a quick eye, and is great on details, regularity, and all the little soldierly *et ceteras* Seeing the small group together by themselves he shouted, " G—— d—— you, why don't you close up with your company."

*Private* (one of the three, saluting)—" General, we're a company."

*General*—" The d—l you are!" looking at them for a moment, his soldierly eye beaming, as he thought of their gallantry and bearing on the field; too full of respect for them, my informant said, to inspect them minutely that time.

One other *morceau.* The story I am going to tell is of an old and inveterate joker, one whose name has appeared often in letters and in stories from the various camps, marches, and bivouacs. In days gone by, it was a humorous, a droll, or a dry saying that was chronicled, and set the table in a roar. Roe, however, was transferred to a different branch of the profession. Formerly he was attached to Quartermaster Haverty's department. Then he was wagon-master. Afterwards he was Captain Martin's forage-master, not an unimportant position, when you consider the great quantity of forage consumed by the animals of the Brigade, its distribution to the various parties entitled to it on requisition and otherwise, and the keeping of the accounts connected with its receipt and distribution. The job becomes more troublesome when you are told that there are always following every army a number of individuals who have animals to which they are not entitled, and others who have more horse-flesh than the law allows them. Well, all the animals somehow manage to exist—and I am bound to say, in many instances, by unauthorized requisitions on the quartermaster's department.  For some time past, Captain Martin and Roe had been painfully conscious of raids upon the forage-tent.  Measures were taken to entrap the thieves, but without effect.  Roe remained up two nights in succession, the sentries were on the *qui vive :* in vain.  In the morning more feed was missing.  The rogue must be shrewd and wary, because not a single trace was left by which to track the purloiners.  They almost gave up in despair, and nearly came to the conclusion that watching, vigilance, care, were thrown away.  No results, but still the quantities missing in the morning.  The next night Roe turned in to take his natural rest.  The large forage-tent was carefully tied up, but in dangerous propinquity to the entrance the careless forage-master kept a tempting bag of the choicest feed: it was within easy reach of the door.  Our forage-master wrapped his blanket about him and was soon in a deep, heavy sleep.  He awoke early in the morning, a little after day-dawn.  He looked towards the door; the tempting bag of the choicest feed had disappeared.  "I thought so," said the forage-master.  He sprang down from his perch, folded up his blanket, went to the door, stooped down for a moment, as if to look for something, and said, "Aha, my cock, so I've caught you at last, have I?"

From the door of the forage-tent to the door of another tent there was the feed, showing the course the bag had taken. Roe had inserted a knife in the bottom of the bag before leaving it so near the door the evening before. The thoughtless thief, in the middle of the night, was unconscious that, as he was carrying off his booty, he was laying a train for his own discovery.

About the middle of February General Meagher returned to the Brigade. He waited on the President at Washington, relative to the propriety of relieving the Brigade from duty, and letting it return to New York to recruit its shattered ranks.

The President received him kindly, and though the reception-room was full on his entrance, His Excellency went over and shook hands with him, entering familiarly into conversation about the Brigade, and promised to take his request into consideration.

On General Meagher's arrival at his headquarters, the men of the different regiments surrounded him and cheered him most enthusiastically. The general said only a few words, telling them that he was heartily glad to be with them once more, never to leave them again until they all went home together. All the officers then visited him and congratulated him on his return.

In the evening the officers treated Gen. Meagher to a serenade, the magnificent band of the One Hundred and Twenty-seventh Pennsylvania Volunteers having been kindly lent them by the commandant of the regiment. The performance of these " warrior bards" was exquisite. They had been all picked out of the enlisted men of the One Hundred and Twenty-seventh Regiment by the leader, and he did, without doubt, make the most perfect band in the army out of his material.

The general, in addressing the Brigade, told them how glad he was to return to them, that his place was always with them, and would be always with them while they were continued in the field; but that he had the strongest hope and the fullest assurances, if any reliance could be placed on the promises of those in power, that he would at no distant day have the gratification of leading them back to the repose, to the less exacting duties that their gallantry, their enthusiasm, their lofty and signal courage had so deservedly won and so richly earned.

General Meagher having awaited an answer for some time to his application to have the Brigade sent home to recruit, and not receiving any, addressed the following letter to the Secretary of War on the subject:

HEADQUARTERS, IRISH BRIGADE,
SECOND BRIGADE HANCOCK'S DIVISION, COUCH'S CORPS,
ARMY OF THE POTOMAC,
BEFORE FREDERICKSBURG, VA., February 19, 1863.

*To the Honorable the Secretary of War at Washington :*

SIR—I have the honor to request that three regiments of the Brigade I command may be temporarily relieved from duty in the field.

I make this application for the following reasons. The Brigade nomnally consists of five regiments—

Sixty-ninth New York Volunteers.

Eighty-eighth New York Volunteers.

Sixty-third New York Volunteers.

One Hundred and Sixteenth Pennsylvania Volunteers.

Twenty-eighth Massachusetts Volunteers.

The aggregate strength of these five regiments is made up of one hundred and thirty-nine officers and one thousand and fifty-eight enlisted men. To this strength, the One Hundred and Sixteenth Pennsylvania Volunteers (now consolidated into a battalion) and the Twenty-eighth Massachusetts Volunteers contribute forty-eight officers and five hundred and twenty-seven enlisted men. The other three regiments, therefore, make up the balance, giving as their aggregate ninety-one officers and five hundred and thirty-one enlisted men.

For duty, including pioneers, drummers, &c........ ... 340

On extra and daily duty............................. 132

Sick and wounded................................. 59

The Sixty-ninth, Eighty-eighth, and Sixty-third are the three original old regiments of the Brigade. They left the city of New York in the months of November and December, 1861, fully two thousand two hundred and fifty strong, including two batteries of three officers and one hundred and fifty men each. Assigned to the division commanded by Major-General Sumner, these regiments entered immediately on active duty, being encamped near Edsall's Hill, beyond Alexandria, Virginia, until the 10th of March, when they proceeded to Union Mills, Manassas, and Warrenton Junction.

Returning to Alexandria early in April, they embarked for Ship Point, on the York River, when, after several days of laborious activity in the commissary and quartermaster's departments of the army, they proceeded to the front, and were engaged at once in the operations for the reduction of Yorktown.

The battle of Fair Oaks was the first battle in which these regiments fought, and these were the only regiments then constituting the Brigade.

A fortnight subsequently the Brigade was re-enforced by the

Twenty-ninth Massachusetts Volunteers; and thus re-enforced, the three old regiments did severe duty before Richmond; this duty requiring of them to defend the front of the army at Fair Oaks, throw up extensive earthworks, perform picket-duty every third day, support the command of Major-General Hooker on three occasions, when he was forcibly pressed by the enemy; and, ultimately hastening to the relief, and covering, in conjunction with the brigade commanded by Brigadier-General French, the retreat of the army corps under Major-General Fitz-John Porter, at Gaines' Hill.

On the retreat of the Army of the Potomac from before Richmond, the Brigade, consisting of the above-mentioned regiments, participated in the battles of Peach Orchard, Savage's Station, White Oak Swamp, Glendale, Malvern Hill, and suffered severely, the loss of commissioned officers being more, proportionately, than the loss of privates.

Whilst suffering in this way, and reduced to an average of three hundred men to each regiment, the Brigade arrived at Harrison's Landing, James River; and, although the undersigned was ordered by Major-General McClellan to proceed to New York shortly after the Army of the Potomac had reached the landing, for the purpose of procuring recruits; and, although the brigadier-general exercised all the influence within his scope to procure such recruits, the Brigade almost imperceptibly benefited by its temporary relief from duty in the field, and the exertions of the undersigned.

Nevertheless, the Brigade most cheerfully and heartily participated in the rapid and sultry march to Newport News, by way of Williamsburg and Yorktown, and with equal alacrity and good-will proceeded to Aquia Creek, and thence to Falmouth, Virginia, where they were ordered by Major-General McClellan to report to Major-General Burnside, in command of the Federal forces in front of Fredericksburg.

Relieved by Major-General Burnside, the Brigade, still consisting of the Sixty-ninth, Eighty-eighth, and Sixty-third New York Volunteers, and the Twenty-ninth Massachusetts Volunteers, returned from Falmouth forty-eight hours after they had reported to General Burnside, and repaired to Alexandria, whence, after a halt of less than eight hours outside the city, they hurried to the support of Major-General Pope, then engaged with the enemy on the plains of Manassas, resting not more than six hours in the rear of Fort Corcoran preparatory to their advance.

On the retreat from the plains of Manassas, the Brigade formed a portion of the rear-guard, and, acting as such, experienced a good deal of harassing from the light artillery and cavalry of the enemy.

First in the advance on the march through Maryland to the battle-field of Antietam, they supported Major-General Hooker at South Mountain, and, two days after, under the immediate command of Major-General Richardson, were conspicuously engaged in that great attack which compelled the enemy, defeated and humbled, to recross the Potomac.

Since then the Brigade, re-enforced by the One Hundred and Sixteenth Pennsylvania Volunteers, and having the Twenty-ninth Massachusetts Volunteers replaced by the Twenty-eighth of the same State, took part in the reconnoissance of Charlestown and the intervening and adjacent country beyond Bolivar Heights, which reconnoissance was so brilliantly and successfully conducted by Brigadier-General Hancock, commanding the division of which this Brigade is the Second Brigade.

In the subsequent advance to the Rappahannock, the Brigade was frequently foremost; and on the evening of November 17th, had the honor of being ordered by Major-General Sumner to proceed with all speed up the road, ford the river, and take the guns which (opposite Falmouth) had been silenced and dismounted by the splendid battery commanded by Captain Petitt.

This order, however, was countermanded half an hour after the Brigade had dashed forward with the greatest enthusiasm to execute it, it being decided by Major-General Sumner that it would be imprudent to throw any portion of the army over the Rappahannock before the entire force was prepared to establish itself on the Fredericksburg side of the river.

The records of the Brigade, thus far, close with the day on which the assault was made on the enemy's lines and batteries; and all his redoubts and fortified works and heights in the rear of Fred-

16*

ericksburg, unless continued picket-duty, from that day to this, may be considered a prolongation of the record.

The official statistics of the five regiments have been inserted in this application ; and, if I do not greatly err, from a partiality generated by my peculiar relationship with the Brigade—having been the founder of it—I think I am justified, and fully justified, in affirming that no brigade in the army of the United States has more assiduously, unremittingly, bravely, nobly done its duty.

No history, however vividly and powerfully written, could do more than these plain and stern statistics do in attestation of the cordial loyalty and devotion unto death of this Brigade, in the good and glorious cause in which it staked its reputation, which is dearer to it than the blood of the bravest soldiers of whom it is composed.

Grounding the application on these statistics and these facts— representing, as they unquestionably do, that the Brigade has ceased to be a Brigade, and hardly exhibits the numerical strength which qualifies it for a higher designation than that of a colonel's command—and with an honest and generous view of the still greater efficiency of the military power of the Government, I do most respectfully and earnestly beg that the three original regiments of the Brigade, viz., the Sixty-ninth New York Volunteers, Eighty-eighth New York Volunteers, Sixty-third New York Volunteers, be temporarily relieved from duty in the field ; and, being so relieved, have the opportunity of restoring, in some serviceable measure, their exhausted ranks.

As long as these regiments are retained in the field, the undersigned is convinced that no accession to their ranks will take place ; and the undersigned feels that it is unnecessary for him to enter into any argument or exposition to confirm this assertion.

He confines himself to the respectful duty of directing the attention of the Secretary of War to the fact, that decimated regiments from Maine, Massachusetts, and Connecticut have been ordered home, so as to enable them to return actively to the service of the Government with a strength commensurate with their reputation, and the cause in which they are engaged.

The brigadier-general commanding what is popularly known as

the Irish Brigade, asks no more for what is left of his brave officers and men than that which has been conceded to other commands, exhibiting equal labors, equal sacrifices, and equal decimation.

In doing so, he does violence to his own heart and nerve. In making and urging an application of this character, any man of soldierly instinct and pride must feel that he has imputations to encounter, which tend to the damage of the good name he has acquired in the midst of many difficulties and dangers, and to which the Brigade, in whose behalf he appeals, has with so liberal a gallantry contributed.

But there is a courage sterner still than that which faces the fire of the enemy. Doing your duty to your men—either to their displeasure or in concurrence with their wishes—oftentimes demands a resolution higher far in a moral estimation than that which the orders delivered on the eve of battle exact.

Such do I feel to be the resolution required of me at this moment, in forwarding and pressing this application, We are in front of the enemy of the Government of the United States. A narrow river alone divides us. Any moment may witness—any accident may precipitate a collision between the two armies. With this possibility before us, the reluctance with which I make this application will be easily conceived, and cannot but be readily admitted.

But, as I have already more than estimated, the reputation of the Brigade, for the remnant of which I appeal, is too vitally identified with the race which it represents, and the cause to which it has devoted its fidelity and its life, for me, as the official guardian of it, to be silent—to refrain from urging such a request as I do now—when to be silent might, and would inevitably, imperil that righteous reputation.

I have alluded to considerations of public and national interest in forwarding this application.

These considerations form a part of the application, which I do not conceive it proper or essential for me to submit at large, or in detail, to the Secretary of War, and shall, therefore, confine myself, as I do conscientiously, and with the deepest and strongest conviction that the relief of the first, second, and third regiments of the

Brigade from duty in the field will result in an important accession to their ranks, and so enable the Irish Brigade to render, in support of the Constitution and the legitimate Chief Magistracy of the United States, services not less faithful and chivalrous than those they have already permanently imprinted with their blood upon the national records of this war.

I have the honor to be your very humble and obedient servant, with the greatest esteem,

THOMAS FRANCIS MEAGHER,
Brigadier-General commanding the Irish Brigade.

## ST. PATRICK'S DAY.

Patrick's day in camp was celebrated with the usual gayety and rejoicing by the few and fearless men composing the Irish Brigade. This time-honored national anniversary was observed with all the exhaustless spirit and enthusiasm of Irish nature. For days previous vast preparations had been made, a race-course marked out, and on every side, written in large, bold characters, was the following announcement:

" GRAND IRISH BRIGADE STEEPLE-CHASE,

"To come off the 17th of March, rain or shine, by horses, the property of, and to be ridden by, commissioned officers of that Brigade. The prizes are a purse of $500 ; second horse to save his stakes; two and a half mile heat, best two in three, over four hurdles four and a half feet high, and five ditch fences, including two artificial rivers fifteen feet wide and six deep; hurdles to be made of forest pine, and braced with hoops."

The quartermaster was sent to Washington for liquors and meats, and brought for the banquet that was to follow the race the following moderate supply, which constituted the fare: thirty-five hams, and a side of an ox roasted; an entire pig, stuffed with boiled turkeys; an unlimited number of chickens, ducks, and small game. The drinking materials comprised eight baskets of champagne, ten gallons of rum, and twenty-two of whiskey. A splendid bower was erected, capable of containing some hundreds of persons, for a general invitation was issued to all the officers of the Army of the Potomac.

The evening previous to the races a committee was held on punch, as to who was the best qualified to mix that important compound. It was unanimously agreed that the general and staff were the best judges, and therefore the most proper to undertake it. It was ruled that the matter be left entirely in their hands. Captains Gosson and Hogan were voted masters of ceremonies, in which they labored so diligently that before the mixture was complete both felt overpowered by their labors and had to be relieved from duty.

The morning commenced with religious ceremonies, after which the different riders proceeded to dress themselves. The dresses were showy, but some rather incongruous. One officer appeared mounted in scarlet, the top of his head crowned with a green velvet smoking cap, the present of his lady-love. The reason he assigned for his peculiar taste was, he was from Galway, and his family had hunted with the Galway Blazers Club, and dressed similarly.

At eleven o'clock the grand stand was crowded with distinguished generals, officers, and about a dozen ladies.

A large concourse of at least ten thousand had assembled to participate in the fun. Previous to the starting, the course was the object of attraction for spectators. Large crowds of soldiers were congregated in the vicinity of the interesting points, which seemed to be, in their estimation, where the leaps were highest and the ditches deepest. The nature of the ground was favorable,—a gently rolling stretch of land, over which the course ran a mile and three-quarters in length ;—and at points about equal distance from each other, eight leaps had been erected or excavated. From the ground whereon the stand was, and where the flags marking the track waved, the hills, here and there crested with a growth of oak or cedar, sloped away towards the Rappahannock. The bluest of blue skies looked down on the gayly-dressed and eager crowds, on the dashing horsemen, whose steeds pranced by the side of others on which were riding gay and brilliant women, on the quiet hills, the peaceful river, the two hostile armies, and seemed to shower its blessings and its beauties on the festive throng assembled for enjoyment and sport commemorative of our national holiday.

The start was named for eleven o'clock: ten minutes before that hour the commander-in-chief of the Army of the Potomac, Major-General Hooker, attended by all the members of his staff not detained at headquarters or elsewhere on duty, and accompanied by Lieutenant-Colonel Bentley, and Captain John C. Lynch, of the Sixty-third, both of whom had waited on General Hooker earlier in the day, arrived on the ground. On the appearance of the commander-in-chief he was greeted with warm cheers, which he gracefully acknowledged as he took his place on the grand stand. Before attempting to describe the sports of the day, it may be as well to notice some of the more prominent and distinguished of the invited guests. And first let us speak of the ladies, who added much, by their vivacity and their picturesque costume, by their brilliancy and witchery, to the entertainments and amusements of the day. Fortunate citizens, dwelling in their quiet homes, and having before their eyes, every hour of the day, graceful and lovely women, can have no idea of the chivalrous emotions which swell the hearts of even the roughest soldier, seeing on rude camp-covered hills the figures, the fair faces, which, it may be, have not been looked on in these regions and by these men for many, many months. If the reader has any conception of these things, he can then easily imagine with what deep, yet subdued gladness, the ladies were greeted by all.

When a fitting opportunity offered, in recognition of the hospitable greeting that was accorded him, General Hooker proposed three cheers for "General Meagher and his Irish Brigade, God bless them."

The following horses only, out of a larger number entered for the first race, open to officers of the Irish Brigade, started:

General Meagher's gray horse, "Jack Hinton;" rider, Captain John Gosson; dress, crimson jacket, sleeves, breeches, and white cap.

Captain Hogan's bay horse, "Napper Tandy;" rider, Lieutenant Ryder; dress, blue jacket, white breeches, green cap.

Captain Martin's bay mare, "Kathleen Mavourneen;" rider, Captain Martin; Solferino jacket, white breeches, maroon cap.

Captain Langdon's black horse, "Nigger Bill;" rider, Lieutenant Byron; plaid jacket, white breeches, pink cap.

Quartermaster McCormick's bay horse, "Sharpsburg;" rider, Lieutenant O'Connor; red jacket, white breeches, blue cap.

Major Mullholland's chestnut horse, "Major;" rider, Quartermaster Wade; blue jacket, white breeches, red cap.

Judges: Colonel Von Schaick, Seventh N. Y. V.; Colonel Frank, Fifty-seventh N. Y. V.

Umpire: Brigadier-General Caldwell.

Clerk of the Course: General Meagher.

A few minutes before eleven o'clock the bugle sounded to the post, the horses were uncovered, and the eager riders mounted. Precisely as the hand denoted the hour, the clerk of the course waved his whip, another sweet, inspiriting note from the bugler, and off they go. Six horses, six gallant riders, the course, the leaps, innumerable throngs of spectators, meet the eye of one standing on the platform. The first leap was a hurdle almost five feet high. They come to it; three clear it beautifully; two saddles are emptied; the bay mare bolts, but is spiritedly and scientifically brought to it, and flies over magnificently. With varying fortune the other leaps and spaces are taken and passed over, the rider of the gray drawing towards him the attention of the throng, by the masterly manner in which he handles his horse. The home-stretch is reached, the gray, hard pressed by the bay, gains the winning-post, and the umpire declares him the winner of the first heat. A wild, enthusiastic cheer goes up from the jubilant throng. The start on the second heat was according to the formula of the first. All the horses cleared hurdle number one in fine style ; the run home was headed by the gray again, this time the little black closing tightly in on him, and the gray was declared the winner, amid thunders of applause for his dashing rider.

To this race succeeded a sweepstakes, open to all, and, as usual, all the incidents of an old-fashioned course happened. Eight horses contested for the prize, which was won by a fine chestnut, ridden by, it is said, a descendant of the Blucher of Waterloo fame.

It was one o'clock when General Meagher announced that all further operations would be postponed for half an hour, and invited the ladies, the generals present, and their staffs, to a collation, prepared and awaiting destruction at his quarters, and thither the goodly company proceeded. In front of the quarters two Sibley tents had been pitched, separated by a space of ten yards, which space was inclosed by an awning. In and under these the guests thronged. Mountains of sandwiches disappeared, no doubt filling up those voids which nature is said to abhor. With the precision and promptitude of file-firing, pop, pop, went explosions that preceded copious draughts of rich wines. In and out, in fact everywhere, went the attentive officers of the Brigade, attending to their visitors. What attracted most attention, however, and gratified every appreciative palate, were potations of spiced whiskey-punch, ladled by Captain Hogan, the Ganymede of the occasion, from an enormous bowl, holding not much less than thirty gallons.

The following amusements followed :

1st. A foot-race, one-half mile distance, best of heats ; open to all non-commissioned officers and privates, the winner to receive $7, and the second $3.

2d. Casting weights, the weights to weigh from ten to fourteen pounds ; the winner to receive $3.

3d. Running after the soaped pig—to be the prize of the man who holds it.

4th. A hurdle-race, one-half mile distance, open to all non-commissioned officers and privates; the winner to receive $7, the second $3.

5th. The wheelbarrow-race—the contestants to be blindfolded, and limited to six soldiers of the Irish Brigade; the winner to receive $5 ; distance to be decided on the ground.

6th. Jumping in sacks to the distance of five hundred yards ; the winner to receive $5.

7th. A contest on the light fantastic toe, consisting of Irish reels, jigs, and hornpipes; the best dancer to receive $5, the second best $3, to be decided by a judge appointed by the chairman.

The amusements of the day were followed by a grand entertainment at night, theatricals and recitations. Many a health was drank, many a friend was toasted, and even the American generals fully entered into the spirit of the hour; flowing bumpers, loving glances at the fair ones, songs and toasts went freely round. Captain Hogan presided at the nectarean mixture, which floated like a spiced island in a huge barrel. Captain Jack Gosson, in his most *recherché* uniform, bespangled with lace, aided and assisted. Around them were a lot of drummer-boys and soldiers. These Captain Jack dispersed in the most dignified manner, while they looked most longingly at Captain Hogan, as he ladled out the punch.

A poetical address was read by Dr. Lawrence Reynolds, of his own composition, giving a history of the career of the Brigade. Dr. Lawrence, of the Sixty-third Regiment, was the poet laureate of the Brigade. This was followed by the following song, written by a poetical rival of the doctor's, and was sung by Captain Blake, in his best style:

### Song of the Irish Brigade.

#### I.

We've never swerved from our old green flag,
　Upborne o'er many a bloody plain ;
'Tis now a torn and tattered rag,
　But we will bear it proudly oft again.

We'll raise it high, this dear old flag,
   From Liffy's banks to Shannon's stream,
'Till victory o'er the pirate rag
   Upon our sacred cause shall beam.

### CHORUS.

   Hurrah! Hurrah! for our dear old flag,
      Hurrah for our gallant leader, too;
   Though 'tis a torn and tattered rag,
      We would not change it for the new.

### II.

We've borne it with the Stripes and Stars,
   From Fair Oaks to Frederick's bloody plain;
And see, my boys, our wounds and scars
   Can tell how well we did the same.
But sure, our chieftain, of his race,
   Was ever foremost 'mid the brave,
Where death met heroes face to face,
   And gathered harvests for the grave.

### CHORUS.

   Hurrah! hurrah! etc.

### III.

We miss full many a comrade's smile,
   The grasp of many a friendly hand,
We mourn their loss, and grieve the while
   They had not died for fatherland.
But o'er their fresh and gory graves—
   We swear it now, and evermore—
To free green Erin, land of slaves,
   And banish tyrants from her shore.

### CHORUS.

   Hurrah! hurrah! etc.

IV.

Now we're pledged to free this land,
  So long the exile's resting-place ;
To crush for aye a traitorous band,
  And wipe out treason's deep disgrace.
Then let us pledge Columbia's cause,
  God prosper poor old Ireland, too !
We'll trample on all tyrant laws :
  Hurrah for the old land and the new !

CHORUS.

Hurrah ! hurrah ! etc.

Letters of apology were received from several officers and civilians who could not attend. Among them the following.

NEW YORK, March 17, 1863.

MY DEAR GENERAL—I regret that it was not in my power to reply to the kind invitation to be present at your celebration of to-day, in time for you to receive it at your meeting. Please convey to your officers my warmest thanks for their kind remembrance of me, and say to them that, whatever may be my future fate, I can never, so long as life lasts, forget my Irish Brigade, whose green flags advanced so steadily and nobly at Antietam. My warmest friendship and admiration will follow your fortunes wherever you may go, and I know that every field in which the Brigade may be placed hereafter will only add new laurels to those already so proudly won.
  I am, my dear general, most truly your friend,
                      GEORGE B. McCLELLAN.

HEADQUARTERS FIRST DIVISION N. Y. S. M.,
        NEW YORK, March 14, 1863.

MY DEAR GENERAL.—I wish most sincerely that I could reply to the kind invitation of yourself and the officers of your gallant

Brigade, by presenting myself at your headquarters on the morning of the 17th, to unite with you and them in the celebration of Ireland's National Holiday.

I have many gratifying recollections of joyous celebrations of St. Patrick's natal day by the genial sons of the Emerald Isle, in other days, ere " faithless sons betrayed us ;" but I should rejoice more in meeting with you and the devoted officers of your Brigade at your quarters in the field, ready to do or die in the cause of liberty, than in the most enthusiastic or luxurious entertainment at the Astor or the St. Nicholas.

> " Oh, the sight entrancing,
>    When the morning's beam is glancing
>    On files arrayed, with helm and blade,
>    And in *Freedom's* cause advancing."

Be pleased, my dear general, to present my warmest felicitations and best wishes to your brave officers, and believe me ever,

Your friend and obedient servant,

CHARLES W. SANDFORD.

---

NEW YORK, March 14, 1863.

GENERAL T. F. MEAGHER:

MY DEAR MEAGHER—I cannot describe the pleasure which I derived from receiving the invitation tendered by yourself and the other officers of the Irish Brigade, to unite with that Brigade in celebrating St. Patrick's Day at headquarters. If it were possible I would gladly be present with you all. But duty keeps me here. That the officers of the Brigade favor me with their esteem, is a circumstance of which I feel very proud. Would that I were associated with them to share their perils, privations, and honors. Thank God, the blood of old Ireland stirs in harmonious association with that of true Americans, in devoted attachment to the Republic, to the Union, and the Constitution. The Irish name will derive additional lustre from this glorious fact. I write in some haste, so as to insure the delivery of the note before the 17th, and ask you and the officers of the Brigade to pledge with me this sentiment :

*The Constitution of the United States* —If it be ever destroyed, the sons of Ireland will not share in the responsibility of its ruin.

Yours affectionately,

JAMES T. BRADY.

---

NEW YORK, March 14, 1863.

BRIGADIER-GENERAL MEAGHER:

DEAR GENERAL—I thank you and the officers of the Brigade very kindly for the generous invitation to join you in your celebration of the National Holiday of Ireland, at the headquarters of the Brigade, Army of the Potomac. The day will not find warmer or more gallant hearts, devoted to its memories, than will be assembled within your camp circle. That circle is a ring of true metal, that has won the admiration of the world. It would have given me great pleasure to be with you in the enjoyment of the festivities of the day, but binding engagements will not permit me to leave the city, and you will therefore accept my sincere regrets. The statement in your invitation, that the "celebration will take place utterly regardless of any vicissitudes of the weather," is, I know, no reckless waste of words, notwithstanding the prevalent visitations of rain and snow, inasmuch as it reminds me of that banquet of the Brigade, which went on utterly regardless of *fire*—the devastating fire of the enemy at Fredericksburg. With every heartfelt wish for your welfare, and that of your officers and men, I am very truly and sincerely,      Your attached friend,

BARTHOLOMEW O'CONNOR.

SENTIMENT—*Irish fidelity and Irish valor*—Like the writ of *habeas corpus*, they can never be suppressed without danger to law and order—more particularly if the law and order are not civil, but *uncivil.*

---

HERALD OFFICE, NEW YORK, March 14, 1863.

To Brigadier-General T. F. MEAGHER

and the officers of the Irish Brigade:

GENTLEMEN—I have the honor to acknowledge the receipt of your kind invitation to participate in the festivities of St. Patrick's

Day at the headquarters of the Brigade; and it is with sincere regret that I am prevented from availing myself of your friendly remembrance of me, owing to the nature of my engagements in this city.

Though not present in person, I shall be with you heart and soul on that occasion, as I have ever been since the organization of the Brigade, through all its varied fortunes; the first to exult in its successes; the first to mourn the loss of the gallant soldiers who have fallen in its ranks; and yielding to none in my devotion to its brave commander.

It is the traditionary privilege of the Irish race to fight in every just cause. It is their proud boast that they always *fight well.* The Irish Brigade of the Army of the Potomac have preserved that golden rule religiously. While thanking you for your cordial invitation, permit me to offer a sentiment which, if it be in order, you will honor me by presenting at your festive meeting on the 17th of March. It is this: " The laurel wreaths won by the *old* Brigade at Fontenoy and Cremona have lost none of their verdure—may the valor of the *new* Brigade make them perennial."

With best wishes for your welfare, and the heartiest sympathy with your coming celebration, I remain, gentlemen,

Very faithfully yours,<br>W. F. Lyons.

---

New York, March 15, 1863.

My Dear General—I duly received the joint note from you and the officers of the Irish Brigade, inviting me to unite in the celebration of St. Patrick's Day at your headquarters on the Rappahannock, and beg to return you and them my most cordial thanks for the thoughtful kindness which kept me in your heads and hearts at such a time and place. I sincerely regret that I cannot be with you in person to see and feel the additional inspiration which the character and situation of Irishmen in arms for a holy cause must give to the ever suggestive memories of Ireland's national holiday.

I am proud of the invitation, conscious of the honor conferred by it, and will treasure up the characteristic missive in which they

17

were conveyed. It evokes many, many memories. Its brief and soldier-like sentences suggest an epic. Dated from where you are, the purport of it points to where you came from. It calls to mind what you are doing for America, and what we attempted to do, and what we hope to do, for Ireland. It conjures up the story of the Irish exodus, and what caused it; and the American treason, and what will crush it. It indicates the wondrous history through which we have passed from 1843 to 1863. What a contrast between the monster meetings in the former, and—be it reverently said—the *mass* meetings we have seen round camp chapels, at which regimental chaplains officiated, preparing and blessing Irish soldiers to go forth and battle for Republican institutions. Many who have heard the old Tribune at Tara and Mullaghmast, have followed the young Tribune at Gaines' Mill and Antietam; many who aspired, with me, to fight for freedom on the Waterford mountains in 1848, have fought, bled, and died for freedom by your side on the Peninsula and in Maryland.

Your note calls to mind a crowd of such facts, with the thoughts and historical contrasts they compel. Of all these contrasts, not one is of deeper significance than that afforded by the circumstances attending the obsequies (Dublin, 1847) of the all-potent moral force Tribune, who declared liberty not worth the expenditure of a drop of blood; and the Requiem Mass in St. Patrick's Cathedral (New York, 1863) for the dead heroes of the Irish Brigade, at which the fallen were exalted as Christian soldiers, who, dying for just principles and their country, glorified God.

In my old age, too, if Heaven shall extend my days into the season of the sere and yellow leaf, this little note will awaken grateful and flattering thoughts to weave a memorial halo round my declining days. It will remind me that at a time of great civil war, when the best government devised by man was waylaid by the most stupendous treason—when the fate not only of that government, but the hopes and blessings its example kindled and its success sustained, was at stake, the Irish rushed in thousands to the standard of Democratic government and civilization—that in the unparalleled conflicts the Irish Brigade was ever foremost in, and once saved the army of humanity, that it was ever prominent, and never disgraced in battle, compelling the admiration of the foes, as well as the honor of the friends of justice; and that the surviving remnant of this immortal band, on a St. Patrick's Day, encamped in view of the slopes whereon was offered their latest holocaust for freedom, thought of me as one not unworthy to join with them in the pious exercises and festive pleasures, the patriotic reminiscences and hopeful aspirations commemorative of the national holiday of Irishmen : this shall stir my old blood. I give you as a sentiment, should this reach you in time—

Long live the Republic, one and indivisible. May the Irish citizens as well deserve its honors in peace, as the Irish Brigade has won them in the war for its defence.

With renewed affection for you and the officers of the Brigade,

Believe me your friend,

JOHN SAVAGE.

Brigadier-General MEAGHER,
Commanding Irish Brigade.

# CHAPTER XVIII.

Battle of Chancellorsville.—Breaking of the Eleventh Corps.—The Irish
   Brigade rescue the Fifth Maine Battery.—Incidents of the battle-field.—
   Resignation of General Meagher.—Regret of the Brigade.—Battle of
   Gettysburg.—The Brigade again engaged.

THINGS remained quiet and monotonous in camp until
the middle of April, when all preparations denoted an
immediate advance. This took place soon afterwards,
and the battle of Chancellorsville followed. I give a
*resumé* of the daily operations of the battle, with the
account which I wrote for the "New York Herald"
at the time.

## THE BATTLE OF CHANCELLORSVILLE.

THE PLAN.—A portion of the army (about half of
it) was to cross the river near Fredericksburg, and
pretend to renew the attempt in which Burnside had
been previously unsuccessful, and accomplish two objects—first, to hold the enemy's force at that point;
and second, to protect our communications and supplies, while the other half of the army should make
a crossing above the fortifications, and, sweeping down

to the rear of Fredericksburg, take a strong position and hold it until they could be re-enforced by the portion of the army engaged in making the feint, which was to withdraw from its position, take the bridges to the point of the river, which had been uncovered by the flank movement; and the whole army would thus be concentrated in the rear of Fredericksburg. The following outline of each day's operations will show to what extent this bold and hazardous plan has proved successful, and in what degree and for what reason it has resulted so unfortunately.

MONDAY AND TUESDAY, APRIL 26 AND 27.—On Monday, the 26th, was commenced the execution of this plan. Three corps, the fifth, eleventh, and twelfth, were ordered to march with eight days' rations to Kelly's Ford, near the Orange and Alexandria Railroad. General Slocum, of the Twelfth Corps, was placed in command, and on Tuesday night, the force intrusted with the important part of executing the flank movement had reached the point at which they were ordered to cross the Rappahannock. Tuesday night, also, three other corps, the first, third, and sixth, were sent to Franklin's crossing, three miles below Fredericksburg, to be ready to undertake the crossing simultaneously with the other corps at Kelly's Ford, on Wednesday morning. General Sedgwick commanded these troops.

WEDNESDAY.—Without serious opposition, both divisions of the army were established on the west bank of the river, and a portion of the flanking corps pushed on from Kelly's Ford towards the Rapidan at Germania Mills.

THURSDAY.—Sedgwick threatened the enemy, and held him near Fredericksburg, while Slocum pressed on from the Rapidan and took his position across the plankroad (the enemy's line of retreat towards Gordonsville) at Chancellorsville. Couch's Second Corps, which had remained at Banks' Ford, now moved up to the United States Ford, and crossed to join General Slocum. General Hooker also joined, and took command of the four corps thus concentrated in the rear of Fredericksburg and across the line of the enemy's retreat. Thursday night there was sharp work on both sides to outmanœuvre each other.

FRIDAY.—The first and third corps were moving from the left wing to join General Hooker at Chancellorsville, while Jackson was taking a circuitous route to reach the rear of General Hooker's line between Chancellorsville and the Rapidan, where Hooker, by night, concentrated all this portion of his army, save the Sixth Corps. At the same time the main body of the enemy had been moved from their works at Fredericksburg.

SATURDAY.—General Hooker occupied the forenoon

in awaiting the attack of the enemy, which was evidently expected in front. The movements of the enemy seemed to indicate that they were retreating; but in the afternoon Stonewall Jackson pounced upon our extreme right and rear, between Chancellorsville and Germania Mills. A most furious and desperate attack was made, and the right of our lines, which was held by the Eleventh Corps, was almost instantly broken, and the panic-stricken men, in utter confusion, with and without muskets, hats, and coats, rushed headlong from under fire down the only road which led to the bridge. The Third Corps, under General Sickles, was interposed in the breach thus made, and the excellent coolness of this officer, with the better qualities which his corps exhibited, saved the further progress of the panic and the rout, and the evil was temporarily stayed. This rout of the Eleventh Corps was the crisis. This was the turning point, from which our succeeding misfortunes can be most distinctly traced. Saturday closed the operations of the first week, with doubtful prospects of the final result, and the previous successes of the right wing seemed destined to end in disaster. Sedgwick, with the Sixth Corps, had at this time withdrawn to the east bank of the river, taken up his bridges, and replaced them again directly in front of Fredericksburg, and prepared for an assault on the morrow of the earthworks back of the town.

SUNDAY.—The assault of General Sedgwick upon the heights of Fredericksburg, which, most probably, was defended but by a few brigades, was vigorous and completely successful. After it, that general marched to join his chief, Hooker; but Lee turned on him in force, cut him off from all communication either with Hooker or with Fredericksburg, and thus isolated, forced him back upon the river at Banks' Ford. Another repulse, too, was sustained on Sunday morning by the army near Chancellorsville. The enemy renewed the attack, and again drove back our lines for half a mile. From the large brick house, which gives the name to this vicinity, the lines of the enemy could be seen sweeping slowly, but confidently, determinedly, and surely, through the clearings which extended in front. Nothing could excite more admiration for the best qualities of the veteran soldier than the manner in which the enemy swept out, as they moved steadily onward, the forces which were opposed to them. The enemy felt confident that they were to be victorious, and our own men had, from some occasion, imbibed the same impression.

MONDAY.—Another day of misfortune, and the day was hardly ushered in before the enemy, in force, came down upon the detachments which had been thought sufficient to hold the works upon the heights of Fredericksburg. First a brigade, then a division, then a

larger force came in upon them, and after strongly
contesting the position, they were compelled to yield
and fall back under the protection of the town. The
enemy formed their line of battle on the outskirts, and
within the town the two brigades of General Gibbon
held them in check as long as could be. Many
wounded men were in the hospitals, and the position
was maintained as long as possible. At length the
ground was given up, the troops were withdrawn, the
bridges taken up, and Fredericksburg was given back
to the enemy. They were now at liberty to turn their
attention to Sedgwick, and they lost no time in concentrating their forces against him. After a most
obstinate fight, in which the enemy almost were successful in destroying his bridges, and the possibility of
his escape, he made good his retreat to the east bank
of the Rappahannock. His losses were appalling.
He suffered terribly, and in their retreat there was
much confusion and disorder among the troops.

TUESDAY.—By this time the aspect of affairs had
become exceedingly dark. The troops were much
dispirited, and although they had held their position
on Monday, the prospect of meeting the combined
forces of the enemy with large re-enforcements, which
they were known to have received, was exceedingly
unpromising. A severe storm appeared also on Tuesday afternoon, swelling the Rappahannock to a torrent,

and threatening to carry away the bridges. Tuesday night, the army of the Rappahannock was withdrawn, and the entire force brought again across the river, with the exception of many dead and wounded.

On the evening of the 30th of April General Meagher invited his staff-officers to a camp supper, preparatory to the march. The Brigade was then formed into marching order, and proceeded under the guidance of Lieutenant Miller of General Hancock's staff. We left camp about one o'clock, and, as our way lay through a thick forest, supposed to be occupied by rebel sharpshooters, we had to proceed with great caution. About twelve o'clock at night we bivouacked in the midst of the forest, and at dawn resumed our march towards the United States Ford. About noon next day we halted, to give the troops time to rest and refresh themselves, and also to have the pontoons completed across the Rappahannock. About six o'clock in the evening we resumed our march, the Brigade bringing up the extreme left of the Second Army Corps.

Our passage across the river by moonlight was magnificently grand; indeed the army deployed in close column along a steep and almost perpendicular hill to reach the river. Seen from the top of this hill, the long line of ambulances and trains, extending for miles, the almost interminable columns of men, with forests of glittering bayonets, the brilliant uniforms of generals and their staff-officers, presented one grand moonlight panorama of unsurpassed beauty. The Brigade picketed for the night commanding a ford at the south side of the river, near the main road from Fredericksburg to Richmond. About noon next day we resumed our march to a place called Scott's Mills —a ford within a few miles of Chancellorsville. We arrived here about ten o'clock on Friday night. As this was an important position, and exposed by a by-road to the left wing of the enemy's lines, the general threw out pickets, loopholed the mill and offices, and fortified them with men. We also had a battery of six guns in position in our front. Towards Chancellorsville we heard some heavy firing all the afternoon, which we subsequently learned was produced by an engagement between the enemy and Sykes' division, General Meade's Fifth Army Corps, which was the first to engage while General Hooker was completing his plans for the formation of his line of battle.

I should have mentioned that the Fifth, Eleventh, and Twelfth Army Corps, under the respective commands of Generals Meade, Howard, and Slocum, crossed near Kelly's Ford, in order to form a junction with the Second corps, under Major-General Couch— the First under General Reynolds, and the Third under Major-General Sickles. The three last corps crossed at the United States Ford—a distance of eight miles from Kelly's Ford. Chancellorsville is about six miles north of the United States Ford, on the military road, and midway on the pike road between Fredericksburg and Gordonsville, being about ten miles from both places. It was a good-looking house, with piazzas and balconies, and a large open plain in front. Beyond this place is a thick forest. Behind the house is another open plain, intercepted by a belt of forest. Behind this is Burns' house, or, as it is called, the White House. The Brigade remained all Friday night and Saturday defending the ford; for it was well known that General Jackson was trying to turn the right wing of our army, and as a road through the forest from the ford, it was an important position to defend.

About eight o'clock on Saturday morning the firing was again commenced in our front beyond Chancellorsville. Our sharpshooters and advanced guards had engaged the enemy in the woods, and were steadily repulsing them. Here the fight continued without intermission until about two o'clock. The enemy were driven back over a mile. From the entrance of the wood we could see column after column forcing back the enemy, who were fiercely disputing every inch of ground. About this time the fight was raging furiously on the right. Hayman's brigade, Third

Corps, was forming into line on the right, the Thirty-seventh New York Volunteers (Irish Rifles) were in front, and before two companies were formed the enemy burst upon them. After a few moments' desperate fighting, the Thirty-seventh had to fall back by a flank movement, and were only supported by the First New York, Fifth and Third Michigan, and Nineteenth Maine. The Thirty-seventh lost heavily in this short but fierce encounter. The Eleventh Army Corps, under command of General Howard, had taken up their position commanding the Gordonsville road, about four miles beyond Chancellorsville. Their left was supported by the Third Army Corps, while the Fifth and Twelfth lay on their rear.

About three o'clock in the afternoon the advance corps of the rebel army attacked the Eleventh Corps. The firing here for some time was terrifically grand. The rebels kept up one continuous and destructive fire of cannon and musketry, which threw the Eleventh Corps into a regular panic. General Howard did all that a brave man could to rally them, but in vain; for they retreated pell-mell back on Gordonsville, abandoning their cannon, ammunition, and wagons. In the midst of this panic I met the brave but ill-fated General Berry coolly and cheerfully advancing to their support. He renewed the attack, keeping the enemy in check. The Seventh New Jersey of this division took six colors.   The Excelsior brigade, the Jersey brigade, Mott's brigade, and Hayman's brigade nobly supported General Berry, who unfortunately fell in trying to gain the position abandoned by the Eleventh Corps.

The breaking of the right wing left our troops in front in danger of being outflanked; so they had to fall back on Chancellorsville.   General Hooker had also to remove his headquarters.   General Meagher had to throw a line across the road and into the wood at Scott's Mills, in order to intercept the panic-stricken fugitives, who came rushing along; but, finding their retreat thus cut off, had to rejoin the army.   The result of the day's fighting was, that our troops had driven back the enemy over a mile in the centre; and, had sufficient re-enforcements been thrown in to follow up our advantage, the enemy might have been crushed. On account of the defalcation of the Eleventh Army Corps, re-enforcements had to be thrown in, in order to maintain our position; for, if Jackson forced our right wing, our centre was too far advanced, and would be crushed.   So our troops had to fall back, forming a more direct line of battle.

SUNDAY, MAY 3.—About five o'clock in the morning the battle was resumed, the batteries in our front vomiting forth their horrid missiles of death.   Indeed, the battle opened so fiercely that the booming of artillery shook the earth around, as if convulsed by an earthquake. About eight o'clock in the morning General Meagher received orders to advance the Brigade to the front, to support the Fifth Maine Battery. As we marched through the columns that lined the way, we were loudly and repeatedly cheered. With our general at its head, the Brigade marched as steadily and coolly as if on parade. As we marched through the woods, shot and shell were poured like hail upon us. When the general reached the end of the road, he turned the head of the column and deployed into the woods. His escapes here were almost miraculous; for, though men were falling on every side, he boldly rode on, all the time cheering the men by word and example. Here a shell burst behind him, where we had just left, killing four of our men.

The Brigade remained in the woods for about two hours, under a most destructive fire of shot and shell, which killed two officers and several men. The Fifth Maine Battery was placed at the opening of the wood, commanding the plain towards Chancellorsville. This battery was well worked, and did good execution; for, not until all the men and horses were killed or wounded did it cease firing. Corporal H. Lebroke and one private alone remained, and finding themselves unable to work the guns, they blew up the caissons. It was then that the Brigade was ordered to their relief. The Brigade again steadily formed line and dashed into the open plain, pouring one destructive fire on the enemy, who were advancing to seize the guns, which drove them back in confusion. Some of our men fell; but the others seized the ropes and dragged the guns with them, General Meagher all the time directing the movement.

Here the remnant of the Irish Brigade—for it numbered only about five hundred and twenty men going into action—did good service to the Union; for, had the rebels seized the battery and turned it upon our army, a regular panic might have ensued, for at the same time several regiments on the right and left were giving way. As we reached the plain at the end of the wood, General Hancock rode up to General Meagher, and very emphatically called out—

" General Meagher, you command the retreat."

The Brigade was next placed in a wood on the left of the White House.

A continual fire of musketry was kept up through the woods. At one time the enemy succeeded on the right in forcing our lines from the wood into the open plain; but our batteries, particularly Randolph's, opened such a fierce, destructive fire on them of grape and canister, that they were literally mowed down in hundreds. A dense, sulphurous fog of smoke obscured the plain, while high above the shouts and cheers of the combatants rose the volcanic din of artillery. This continued 'all through Sunday, until night threw its welcome veil of silence over the combatants. From the dense volumes of smoke that arose from Chancellorsville House and the forest in our front, it was evident that they were on fire. This was the more melancholy, as the house was used as a hospital, and the wood was full of our dead and wounded. So thick was the smoke from the burning forest and the continual firing, that the plain was obscured. Indeed, it was sad to reflect that our brave wounded companions were left to perish the most horrible of all deaths. Yet, such are the awful casualties of war. Our troops were engaged all Sunday night and Monday morning in throwing up a strong line of breastworks on the right and left. These were lined with troops, with re-enforcements behind, so that this position seemed almost impregnable.

The enemy's batteries continued to shell us fiercely all through Monday, killing and wounding several of our men, and struck the trees near General Meagher. Rain fell in torrents on Tuesday, making a regular pond of the camp. As we were not allowed any tents, we had to rest ourselves as best we could upon the wet ground, under one of the most drenching rains I have ever witnessed. There was an ominous silence throughout the camp on Tuesday, now and then enlivened by a fusilade of musketry between our pickets and the enemy's. We were so wearied and exhausted on Tuesday night, that we threw ourselves upon the wet ground. About ten o'clock we were aroused by an aid, who ordered us to be ready for marching in half an hour. We jumped up, saddled our horses, and remained so for nearly two hours, when a further order came that we would not march for the night. We lay down again in our wet blankets, pools of water around us, and were trying to compose ourselves to sleep, when we were again ordered to get ready for the march. Never did an unfortunate army suffer a more wretched or wearisome march. We had to march along a new road just cut through the forest; the rain was pouring upon us in torrents, converting the road into a regular mass of sticky mud and pools of water; men and horses rolled over in trying to drag themselves through it, and I am sure several of them must have perished. Next day we recrossed the Rappahannock, the men wearied and dispirited, and the different commands returned to their old camps.

Never did an army go into action in better spirits, or more confident of success, than the Army of the Potomac under General Joe Hooker. His popularity with the army was great, and their confidence in him unbounded. His fine martial bearing commanded their respect, his fighting qualities their admiration, and his courteous, gentlemanly demeanor their love. With such a splendid army, full of confidence in themselves and their general, every one felt sure of a glorious victory. The admirable disposition made by General Hooker of his troops for battle confirmed this good opinion, but jealousies and private piques among some of his generals, and some other causes, marred his well-laid plans, and converted what promised to be a glorious victory into a shameful defeat. Sedgwick, who commanded the left wing at Fredericksburg, by unaccountable delay, lost an opportunity of occupying the heights, and his retreat across the river does not appear to be in accordance with his instructions. Again, the defalcation of the Eleventh Corps on the right flank had a disastrous *morale* on the whole army; add to this the want of co-operation by the cavalry, from whom so much had been expected, the differences and jealousies of certain generals, General Hooker being stunned at a critical moment by the bursting of a shell, the torrents of rain that flooded the country and threatened to sweep off the pontoons,—all contributed to frustrate General Hooker's well-laid plans, and to compel him to seek safety for his army by recrossing the river.

### INCIDENTS.

Every battle-field is full of incidents of the most painful kind, or hairbreadth escapes.

As we dragged out the battery, the cheering and excitement were unbounded, and the rebel batteries continued raining shot and shell around us. Here Captain Lynch was killed, being cut right through the centre with a solid shot.

When we fell back to the woods I was leaning against a tree, General Meagher at the other side talking to me, when a bullet struck the tree over our heads. I remarked—

"General, that was fired by a sharpshooter; they have range of you; we'd better leave this."

"Oh, no; it's but a chance shot."

Just as he spoke another bullet lodged behind our heads.

"They are improving, general," I remarked.

"Well, yes; I think it is time to leave now."

"I thought so long since, general."

I was riding across the plain in front of Chancellorsville House, when a shell burst right in front of me. Fortunately there was another officer just before me, who got the whole contents of it.

Captain Byron, of the Eighty-eighth, had a tan slut named Fan. Fan went into every battle, and while the firing was brisk lay down behind a big log or in some other secure place; and when a lull would follow she'd sally out, and run along the regiment to see if any of her friends were killed or hurt.

She was very much attached to a man of the company, who during the firing fell mortally wounded. When Fan came up to him, she threw herself on him and cried, she wept and licked him, while the poor fellow would throw out his hand to pat her as he feebly exclaimed, " Poor Fan ! poor Fan !"

The scene in the woods was fearful to contemplate; after we were driven back, the woods took fire, burning up our dead and helpless wounded. As they were between both lines, there was no chance of aiding them. We could hear the shrieks and groans of the poor fellows in their desperate agony. I am told that over seven hundred charred and burned bodies were afterwards found at this spot.

After the battle of Chancellorsville, General Meagher again applied to be allowed to recruit his brigade, now reduced to a battalion of a few hundred men. Not receiving a favorable answer, he tendered his resignation, which was accepted in the following order:

ADJUTANT-GENERAL'S OFFICE,
WASHINGTON, D. C., May 14, 1863.

Sir—Your resignation has been accepted by the President of the United States, to take effect this day.

I am, sir, very respectfully, your obedient servant,

JAMES A. HARDIE,
Assistant Adjutant-General.

To Brigadier-General T. F. MEAGHER,
United States Volunteers.

On the evening of the 19th the general assembled his little command, four hundred strong, and took leave of them. The scene was deeply interesting. Few present were unmoved. The Brigade having been formed into a hollow square, inside stood its general— the pride of the last of the brave men whom he had over and over again led to the deadliest assaults— there he stood, to withdraw from their command, which had been his highest ambition; and this withdrawal was in proof of his devotion to them, and a protest against the exaction of an accumulation of labors which should fairly devolve upon a full brigade. General Caldwell and other visitors were also within the square, and after some excellent music had been discoursed by the fine band of the Fourteenth Connecticut Volunteers, General Meagher spoke as follows his parting address:

*To my Officers and Soldiers,*
  *My Countrymen and Comrades in Arms:*

A positive conviction of what I owed to your reputation, to the honor of our race, and to my own conscience, compelled me a few days ago to tender to the President of the United States my resignation of this command. I shall not recapitulate the reasons which induced and justified me to do so. It would be superfluous. There is not a man in this command who is not fully aware of the reasons which compelled me to resign, and there is not a man who does not thoroughly appreciate and approve it. Suffice it to say that, the Irish Brigade no longer existing, I felt that it would be perpetuating a great deception were I to retain the authority and rank of a brigadier-general nominally commanding the same; I therefore conscientiously, though most reluctantly, resigned my command. That resignation has been accepted, and as your general I now bid you an affectionate farewell. I cannot do so, however, without leaving on record the assurance of the happiness, the gratitude and pride with which I revert to the first days of the Irish Brigade, when it struggled in its infancy and was sustained alone by its native strength and instincts ; and retrace from the field, where it first displayed its brilliant gallantry, all the efforts, all the hardships, all the privations, all the sacrifices which have made its history—brief though it be – sacred and inestimable. Sharing with the humblest soldier freely and heartily all the hardships and dangers of the battle-field—never having ordered an advance that I did not take the lead myself—I thank God that I have been spared to do justice to those whose heroism deserves from me a grateful commemoration ; and that I have been preserved to bring comfort to those who have lost fathers, husbands, and brothers in the soldiers who have fallen for a noble government under the green flag. My life has been a varied one, and I have passed through many distracting scenes. But never has the river that flowed beside my cradle, never have the mountains that overlooked the paths of my childhood, never have the old walls that claimed the curiosity and research of maturer days, been effaced from my memory. As at first—as in nature—the beautiful and glorious picture is indelible Not less vivid, not less uneffaceable, will be the recollection of my companionship with the Irish Brigade in the service of the United States. The graves of many hundreds of brave and devoted soldiers, who went to death with all the radiance and enthusiasm of the noblest chivalry, are so many guarantees and pledges that, as long as there remains one officer or soldier of the Irish Brigade, so long shall there be found for him, for his family and little ones, if any there be, a devoted friend in

THOMAS FRANCIS MEAGHER.

At the conclusion of the address, and after the men had given vent to their feelings by vociferous cheers, the officers came forward and shook hands with the general, bidding him an affectionate adieu. Then the general passed along the lines and shook each and every soldier by the hand, saying "Good-by" and "God bless you" to each; and during all this, many a manly eye was filled with tears. The general then turned over the command to Col. Patrick Kelly, of the Eighty-eighth, who promptly dismissed his little column.

Previous to taking his departure, the following addresses were presented to him by the different regiments:

### FAREWELL ADDRESS OF THE OFFICERS OF THE SIXTY-NINTH, SIXTY-THIRD, AND EIGHTY-EIGHTH REGIMENTS, NEW YORK STATE VOLUNTEERS, IRISH BRIGADE.

> CAMP OF THE IRISH BRIGADE, FIRST DIVISION,
> SECOND ARMY CORPS, ARMY OF THE POTOMAC,
> FALMOUTH, VA., May 20, 1863.

*To Brigadier-General Thomas F. Meagher,*
*late Commanding Irish Brigade:*

The undersigned officers of the original regiments of the Irish Brigade, in the field, having learned with deep regret that you have been compelled by reasons of paramount importance to tender your resignation as General of the Brigade, and that the Government having accepted your resignation, you are about to separate yourself from us, desire in this manner, as the most emphatic and courteous, to express to you the sorrow we personally feel at your departure, and the sincere and heartfelt affection we entertain, and shall ever entertain for you under all circumstances, and changes of time and place.

We regard you, general, as the originator of the Irish Brigade in the service of the United States; we know that to your influence and energy the success which it earned during its organization is mainly due; we have seen you since it first took the field—some eighteen months since—sharing its perils and hardships on the battle-field and in the bivouac; always at your post, always inspiring your command with that courage and devotedness which has made the Brigade historical, and by word and example cheering us on when fatigue and dangers beset our path; and we would be ungrateful, indeed, did we forget whatever glory we have obtained in many a hard-fought field, and whatever honor we have been privileged to shed on the sacred land of our nativity, that to you, general, is due, to a great extent, our success and our triumphs.

In resigning the command of the remnant of the Brigade, and going back to private life in obedience to the truest dictates of honor and conscience, rest assured, general, that you take with you the confidence and affection of every man in our regiments, as well as the esteem and love of the officers of your late command.

With this sincere assurance, we are, general, your countrymen and companions in arms—

P. Kelly, Colonel, Eighty-eighth New York, Irish Brigade; R. C. Bentley, Lieutenant-Colonel commanding Sixty-third New York, James E. McGee, Captain, commanding Sixty-ninth New York; William J. Nagle, Captain, commanding Eighty-eighth New York; James Saunders, Captain, Sixty-ninth New York; John Smith, Major, Eighty-eighth New York; P. J. Condon, Captain, Sixty-third New York, Company G; John H. Donovan, Captain, Sixty-ninth New York; Richard Moroney, Captain, Sixty-ninth New York; John H. Gleeson, Captain, Sixty-third New York, Company B; Maurice W. Wall, Captain and Acting Assistant Adjutant-General; D. P. Conyngham, Captain, Acting Aide-de-Camp; Thomas Touhey, Sixty-third New York, Company I; John J. Blake, Captain, Company B, Eighty-eighth New York; Robert H. Milliken, Captain, Sixty-ninth New York; Garrett Nagle, Captain, Sixty-ninth New York; John Dwyer, Captain, Sixty-third New York; Michael Gallagher, Captain, Eighty-eighth New York; Laurence Reynolds, Surgeon, Sixty-third New York; F. Reynolds, Surgeon, Eighty-eighth New York; Richard Powell, Assistant Surgeon, Eighty-eighth New York ; James J. Purcell, Assistant Surgeon, Sixty-third New York ; Charles Smart, Assistant Surgeon, Sixty-third New York ; Richard P. Moore, Captain Sixty-third New York, Company A ; John C. Foley, Adjutant, Eighty-eighth New York ; John W. Byron, First-Lieutenant, Eighty-eighth New York, Company E ; D. F. Sullivan, First-Lieutenant, and Regimental Quartermaster, Sixty-ninth New York ; James J. McCormack, Lieutenant and Quartermaster, Sixty-third New York : John O'Neil, Lieutenant, Eighty-eighth New York ; William McClelland, Second-Lieutenant, Eighty-eighth New York, Company G ; John Madigan, Lieutenant, Eighty-eighth New York : James J. Smith, First-Lieutenant and Adjutant, Sixty-ninth New York ; Edmund B. Nagle, Second-Lieutenant, Eighty-eighth New York, Company D ; Miles McDonald First-Lieutenant and Adjutant, Sixty-third New York ; John J. Hurley, First-Lieutenant, Sixty-third New York, Company I ; Edward B. Carroll, Second-Lieutenant, Sixty-third New York, Company B ; James Gallagher, Second-Lieutenant, Sixty-third New York, Company F ; John Ryan, First-Lieutenant, Sixty-third New York, Company G ; Matthew Hart, Second-Lieutenant, Sixty-third New York, Company K ; Bernard S. O'Neil, First-Lieutenant, Sixty-ninth New York ; John Dillon Mulhall, First-Lieutenant, Sixty-ninth New York ; Matthew Murphy, First-Lieutenant, Sixty-ninth New York ; Luke Brennan, Second-Lieutenant, Sixty-ninth New York ; Robert Laffin, Second-Lieutenant, Sixty-ninth New York ; W. L. D. O'Grady, Second-Lieutenant, Eighty-eighth New York, Company H ; P. J. O'Connor, First-Lieutenant, Sixty-third New York, Company D ; Edward Lee, First-Lieutenant, Sixty-third New York, Company A ; Patrick Maher, First-Lieutenant, Sixty-third New York, Company G ; David Burke, Lieutenant, Sixty-ninth New York ; Martin Scully, First-Lieutenant, Sixty-ninth New York ; Richard A. Kelly, First Lieutenant, Sixty-ninth New York ; Joseph M. Burns, Lieutenant, Sixty-ninth New York ; James E. Byrne, Lieutenant, Eighty-eighth New York ; Dominick Connolly, Second-Lieutenant, Sixty-third New York, Company H ; John J. Sellors, Second-Lieutenant, Sixty-third New York ; William Quirk, Captain, Sixty-third New York, Company E ; Patrick Chambers, First-Lieutenant, Sixty-third New York, Company H ; Patrick Callaghan,

First-Lieutenant, Company G, Sixty-ninth New York ; Patrick Ryder, Captain, Eighty-eighth New York; Patrick M. Haverty, First-Lieutenant, and Regimental Quartermaster, Eighty-eighth New York.

----

## NON-COMMISSIONED OFFICERS OF THE EIGHTY-EIGHTH REGIMENT TO GENERAL MEAGHER.

CAMP OF THE EIGHTY-EIGHTH NEW YORK STATE VOLUNTEERS,
May 21, 1863.

*To Brigadier General Thomas F. Meagher :*

BELOVED GENERAL—Seldom, if ever, has a more mournful duty devolved on a soldier than now devolves on a few of that devoted band of Irishmen that rallied at your call around the green flag of our native land, and who are here now to evince their sincere and heartfelt sorrow at the loss of an indomitable leader, a brave companion, and a stern patriot, as well as to extend their congratulations at your returning in all your manly pride and spotless integrity to the domestic scenes of your own fireside.

Appreciating as we do the motives that actuated your resignation, nevertheless, we feel that whatever advantages may accrue to us, if any, are purchased at too great a cost, and tells deeply the feelings and relations that existed between the general and his men.

The first to lead us to victory, we fondly hoped it would be your proudest honor, as it was your highest ambition, to lead us back again to our homes ; but, through the inscrutable wisdom of an all-wise War Department, it will be reserved for you instead to welcome back what has been, or will be, left of what was once known, and proudly so, as Meagher's Irish Brigade.

Present to our lady patron, Mrs. Meagher, our happiest congratulations at your safe return ; and assure her, through us, that what is left of the Eighty-eighth will still endeavor to hold, by a high soldierly bearing, that claim on her affections as of old, when you yourself led us to battle.

In conclusion, general, we tender to you the following resolutions, and, believe us, they are not the selfish offerings of interested followers, nor the cool, well-digested, and carefully worded productions of sage and matured veterans ; but they are, general, the spontaneous offerings of young heads, young hearts, and young blood, that will always rally at your call around that flag for which you have sacrificed so much, and braved so many dangers ; and trusting, general, that the recollections of this meeting will in after years compensate for many days of wearied toil and profitless hardships, it is, therefore,

RESOLVED—That we, the non-commissioned officers of the Eighty-eighth Regiment New York State Volunteers, duly authorized and appointed in behalf of the regiment, express in words too feeble to convey their sorrow, their regret, at the retirement of their General, Thomas Francis Meagher.

RESOLVED—That in tendering his resignation he was prompted by the highest chivalric principles and unselfish aims, and, consequently, meets the approbation of his men.

RESOLVED—That the foregoing resolutions and address be presented by a committee of the non-commissioned officers of the Eighty-eighth Regiment New York State Volunteers.

Signed on behalf of the regiment—

Patrick McCabe, Sergeant-Major ; Thomas Smith, Quartermaster-Sergeant ; Richard A. Dowdall, Hospital-Steward ; John McDonnell, Commissary-Sergeant. First Sergeants—William J. O'Conner, Company A ; Richard Finnen, Company B ; Benedict J. O'Driscoll, Company C ; R. McDonald, Company D ; George Ford, Company E ; James Carr, Company F ; Lawrence Buckley, Company G ; John Meighan, Company H ; Michael McGrane, Company I ; Henry Southwell, Company K. Sergeants—John Desmond, Company C ; Richard S. Harrison, Company C ; James Fox, Company C ; Patrick O'Neill, Company B ; George Geoghegan, Company B ; Hugh Curry, Company K ; Timothy J. Murray, Company I ; Dennis Leonard, Company I ; Thomas McDonald, Company I ; John McGowan, Company D ; John B. Sparks, Company A ; Joseph Hyland, Company E ; Edward Wilson, Company E ; John Morton, Company E ; Thomas Hart, Company E.

RESOLUTIONS OF THE OFFICERS OF THE ONE HUNDRED AND SIXTEENTH REGIMENT, PENNSYLVANIA VOLUNTEERS, IRISH BRIGADE.

HEADQUARTERS 116TH PENNSYLVANIA VOLUNTEERS,
IRISH BRIGADE, HANCOCK'S DIVISION,
SECOND ARMY CORPS, May 18, 1863.

At a meeting of the commissioned officers of the One Hundred and Sixteenth Pennsylvania Volunteers, Major St. Clair A. Mulholland was called to the chair, and First-Lieutenant Louis J. Sacriste was appointed secretary. The following preamble and resolutions were proposed and unanimously adopted :

WHEREAS, By the acceptance of the resignation of our beloved general, Thomas Francis Meagher, we have been deprived of one who was always solicitous for our comfort and welfare ; therefore, be it

RESOLVED—That by the resignation of Brigadier-General Meagher this Brigade, and especially this regiment, experiences an irreparable loss—one which is felt alike by officers and men ; we have been deprived of a leader whom we all would have followed to death, if necessary ; a leader whose name was sufficient to strike terror into the hearts of his foes, and excite admiration in the hearts of his co-patriots in arms.

RESOLVED—That in the discharge of his official duties he exhibited alike those qualities which only a true soldier can possess—when on duty a strict disciplinarian, and when off duty an affable, agreeable, and kind companion.

RESOLVED—That as a soldier he was foremost in the battle, offering his life as a sacrifice for the cause of liberty and the Constitution of his adopted country—which country has lost by his resignation one of its most patriotic generals, one of its most daring soldiers, and the army one of its brightest ornaments.

RESOLVED—That in his retirement to civil life he carries with him our most sincere wishes for his future welfare, and we earnestly hope that his future life may be as successful as his past career has been brilliant and honorable.

St. Clair A. Mulholland, Major, commanding One Hundred and Sixteenth Pennsylvania Volunteers ; John Teed, Captain, commanding Company G, One Hundred and Sixteenth Pennsylvania Volunteers ; S. G. Willaner, Captain, commanding Company A, One Hundred and Sixteenth Pennsylvania Volunteers ; Garrett Nowlan, Captain, commanding Company B, One Hundred and Sixteenth Pennsylvania Volunteers ; Louis J. Sacriste, First-Lieutenant, commanding Company D, One Hundred and Sixteenth Pennsylvania Volunteers ; Richard H. Wade, Lieutenant and Quartermaster, One Hundred and Sixteenth Pennsylvania Volunteers ; H. D. Price, First-Lieutenant and Acting Adjutant, One Hundred and Sixteenth Pennsylvania Volunteers ; Francis Crawford, First-Lieutenant, One Hundred and Sixteenth Pennsylvania Volunteers ; George Roeder, First-Lieutenant, Company A, One Hundred and Sixteenth Pennsylvania Volunteers ; William B. Hartman, Assistant Surgeon, One Hundred and Sixteenth Pennsylvania Volunteers ; William H. Tyrrell, Second-Lieutenant, Company C, One Hundred and Sixteenth Pennsylvania Volunteers ; George Halpin, Second-Lieutenant, Company A, One Hundred and Sixteenth Pennsylvania Volunteers ; Thomas McKnight, Second-Lieutenant, Company B, One Hundred and Sixteenth Pennsylvania Volunteers.

When General Meagher resigned his command of the Brigade it was reduced to about five hundred men. Its original strength was—Sixty-ninth, about seven hundred and thirty ; Eighty-eighth, eight hundred ; Sixty-third, close on one thousand ; Captain Hogan's battery, one hundred and forty-four men ; Captain McMahon's, one hundred and fifty-four. The Twenty-eighth and Twenty-ninth Massachusetts and One Hundred and Sixteenth Pennsylvania were nearly full regiments when they joined the Brigade.

## CHAPTER XIX.

General Meagher leaves.—The Brigade at Gettysburg.—Father Corby gives it his benediction before the battle.—The Brigade at Mine Run and Rapidan.—Retires to winter-quarters previous to its departure for New York.

NOTHING of importance transpired in military circles for some time after this. The Brigade remained in camp—now a brigade only in name. After the resignation of General Meagher its history as a brigade ceases until the opening of Grant's campaign, when its partly recruited ranks again distinguished themselves in the fierce and bloody battles before Richmond.

However, the Brigade continued to follow the fortunes of the Army of the Potomac, and to participate in the different engagements. At Gettysburg it took an active part in the fierce assault made by the Second Corps.

The handful of men, before going into that fierce battle, knelt down; the excellent chaplain, Father Corby, piously raised his hands, and gave them his benediction. They then jumped to their feet, closed up their lines, and charged.

I will give a short *resumé* of this great battle of the war.

General Hooker was removed while the army was on its march to Gettysburg.

He was replaced by General Meade, an officer of Irish descent.

On Wednesday, 1st of July, 1863, the advance corps of our army (the First and Eleventh), after a harassing march, came up with the enemy; but, being vastly outnumbered, were repulsed, with a large loss, including Major-General Reynolds and a number of his most gallant officers. The broken corps, however, fell back on the approaching columns under the personal lead of General Meade. A new position was rapidly chosen, and the troops massed and in perfect order of battle by the afternoon of Thursday, at this side of Gettysburg, near the cemetery. Our centre occupied the heights; the Second and Third Corps, under General Sickles, formed the left wing; while the First and Eleventh Corps were on the right. The other troops which had not yet arrived were appointed to fall in, as they appeared, as reserves.

About half-past four P. M., our line, which had commenced an advance, was met by a terrific cannonade, opened on its centre and left, from the rebel batteries, masked with woods and grain fields. Our rifled-guns replied with effect, and for two hours the air seemed literally filled with screaming messengers of death. Then, with a defiant yell, the rebels rushed forward to attack the extreme left of our line; but Sickles' forces gallantly withstood the shock, and a large number of pieces of artillery being immediately placed in position made terrible havoc in the opposing ranks. Our centre and left centre then advanced with loud cheers and pushed the enemy from point to point through the valley and up the heights beyond, where many of them were bayoneted and taken prisoners, while secreting themselves behind trees and ledges. A space of several hundred yards existing between the left of the Second Corps, Third Division, and the right of the next corps on the left, the rebels threw forward heavy columns of infantry, overpowering the skirmishers and filling the gap, delivering at the time a deadly flank fire on our forces. Here General Zook, of New York, and other gallant officers fell.

Our forces now fell back a short distance, when they were relieved with fresh troops. Meanwhile the rebels were slowly gaining ground on our left, and it seemed as if our decimated and dispirited ranks would be forced back, when suddenly the Fifth Corps came pouring forward on the Baltimore Turnpike, and threw themselves into the breach with a power and energy that nothing could withstand.

Our artillery worked with an energy almost superhuman, and four times the rebels charged upon that part of our artillery across the plains, but were each time repulsed with great slaughter, and Lee's great flank movement was met and checkmated.

General Meade superintended the movements during the entire day, and night closed with the advantage on the side of our arms, and our forces occupied Gettysburg.

On the morning of Friday, the 3d inst., at daylight, the batteries on the right of the rebel line opened on our left, and their infantry and sharpshooters attacked our right wing. They did so with a sudden impetuosity and gallantry that drove our skirmishers and front line from their intrenchments, and it was only by the aid of our splendidly served batteries and the persistent valor of the Twelfth Corps that the ground was retaken.

Several hours of continued silence followed this repulse. At one o'clock the enemy fired two shots, apparently as signals for the grandest artillery fight ever witnessed on this continent. Before a minute had elapsed, it is estimated that over eighty guns opened on us. Our batteries returned the compliment with interest. The air seemed literally thick with iron, and for more than an hour it seemed impossible that man or beast could live through it. Under cover of this *feu d'enfer.* Lee advanced his columns of infantry, and made several desperate attempts to carry our lines by assault; but each successive attempt was repulsed with terrible havoc to their ranks. After an hour's terrific cannonading the fire grew less intense for a short time, but was again renewed for a little while, with great spirit, during which another assault was made by their infantry. This, however, was repulsed with slaughter, and hundreds of the rebels threw down their arms and asked for quarter. Nearly the entire brigade of General Garnett surrendered, and Garnett, himself wounded, barely made his escape.

During this fierce assault—the boldest and grandest of the war—the Brigade held a copse of wood, which was swept by a part of the enemy's line. Here they defiantly stood, and as the enemy closed upon them they poured a most destructive volley into them, contributing materially to their confusion.

After the two repulses, the enemy withdrew his forces from the battle-field, leaving General Armistead and three thousand prisoners in our hands. In the interim, the enemy, as well as ourselves, had suffered heavily in prominent officers. General Barksdale, of Mississippi, had been killed, and his body was within our lines. In addition to the three thousand prisoners mentioned above, General Meade claims one thousand six hundred more, captured previous to the great fight on Friday. On our side, Generals Sickles, Hancock,

Gibbon, Meredith, Butterfield, Barlow, Graham, and Warren were wounded.  Generals Reynolds, Doubleday, Paul, and Zook were killed.  General Sickles was so badly wounded in the leg that it was subsequently amputated.

Here the remnant of the Brigade nobly did its duty, though exposed to the fiercest fire of the enemy.  On the 2d of July, the Second Corps was ordered up to support the Third Corps, which was engaged in the front, and in danger of being crushed and overpowered by overwhelming force.  The First Division—of which the Brigade was a part—occupied the left of the corps.

To the left of the Second Corps was a commanding eminence, and a position of importance.  A brigade of the Third Corps occupied this with a battery of artillery.  The rebels massed their troops and attacked the position.  So fierce was their charge, that they would have succeeded had not the First Division of the Second Corps advanced in support of their comrades.

In this charge the right was occupied by the Irish Brigade, commanded by Colonel Patrick Kelly.  The enemy occupied a strong position, sheltered by rocks and a belt of wood.  They were charged by the Brigade, which, after a heavy fight, succeeded in forcing back the enemy.

After the battle of Gettysburg, General Meade followed up the retreating rebels beyond the line of the Rappahannock. We were ready to support the advance; but the enemy gave us no chance, as they rapidly fell back, fiercely pursued by our cavalry. We had some firing between our pickets and the enemy's; but as soon as the Irish Brigade was sent on picket this ceased, for they and the enemy's pickets never fired at each other. When I asked an old soldier the cause, he replied : " Arrah, the moment we go out, we stack our arms, and they does the same. What good would it do to kill a few poor devils? and sure it looks like murder." This is poor Paddy's logic on the matter.

This was followed by the Mine Run campaign, but General Meade had to fall back, and on Monday, 12th November, the army had recrossed the Rapidan. Still it was followed up, with its flank threatened, and so it pursued its rearward march. On Tuesday, 13th November, the enemy's dismounted cavalry gave some annoyance and caused loss; and on the following day they made their appearance in pretty strong force, with artillery, which, from advanced and chosen positions, raked and assailed the Second Corps, then acting as the rear-guard of the infantry force. As the corps were at breakfast that morning, they first felt the immediate proximity of the enemy, whose shot and shell came ploughing through the advanced ranks, formed of the Fifty-second N. Y. V., " a conscript regiment," the men of which wavered and fell back on the old commands.

As this occurred, Colonel Frank, who commanded the Third Brigade, rode in their front and rallied them, crying out, "Stand, boys! follow me." Beyond them was the Second Brigade—or Irish Brigade—who coolly stood to their guns. Colonel Miles, too, rallied the lines. In a moment the panic subsided and the men stood coolly in their lines, though the shot and shell of the enemy were knocking them over pretty fast. Here my horse and some men beside me were killed by a shell. The lines now fell back behind the crest of the hill, and Ricketts' Battery having taken position, returned the enemy's killing compliments with interest. On the evening of the same day was fought the battle of Bristow Station, in which we were victorious.

We captured a battery of six guns, two battle-flags, killed two rebel colonels and took one colonel and about 750 men prisoners. In the capture of the guns the valor of our men was displayed to a remarkable degree. After the enemy had been driven from a position on which they had planted a battery —which was done by our artillery and infantry— General Warren ordered a detail to be made of ten men from each regiment of the corps to bring off the pieces. The work to be done was a hazardous one, but the boys shouted, as they started at a double-quick. The woods in the rear of the battery were full of graybacks, who, in all probability, would attempt to prevent their pets from falling into the hands of the Yankee soldiers. Our infantry and artillery would be powerless to help, as a shot from either would be as likely to kill one of our own as one of the rebel troops. But the selected men went off in the direction of the prizes, reached them, seized them, turned them towards their foe, fired a parting salute from such as the enemy, in his haste, had left loaded, then dragged them away by hand.

This was followed by another move in December, beyond the Rapidan, in which the enemy were driven back to their intrenched works, without bringing on any general engagement, and thus ended the campaign of 1863, and the services of the Irish Brigade under Brigadier-General Thomas F. Meagher.

## CHAPTER XX.

Introductory.—Gigantic efforts to crush the Rebellion.—Recruiting.—
Re-enlistment of veterans.—The Irish Brigade first to re-enlist.—Terms
of re-enlistment.—Return of the Brigade to New York.—Popular in-
difference.—Grand Banquet to the veterans by their officers.—Speeches
of General Meagher, &c., &c.

THE close of 1863 found the Army of the Potomac
encamped in winter-quarters, north of the Rapidan,
resting and recruiting, after its recent movements,
which, as is well known, were neither successful nor
creditable to the commanding generals. The exacting public, through their organs and mouthpieces,
loudly expressed their dissatisfaction ; and the War
Department appeared to think that a more gigantic
effort should be made, as well to subdue the rebellion
as to satisfy the popular wish and expectation. Nor
was the enemy less remiss in making preparations for
the coming struggle, which, from all indications,
promised to be not only deadly and desperate, but
finally decisive for one or other of the combatants.
Accordingly, recruiting for the Union Army was immediately recommenced with renewed energy at all

the principal depots, and the veterans were offered the most flattering inducements to re-enlist for another term. This re-enlistment first commenced in the Army of the Potomac, and I believe I am safe in say-ing that the Irish Brigade was the first to take the initiative. This noble example was immediately and steadily followed, until nearly two-thirds of the army had declared itself ready to re-enlist for the war.

The terms of re-enlistment were very liberal, the veterans receiving a large bounty and a furlough of thirty days, wherein to revisit home, family, and friends. No delay was made, the papers were com-pleted with the utmost zeal and activity, and the re-enlisted veterans of the Irish Brigade reached New York in safety, and in the most exuberant spirits, January 2d, 1864. Here, no elaborate reception of grateful enthusiasm greeted the handful of heroes— gallant remnants of many a bloody engagement. A brief paragraph in the morning papers announced to the citizens of New York that the Sixty-ninth, Sixty-third, and Eighty-eighth Regiments, represented by a few hundred veterans, were returning to their homes for a short period, to return again to the field with in-creased numbers and renewed ardor. The sparse and grimy columns were escorted by a company or two of the Sixty-ninth militia, and the immediate relatives of the members.

The officers who returned with the several commands were: Lieutenant-Colonel R. C. Bentley, commanding Sixty-third Regiment, together with Captains Touhey and Brady, Adjutant McDonald, Surgeon Reynolds, Lieutenants Lee and Chambers, and one hundred re-enlisted veterans. A company of fifty remained in the field, under the command of Captain Boyle.

The Sixty-ninth consisted of about the same number of men, under command of Captain Richard Moroney, Adjutant James J. Smith, Lieutenants O'Neill, Mulhall, Brennan, Mansergh, Quartermaster Sullivan, and Assistant-Surgeon J. J. Purcell.

The Eighty-eighth was under the command of Colonel Patrick Kelly, Captains Ryder, Burke, Lieutenants J. W. Byron, O'Grady, &c., Surgeon Richard Powell and Chaplain William Corby.

In order to make up for the lukewarmness on the part of the authorities, who were openly and malignantly opposed to the national cause and its supporters, the officers of the Brigade, those who had served and those still in service, met at the Whitney House, in Broadway, " for the purpose of taking immediate steps to welcome back to their homes, in a fitting manner, the faithful and brave men of the Brigade, and to tender them that tribute of hearty friendship and hospitality, which their noble conduct, for over two years, in the camp and in the field, in the fullest measure entitled them to receive at the hands of their officers." There was a full attendance of all the officers of the Brigade then in New York. General Meagher presided, and it was unanimously resolved, " that the object for which the meeting had been called should be carried out in the most effective manner. As a mark of the respect and friendship entertained by the officers for the men, by whose unflinching valor, steady discipline, and hardy endurance the fame of the Irish Brigade had been upheld during two years of the severest service—a respect and friendship which they could appropriately evince, now that a respite from the duties of the camp had restored the relations of equality, which, as citizens, they bore to each other—it was determined to invite the enlisted veterans of the Brigade, and those men who, through loss of limbs or health, had been honorably discharged the service, to a grand banquet, to be given in their honor by the general and commissioned officers."

This novel entertainment, which was at the same time a most grateful and touching tribute from brave officers to their humble but heroic comrades, took place at the appointed time in Irving Hall, January 16th, 1864. The following officers formed the committee of arrangements : Brigadier-General Thomas F. Meagher ; Surgeon William O'Meagher, Sixty-ninth ; Captain

James E. McGee, Sixty-ninth; Captain W. J. Nagle, Eighty-eighth; Captain Thomas W. Cartwright, Sixty-third; Captain Richard Moroney, Sixty-ninth; Dr. Philip O'Hanlon, Jr., Sixty-third; Captain M. W. Wall, Eighty-eighth; and Captain James B. Turner, A. A. G., Secretaries.

The men assembled at the City Hall about noon, where they formed in order, under command of Captain Moroney, and were reviewed by the mayor. Thence, headed by Dodworth's band, and accompanied by a number of the officers, they proceeded up Broadway to the banquet-hall, were they arrived a little after one o'clock, and were marched into the dining-hall, where a number of those disabled by the loss of limbs were already assembled. Five tables extended down the length of the hall, and at these the privates, to the number of about two hundred, were seated, the non-commissioned officers occupying a head table stretching across the room in front of the stage, on which was placed the band. The hall was tastefully decorated with flags—the war-worn banners of the Brigade and the newer ones presented by the merchants of New York appearing conspicuous among the gay ensigns which made the room brilliant. From the galleries, all round, hung American shields, with the names of the different engagements in which the Brigade had participated inscribed on them, as follows: "Yorktown,"

"Fair Oaks," "Gaines' Hill," "Savage's Station,"
" Peach Orchard," " Glendale," " White Oak Swamp,"
" Malvern Hills," "Antietam," " Fredericksburg,"
" Chancellorsville," " Bristow Station." On the centre
of the ladies' gallery, opposite the chairman's position,
was a military trophy, sustaining a shield, on which
was the name of " Gettysburg."

The galleries were filled with ladies, the mourning
weeds of many of whom testified to the loss of some
loved one, who, perhaps, in the pride of youth and
high spirit, had marched with the Brigade two short
years since. Mrs. Meagher and the ladies of some of
the officers occupied the stage-boxes.

Sergeant-Major O'Driscoll presided. When the
good things provided had received due attention, and
that portion of the entertainment arrived that is
usually designated "the feast of reason and the flow
of soul," General Meagher and the principal officers of
the Brigade entered the hall, accompanied by a number of gentlemen who had been invited to witness the
proceedings. Among them were Messrs. Daniel
Devlin, John O'Mahony, Hon. C. P. Daly, Captain
James B. Kirker, Captain W. F. Lyons, Rev. T. Quinn,
of Rhode Island; John McAuliffe, John Hennessy,
W. J. Hennessy, W. J. Florence, Barney Williams,
D. Bryant; Colonel Bagley, Sixty-ninth N. Y. N. G.;
Captain Tully, do. ; Colonel Brewster and Colonel

Farnham, of the Excelsior Brigade; Colonel Hammill, Sixty-sixth N. Y. V., and others whose names we cannot recall.

Sergeant-Major O'Driscoll, having called the company to order, General Meagher came forward and addressed them as follows:

"Sergeant O'Driscoll, non-commissioned officers, and privates, re-enlisted veterans of the Irish Brigade: Heartily concurring in the general wishes and instructions of my brother-officers of the Committee of Arrangements, of which I have the honor to be the chairman, I bid you welcome, a thousand times welcome to this table. Prohibited by the rules, as well as by the etiquette of military service, of testifying in the field to the services and devotion of the men constituting our commands, we avail ourselves of the first moment at our disposal to thank you, the rank and file, the bone and sinew, the stout hearts and the iron arms of the Armies of the Republic. The fortune of the private soldier is, indeed, an humble, and, I might almost say, a penal one. Having to endure the sunrays on the march, the blinding snows and chilling winds of winter, to plunge into the swollen torrent, or traverse the arid plains, nothing can possibly sustain him, unless it be a high and holy sense of the rectitude of the purpose in which he has taken up

arms, and with which he strikes. No glowing vision
of a monument erected by a nation, nor even by his
comrades in arms, can allure him to the dangerous
path. The private soldier of any army, but above all,
the private soldiers of the army whose banners are
consecrated to the laws which are the expressions to
us of the safeguard of popular rights, and the cause,
in an eminent degree, of civilization and liberty—per-
vading the soldiers of the armies everywhere, but especially in the armies called together by such a cause,
it may, indeed, be said of them, what an eloquent
European said of those who fell before the walls of
Buda, the consciousness of doing right impressed on
their dead features—that they were the nameless demigods of Liberty. No monument rises up in the anticipation of his future; he cannot expect that when
he returns either brave hands or fair hands can wreathe
the bays upon his bent or aching brow, or even antici-
pate that he will be remembered by those who most
heartily bade him leave the threshold of his home, and
go forth and do his duty like a man. Nevertheless,
there is a fame milder, and, perhaps, more sacred than
that which descends in bounteous plenitude upon the
head of the conspicuous officer, or upon those who
have signally distinguished themselves in battle.
There is not a private here, I do not believe that there
is a private in any of the national armies, who has

been under the fire of battle, and has returned maimed or in the freshness of his vigor to his home, who will not enjoy the fame with which the loving wife or venerable mother, or, prouder still, with which his children will remember his deeds. Soldiers, you may not have municipal authorities to welcome you at the gates, even of this imperial and hospitable city; you may not have regiments to go forth in all the finery of military paraphernalia to welcome you, after your onerous, tiresome, exacting duties; but with a love multiplied infinitely, multiplied by the dangers you have encountered, the labors you have resolutely and heroically performed, by the sacrifices of health and limb that you have incurred for the country that has given you shelter, and has maintained for you a magnificent sanctuary—for all these the wife of your choice will clasp you, as I am sure she has already done in hundreds of instances, still more dearly to her heart; for all that, with a still deeper sanctity, the wavering hand of the old woman who nourished you at her breast will impart her welcome on the threshold, and, perhaps, her farewell benediction. With tears she may impart it, but ah! they will be tears glowing with enthusiasm, and with an old mother's love. This, I say, is the fame, the milder, more obscure fame—if that be not a contradiction of terms—but, nevertheless, by reason of this, the more sacred

fame, which will be perpetuated for a generation or
two, or more, in the household, and amongst the relatives of the private soldier. In addition to this, of
much less consequence and of much less value, but
that which, I trust, will outlive in your happier recollections the war you return temporarily from to your
homes, is the gratitude which I am glad to express in
emphatic terms—the gratitude of the officers, who,
without your fidelity to them, without your heroic
bearing in the face of the enemy, without your unfaltering persistence, even though the danger threatened to overwhelm you, without which their reputation would have been but as idle wind. Upon the
graves and empty firesides of the private soldier, are
raised the trophies of the officer, whether of low or
superior rank. The officers of the Irish Brigade shall
ever hold it to be one of the most happy, as it is
surely one of the most proud recollections that can
possibly be linked with our relationship, that we have
been the first in a conspicuous way to acknowledge
the indebtedness of the officers to the private soldiers
of the Brigade. And I, who once commanded you,
do not hesitate to say, as I did not hesitate to say in
the presence of some of the highest authorities of the
Republic, that indeed promotion might be given to
me—a high rank in the army might be accorded; but
history has no power to bestow upon me any higher

19

distinction than that I have been the general in command of the Irish Brigade."

Sergeant-Major O'Driscoll, in the name of the non-commissioned officers and privates, returned thanks to General Meagher and the officers of the Brigade, and ended by proposing the health of General Meagher, which was toasted with cheers.

General Meagher briefly thanked the company for their good feelings towards himself. He then said he would ask them a question with regard to a charge that had been privately circulated regarding him—namely, that he had recklessly exposed the lives of the officers and men of his command. (Cries of "No, no.") He called on all present—officers as well as privates—to say whether he had ever brought them into danger, except when he had been ordered there? (Renewed cries of "No.") When he had brought them where danger was to be encountered, was he not the first in himself at the head of the column? ("Yes, yes.") He thanked them for this contradiction to the malicious falsehoods which had been asserted against him, and he hoped that this answer of the Irish Brigade would be sent not only over this land, but over Europe, where the enemies of the country had sympathizers and abettors.

Colonel Patrick Kelly, of the Eighty-eighth, was

then introduced, and was received with the most enthusiastic demonstrations of welcome from the men. He made a few remarks, and proposed—

" Our Dead Comrades—officers and soldiers of the Irish Brigade—their memory shall remain for life as green in our souls as the emerald flag, under which, doing battle for the United States, they fought and fell." Music—Dirge.

Colonel Nugent then came forward and was warmly received. He expressed the pleasure it gave him to meet the men of the Sixty-third, the Eighty-eighth, and his old command, the Sixty-ninth, and concluded by proposing as his toast :

" No negotiation, no compromise, no truce, no peace, but war to the last dollar and the last man, until every rebel flag be struck between the St. Lawrence and the Gulf, and swept everywhere, the world over, from land and sea."

Captain Magee proposed the health of Hon. Daniel Devlin, which was cordially drank.

Colonel Bentley, of the Sixty-third, then came forward and was received with cheers. He said, as the only officer of the Brigade not of Irish birth, he was proud of their achievements in this war. When history shall be written, the name of the Irish soldier shall take a high rank in the history of this war and country. In closing, he proposed the following toast :

"The Emmets of the Irish Brigade; they have been as true to the liberties of the country, as in another family and another generation they were true to the liberties of Ireland."

"Captain Gregg, assistant inspector-general of the Brigade, then proposed—

"The Irish soldiers in the national armies, North, South, East, and West; among them those of the Excelsior Brigade, Third Corps, Army of the Potomac."

Barney Williams was then introduced, and sang "The Bowld Soldier Boy," which was applauded to the echo.

Colonel Brewster, of the Excelsior Brigade, was then introduced, and was rapturously cheered. He said the two Brigades were twins in origin and services, for in the names he saw around him on the walls, he recognized those of the battles in which the Excelsior Brigade had served side by side with the Irish Brigade. Of that Brigade, one-half, at least, were Irish; his own regiment, he knew, were more than half Irish; and better soldiers, or men who went into a fight with heartier enthusiasm, he never knew. In conclusion, he proposed—

"The Irish Brigade; what there is left of it."

Colonel John O'Mahony was then introduced, and concluded a very appropriate speech by giving "The Memory of General Michael Corcoran, one of the noblest and best of men, whether considered as an Irishman or as an American. May you bear a part in fulfilling, under the leadership of the dauntless Meagher, the two dearest hopes of his heart—the restoration of the American Union and the liberation of Ireland!

The memory of General Corcoran was honored in solemn silence, all present rising and remaining standing while the band played a mournful dirge.

The health of Father Corby, chaplain of the Eighty-eighth Regiment, was then toasted.

The reverend gentleman briefly returned thanks.

General Meagher then proposed " The American Press," and called on Captain Lyons, of the *Herald*, who briefly responded. The healths of the merchants of New York, who presented the new flags of the Brigade; of Colonel Hammill, of the Sixty-sixth; of " Private Myles O'Reilly," and others, were drank. Captain Gosson was loudly called for by the soldiers, and made a humorous and characteristic speech, which was loudly cheered.

The company soon after dispersed.

Letters of apology were received from General Sickles and James T. Brady, who had been invited to be present. A letter was also received from John Savage, who was prevented from being present by absence from the city.

# CHAPTER XXI.

Reorganization of the Brigade.—Return to Virginia.—Winter-quarters and winter sports.—Recruits.—Kilpatrick's raid.—Lieutenant-Colonel James Kelly in command.—Colonel Tom Smyth succeeds him.—Presentation of a green flag to Twenty-eighth Massachusetts.

STEADY progress was made in reorganizing the Brigade during the months of January and February, under the able management of Colonel Nugent, Captain McGee, Adjutant Smith, and their assistants.

The Sixty-ninth Regiment was rapidly filled up to the minimum by the addition of several new companies, and the Brigade, on the expiration of the veteran furlough, returned to camp in the field early in February, while many officers remained behind to forward the recruiting of still further levies. Several old and new officers received commissions in the various regiments, among whom were Captains Wall, Blake, R. A. Kelly, John C. Foley, B. S. O'Neill, R. H. Milliken, John Smith, J. H. Gleeson, etc.

On the return of the first instalments of the new Brigade to Virginia, nothing particular was to be done in the army, except the construction of winter-quarters and picket duty. There was plenty of time for amuse-

ment, to which every one devoted himself with an
ardor characteristic of military life. Ball parties and
horse-racing filled up the time pleasantly, and served
to attract numbers of visitors, even from considerable
distances. Thus, at a grand ball given at the Second
Corps headquarters, about this period, numbers of distinguished citizens were present from Washington,
Philadelphia, New York, etc. Nor was the Brigade
remiss or backward in taking a prominent place in
this pursuit of pleasure. Indeed, both the Brigade
and the Legion were notorious throughout the army
for the pleasurable state of excitement which was constantly kept up in and around their precincts, and
when frolic and whiskey were not to be found in either,
every thing looked blue generally, and "all was quiet
in the Army of the Potomac." Who, for instance, can
forget the celebrations of "Patrick's Day," in the
Brigade, when deputations of horse, foot, and artillery
from all parts of the army thronged to witness or join
the various sports of the day? And it was no unusual
circumstance to see as many thus placed *hors du combat*
as in a decent skirmish with the enemy. The "Day"
was always inaugurated with all due decorum—first
by a grand Mass and panegyric in honor of the illustrious apostle; but when this solemn duty was accomplished to the satisfaction of our worthy and venerated
chaplains (who sometimes witnessed the more exciting

part of the festivities), a loose rein was given to pleasure, and the fun was both fast and furious. This part of the celebration, however, was not devoid of an intellectual element. Excellent speeches, toasts, and poetical effusions distinguished the occasions in the most marked and agreeable manner. Certainly one of the best speeches I ever heard was delivered at the banquet of 1864 by General Caldwell, then commanding the division—a brilliant and masterly exposition of Celtic wit, eloquence, intellect, and patriotism. And Doctor Reynolds, as the poet laureate of the Brigade, furnished several meritorious poetic effusions for this and other occasions.

Meantime new companies were added to the Brigade: the regiments were nearly filled up to the minimum number, so as to enable the several commands to have higher officers. Nor was this activity confined to the New York regiments. Both the Twenty-eighth Massachusetts and the One Hundred and Sixteenth Pennsylvania Volunteers received large additions to their thinned ranks; and thus the new promised to rival— in numbers at least—the palmiest days of the old Brigade.

About the close of the month of February, the cavalry under Kilpatrick and Colonel Dahlgren, made a dashing raid in the rear of Lee's army, completely cutting off his communications for several days, penetrating the outer defences of Richmond, causing an immense amount of damage to the enemy. This exploit for a time excited high hopes of a speedy termination of the rebellion ; or at least, a successful beginning of an active campaign for the same results. But its immediate consequences did not justify the expectation, and quiet again reigned in both armies.

About this period Lieutenant-Colonel James Kelly, Sixty-ninth Regiment, rejoined the Brigade, having been relieved from duty at Ann Arbor, Mich., where he was in command of the post, which was then a recruiting depot. He commanded the Brigade for a short time, but in that short time the effects of his energy and discipline were everywhere apparent. When he was ordered to report to his regiment, the Sixteenth Infantry, in which he was captain, the principal officers of the Brigade then in the field held a meeting and expressed their heartfelt sorrow for his loss in a series of complimentary resolutions.

After Colonel Kelly's departure Colonel Thomas A. Smyth, of the First Delaware, was appointed to the command of the Brigade, to the delight of every officer and man in it. A vast improvement was soon apparent in every department, for Smyth was not only a brave officer—in fact, heroically brave—but in every respect a thorough disciplinarian, as far as all the details and duties of a soldier are concerned. His

modest, affable, and unassuming manners, combined
and blended with his fine soldierly qualities and commanding appearance, soon rendered him so popular
with the Brigade, so identified him with its fame and
future aspirations, that no man could be found fitter
to represent it, fitter to lead it to victory and glory.

During the remainder of March and the month of
April there was no movement of any consequence, in
the Army of the Potomac. But there was an active
campaign of amusement, and both men and officers
devoted themselves with ardor to such sports as the
service at all tolerated, enjoying the fleeting hours up
to the very latest moment of departure from camp,
with unabated devotion to pleasure. Many a great
and exuberant spirit thus employed the brief period of
quiet, whose life and light were forever soon extinguished in the bloody drama that succeeded this prel-
ude of calm and enjoyment.

In Boston, during the month of April, Colonel
Byrnes, who had obtained a special leave of absence
for the purpose, was making every effort to recruit for
the Twenty-eighth Massachusetts, which was as much
reduced as the New York regiments. He succeeded
at length, through the influence of the original founders of the regiment, among whom were P. Donohue,
and Martin Griffin, Esqs.

Before Colonel Byrnes should return to the field

these friends resolved to have made for the regiment a green flag, and present it publicly, with all due ceremony. This presentation was made on the 5th of April, at the Parker House, and the presentation address was delivered by Martin Griffin, Esq., who tendered the flag as a token of the respect and admiration in which both Colonel Byrnes and his command were held by the donors. The green flag of Erin was dear to many chivalrous hearts, and the gift was confided fully to the keeping of brave men. Though Ireland, as a separate nation, had no existence, still the flag was honored by all her sons, nor was it disloyalty to the Stars and Stripes, for the two banners should float together.

Colonel Byrnes replied as follows :

"Sir—In behalf of my fellow-soldiers I thank you, and, through you, the kind friends who have presented us this beautiful flag. It will be dearly cherished ; and, in their name, I promise it shall be gallantly defended. I can promise no more, sir, than to assure you that it will be a fresh incentive to the brave men who are perilling their lives in defence of that flag which typifies Union and liberty, and beneath which the shamrock has ever bloomed. In a few days, sir, that flag will throw its emerald folds to the breeze, and the smoke of battle will encircle it ; its freshness and beauty may be tarnished, but while there is an

Irish arm to strike in its defence, its honor shall never, never be sullied nor impaired. I can only point to the past history of my regiment to vouch for the future. Neither Massachusetts nor the historic fame of our race need to blush for such a regiment. And, sir, your kindness to-night has imposed new obligations upon us. We shall endeavor to merit the one and uphold the other. Again, sir, I thank you for the flag, and trust that one day we shall return it to the care of Massachusetts, crowned with the laurel of victory—of Union and liberty forever."

After this, Colonel Byrnes was detained in Boston until the middle of May, when he returned to the Brigade. Being senior to Colonel Smyth, he of course resumed the command, which, unhappily for him and them, he was not destined long to hold.

# CHAPTER XXII.

Opening of the campaign.—The army crosses the Rapidan.—Battles of the Wilderness.—Spottsylvania.—Casualties.

EARLY in May the Army of the Potomac started to cross the Rapidan, in light marching order, accomplishing this movement with quiet celerity on the 4th, and confronting the enemy in the Wilderness of Chancellorsville on the 5th. The Sixth Corps, under Sedgwick, held the right of our line; the Fifth, under Warren, the centre; while Hancock, with the Second Corps, occupied the left; and Burnside, with the Ninth Corps in reserve, brought up the rear. The enemy did not wait to be attacked, but with his usual impetuosity fell on Warren first. A fierce engagement, which lasted for an hour, was the result, when the enemy withdrew to prepare for an attack on another part of the line. In this action, among several general officers wounded were Colonels Guiney, Ninth Massachusetts, and Lombard, of the Fourth Michigan. The enemy next attempted to get between Hancock and the centre and right of our line, but the movement was discovered in time, and a division of the Sixth Corps kept him in check until the Second Corps came up. Hancock's division, under Barlow, Gibbons, and Birney, fell into line immediately, advanced across a swamp overgrown with heavy timber and thick underbrush, and engaged the enemy, then massed in heavy columns, under General Hill. Owing to the nature of the ground, artillery could not be used to advantage on either side; accordingly a steady stunning roar of musketry was kept up for some hours, until night closed the scene. This action lasted from five in the afternoon until dusk; the rebels, finally, being obliged to return, baffled before the impetuous bravery of the Second Corps.

Next day (Friday, 6th May) the Second Corps commenced the attack at dawn, and soon the engagement became general along the whole front; Hancock driving the enemy over a mile and a half, and then holding his ground against all efforts made to outflank or pierce his lines. All day long the contest raged with little intermission, till towards evening, when the hardest fighting of the campaign commenced, the rebels sweeping down on Hancock in four imposing lines. Before these advancing waves our skirmishers slowly retired to the front line of defences, where our men awaited the onset; when within musket-range, the enemy opened a vigorous fire on our men, who replied with fatal effect, until Longstreet's forces were so severely handled that the reserves were ordered up.

The contest was thus kept up for nearly an hour, when, in one position of the line, near where the Wilderness had been set on fire and our breastworks had been demolished, the rebels pushed in with a shout of anticipated victory, and planted their colors on our works. At this point our first and second lines fell back; but a couple of batteries, already in position, opened a destructive fire, and two of Colonel Carroll's regiments charged, with a cheer, upon the enemy, who were thus driven back in gallant style, and the position regained.

During the night of the 7th Lee fell back to Spottsylvania Courthouse, and on Sunday morning (8th) both armies prepared for battle. On this day the Fifth and Sixth Corps were mainly engaged, and in this action Major-General Sedgwick was killed.

On Monday (9th) there was only skirmishing and no active engagement, the enemy holding their strong positions around Spottsylvania.

On Tuesday morning (10th) the battle was opened by our forces along the whole line. The First Division (Second Corps), in which was the Irish Brigade, crossed the Po River on the previous night, and took a position, from which they enfiladed the enemy's right. An attempt to break his centre was then ordered, and the right was also advanced in the afternoon. The enemy was driven into his intrenchments, and a portion of the Sixth Corps succeeded in getting into the enemy's rifle-pits, spiking several guns, and capturing over a thousand prisoners. This battle was very desperate, but indecisive, and our men suffered terribly throughout.

Meantime, the cavalry under Sheridan turned the enemy's right, getting into his rear, doing considerable damage to railroads, stores, and spreading terror among the inhabitants, while the main part of our army rested on Wednesday (11th).

Next morning (12th) the contest was renewed at dawn, Hancock opening the battle with such determined activity that by eight o'clock he had routed the best troops of the rebel army, among them the Stonewall Division, led by General Ewell, capturing three generals, thirty guns, and prisoners amounting to about four thousand. Then the rebels massed their troops against him in such numbers that he found it difficult to retain the advantage gained, and the Sixth Corps was sent to his assistance. Thus, about eleven o'clock A. M. the battle raged with undiminished fury in Hancock's front, until dusk; was renewed at nine P. M., and continued until nearly three A. M., both parties contending during the night for the possession of a line of rifle-pits from which Hancock had driven the enemy in the morning. The rebels fell back at length, and our men followed them steadily through the woods, skirmishing as they advanced for a distance of nearly four miles, when Lee took up a new position.

David Power Conyngham as a *New York Herald* correspondent with the Army of the Potomac, 1863. Conyngham is seated second from the left (Courtesy Library of Congress)

The 69th N.Y.S.M. leaves New York City for the war, 1861 (Courtesy Mass. MOLLUS Collection, USAMHI)

Michael Corcoran, Colonel of the 69th N.Y.S.M. and Brigadier
General commanding Corcoran's Legion (Courtesy Massachusetts
Commandery, Military Order of the Loyal Legion Collection, U.S.
Army Military History Institute, Carlisle Barracks, Pa. [hereafter
Mass. MOLLUS Collection, USAMHI])

Brig. Gen. Thomas Francis Meagher, first commander of the
Irish Brigade (Courtesy Mass. MOLLUS Collection, USAMHI)

# 2D IRISH REGIMENT

**FAUGH A BALLAUGH**

## Of Massachusetts IRISH VOLUNTEEERS
### By Order of GOVERNOR ANDREW.

## HEAD QUARTERS AT MARBLE HALL
### HOWARD STREET, NEAR THE HOWARD ATHENAEUM, BOSTON,
Where every accommodation will be afforded to Recruits who desire to enlist for the War.

THIS REGIMENT WILL BE COMMANDED BY

# COL. T. S. MURPHY,
Late Commander of the New York Montgomery Guards, a gentleman qualified to command any Regiment.

## 100 DOLLARS BOUNTY.    Pay and Rations upon Enlistment.
The people of many of the towns and cities of the Commonwealth have made ample provision for those joining the ranks of the Army. If any person enlists in a Company or Regiment out of the Commonwealth they cannot share in the bounty which has been thus liberally voted.

**The Recruits for this Regiment will go into Camp at once** at CAMP CAMERON, Cambridge, and all who desire to serve in the ranks of this Regiment should make application to _____ Deputy Recruiting Agent.

In _____ Office at _____

# PATRICK DONOHOE, - - DR. W. M. WALSH.
M. H. KEENAN'S CARD AND JOB PRESS, 104 WASHINGTON STREET, BOSTON.

Recruiting Poster for the 28th Massachusetts Volunteers, showing traditional Irish symbols (Courtesy Massachusetts Historical Society)

Recruiting poster for the 69th New York Volunteers, illustrating some of the appeals by which Irish-Americans were to be induced to fight for the Union (Courtesy Kenneth H. Powers, Westport, Conn.)

Col. Robert Nugent, 69th New York Volunteers, commander of the Irish Brigade in 1863 and 1864–65 (Courtesy Roger D. Hunt Collection, USAMHI)

Col. Patrick Kelly, 88th New York Volunteers, commander of the Irish Brigade in 1863–64 (Courtesy Division of Military and Naval Affairs, New York State Adjutant General's Office, Albany, N.Y.)

Col. Richard Byrnes, 28th Massachusetts Volunteers, commander of the Irish Brigade in 1864 (Courtesy USAMHI)

Brig. Gen. Thomas Smyth, commander of the Irish Brigade in 1864 (Courtesy Mass. MOLLUS, USAMHI)

"The Grand Stand," St. Patrick's Day in the Irish Brigade, 1863. Drawing by Edwin Forbes (Courtesy Library of Congress)

"The Steeple Chase," St. Patrick's Day in the Irish Brigade, 1863. Drawing by Edwin Forbes (Courtesy Library of Congress)

Requiem Mass in St. Patrick's Cathedral for the dead of the Irish Brigade after the Battle of Fredericksburg (From *Frank Leslie's Illustrated Newspaper*, February 7, 1863)

Rev. William Corby, C.S.C., chaplain of the 88th New York Volunteers (Courtesy University of Notre Dame Archives, Notre Dame, Indiana)

Rev. James Dillon, C.S.C., chaplain of the 63rd New York Volunteers (Courtesy UNDA)

Officers of the 69th New York Volunteers (Courtesy Library of Congress)

Officers of the 63rd New York Volunteers (Courtesy Mass. MOLLUS Collection, USAMHI)

Officers of the 28th Massachusetts Volunteers (Courtesy Mass. MOLLUS Collection, USAMHI)

Col. St. Clair Mulholland, 116th Pennsylvania Volunteers (Courtesy Civil War Library & Museum, MOLLUS, Philadelphia)

Major James Quinlan, 88th New York Volunteers (Courtesy Mr. and Mrs. G. E. Quinn, Warwick, N.Y.)

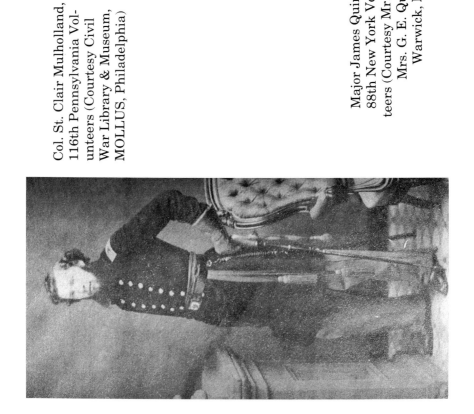

Capt. Jeremiah W.
Coveney, 28th Massachu-
setts Volunteers
(Courtesy USAMHI)

Maj. James Cavanagh,
69th New York
Volunteers
(Courtesy USAMHI)

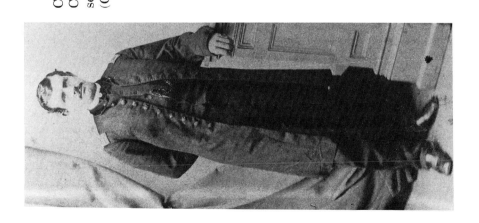

Lt. Col. George W. Cartwright, 28th Massachusetts Volunteers (Courtesy USAMHI)

Major Thomas Lynch, 63rd New York Volunteers (Courtesy Div. of Military and Naval Affairs, New York State Adjutant General's Office, Albany, N.Y.)

Lt. Henry McQuade, 69th New York Volunteers (Courtesy Wendell W. Lang, Tarrytown, N.Y.)

Capt. Garrett Nowlen, 116th Pennsylvania Volunteers (Courtesy Art Costigan Collection, USAMHI)

Capt. Patrick Ryder, 88th New
York Volunteers (Division of
Military & Naval Affairs, New
York State Adjutant General's
Office, Albany, N.Y.)

Maj. John H. Donovan, 69th
New York Volunteers (Courtesy
Martin L. Schoenfeld Collection,
USAMHI)

Capt. John Dwyer, 63rd New
York Volunteers (Division of
Military & Naval Affairs, New
York State Adjutant General's
Office, Albany, N.Y.)

Maj. Thomas Touhy, 63rd New
York Volunteers (Courtesy Division of Military & Naval Affairs, New York State Adjutant
General's Office, Albany, N.Y.)

Monument of the New York regiments of the Irish Brigade at Gettysburg

Monument of the 28th Massachusetts Volunteers at Gettysburg

Monument of the 116th Pennsylvania Volunteers at Gettysburg

## CHAPTER XXIII.

On the 13th and 14th there was little active fighting, owing to the badness of the roads.

During this temporary lull, the contending armies still kept their positions in the vicinity of Spottsylvania Courthouse, where Lee had strongly intrenched himself. The Army of the Potomac rested as follows: On the right, the Ninth Corps, under Burnside; the centre and left were held by the Fifth and Sixth Corps, under Warren and Wright; while the Second Corps was on the extreme left.

Before dawn on the 15th Hancock, moving under cover of the night, took up a position on the right. The troops rested in the very fortifications from which only a few nights before they had taken so large a number of prisoners, and at four o'clock A. M. their skirmishers advanced. Then artillery opened on both sides. The First Division, with the Irish Brigade, held the extreme right; the Corcoran Legion, which had come up from Fairfax Courthouse the night before, was assigned to the Second Division. During this day's engagement the Legion fought with conspicuous gallantry, side by side with the Brigade.

Two hundred yards of cleared space was to be traversed before the first line of the enemy's breastworks could be gained; a battery of four brass pieces played on our men incessantly, as they advanced on the double quickstep. At this time the sharpshooters were busy: although there was not sufficient light to enable them to sight their pieces with accuracy, still many owed their deaths to this uncertain firing. At last the field is crossed, the rebels fly from their first intrenched position, and our men clamber over, cheerily, capturing a few dilatory sharpshooters who lingered too long at their post. Again they charge after the retreating but still fighting foe; and the line is not quite as orderly as might be desired, owing to the unevenness of the ground, which was in various places covered with dense pine-woods. But the veterans of the Second Corps, unmindful of the driving tempest of bullets, shot, and shell, reformed their disordered ranks, pushed steadily on, and soon took possession of the second line of fortifications. In this charge many officers and men were killed and wounded, and several, who were too seriously wounded to be removed from the field, were taken prisoners. Here

Captains Kelly and Blake, of the Sixty-ninth, received their death-wounds. Major A. J. Lawler, of the Twenty-eighth Massachusetts, was killed; Lieutenant Annand lost a leg; while Captains W. S. Bailey, Cochrane, and Fleming, of the same regiment, were severely wounded.

In the Legion the losses were also heavy. Colonel Matthew Murphy, commanding Brigade; Lieutenant-Colonel DeLacy, One hundred and Sixty-fourth, a cool intrepid soldier, formerly major Thirty-seventh New York; Lieutenant Dunn, Adjutant of One Hundred and Seventieth; Captain Thomas Lyford, One Hundred and Sixty-fourth, being more or less severely wounded.

In other regiments several prominent officers were killed and wounded; among them were Captains O'Shea, an ardent patriot, from Cork; Tobin and Dunn, of the Forty-Second New York; Lieutenant J. Kelly, of the Eighty-Second New York, killed; and several others wounded.

Lieutenant King thus wrote to his brother a description of this action: " On that morning, after a wearying march, we reached a clearing in front of the enemy's breastworks—perhaps I ought to say fortifications—for these works were, indeed, immensely strong, and extended for miles. These we, who were of the First Division, were ordered to take. Our men of the

Brigade had to rush at them through a storm of grape and rifle-balls. Men dropped in scores, but the rest never faltered; and on our springing into the outer ditch, the rebels, after dreadful havoc in their ranks, broke, and in swarms took to the woods in the rear. For some time we held their works, but, on their being heavily re-enforced, they returned and drove us out. Again we drove them from the rifle-pits, but only after terrible slaughter, in which our Brigade got very much shattered, and I found myself with Blake and about a dozen of our company. It was then Blake showed himself a soldier. We rallied some men belonging to several regiments, together with our own, and Blake led us through a shower of balls to the opposite side of the works, intending to follow the enemy to the woods; and would have done so, but I persuaded him to desist, as he would thereby place himself too far in advance of the line. He then took the regimental flag, which was the only color on that part of the line, and got up upon the highest part of the work, and stood there waving it and calling us, 'Come on, boys, and I will show you how to fight.' Giving up the flag to the sergeant, he then went in with any men he could find; and while a most infernal fire raged from both sides he fought conspicuously in the extreme front, till he was struck in the knee. I immediately got some help, and was in the act of carrying him off

# CHAPTER XXIV.

Tolopotomy Creek—Cold Harbor.—Assaults on Petersburg.—Lists of casualties.

From Spottsylvania Lee withdrew beyond the North Anna, and the Fifth and Second Corps followed him up on the evening of the 21st. The Fifth crossed first and was fiercely attacked; but with the assistance of the Second and Sixth, the enemy was repulsed with loss. On the evening of the 26th, the army recrossed the river, moved by way of Hanovertown, crossed the Pamunkey River, had a brisk engagement at Tolopotomy Creek, where the Brigade was engaged, advanced to Hanover Court-house, and found the enemy in position north of .the Chickahominy, on the 31st. Late in the evening, our left was attacked, and in return, our whole line moved, and the enemy was driven from some of his intrenchments.

On the 3d was fought the disastrous battle of Cold Harbor, when the Brigade and Legion suffered terribly, while charging up hill and holding a position on the crest for two hours, against fearful odds; when at length they were obliged to fall back, losing as heavily in retiring as in the advance. In this attack Colonel Byrnes, commanding Brigade, fell mortally wounded, and Colonel James McMahon of the One Hundred and Sixty-fourth New York was shot dead on the enemy's intrenchments, where "with his own hand he had planted his colors."

During the fight at Cold Harbor, Col. Patrick Kelly arrived and immediately assumed command of the Brigade; Lieutenant-Colonel McGee also taking command of the Sixty-ninth.

After the battle of Cold Harbor, the troops enjoyed some rest, while preparations were in progress to make another flank movement across the James River. This was effected on the 16th, without encountering any serious opposition. In this movement the troops marched upwards of ninety miles in three days, and fought a big battle in front of Petersburg on the evening of the 16th. Here again "somebody blundered," and thus again thousands of brave men were ruthlessly sacrificed.

Here, in consequence of the failure of the Ninth Corps to co-operate with the Second, the latter suffered heavily, especially the First Division, which was ordered to charge where the works were very strong, and in a place where a converging fire decimated its ranks. In this charge fell Col. Patrick Kelly, a thorough soldier, whose cool courage, gentle manners, great natural modesty, honesty, and simplicity of character, had endeared him to all who knew him.

On the 22d the Second and Sixth Corps made a movement towards the Weldon Railroad; but the enemy, taking advantage of a gap between them, struck the First Division (Second Corps) in the flank, and captured several prisoners, among whom were Captain Wall, of the Sixty-ninth, and Lieutenant Grainger, of the Eighty-eighth.

Among the killed in the Wilderness and Spottsylvania were Captain James B. Turner, A. A. G.; Captain Boyle, Sixty-third; Captains C. V. Smyth and McIntyre, Twenty-eighth Massachusetts, mortally wounded, died in the hospitals in Fredericksburg; Major P. Ryder, Eighty-eighth; Major Thos. Tonhy, Sixty-third, shot through the lung, surviving only to reach his home; Capts. Pat'k Kelly and John Blake, Sixty-ninth, both mortally wounded and taken prisoners; Captain Kelly died at a rebel field-hospital, and was buried at Massaponax church, near Spottsylvania; Captain Blake survived to reach Richmond, where he died, it is reported, on the operating table; Lieutenant Richard P. King, of Blake's company, died in Fredericksburg, of gunshot wound of spine, and was buried in the Catholic cemetery there by Captain John C. Foley; Lieutenant John Sparks, of the Eighty-eighth, died at the field-hospital, and was buried there; Major

20

Lawler, of the Twenty-eighth, was killed on the morning of the 18th, near Spottsylvania.

Among the wounded were Colonel Thomas Smyth, commanding Brigade; Colonel Mulholland, of the One Hundred and Sixteenth Pennsylvania; Lieutenant Cartwright, Twenty-eighth Massachusetts.

Among the officers of the Legion wounded at Spottsylvania, were Colonel Matthew Murphy, Colonel Flood, Major O'Dwyer, etc.

At Cold Harbor, among the killed were Colonel Byrnes, commanding Brigade; Captain J. Magner and Lieutenant J. S. Wast; while Captains T. F. Page, J. W. Coveney, Lieutenants P. Kirley, J. Traynor, E. O'Brien, Twenty-eighth Massachusetts, were severely wounded; O'Brien having a foot amputated.

In the One Hundred and Sixteenth Pennsylvania, Lieutenant Colonel Dale, missing, supposed killed or wounded; Captains T. E. Crawford and Lieb, Adjutant L. J. Sacyste, and others, wounded.

In the Sixty-third, Lieutenant James M. Smart was killed; Lieutenants W. Grogan and D. P. Root wounded.

In the Eighty-eighth, Lieutenant James E. Byrne was killed.

In the Sixty-ninth, Major John Garrett, commanding regiment; Captain R. H. Milliken and Lieutenant E. O'Connor wounded.

The Brigade lost thus far one thousand men and officers, or one-third of its entire strength, in killed, wounded, and missing.

In the Legion, the losses were also very numerous. The command of the One Hundred and Sixty-fourth devolved on Captain Michael Doheny, whose gallantry was officially reported; Lieutenant Abraham, of the same regiment, was captured. In the Sixty-ninth militia, Captains E. K. Butler, J. H. Nugent, and John Sargent were killed, while several officers of the One Hundred and Fifty-fifth were wounded or captured.

Before Petersburg were killed Colonel Pat'k Kelly, commanding Brigade; Captain B. S. O'Neill, Sixty-ninth ; Adjutant Miles McDonald, Sixty-third. Among the wounded were Captains O'Shea and O'Driscoll, of the Eighty-eighth, the latter having his foot amputated; Lieutenant-Colonel McGee, of the Sixty-ninth, by a piece of shell; Lieutenants Brennan, Sloceny, and M. H. Murphy, of the same regiment. In the Legion, Major William Butler, of the Sixty-ninth militia, was severely wounded.

# CHAPTER XXV.

### Sketch of the Corcoran Legion.

HERE it is deemed proper to introduce a short sketch of the Corcoran Legion and its services until it joined the Army of the Potomac, so as to fill up what would be otherwise an imperfect record.

When Colonel Corcoran returned from captivity, after an imprisonment of over twelve months, he was received with the highest honors everywhere by the whole people. His progress to New York was a triumphant ovation, but in the latter city his reception surpassed every thing. He had received his commission of brigadier-general, with rank and pay, from the first battle of Bull Run, so that as soon as the festivities had to some extent subsided he set to work to raise his Brigade; and, accordingly, by the end of August, 1862, the "Corcoran Legion" was inaugurated. Deputations of recruits, companies, battalions, etc., thronged to New York from the neighboring cities, and from

Philadelphia, Boston, and other places. So popular was the command, that in two short months the Legion was on its way to the front, and reported to General Dix at Fortress Monroe about the middle of November.

The regiments composing the Legion were the Sixty-ninth National Guards, Colonel Matthew Murphy; the One Hundred and Fifty-fifth New York Volunteers, Colonel William McEvily; the One Hundred and Sixty-fourth New York Volunteers, Colonel John P. McMahon; the One Hundred and Seventieth New York Volunteers, Colonel McDermott; the One Hundred and Seventy-fifth New York Volunteers, Colonel M. K. Bryan. This latter regiment was not quite completed at the time of starting.

It was at first proposed to raise eight regiments, and so many organizations did leave New York, but it was subsequently decided to consolidate all into the regiments above stated, and even the One Hundred and Seventy-fifth was afterwards transferred into another command, so that only four regiments, in reality, constituted the Corcoran Legion up to the close of the war.

After about six weeks' sojourn on the Peninsula, the Legion was ordered to the vicinity of Suffolk, where the general received a deputation from the Common Council of New York, who came to present him with a sword. This presentation took place on the 19th of January, 1863, at a brigade review, the command being formed in hollow square. Major-General Peck, commanding division, with his entire staff and nearly all the officers of the division, were present. William Walsh, President of the Board of Aldermen, made the presentation in a patriotic speech, and General Corcoran responded with much feeling.

On the 29th of January, General Corcoran was placed in command of several details of men from the various regiments of the division, for the purpose of checking a movement made by the rebels under Pryor across the Blackwater. At four o'clock A. M. of the 30th, after marching most of the previous night, the troops struck the enemy near a deserted house, from which the action that followed took its name. In this first fight the men acquitted themselves creditably against a much superior force, and after a sharp engagement succeeded in repulsing the enemy, with the loss of over one hundred men.

The position selected by the enemy was an excellent one, and they were found to be in considerable force in cavalry, infantry, and artillery. Skirmishing commenced about five A. M., and was continued quite briskly for nearly two hours, until the enemy began to slacken their fire, and finally gave up the position, retiring to Franklin. A troop of the Eleventh Pennsylvania

Cavalry, under Colonel Spear, followed them up, capturing several prisoners.

The casualties were:

Sixty-ninth New York Artillery—killed, Sergeant Woods, Company B; Thomas Stone, Company C; William Campbell, Company C; wounded, Corporal Thomas Mahon, Company D; H. Coleman, Company D (died in hospital next day); J. D. Cassidy, D. R. Renn, D. Philip Griffin, Company E; Corporal Kelly, Company F; Corporal John Carroll,  Company E; Eli W. Pitts, Company B, thigh amputated; John Kearns, Company B, arm amputated.

One Hundred and Fifty-fifth New York Volunteers—killed, private Grimes; wounded, B. Miller, Company B; I. Walsh, Company B.

One Hundred and Sixty-fourth New York Volunteers—H. Schneidler, Company F; Captain Blodgett, A. A. G., of General Corcoran's staff, was slightly, and Captain Kelly, of the Sixty-ninth, severely wounded.

Several officers and men of the other commands were killed and wounded.

After the engagement, Major-General Peck issued the following congratulatory order:

HEADQUARTERS, SUFFOLK, VA., Feb. 5, 1863.

GENERAL ORDER No. 5.

The commanding general desires to thank Brigadier-General Corcoran and the troops assigned to his command, for their good conduct and gallant bearing in the engagement of the 30th of January, 1863, at Deserted House, which resulted in driving the enemy to the Blackwater. Most of the regiments were under fire for the first time, and furnished those so unfortunate as not to have a part in the expedition with examples of patriotism worthy of imitation.

By command of

MAJOR-GENERAL PECK.

BENJ. B. FOSTER, Major and A. A. G.

In April, Suffolk was invested by thirty thousand Confederates, under Longstreet and Hill, who laid regular siege to the place. During the siege, General Corcoran, who had been assigned to the command of the First Division of the Seventh Corps, made a reconnoissance with about five thousand men, in order to find out the strength and positions of the enemy, and had a brisk engagement on the Edenton Road, in which the enemy were driven from their breastworks and their position. For this action the general again received the congratulations of the department commander at Suffolk. At length, Longstreet raised the siege, and Corcoran started in pursuit to clear the neighborhood of his presence, which was finally effected. The enemy never afterwards crossed the Blackwater but he was whipped by "Corcoran's boys." Corcoran's stalwart Irishmen were dreaded by the foe and relied on by the Government, and the Irish Legion was always victorious and never retreated.

The evacuation of Suffolk being decided on, this

important duty was allotted to General Corcoran and his Legion, who, alone, were left to guard a place which, three weeks before, was garrisoned by forty thousand; and it was accomplished with extraordinary care and dispatch.

He was next placed in command of the defences of Portsmouth, and the men were engaged in strengthening these when the command was ordered to the Department of Washington, where they arrived on the 16th of July, and were assigned to General King's division; and lastly, General Corcoran was placed in command of the outpost defences at Fairfax Courthouse. Here occurred the sad accident that put an end forever to an honorable career, and deprived the Legion of their beloved commander. For several days he had been preparing to receive, at Christmas, several distinguished guests from New York and elsewhere, and had just accompanied General Meagher to Fairfax Station, which lay on his route of inspection, when he was thrown from a spirited horse, and died from the effects of the accident, December 22, 1864.

His death caused a profound feeling of sorrow everywhere, especially in New York, where a grand funeral awaited his honored remains, and a brilliant oration by his friend, General Meagher, was a fitting tribute to his memory.

After General Corcoran's death, the command of

the Legion devolved on Colonel Mat. Murphy, who worthily upheld his own and the reputation of the command.    The Legion continued to perform the same duties as heretofore, occasionally pursuing Moseby, Steuart, and other raiders; again, guarding a long line of the Orange and Alexandria Railroad. In one of their skirmishes with Rosser's brigade of rebel cavalry, Captain McNally's Company of the One Hundred and Fifty-fifth displayed great coolness, courage, and pluck in repelling an attack of very superior numbers.    After this nothing of unusual moment occurred in the Legion during the spring of this year, until the command joined the Army of the Potomac, near Spottsylvania, about the middle of May, as previously stated.

# CHAPTER XXVI.

Consolidation of the Brigade.—Recruiting.—First movement to Deep
Bottom.—Explosion of Burnside's mine.—Disasters.

IN the Army of the Potomac quiet still reigned, disturbed only by the occasional interchange of a few shots between the sharpshooters.

In the Irish Brigade, after the death of Colonel Kelly, the several commands were so reduced in numbers that it was decided to consolidate them into battalions. Accordingly, the three New York regiments were consolidated under the command of Captain Moroney, and the Brigade itself consolidated with Carroll's. This ungracious and ungenerous measure naturally caused much indignation; but after the numerous casualties among the principal officers, there was no one in the field of sufficient influence to protest against or prevent its hasty accomplishment. However, Colonel Nugent, who had been appointed to forward the draft in New York, together with Colonel McGee and other officers, set to work to refill the depleted regiments to the minimum at least, and thus start the Brigade again. Recruiting forthwith commenced with extraordinary success, and a large number of new men were thus added to the old commands, swelling their decimated ranks, to the entire satisfaction of all.

Major John W. Byron, who had just then been promoted to the majority of the Eighty-eighth, next commanded the consolidated regiments, he being the only field-officer present with the Brigade.

During the remainder of the month of July the Brigade remained quiet, only occasionally moving when the corps took up a new position, either for military purposes or to obtain suitable camp-grounds or supplies. These movements were mainly strategical, for the purpose of misleading the enemy and diverting his attention from the mining operations which had been carried on for some time in front of the Ninth Corps. The principal movement of this character was Hancock's first expedition across the Appomattox and James rivers to Deep Bottom, in the neighborhood of Butler's canal, near the end of the month. This was a very long, fatiguing night-march, in which the Brigade performed its usual prominent part, and was done with such celerity that the enemy was taken completely by surprise, and Hancock succeeded in taking his first line of works, four twenty-pounder Parrott-guns, and two hundred prisoners, thus forcing him to retire to a stronger position. The movement was originally intended for a feint, but it assumed all the characters of an attack in force, inducing the enemy to bring from the front at Petersburg a large force to oppose it, and thus lessen the resistance to the premeditated assault of Burnside after the explosion of the mine.

From Deep Bottom the Brigade returned, after another tiresome night's march, and reached the front at Petersburg at early dawn of a beautiful Sunday morning, just in time to witness, from afar, the terrific explosion and the disastrous assault that followed it.

According to the programme this assault was to follow the explosion instantly; but from some unknown cause Burnside delayed till the enemy recovered from their panic. The colored division, after carrying the first line by assault, became disorganized, owing to the absence of officers, thrown into confusion, and fell in numbers before the well-directed fire from the second line of the enemy's works. The confusion was now inextricable, and the carnage terrible; the troops breaking in disastrous rout, and leaving many officers in the hands of the enemy. The colored division lost about twelve hundred, while the total loss in the corps was set down at five thousand, the white troops having had to bear the brunt of the fighting when the former fell back.

# CHAPTER XXVII.

Rebels again invade Maryland and Pennsylvania.—Explosion of a Rebel
mine at Petersburg.—Explosion of ammunition at City Point.—Second
expedition to Deep Bottom.—Casualties.

EARLY in August the rebels, under Generals Early
and Breckinridge, again invaded Maryland and Pennsylvania. The troops stationed in the Shenandoah
were driven back with heavy loss, after a fierce resistance to the invaders, who penetrated as far as Cham-
bersburg, which they laid in ashes. The object of the
raid being to secure the rich crops of the Shenandoah,
and this having been accomplished, the enemy gradually recrossed the river and returned leisurely down
the valley. Just then General Phil. Sheridan, who
had been in command of the cavalry of the Army of
the Potomac, was appointed to the chief command of
the department of the Potomac, and without a moment's delay, prepared to follow them up with his
usual energy.

In the Army of the Potomac, after the movement at
Deep Bottom, the Irish Brigade had some rest from

active military operations. It was, however, sufficiently near the enemy to be kept constantly on the alert, and on several occasions the men were killed and wounded in their huts, which, owing to their close proximity, and for greater security, were made like bomb-proofs, mostly under ground.

On the 8th of August a rebel mine was exploded in front of the Fifth Corps, which, however, did no great damage, and the casualties were few.

At City Point occurred a fearful explosion of ammunition on an ordnance barge, causing immense destruction of life, and property to the amount of several millions. The Twentieth N. Y. S. M. suffered very severely.

On the 13th of August the Brigade received sudden orders to accompany the Corps on another expedition, the object of which was at first involved in a good deal of mystery. The troops were to carry all their baggage, and take transports at City Point for their destination. Accordingly, the line of march was taken from the arid and uncomfortable plains of Petersburg, and about noon the various commands bivouacked around City Point, and immediately after some light refreshment proceeded on board the transports, which forthwith steamed down the James River, as if their object was to leave Petersburg and Richmond behind them—for a time, at least. Meantime, conjecture was busy as to the destination of the corps ; some thought that it was to be transferred to Maryland, under Sheridan, and others that North Carolina was to be their future camping-ground ; but the favorite and more agreeable supposition appeared to be, that the corps was to return to Washington for the purpose of recruiting its decimated regiments, and thus the most pleasant anticipations were entertained in view of the expected change. But these flattering expectations were soon doomed to disappointment. The fleet shortly anchored for the night nearly opposite Wilson's Landing, about twelve miles below the Point. Here they remained quietly that evening until about midnight, when the anchors were weighed, the engines reversed, and the fleet returned up the river, and about dawn of the 14th reached the well-known banks of Deep Bottom. The mystery was now solved. The troops disembark, the line of march is formed, and forward is the word. After a short march the troops halt for a hasty breakfast, and again start towards Richmond. After about two hours' steady marching, under a blazing sun, the division comes within range of the enemy's guns, mounted on formidable earthworks, advantageously situated on elevated ridges that appeared almost impregnable. The batteries open furiously, while shot and shell and a steady fire of musketry threaten every moment to annihilate the remnant of a once powerful division. With admirable coolness and unconcern the veterans climb the steep ascent, bent almost double for the effort, gain the crest of the first ridge, from which the enemy's front line are dislodged without a shot fired. A little further on is a line of rifle-pits swarming with the enemy, from which a continued fusilade is poured on the devoted band, who push forward with the same grim steadiness, and still without a shot, charge, with a shout that completely drowned the loudest din of shot and shell, and Whitworth bolt and rattling roar of musketry: with a rush like a sweeping tempest this handful of Irish soldiers spring upon the foe, and the line of works is ours. An unusual stillness succeeds, and General Barlow, dismounted with his staff, just beneath the crest of the first ridge, started up from his reclining position to ascertain the cause. With a malignant satisfaction, characteristic of a narrow intellect, he suddenly exclaimed, " That d——d Irish Brigade has broken at last!" Just as he uttered the words, a mounted officer rode up to the group in time to catch their import, and Adjutant Smith, of the Sixty-ninth, who happened to be the rider, covered with sweat and black with the smoke of battle, promptly and manfully, almost disdainfully, replied, " General, the Irish Brigade has taken the first line of the enemy's works, and I have come back for further orders." The general was so confounded at the sudden contradiction of his spiteful slander, that for a considerable period he did not regain his self-possession. The general, though commonly counted a brave, fearless soldier, as his previous career would certainly indicate, was exceedingly unpopular, not only with the Brigade, to which he rarely omitted an opportunity of showing his dislike by the exhibition of many petty acts of tyranny and persecution, but with the whole division, by his reckless management of a splendid command. Even to his immediate staff he was rude and overbearing, frequently and needlessly risking their lives in the execution of many useless commissions.

After this engagement, which took place near the New Market Road to Richmond, the casualties in the Brigade were remarkably small, owing as much to their steadiness and coolness as to the rapidity with which the assault was made. When the charge was ordered it was executed, like a flash scorching and blinding every obstacle within its range. The total losses were two privates killed, and twenty-one wounded, Lieutenant Harry McQuade, of the Sixty-ninth, alone of the officers, receiving a flesh wound of the thigh. In the Legion the losses, though greater, were not very numerous; on the march several had been fatally sun-struck.

Shortly after the charge made by the Brigade the

Second Division, especially the Legion and Colonel
Tom Smyth's brigade, came up to support the First.
Smyth himself was conspicuous as usual, riding around
in front of his brigade, the very beau ideal of a chivalric soldier.

On the 15th, part of the Tenth Corps, under General Birney, composed of General Terry's division,
commenced the attack on the left of the line, near the
position occupied by the Second Corps, by which he
naturally expected to be supported, in case of need.
The first line was soon carried, together with an
advanced work containing four 8-inch howitzers,
which were brought off safely, notwithstanding frequent fierce attempts of the enemy to retake them.

The Tenth Corps had now joined its right with the
left of the Second, and received orders to withdraw
during the night and mass in rear of the latter; and
when this was satisfactorily effected, the remainder of
the day was spent in manœuvring for position.

On the 16th, the Tenth Corps and a brigade of the
Third Division, Second Corps, under Colonel Craig,
were chiefly engaged, capturing the enemy's main
works, four standards, and two hundred and sixty-seven
prisoners. Meantime the enemy, receiving re-enforcements from their right, near Petersburg, massed
heavy columns in Birney's front, bore down on him
with overwhelming force, both in front and flanks,

calling on our troops to surrender. The answer was a cheer and a volley of musketry, and our men slowly retired to the captured works, from which repeated attempts failed to dislodge them. During this engagement General Craig of the Third Division, Second Corps, was shot through the head. At length they found a weak point on the left of the line, from which they delivered a fatal enfilading fire; so, to save a needless loss of life, our men were compelled to withdraw to the main line, distant about two huudred yards.

On the 17th, under a flag of truce, both parties buried their dead, and estimated the various losses, which must have been very considerable on both sides.

In the Legion, Major John T. J. Connery, son of Dr. E. D. Connery, ex-coroner of New York, was mortally wounded. He died at Washington, September 9th, 1864.

# CHAPTER XXVIII.

Battle of the Weldon Railroad.—Casualties.—Prisoners.

ON the 18th of August the Fifth Corps moved to and across the Weldon Railroad, south of Petersburg, near Reams' Station, and having taken position, then commenced the destruction of the road. The enemy next day came down in force and attacked our troops, but were handsomely repulsed at first. Meantime, the Second Corps, having returned from Deep Bottom, were ordered to take a position on the left of the Fifth, and assist in the work of destruction. While the First and Second Divisions of the Second Corps were engaged in destroying the railroad, they were suddenly attacked in flank and rear. Some breastworks had been thrown up at Reams' Station, and here they awaited the attack of the enemy, who assaulted the position three times and were each time successfully repulsed. Then followed a desperate charge, during which they were mown down by the steady fire from our breastworks, but they pushed on with the most frantic bravery, and the right centre having given way, the works had to be abandoned, and our men withdrew to a neighboring wood, from which they subsequently made another sally on the enemy; but night coming on, terminated the conflict.

In this disastrous fight the Brigade and Legion suffered very severely, but their greatest losses were in the number of prisoners. The remnant of the Brigade, led by Major Byron, fought magnificently, and General Miles has testified to the fact that the rebels on their front were throwing down their arms, preliminary to surrender, when another brigade stationed near them gave way, and thus encouraged the enemy, who poured in on all sides in overwhelming numbers, and finally compelled them to fall back.

The principal casualties were, in the Irish Brigade: Adjutant J. J. Smith, of the Sixty-ninth, who thus far seemed to have had a charmed life, severely wounded in the leg; Adjutant Bermingham, Eighty-eighth; Lieutenant John Miles, Twenty-eighth Massachusetts, wounded; Captain Nowlan, One Hundred and Sixteenth Pennsylvania, killed. Major Byron, of the Eighty-eighth, commanding Brigade; Lieutenant E. O'Connor, of the Sixty-ninth, and others, were captured.

Of the corps staff, Captain Brownson, A. D. C., a brave officer and a universal favorite, was killed, and Colonel Walker, A. A. G., who had risen from the ranks, taken prisoner.

CORCORAN LEGION.—Of the disasters which occurred in the Corcoran Irish Legion, in the same battle, the following letter, dated Sunday, August 28th, gives the best description we have seen. It was addressed to Mr. Matthew Byrne, of Buffalo, brother of Lieutenant-Colonel Byrne, One Hundred and Fifty-fifth New York Volunteers:

FRIEND MATTHEW—I now undertake the painful duty of informing you of the severe loss our Brigade met with on Thursday, 25th. That day the first and second divisions of our corps lay at Reams' Station, on the Weldon Railroad—about five thousand five hundred muskets—our division (Gibbon's) being very small—and twelve pieces of artillery, with some cavalry under General Gregg, General Hancock commanding the whole. Early in the morning our pickets were driven in at all points, and the rebel sharpshooters annoyed our batteries considerably. Then commenced the fight in reality. We lay on the right angle of the first division. The enemy charged six times on our right, and were repulsed with slaughter. But then they brought up their batteries, I should say twenty or twenty-five pieces, and opened on us simultaneously. They were in such force they overlapped our line on the right and left, and came up in our rear. Then commenced the slaughter. From front and rear they came swarming in with their yells, and seizing the artillery, turned it immediately on our men. The lieutenant-colonel was captured while endeavoring to get the men to stand by the guns. Captain McConvey was wounded severely and carried about a mile, when the men who were carrying him had to leave him, as the rebels were in our rear, and right on top of us. He gave his money to the adjutant of the one Hundred and Fifty-second New York, who was captured with it afterwards, and Captain McConvey, also, taken prisoner. Captains Doran, Page, Pelouze, Quintz, Flynn, Hartford, and Davis were captured. Lieutenant Quinn was wounded in the arm, and got off. We lost forty-one men out of seventy-five. Company I lost James Clark, P. Donohue, and David Smith, missing; J. Ryan and George Barry wounded, but got off the field. Company K lost Sergeant McGowan, P. Kiernan, Amengo Bogert, James Cotter, P. Dolan, Louis Katrick, missing; Sergeant Seymour was captured, but got away again. The One Hundred and Sixty-fourth has only one officer left—Captain Burke. Thomas Cantwell was wounded, and got off. The Brigade loss was five hundred men. The One Hundred and Seventieth has one officer and about thirty men out of one hundred and fifty. We saved our colors, so did the Sixty-ninth and One Hundred and Seventieth.

Prisoners taken told our officers that we were fighting Hill's whole corps, and two divisions of Beauregard's command. I hope and trust that my comrades and your friends will not be let rot in a Confederate prison. They captured from us eight or ten pieces of artillery and one thousand seven hundred prisoners.

Many of our troops would not leave the pits at all, preferring capture and imprisonment to running the chances of getting out from under the destructive artillery fire that was concentrated on us from all points front and rear, right and left. General Hancock led a charge in person on the right, and General Gibbon exposed himself fearlessly, but the day was gone against the noble Second Corps. Captain Emblee, of General Gibbon's staff, led the One Hundred and Sixty-fourth and the Eighth New York artillery troops on the charge; but it was useless, as at that time the enemy were swinging in our rear. Their artillery checked their rear from capturing more of us, as they mowed down their own men with the artillery they captured and turned on us. I hope, dear friend, that I will never get in such another "tight place." General Gibbon cried; Hancock to-day and yesterday will let no one approach him. This is the first time the old corps was ever whipped; but the odds were three to one in artillery and men. I have tried to give you as true a statement as possible. Charley Priest is safe; also the following men of Companies I and K: Sergeant P. Kelly, Sergeant Opping, Sergeant Seymour, John Donohue, William Heffernan, Allan Gray, James Griffin, John Monohan, Dan Frawley, and John Gallaher; we have four officers and thirty-eight men left. Please show this letter to Captain McNally when you get through.

Dr. Hasbrouck, of the One Hundred and Sixty-fourth, was ordered to take charge of the wounded. When he comes back, I may find something more definite in relation to the lieutenant-colonel and the men. If so, I will let you know at the earliest opportunity. Hoping you will have patience, and take the brightest side of the picture,

I remain your friend,

DEAN WILSON,

Second-Lieutenant, One Hundred and Fifty-fifth, N. Y. S. V.

---

Captain Emblee, above alluded to, was a gallant Irish officer, who had served in the Eighty-second Regiment New York Volunteers. The following is an official statement of the casualties among the officers of the Legion on the above-named battle-field :

ONE HUNDRED AND SEVENTIETH NEW YORK VOLUNTEERS.— Major J. B. Donnelly, wounded and prisoner; Captain James H. Keely, Captain Turner, Adjutant Dunne, Lieutenants Quigley and Whelan, also wounded and prisoners. The command went into the fight some seventy strong, and lost more than half.

SIXTY-NINTH N. Y. S. M.—Captain Whelpley, killed ; Lieutenant D. Sweeney, killed ; Captain Canton and Lieutenant O'Farrell, wounded ; Lieutenant E. Kelly, captured.

ONE HUNDRED AND FIFTY-FIFTH NEW YORK VOLUNTEERS.— Major Byrne, Captains Page, Doran, Pelouze, and Lieutenant O'Flynn, captured.

ONE HUNDRED AND SIXTY-FOURTH NEW YORK VOLUNTEERS.— Major Beatty, Captains Kelly, Hearne, O'Reilly, and others, captured.

The Legion numbered after the fight about two hundred men.

21

# CHAPTER XXIX.

Anniversary of the Brigade.—Generals Meagher, Hancock, Birney, Gib-bons, Mott, De Trobriand, etc., present.

EARLY in September several visitors sojourned with the Brigade, among whom was General Meagher, who had been on a visit to General Hancock, and was then preparing to start for the Southwest, to report to General Sherman. The occasion was deemed a favorable one to extemporize a celebration in memory of the formation of the Brigade; and, accordingly, a committee of officers met together hastily on the evening of the 3d, and arranged the preliminaries for an anniversary celebration next day, which happened to be Sunday. This committee were Captain John Smith, Eighty-eighth, chairman; Lieutenant John C. Foley, Sixty-ninth, secretary; Captain Benjamin, Sixty-third; Dr. Powell, Eighty-eighth; Dr. Purcell, Sixty-ninth; Captain Desmond, Eighty-eighth; Lieutenant Mc-Quade, Sixty-third; Lieutenant Clarke, Sixty-ninth Invitations were dispatched in all directions, and at the appointed time quite a large and distinguished company was assembled to do honor to the occasion.

Among these were Generals Hancock, Birney, Meagher, Gibbons, Mott, Miles, De Trobriand, etc.

At eight o'clock, A. M., the company began to arrive in camp, which was enlivened by music from the division band, under the accomplished Higgins, from Boston. A solemn High Mass was first celebrated by the chaplains, the Rev. Fathers Willet and Corby, at which the soldiers and officers of the Brigade and their guests assisted—the several regiments attending under their respective officers, and the band furnishing appropriate music. At the conclusion Father Corby spoke, at length, on the duties which, as soldiers, the Irish Brigade owed to their race, creed, and adopted country ; how by morality and proper Christian deportment they should furnish an example to others, and thus be a credit, not alone to themselves, but an honor to their nativity. As to their military duties, he would forbear to speak, but would leave that subject to the proper officers. Of their higher and holier obligations, it was his peculiar province to continue to remind them. He concluded a very able and elegant discourse, by trusting they would perform all their duties, while in the service, in such a manner as to earn for themselves the approval of their own consciences, the esteem of their fellow-soldiers, and then return to private life, respected and useful citizens.

After Mass the visitors were conducted to the banquet hall, composed of a raised platform, tastefully decorated with evergreens, and ornamented with banners, flags, guidons and other military insignia. Here the company partook of a plentiful collation, which, if not as elegant as Delmonico could furnish, made up the deficiency in abundance of hospitality.

Assembled in front were the soldiers generally, who had been specially exempted from military duty, in honor of the occasion. Altogether, it was a scene of gayety and general enjoyment, distinctively characteristic of Irish gatherings.

After the collation the company made their appearance on the platform, and the generals were greeted with a round of cheers, again and again repeated.

When the applause had subsided, General Meagher was introduced by Dr. Reynolds, and the cheering was again renewed. Upon order being restored, the general proceeded to address them, and said he did not come there to make a speech, but to bear testimony to the truth. He was glad they had anticipated him by cheering General Hancock, who had so well and successfully led them to victory on many a battle-field. He did not come there to speak to them on political subjects, as he was prohibited from so doing, so long as he wore his uniform; but he would revert to the past, and for a brief period indulge in some of its pleasant reminiscences. It was on that day, three years ago, he received a commission from Secretary Cameron, to raise an Irish Brigade--"Irish" was specifically mentioned—and he was proud to say that they had never disgraced the high position which he had taken for them. He had, as it were, pledged himself that they would never violate the trust which had been placed in them by the land of their adoption; and he was proud to boast that, from that day up to the present, they had not abused his confidence. Every battle-field, from Bull Run to Reams' Station, but added another laurel to the wreath which this war would transfer for them to posterity. They had redeemed all his pledges, and had won for themselves undying glory. They had proved themselves worthy descendants of their forefathers, both in valor and patriotism; and he was proud to say that no other country had contributed so much to the honor of the flag of America as Ireland. Not a star had been shaded by them—it had lost nothing of its lustre by floating beside the green flag of Erin, and he hoped America would not forget it. There was another thing which he wished to call the attention of his hearers to, and that was the fact that the Irish Brigade had never lost a color, notwithstanding the many trying ordeals through which they had passed; and to-day, as that day three years ago, the same green flag waved side by side with the same American flag over their heads. When he was coming amongst them he expected to meet some of his old friends in arms, but he was sorry to say that he could notice but very few familiar faces there. He knew and felt the sad change; but he also knew that they died and suffered in a noble cause, and that was an alleviation of the pangs which he might otherwise feel. He would say no more to them, as he did not intend to make a speech, but would conclude by calling for three cheers for Major-General Hancock.

When these were given with a hearty will, General Hancock rose in answer to the repeated calls of the auditory, and delivered a short address, dignified and soldierly, which was frequently interrupted by applause.

General Miles, being loudly called on, said he had not intended to address them at all, but he was glad to have an opportunity to bear testimony to the unflinching bravery of the Irish troops on all occasions, and particularly to that of the Brigade at the most recent battle—that of Reams' Station. He was a witness to it on that occasion; he saw them hold their position against the advancing foe; and so destructive was their resistance, that, after the determined enemy had tried, but tried in vain, to force the position held by the Irish troops, he could see him laying down his

arms, when the troops broke on the left of the Brigade.
The rebels suffered fearfully at the hands of the Brigade; and it was not its fault that Reams' Station
could not be claimed as an undisputed victory.

General Miles took occasion to pay a very handsome
compliment to Captain Benjamin, of the Sixty-third,
for bravery displayed while on picket at Reams'
Station during the day of the fight. Captain Benjamin, with his little band, was driven back three
times, and cut off from our lines once; but, owing
to his coolness and good judgment, managed to
effect his escape and hold the position. Sergeant
McHugh, of his regiment, and a boy belonging to the
Seventh New York, were captured by a rebel cavalry
man, but Captain Benjamin followed them up until
one of his men shot the captor's horse, and he was
forced to fly for his own safety. Thus, by the bravery
of Captain Benjamin, Sergeant McHugh and the boy
were recaptured.

Short addresses were delivered by Generals Gibbon,
Birney, Mott, and De Trobriand, who humorously remarked that his Irishmen claimed him as one of them,
by changing his cognomen, which they insisted was
originally Irish, and but slightly Frenchified. Thus,
De Trobriand was nothing more nor less than D. T. R.
O'Brien, a name quite familiar in Thomond, Ormond,
and Desmond. Finally Dr. L. Reynolds made a stir-

ring speech, full of his usual wit, eloquence, poetry, and patriotism.

Col. Tom Smyth arrived late in the evening, having been detained by urgent military duties, just when the Eighty-eighth were receiving their quota of the diluted commissary with which they were moderately regaled in honor of the anniversary. Immediately on his appearance, the men, forgetful of their engrossing occupation, crowded around to greet their former and beloved commander, while Smyth, who would rather face a battery than make a speech, waved his hand and retired with more precipitancy from his friends than he ever did from his foes.

A gratifying incident of the celebration is recorded by Dr. L. Reynolds, who states that General Hancock informed him that as soon as he had received the Doctor's song, " There's not a star for you, Tom Smyth," he immediately wrote to Washington, recommending Col. Smyth for promotion, which recommendation he took care to have indorsed by General Meade, and also by General Grant. " So," added the general, " you may inform him that his commission may arrive at any moment." The commission soon came, and in honor of its reception General Smyth received several handsome presents from his military friends. A full uniform, including sword, belt, and pistols, a beautiful horse from his staff-officers, and another magnificent charger from the soldiers of the Sixty-third Regiment. He also received a third horse from his own regiment, the First Delaware.

The festivities were at length brought to a close, and the company separated, highly pleased with the day's entertainment.

Late that evening news was received of the capture of Fort Morgan, near Mobile, on which a general congratulatory order was issued from Army Headquarters.

21*

## CHAPTER XXX.

Letters from Prison.—Movements on the right and left.

During the remainder of the month of September nothing of note occurred in the Brigade, beyond the usual routine of guard and picket duty, which were, however, at this time, almost as bad as constant skirmishing, and so exposed was the position of the camp, that very frequently both men and officers were killed and wounded in their tents and quarters.

Several letters were received at this time from the officers and men captured on the 22d of June, and the 25th of August, at Reams' Station, on the Weldon road. From these we learned that Captain Maurice Wall, Sixty-ninth, and Lieutenant Grainger, of the Eighty-eighth, were then in Charleston, from which place they subsequently escaped into General Foster's lines, after suffering severe hardships and encountering numerous adventures.

Major Byron wrote the following characteristic letter from Richmond, where our gay and fascinating friend was fêted to his heart's content, as the last living

:presentative of the Byron peerage, notwithstanding t le earnest protestations of several sour and malig- n ant editors, who were highly indignant that such un- u:ual courtesy should be extended to any Yankee offi- cer by the *élite* of Southern aristocracy. Doubtless owing to his good looks, gallant demeanor, and favor with the ladies, the major was soon restored to liberty.

LIBBY PRISON, RICHMOND, VA., Sept. 3, 1864.

MY DEAR L———: No doubt you have heard ere this that I am en- joying the hospitality of "Libby," or, as the Richmond *Enquirer* has been pleased to term it, "permitted to enjoy its freedom." Well, I have not much to complain of as yet: I anticipated worse. Lynch and Connor, of the Sixty-ninth, and Concklin, of the Eighty- eighth, with a number of the "Legion," partake of the same privi- leges; and although they cannot appreciate them, they rest gloomily content—a matter of absolute necessity. Wall and Granger have been sent further South.

Send the inclosed note to Dr. Powell, of my regiment, and oblige

Your friend,  JOHN WHITEHEAD BYRON,

Major 88th N. Y. V. I. B.

The accompanying notes were received from Colonel Byrne, of the Legion, and Captain Maurice Wall, of the Brigade, about the same period:

LIBBY PRISON, RICHMOND, VA., Aug. 28, 1864.

MY DEAR BROTHER—I arrived at the above place yesterday evening, and in good health and spirits. I received no wound in the battle of the 25th; Capt. McConvey was severely wounded, and I have since learned that he died from its effects. If such is the case, I am sorry, and I hope it may be otherwise. About thirty of our regi- ment were taken prisoners, six of whom are officers: Capt. Doran, Capt. Page, Lieut. Flynn, Lieut. Davis, Lieut. Hartford, and your

humble servant. Capt. Kelly and Lieut. Cantwell, of the One Hundred and Sixty-fourth, are also prisoners here, taken at the same time. Capt. Granger of the One Hundredth N. Y. Vols., is also here. All seem to be first-rate and looking well. I cannot state the length of time I am to remain in this place. Neither can I state the time I may be exchanged. But I feel satisfied to pull it through and await my fortune. You must not fret or feel discontented, for I assure you I am all right. JOHN BYRNE,
Lieut.-Col. 155th N. Y. V., Irish Legion.

CHARLESTON JAIL, Sept. 24, 1864.

MY-DEAR BROTHER—Since I became a prisoner—now over three months—I have not received a word from you or home, and I cannot for the life of me imagine what is the cause of it. I am enjoying good health, and would feel in much better spirits if I could only hear from home. Our present abode is better than the one we were in when last I wrote you, having better water, more room, and an improvement in our food, which consists of corn-meal, flour, and bacon, in small quantities. It is served out to us for ten days, and with the strictest economy we can make it last about nine ; the other day is devoted to cursing the Confederacy and our misfortune in falling into the hands of the Philistines. Our time is taken up, principally, in cooking, washing, and other industrial occupations. When the latter duty comes, I have to do as the old story goes— " go to bed while your shirt is drying ;" and, as to tailoring, I have just completed an elaborate piece on the back of my unmentionables; for you must remember that this is the part most used to hardship among us prisoners. You can often see a black pants with a blue seat, and *vice versa ;* but if you ask its wearer what is the reason of the change in colors, he will probably get off some joke by stating he belongs to the horse-marines, and he always has his headquarters in the saddle.

But our sufferings, of which I keep all to myself until I see you, are nothing compared with those of the enlisted men in Andersonville, Ga. Up to the 30th of July, there were 10,000 men buried there. The space they had to live in was only 13 acres, and in this pen were confined some 30,000 of our poor fellows. The water running through this was of a swampy, foul nature ; and this they were compelled to wash in, use as a ——, and drink. Many men often begged of the guard for " God's sake" to shoot them, and put them out of pain, they being smitten by disease, with no shelter, and being almost devoured with vermin. Oh, God! the horrors of that place, if told in detail, would make the blood run cold. Of the number taken with me, one-half are now sleeping their last sleep. Dear Brother, God has been particularly kind to me in sparing me through the shock of battle and the misery of a prison-house.

\* \* \* \* \* \* \* \* \* \*

I will await anxiously your letter. Address it to Capt. Burger, A.A.G. of Gen. Foster ; have two envelopes—the one addressed to me, leave open, and do not say any thing about military or political movements.

I remain, your fond brother,        MAURICE

In the Legion, Captain John Coonan, a dashing veteran officer of the Sixty-ninth National Guard, was promoted to the Lieutenant-Colonelcy. In the Brigade, Captain John H. Gleeson, of the Sixty-third, was promoted to the majority of that regiment.

On the morning of the 17th every one was startled by the news that, on the previous night, Wade Hampton, with a considerable force of cavalry, had captured nearly three thousand beeves from the rear of the army ; and, though pursued by our cavalry and some infantry, succeeded in making good his escape.

In the latter part of the month various successful and unsuccessful movements took place on the right and left of the line.

During the night of the 28th, the Tenth and Eighteenth Corps crossed to the north side of the James; and next morning the Eighteenth Corps, under General Ord, carried the outer line of works below Chapin's Farm. In this action, Fort Harrison—containing sixteen guns—and over two hundred prisoners were captured. The Tenth Corps, under Birney, at the same time assaulted and carried the works on Newmarket Heights, and Kautz, with the cavalry, reconnoitred within two miles of Richmond. On the 30th the rebels assaulted a weak point in both corps; but were repulsed with great slaughter. On the left the Fifth and Ninth Corps advanced from their position on the Weldon Railroad, and encountered the enemy at Peebles' Farm, where an attack was made on their position, the rebels falling back to their fortifications, covering the Southside Railroad. Here the battle was renewed, and a brilliant charge made on the works, which failed. As the Fifth and Ninth Corps withdrew, the Confederates made a counter-charge, and, penetrating the Federal lines, took a considerable number of prisoners. An unsuccessful attack was made next day on Ayres' division of the Fifth Corps, and in the afternoon Hampton's cavalry, engaging Gregg's, was driven back. In one of these engagements Colonel Welch, of the Sixteenth Michigan, commanding a brigade, was shot dead on the parapet of the enemy's works.

# CHAPTER XXXI.

Colonel McGee in command of the Brigade.—Mustered out.—Col. Burke
succeeds.—Is detached.—Contemporary movements.—Battle of Hatcher's Run.—The Legion engaged.

AT this period the consolidated regiments were under
the command of Colonel James E. McGee, who had
been wounded at the storming of Petersburg, and
had subsequently been assisting Colonel Nugent in
the reorganization of the Brigade. Colonel McGee had
reported to his regiment early in September, and forthwith was appointed to the command of the Third and
Fourth Brigades, in which he soon became exceedingly popular. Indeed, his military abilities were well
known, not only in the corps, but in the army generally. On the 19th of October the colonel was mustered out of service, by reason of the expiration of his
term of three years. With him were also mustered
out Captain Richard Moroney, Adjutant J. J. Smith,
Quartermaster Sullivan—all of the Sixty-ninth ; Captain Watts, of the Sixty-third, and a few others—thus
leaving the Brigade almost destitute of the old officers.

The command of the consolidated regiments then devolved on Lieutenant-Colonel Denis F. Burke, of the Eighty-eighth, who had been recently promoted. After this nothing of moment occurred in the Brigade, with the exception of the occasional arrival of recruits from New York.

In the army itself there was a deep quiet until October 7, when the enemy made an attack on Terry's division and Kautz's cavalry, on the Darbytown road, north of the James. Kautz, outnumbered, had to withdraw, losing eight guns. Terry's division, being better protected, suffered but slightly, maintaining its position and driving the enemy from the field, with a loss to them of one thousand.

During the latter part of September, Sheridan had been gradually driving the enemy out of the Shenandoah, destroying all the grain and other provisions in the southern part of the Valley. He then retreated, and was immediately followed up by Longstreet— who had succeeded Early—and by Rosser's cavalry. Sheridan attacked this column on the 9th, and gained a complete victory, capturing over three hundred prisoners, eleven guns, and forty-seven wagons. He then fell back to Cedar Creek, and on the 19th the enemy, under Early, again attacked in force, in Sheridan's absence, turning the left of the line, driving his army four miles, and capturing twenty pieces of artillery. Sheridan arrived from Winchester about noon, and reformed his line, when the attack was again renewed by Early. He was repulsed; and at 3 P. M. Sheridan attacked the enemy with great vigor, driving and routing them, capturing fifty pieces of artillery, and very many prisoners. For this exploit, which produced a most thrilling sensation of gladness everywhere, Sheridan was officially congratulated by the President, and immediately promoted to a full major-general's commission in the regular army, *vice* McClellan, resigned.

On the 27th of October movements were made both on the right and left flanks of the army. The main attack was made on the enemy's right, by the Second, Fifth, and Ninth Corps. The Second, with Gregg's cavalry, started at 2 P. M. on the 26th, leaving only Miles' division in camp, and moved southwestwardly towards Hatcher's Run, followed by the Fifth and Ninth Corps. The next morning, Gregg, keeping away to the left, skirmished with Hampton's cavalry at the bridge over the run, and soon joined the Second Corps, which had reached the Boydton Plankroad. The run was crossed early in the morning by the Second Division, under General Egan; and Mott, with the Third Division, captured the rebel works at Armstrong Mills; but Egan, across the run, was unsupported by Crawford's division of the

Fifth Corps, which failed to connect with the Second. The enemy, taking advantage of this, attacked Mott's division about four P. M., just when the corps was about to advance; so Mott was driven, and Egan thus exposed, and far to the front, was given up for lost. He, however, equal to the emergency, changed front and repulsed the enemy, who retreated, leaving nearly a thousand prisoners in his hands. In this engagement the Second and Third Divisions lost severely, and the Legion had several killed and wounded. The following letters, addressed to Colonel M. Murphy, then at home on sick leave, elucidate the part taken in the engagement by the Legion:

SIXTY-NINTH REGIMENT, N. Y. N. G. A., C. I. L.,
SECOND BRIGADE, SECOND DIVISION, SECOND CORPS,
NEAR PETERSBURG, VA., October 31, 1864.

COLONEL MATTHEW MURPHY:

DEAR FRIEND—You had scarcely reached City Point when an order came to strike tents and be ready to move at a moment's notice; but, of course, as it usually happens, we did not leave camp until dark, and then we were marched and counter-marched until about three A. M., when we halted in front of the Avery House, and remained there until nine A. M., when we were again marched to the front, in rear of corps headquarters. We remained here until the evening of the 26th inst., when, with the rest of the division, and the third division of our corps, we marched to the left, and halted about ten P. M. on the Halifax road, about three miles from the "Yellow Tavern." We rested here until two A. M. of the 27th inst., when we continued to march still further to the left. About five A. M. our skirmishers engaged those of the rebels, driving them from one line of works and capturing about sixty prisoners. In the mean time, the Sixty-ninth and One Hundred and Seventieth went out to protect the flanks. We continued to advance for about three miles, when we came to a large field, with no breastworks, where the enemy was in strong force. Here the division was ordered to charge, which they did with a shout that seemed to terrify the rebels, for they ran like thunder. We charged a second time, with like success, capturing about one thousand five hundred prisoners, with colors, and a wagon-train. During this terrible fight, thank God, the loss of the Legion was small; we had only one man killed and about forty wounded. Among the wounded were Captain Purdy, in the breast, and Lieutenant Cunningham, One Hundred and Seventieth, in the breast, also. The dead man belonged to the One Hundred and Fifty-fifth, Company I. The Eighth New York lost about fifty.

The Brigade never fought better, but particularly the One Hundred and Sixty-fourth and Tim Burke, who received the congratulations of General Egan. Burke, with six men, captured a caisson, and would have brought off two guns, but they were ordered back. Lieutenant Conlin, of the One Hundred and Fifty-fifth, captured a color and one hundred and fifty men, and was himself a prisoner for about three hours.

We left the field about midnight, and fell back to the Fifth Corps line. At one time I thought it would be another Reams' Station affair, for we were entirely surrounded. The rebels came to within two hundred yards of the hospital and shelled it, driving the doctors and their attendants into the woods. I have just learned the name of the fight from an order congratulating the division for their gallantry in driving the *élite* of the rebel army, although at one time surrounded. It is called the battle of "Hatcher's Run."

Hoping that you are convalescing, I remain your friend,

N.

---

NEAR CITY POINT, VA., October 29, 1864.

COLONEL M. MURPHY:

COLONEL—I have better news to send you this time than I expected. Your Brigade was in the advance the entire day of the fight. They acted remarkably well, made two charges on the rebs, and routed them each time; for which they were complimented by General Hancock. The casualties are small. I could not learn the number of killed accurately, but suppose it to be about ten—all enlisted men. The following officers are wounded, but not dangerously: Captain Purdy, One Hundred and Fifty-fifth Regiment; Lieutenant Cunningham, One Hundred and Seventieth regiment; and Lieutenants Rector and Safford, Eighth Regiment. Your orderlies had two horses killed. The affair looked serious at one time, but it turned out to be a victory for us. We captured over one thousand rebs, besides commissary stores, wagons, etc. The Brigade is now back in the field of the fight of the 16th of June. The wagon-train is back again in its old park, and every thing looks as if there was no fight or move during the past week

Father Gillen returned to-day; also, Lieutenant Goodwin. All your friends are well. I hope your health is improving.

F.

---

The following official orders were subsequently issued by the State Department of New York, congratulating the commanding officers of the One Hundred and Sixty-fourth and One Hundred and Seventieth regiments for their gallant conduct at Hatcher's Run:

> GENERAL HEADQUARTERS, STATE OF NEW YORK,
> ADJUTANT-GENERAL'S OFFICE,
> ALBANY, November 15, 1864.

COLONEL J. P. McIVOR, commanding One Hundred and Seventieth Regiment, New York Volunteers:

COLONEL—A communication has been received at these headquarters, from Brigadier-General T. W. Egan, commanding Second Division, Second Army Corps, Army of the Potomac, dated October 29, 1864, wherein he speaks in the highest terms of the conduct of the One Hundred and Seventieth Regiment New York State Volunteers, in the late operations before Petersburg.

I am instructed by his Excellency Governor Seymour to express his gratification, and to tender his thanks to the officers and men of the regiment for this additional evidence of the good conduct of New York troops in the discharge of their duties.

I am, colonel, very respectfully, your obedient servant,

(Signed) JOHN T. SPRAGUE,

Adjutant-General.

A similar order was addressed to Captain Robert Heggart, commanding One Hundred and Sixty-fourth regiment.

# CHAPTER XXXII.

Presentation to Colonel Burke.—Sortie by the Eighty-eighth.—A successful ruse of the enemy.—Arrival of Colonel Nugent and reorganization
of the Brigade.—Promotions.—Original members of the Twenty-eighth
Mass. mustered out.—Reconnoissance.—Escape of Captain Wall and
Lieutenant Grainger.—Dutch Gap Canal a failure.—Capture of Fort
Fisher.—Raid on City Point by rebel iron-clads.—Gen. Hancock leaves
the Corps.—Movement to Hatcher's Run.—Promotions in the Sixty-
ninth.—Desertions from the enemy.

In the latter part of October the soldiers of the
Eighty-eighth presented the commanding officer, Colonel D. F. Burke, a magnificent horse and full set of
equipments, in presence of the other regiments of the
Brigade, on dress parade.

Shortly after this, Colonel Burke was recommended
for a brevet appointment. He had been detached
some time with his regiment in command of Fort
Sedgwick, in front of which he received orders to
attack the enemy on the night of the 29th. This he
did with such success and gallantry that he was highly complimented by the division commander, who sent
the following recommendation to General Hancock:

[Official.]

HEADQUARTERS, FIRST DIVISION,
SECOND ARMY CORPS, October 31, 1864.

MAJOR SEPTIMUS CARNCROSS, A. A. G., Second Army Corps:

MAJOR—In compliance with instructions contained in circular of this date, I have the honor to submit the following recommendations:

That Lieutenant-Colonel Dennis F. Burke, Eighty-eighth Regiment New York Veteran Volunteers, receive the rank of brevet colonel, for gallantry in action, October 29, 1864. Colonel Burke, with a party of one hundred men, attacked and captured a portion of the enemy's line, opposite Fort Sedgwick, taking some prisoners and holding the line until ordered to withdraw.

Very respectfully,                       NELSON A. MILES.
WM. R. DRIVER, A. A. G.                Brig.-Gen. Com.

In the same charge Lieutenant Robert J. O'Driscoll was killed, while acting adjutant to Colonel Burke. Lieutenant O'Driscoll was the first on the enemy's works, and fell by a shot from an unerring sharpshooter. He was one of the bravest and most courteous officers of the Eighty-eighth New York.

Lieutenant George Ford, of the same regiment, was taken prisoner, but succeeded in making his escape, by crawling into the lines on his hands and knees, having been under fire for several hours.

On the 30th of October, while a large number of the Brigade was on picket in front of Petersburg, the enemy penetrated the picket lines—either through the treachery or negligence of a sergeant in charge of one of the posts—and proceeded most adroitly and quietly to relieve the several posts they came to, telling the men to fall in behind the officer in command of the party, in the usual manner. The men unsuspectingly fell into the snare, and thus, in a short time, quite a gap was made in the lines; and, of course, a large number of prisoners taken. At length Lieutenant Murtha Murphy, Co. G, Sixty-ninth, who had charge of a portion of the line, suspecting something wrong from the sudden disappearance of so many pickets from their posts, gave the alarm, and immediately ordered his men to commence firing, to which the enemy responded briskly, and quite a fierce skirmish followed, in which, amid the confusion, the enemy succeeded in retaining the prisoners previously taken. In the *mêlée* Murphy was wounded in the head, but not severely. He succeeded, however, in turning what might have resulted in a great disaster into a minor accident and a repulse of the enemy, who were thus foiled in the prosecution of a well-laid scheme. Among the officers captured were: Lieutenants Harry McQuade, David Lynch, Thomas McGrath, Thomas McKinley, George M. Patchen, of the Sixty-ninth, &c.

Early in November Colonel Nugent arrived from New York, with a fine horse presented him by some of his friends, and forthwith set to work to reorganize the Brigade. The three New York regiments were nearly full — especially the Sixty-ninth — and the Twenty-eighth Mass., under Colonel Cartwright, had been considerably re-enforced by recruits. The One Hundred and Sixteenth Penn. was not again added to the Brigade, because Colonel Mulholland, then commanding, would rank Colonel Nugent. Instead of the One Hundred and Sixteenth, the Seventh New York Heavy Artillery was ordered to report to Colonel Nugent, and thus the ranks of the Brigade, as far as numbers were concerned, seemed fuller than before.

The Colonel's staff consisted of John C. Foley, of the Sixty-ninth, A. A. G.; Captain Oldershaw, of the Eleventh N. J. (a popular and efficient officer), Inspector; Lieutenant Walsh, of the Eighty-eighth, Acting Quartermaster; Lieutenant Courtenay of the Seventh, and Lieutenant McQuade, of the Sixty-third, Aids.

In the Legion it was announced that Colonel Hugh C. Flood, of the One Hundred and Fifty-fifth Regiment, had died in New York, on the 5th instant, of wounds received at Spottsylvania.

At this time Sherman was making his grand march to the sea, through Georgia, and, in the mean time, the other armies of the Union appeared to stand still, in anticipation either of a brilliant success or a terrible failure.

In the Irish Brigade the progress of reorganization

22

went on steadily, so that, early in December, the commissions of several officers, too long delayed, were at
length received. Among the promotions were: Major
Richard Moroney, in the Sixty-ninth; Lieutenant-
Colonel Gleeson, in the Sixty-third, in place of Lieutenant-Colonel Bentley, resigned; Major Fleming, of
the Twenty-eighth Mass. Several non-commissioned
officers in their respective regiments had been also promoted; among them were: Sergeant-Major Murphy,
Hospital Steward Daniel Dolan, Quartermaster-Sergeant Maybury, Sergeants John McCann, John
Meagher, in the Sixty-ninth; Sergeants Kiernan, Collins, Dillon, Halley, Meagher, Gleeson, and others, in
the Sixty-third; Sergeants Miles, Meagher, and others, in the Twenty-eighth Mass.

At this period Colonel Cartwright, some other officers, and several men belonging to the latter regiment,
whose term had expired, left the Brigade and proceeded to Boston, to be mustered out. Before they
started, however, rumors were rife of an approaching
engagement, so that Colonel Cartwright and his brave
fellows volunteered to remain yet a little longer, and
were consequently placed in charge of Forts Welch,
Cummings, and Gregg; and when the expected movement had taken place, they returned home with accumulated honor.

The movement turned out to be a reconnoissance

of the First Division, to Hatcher's Run, where the rebels were met in small numbers and driven from their outward defences. The movement appears to have been intended as a demonstration simply in aid of that under General Warren, who, with the Fifth, Mott's Division of the Second Corps, and Gregg's cavalry, made a raid on the Weldon Road, on the 7th of December, crossing the Nottaway River, through Sussex Courthouse, thence to Nottaway Bridge, where the enemy was found posted, and driven back. The bridge—two hundred feet long—was destroyed; together with eight miles of the railroad south of the bridge. Next day two other bridges—each sixty feet long—Jarrett's Depot, and several miles more of the railroad—twenty in all—were thoroughly destroyed; and after a further reconnoissance to the Meherrin River and Hicksford, where the enemy were found strongly posted, with artillery, the expedition returned to camp on the 10th. On the return the town of Sussex Courthouse was burned, in retaliation for the brutal murder of several of our soldiers by the enemy. This exploit cut off Lee's army from Eastern North Carolina. The loss on our side was about one hundred men, killed, wounded, or captured.

About the middle of this month several Union officers escaped from Columbia, S. C., among whom were Captain Maurice W. Wall and Lieutenant C.

M. Grainger. The first attempt was made on Fort
Fisher by General Butler, which resulted unsuccessfully. The general was immediately relieved of his
command, and General Ord appointed to succeed him
in command of the Army of the James.

The first of January, 1865, found the army of the
Potomac quietly resting in camp.

In the army of the James, the bulkhead of the Dutch
Gap Canal was exploded by six tons of powder, but
the returned earth choked it up again, and it now remains one of the unfinished exploits of the war.

On the 15th Fort Fisher and several other fortifications on the Cape Fear River were successively captured by a detachment of the army of the James, under
General Terry, assisted by a fleet under Commodore
Porter.

On the 23d the army was startled by a formidable
raid on City Point, of three rebel iron-clads and a gunboat. It turned out a failure, however, for the batteries on both sides of the James soon brought their guns
to bear, and after a short struggle, in which two of the
iron-clads got aground, and the gunboat was blown up,
the expedition was abandoned.

Meantime, General Hancock, who had been for a
considerable period disabled by a wound received at
the battle of Gettysburg, which rendered him unfit for
active service, especially such as was now expected

from the army generally, and from his corps in particular, received orders to raise a veteran corps for special service. He was succeeded in command of the corps by General Humphries. A farewell entertainment was given to the general previously to his departure, at the headquarters of the First Division, at which the principal officers of the corps were present, and appropriate resolutions of regret for the loss of such a commander feelingly offered. The general, who was deeply affected by the demonstration, expressed his heartfelt sorrow to part with his old command, with which his name and reputation had been so long identified. He would never forget them while he lived, would never cease to boast of their well-tried courage and splendid successes in many a hard-fought contest, and even though absent, owing to unavoidable misfortune, would be always present with them in spirit, to rejoice in their future glory, and to mourn their inevitable losses. He concluded by introducing his successor, General Humphries, into whose hands he felt perfectly confident to intrust them and their future fortunes. After this Hancock was appointed to the command of the Middle Department, with headquarters at Winchester, in the Valley.

On the 5th of February the Fifth and Second corps made another movement to Hatcher's Run, advancing until they came near the intrenched lines of the enemy ; then halting, threw up intrenchments. The enemy attacked them and were repulsed, and our line was extended nearly four miles. In this movement the Brigade and Legion were under fire, but their losses were comparatively slight, the casualties being only ninety in the whole corps.

It was quite a remarkable coincidence that, in these engagements at Hatcher's Run, the troops on both sides were chiefly Irish. Here the Second Corps, for the first and last time, had some of its flags captured, and it was subsequently ascertained that the captors were Mahone's division, composed mainly of Irishmen. Between the division and the Irish regiments of the Second Corps quite a warm friendship existed. On picket there was no shooting nor any other hostile demonstration between them. The soldiers on both sides mingled freely, exchanged newspapers, coffee, tobacco, and sometimes whiskey. Still, when it came to actual fighting, they fought like bulldogs, and worried one another to their heart's content. Numbers of this same division, wrought upon in this free intercourse by old acquaintances and relatives, deserted to our lines; and it is said that Finigan's Brigade had arranged to leave in a body, on a certain night agreed upon, but the plot was said to have been discovered or suspected, and the command was removed to another part of the line.

The Brigade, at this period, mustered about sixteen hundred muskets, and the Legion, which had not received any recruits during the campaign, could scarcely muster half that number.

During the last expedition to Hatcher's Run, Colonel Nugent had been on leave of absence for a few days, and meantime the command of the Brigade devolved on Colonel Duryea, of the Seventh New York Artillery.

In the Sixty-ninth Regiment, Lieut.-Colonel James J. Smith at length received his commission, and reported to his regiment. In the same command the following officers were also promoted: Lieutenants Murtha Murphy, J. D. Mulhall, Harry McQuade, P. H. Sweeny, E. O'Connor, David Lynch, J. C. Foley, M. H. Murphy, to the rank of Captain; Lieutenant Daniel Doran, commissioned as adjutant; Robert McKinley, George M. Patchen, Thomas McGrath, John Nugent, Owen McNulty, P. Ward, M. Leddy, M. Walsh, W. Herbert, John Conway, Robert Murphy (of the Legion), George Nevins, Terence Scanlon, and M. McConville were promoted to the grade of First and Second Lieutenants, graduating from the ranks, in which most of them had been long-tried veteran soldiers.

In the beginning of March, severe storms for a time prevented the usual manœuvring and consequent active operations, and for several days the army remained mud-bound. Intelligence was received in camp that the captured officers and men belonging to the Brigade and Legion had been exchanged, and were then enjoying a furlough of thirty days, in which to recruit after their sojourn in Southern prisons. Information was also received of the murder of Lieutenant Davis of the Legion, at Andersonville prison, where, without any provocation, it is said, he was shot dead by a sentry, who received a furlough as a reward for the exploit. This brutal murder caused a profound feeling of sorrow among Lieutenant Davis' comrades, by whom he was beloved for his gentle and inoffensive manners, and in the army generally, intense indignation. Nor did the President and Cabinet escape severe condemnation for their cruel policy in repeatedly refusing an exchange of prisoners. Protests were all in vain, however; even the deputation that had previously arrived from Andersonville, from the prisoners confined there, had not been received by the authorities at Washington.

Desertions from the enemy's lines were now becoming so numerous, that unsophisticated people began to think the rebellion on its last legs, and very little more fighting need be anticipated. At the same time, rumors of dissensions in the rebel councils were becoming rife, while destitution of almost every military resource seemed to threaten the Confederacy with utter ruin. As yet, however, a most determined front was everywhere maintained, and the rebel positions appeared as unassailable as ever, owing to the vigor and commanding genius of one man, who, when time has calmed the fanaticism of party, may yet be recorded as the greatest of American soldiers. Whatever may be thought of Lee's obligations to the general government, or of his guilt in taking up arms against it, it cannot be denied that he maintained his cause with singular ability and honesty of purpose, in spite of the terrible odds against him, and the lack of proper support from his own government.

22*

## CHAPTER XXXIII.

Patrick's Day.—Capture and recapture of Fort Steadman.—The Brigade engaged at Skinner's Farm.—The Legion at the Run.—Casualties.—The winding up.—Engagements of the 29th, 30th, and 31st.—Storming of Petersburg.—Evacuation, retreat, and pursuit of the enemy.—The pursuit.—Engagements at Amelia Springs, Sailor's Creek, &c.—Surrender of Lee.—Return of the Army.—The Grand Review.—The Brigade mustered out.

THE last celebration of St. Patrick's Day in.camp was observed with all due solemnity, and the usual sports peculiar to the occasion.

After the anniversary High Mass, which was this time celebrated by Father Willet alone, Father Corby of the Eighty-eighth having resigned and returned to his monastery in Indiana, the various regiments of the Brigade mustered on the race-course, where a stand-house was erected; underneath this was a spacious refreshment-room, in which the officers of the Brigade dispensed sandwiches and whiskey-punch to the invited guests.

Amongst the visitors were Generals Meade, Humphries, Warren, Crawford, Griffin, Bartlett, Webb, Miles, Mott, Meagher, Ayres, Hunt, Smyth, Hayes,

De Trobriand, Pearce, Macy, Winthrop, and Ramsey. Colonel Nugent was clerk of the course.

Several flat and hurdle races followed the opening of the sports, the horses making fine time, especially Colonel Nugent's horse "Harry," who won once or twice. Two or three accidents marred the pleasure of the day, by one of which, Second Lieutenant McConville, of the Sixty-ninth, received a fracture of the skull, which terminated fatally shortly afterwards. Colonel Van Schaik, of the Seventh N. Y., was also severely injured.

On the 25th, after various notes of preparation in the shape of numerous orders, the Second, Sixth, and Fifth Corps made an extensive movement in advance, and again in the direction of Hatcher's Run. This movement was at first apparently offensive, preparations having been made for active operations several days previously, but it subsequently turned out to be rendered necessary by the capture by the enemy of Fort Steadman and other works near the Appomattox, early in the day. They were recaptured, however, by the Third Division of the Ninth Corps, under General Hartranft, who took eighteen hundred prisoners, and inflicted a general loss on the enemy of over three thousand, while our loss was less than one thousand. The several guns were recaptured intact.

While this action was in progress, the First Division

of the Second Corps had a brisk engagement at Skinner's Farm, near Hatcher's Run, where again, as of old, the Brigade added fresh laurels to its former chaplets, covered itself with glory in a stand-up fight of several hours' duration, and was publicly thanked on the field. The contest was conspicuous to the rest of the corps, who appeared to be, as it were, spectators at an exciting melodrama in a huge theatre, and on every side the most flattering admiration was expressed for such a splendid spectacle of unflinching bravery.

Captain Mulhall, of the Sixty-ninth, commanded the party of skirmishers, and was very severely wounded in the leg, a ball shattering the bones very badly. He fell, as it happened, in advance of his party, and between a deadly fire from both sides, by which several were killed and wounded. The captain lay in this position for hours, expecting every moment to be made a living target, but at length the enemy gave way. In this action the Brigade lost heavily, although the officers escaped as if by a miracle. About eight o'clock that night the Brigade was relieved, returning to the old camp near Patnall's Station.

The losses were—killed: Twenty-eighth Mass., seven; Sixty-ninth N. Y., seven: all enlisted men.

Wounded—Sixty-ninth, Captain J. D. Mulhall, Lieutenant Leddy, and thirty-one of the rank and file.

Among the latter were several veterans, and of these the death of Sergeant John Miller was most regretted. Sixty-third N. Y., one ; Eighty-eighth, four ; Twenty-eighth Mass., Captain John Miles, Captain Connor, and thirty-three men.

The Legion was engaged near the Run, and in the action several officers were killed and wounded. Among these the principal were Colonel Matthew Murphy, severely wounded in the knee-joint, who died subsequently at City Point, to the great sorrow of all who knew him ; Captain McTaggert, and others.

After the events of the 25th the army of the Potomac forthwith assumed the offensive. Sheridan's cavalry had joined the army after his daring raid around Richmond, and was immediately dispatched on the 29th towards Dinwiddie Courthouse, with the Fifth Corps acting as an infantry support. The Second Corps moved on the same morning across Hatcher's Run, following up the Fifth, and their places in front of Petersburg were supplied by four divisions from the army of the James.

Sheridan found the enemy in full strength, and on the 30th there was considerable skirmishing along the line, after which the Fifth Corps, though at first repulsed, gained a portion of the Boydton Plankroad, from which, on the 31st, it advanced westward against the White Oak Road. Encountering the enemy at

Gravelly Run, an engagement took place which terminated in a repulse of the Fifth Corps. Sheridan was thus exposed, and it was with great difficulty he was able to hold his ground. Irritated at this, Sheridan at once relieved General Warren, whose unaccountable slowness on this eventful day was said to have caused the temporary check, and General Griffin was appointed to succeed him. During the action just mentioned the First Division of the Second Corps, with the Brigade, was ordered to support the Fifth Corps, and while the latter attacked the enemy in front the division attacked him on the left flank. In this action the First Division captured a flag and several prisoners. Then Sheridan, having reformed his line, moved against the enemy with his usual vigor, at Five Forks, which position covered the Southside Railroad. The cavalry first drove the enemy into his intrenchments, and then the infantry, promptly brought up, flanked him on the right, and captured six thousand prisoners. In this flanking movement, the Second Corps marched and skirmished constantly in the dense woods and swamps near Hatcher's Run.

In General Humphrey's report of the movement of his corps on the 30th and 31st, he speaks in the highest terms of the part taken by the First Division, which, when Crawford's Division of the Fifth Corps had fallen back, threw itself forward, and not only repulsed the enemy, but drove them back a mile and a half beyond the Vaughan Road, and retained the ground thus taken until the line was subsequently rectified.

The course taken by General Sheridan in relieving Warren was very much regretted by the army generally, and by none more than the Brigade, by whom Warren was held in high estimation. The splendid fighting of the Fifth Corps during these momentous days added greatly to the general success; and it must not be forgotten that the corps was placed in a most critical and trying position on the extreme left of the line, wherein it was necessary for the general, as he did, to all appearance, to exercise the most rigorous caution, sound discretion, and at the same time exhibit to the dispirited and wavering a conspicuous example of coolness, courage, and resource in action.

As soon as Sheridan's victory at Five Forks was known, General Grant ordered an attack along the whole line in front of Petersburg. Accordingly, from the Appomattox to Hatcher's Run, a tremendous cannonading commenced early on the 1st of April, and from the brazen and iron throats of nearly a thousand guns of every calibre, a continuous rain of shot and shell, and bolt of every size, shape, and destructive composition, poured on the devoted defenders, until four A. M. on the 2d April. Apprehensive, however, that Lee might withdraw his force and fall upon Sheridan, Grant ordered the First Division of the Second Corps to support the latter a second time.

At dawn on the 2d of April the assault was commenced by the Ninth Corps, who carried the outer line of intrenchments in their front; but an inner line was found too strong for immediate capture. Then the Sixth Corps, on the left of the Ninth, took up the attack, and carried every thing before them, to the Boydton Plankroad, from which they turned to the left, flanking the enemy's intrenchments, and capturing many guns and several thousand prisoners. Ord's Corps followed up the assault, until every thing between Petersburg and Hatcher's Run was captured, killed, or routed. Then the Second and Third Divisions of the Second Corps west of the Run stormed and carried the remaining defences of the enemy on that side, while the First Division pursued the fugitives northward to Sutherland Station, on the South-side road, where they overtook them, capturing, by a spirited charge, two guns and six hundred prisoners. Here Captain Foley, Lieutenant Meagher of the Sixty-ninth, Lieutenant Gleeson of the Sixty-third, and Lieutenant George Beatty, of the Twenty-eighth Massachusetts, were slightly wounded. The other casualties were only few.

Meantime, the other troops proceeded towards

Petersburg, and an attack was made on two of the Southside works by a portion of Ord's command under Gibbon. One of these—Fort Gregg—was held by Harris's Mississippi Brigade, numbering two hundred and fifty men, and this handful of heroes defended it with such courage and perseverance that Gibbon's forces were repeatedly driven back. At length, at seven A. M., a renewed charge carried the work, when its defenders were found reduced to thirty men, while Gibbon's loss was about five hundred. The other work surrendered immediately, and the Union lines were drawn close around the city. Here, baffled and beaten, Lee still made a firm stand, from which the Union forces were as yet unable to dislodge him. He even attacked the Ninth Corps with such vigor that it was with great difficulty it maintained its position, and the garrison at City Point was ordered up to its support. In this charge fell General A. P. Hill, who then died like a soldier, after four years of distinguished service around the rebel capital; and his was the last blow in defence of Petersburg and Richmond. At 11 A. M., on that same Sunday morning, a message was received by Mr. Davis, while assisting at the service in St. Paul's Church, announcing that Lee was about to evacuate Petersburg and that Richmond was lost.

Next morning, April 3d, Petersburg was taken— empty—while Lee's army, now numbering about thirty

thousand men, mustered at Chesterfield Courthouse,
sixteen miles on its retreat to the Southwest. "I have
got my army safe out of its breastworks," said he, "and
in order to follow me my enemy must abandon his
lines, his railroads, and the James River."

After the action near Sutherland's Station, on the
Southside Road, the First Division, with the Brigade,
rejoined the corps, and started again in pursuit of the
flying enemy, following up the cavalry and the Fifth
Corps, under Sheridan. On the afternoon of the 4th,
the Brigade, at the head of the column, reached Jet-
tersville, on the Danville Railroad—where the Fifth
Corps had been resting some short time previously.
Just as the head of the column arrived at the village,
an officer of rather unpretending exterior and address,
with expressive features, active movements, and broad
figure, rode up and inquired of Colonel Nugent what
troops he was leading. He answered—" The Irish
Brigade, First Division, Second Corps." "Ah, indeed!" with a smile. "And you are General Sheridan,
I presume?" "Yes." The general next inquired for
General Humphrey, and then ordered the troops to
file off into a belt of woods adjacent, to form line of
battle and await an attack of the enemy, who were at
this time around Amelia Courthouse. As soon as the
men learned that Sheridan was present, there was at
first a murmur of admiration and an intense desire to

see the sturdy Irish-American, of whose exploits they had heard and read so much, then a spontaneous cheer broke from a thousand throats, while the general rode off hastily, acknowledging the compliment. The expected attack, however, did not take place, and early on the morning of the 5th, after a good night's rest, the Brigade started with the division, by by-roads, towards Amelia Court-house. They soon came in sight of the enemy's train, which at this time was in motion on the road to Amelia Springs. Forthwith a battery was ordered into position, which, after a little delay, commenced shelling the train. Then the Brigade and the other brigades of the division were ordered in pursuit, and all day long, and next day—the 6th—kept up a constant skirmish with the enemy's rear, now at Amelia Springs, then on to Deatonsville, occasionally losing some of the men—killed and wounded—until the enemy was driven towards Sailor's Creek, when Sheridan's forces gave them another mauling, capturing the remains of Ewell's corps, himself and four other general officers. " This result was largely due to the energetic movements of the Second Corps, which, moving to the right, had pressed the enemy closely in a rear-guard fight all day till night, when it had attained a position near the mouth of Sailor's Creek ; then the enemy was so crowded in, that a large train was captured and many hundreds were taken prisoners.

The trophies of the Second Corps included, in addition, several pieces of artillery and thirteen flags." Of these the Brigade captured the largest number, and some of the officers were subsequently dispatched with the trophies to Washington, where they received a decoration from the War Department.

The loss in the Brigade during the skirmishing on the 5th and 6th was slight: one officer, Lieutenant Robert Murphy, of the Sixty-ninth, seriously, and some of the men slightly wounded. On the 7th, Lieutenant-Colonel Fleming and Captain McFadden, of the Twenty-eighth Massachusetts, were wounded, but not seriously.

On the 6th, near Sailor's Creek, the corps lost one of its best and most beloved officers, in the person of General Tom Smyth, who was mortally wounded in the neck, on the picket-line, and died subsequently, even in the arms of victory. It would be impossible to picture the grief this unexpected calamity caused to his immediate command and to the Brigade, by whom he was almost idolized. Every thing else was forgotten, and even victory itself could not repay the survivors for the loss of such a gallant commander, and a noble specimen of a man and a soldier. Peace to his great soul, ever-increasing honor to his name, and to his widow and orphan the most heartfelt condolence of his companions in arms!

Next day, the 7th, the enemy still flying, the Second Corps came up with them near High Bridge, over the Appomattox, on the Danville road, just as they were burning the bridge. One span had been already destroyed, and they were preparing to burn the wagon-road bridge, when the corps appeared and prepared for action. The enemy, in considerable force, were drawn up on the heights of the opposite bank of the river, behind intrenchments, while their skirmishers held the bridge, ready to dispute the passage. These were, however, quickly driven off by the second division; and after a short resistance the main force hastily retired, leaving eighteen guns in the hands of the victors.

The corps again took up the pursuit, with the First and Third Divisions, on the Old Stone road, to Appomattox Courthouse, while the Second was directed on Farmville, three miles distant. Here the enemy were in considerable force, burning bridges, and guarding a wagon-train moving towards Lynchburg; but, on the approach of the Second Division, the plan was abandoned. One hundred and thirty wagons were destroyed, and the troops then rejoined the main body of Lee's army. This was found intrenched in a strong position, which Humphrey endeavored to flank with the First and Third Divisions; but the odds against him were too many, so the attempt failed, with the loss of about six hundred of the First Division, three regiments having been very badly cut up in the charge. During the night, however, he again retreated.

Next day, the 8th, the Second and Sixth Corps followed up the fugitives closely, while Sheridan was hastening towards Lynchburg to stop every outlet of escape, and thus capture the entire army. Meantime negotiations had been opened between Grant and Lee, which were not as yet of a satisfactory or decisive nature, because Lee had determined to escape at all hazards, and still continued his flight with all the haste it was possible to make. Soon, however, he was entirely surrounded,—Sheridan's force confronting him towards Lynchburg, while the rest of the army pressed on his rear; and but one escape remained, and this was to cut his way through Sheridan's lines. The attempt was made on the morning of the 9th by a body of troops about eight thousand strong, under General Gordon, who had orders from Lee to cut his way through at all hazards. This was immediately begun with such impetuosity that the cavalry, previously dismounted to resist the attack, was forced back. At this junction, Sheridan arrived from Appomattox, whither he had been to hurry up the infantry. He directed his troopers to fall back gradually, at the same time resisting steadily, so as to give the infantry time to come up and form its lines. When this was effected, Sheridan ordered the cavalry to mount, and charged on the enemy's left flank. Then a party with a flag of truce emerged from the Confederate lines, to present a letter from Lee, with a view to surrender on the terms already proposed. Hostilities ceased, Generals Grant and Lee met at McLean's house, in Appomattox Courthouse, and a formal surrender took place on the following terms : Rolls of all the officers and men to be made out in duplicates, one copy for each party; the officers to give their individual paroles not to take up arms against the United States until properly exchanged, and all company and regimental commanders to sign a like parole for the men of their commands; the arms, artillery, and public property to be packed and stacked, and turned over to the proper officers appointed to receive them. This was not to include the side-arms of the officers, nor their private horses or baggage; this done, each officer and man was to return home, to remain undisturbed so long as they observed their paroles and the laws in force where they were to reside. Victors and vanquished then mingled freely together; rations of all kinds were issued to the half-famished Confederates, and the rest of the afternoon of this eventful day was spent in deeds of kindness and mutual rejoicing that the end had at last been reached, and peace was to reign once more.

After the surrender of Lee the Army of the Potomac prepared to return, but as yet Johnston's army had not surrendered to Sherman; and while this was an uncertainty, the Sixth Corps was detached to Danville, so that, in case of hostilities being resumed in North Carolina, a force might be on hand to aid Sherman. The remainder of the army rested for some days, near Burkesville, and then started to return by way of Richmond. Meantime, Johnston's surrender was announced, and the Sixth Corps rejoined the Army of the Potomac.

At Burkesville the army was stunned and horrified at the news of the atrocious murder of President Lincoln.

After a tiresome march overland, the Army of the Potomac reached Alexandria shortly afterwards, having paraded through Richmond, where it was received with a certain amount of enthusiasm.

Encamped quietly within a few miles of Alexandria, the Brigade and Legion had now plenty of time to devote to pleasure, reminiscences of the past, and sad memories of departed comrades. Promotions, in regular order and by brevet, rewarded merit in every grade. First in the line of promotions came Colonel Nugent, who, though entitled to a full commission, received the brevet rank of brigadier-general. In the Eighty-eighth, Lieutenant-Colonel Burke had already had his full commission as colonel, from the State; but, in addition, he received a brevet appointment in the

U. S. Volunteers. Major J. W. Byron, of the same regiment, was promoted to the rank of lieutenant-colonel; Captain Brady, of the Sixty-third, was appointed lieutenant-colonel; and Captain Terwilliger, major. Captain Black, of the Twenty-eighth, was brevetted to a majority, and Captain McQuade, of the Sixty-third, both in the brigade-staff, received a similar appointment.

In the Legion, also, several brevet appointments were made; among them, that of Colonel McIvor, to the rank of brigadier-general.

On the 23d of May a grand review of the several armies took place at Washington, in presence of President Johnson and Cabinet, the representatives of foreign powers, and an immense concourse of citizens from all parts of the country.

The Brigade returned to New York early in July, assisted at the celebration of the Fourth, and was afterwards mustered out of service.

---

I have thus briefly sketched the services of the Irish Brigade and the Irish Legion, during the vigorous campaigns under Grant, in 1864-5. I have labored to be as correct and impartial as possible; and if I have, in any way, failed in the prosecution of this important task, it has been through no feeling of partiality, but from want of space, and more extensive materials.

W. O'M.

# APPENDIX.

---

THE Irish Brigade* participated in the following general engagements, besides in several minor actions and skirmishes:

1862.—Siege of Yorktown, ending May 6th.

   "     June 1st, battle of Fair Oaks.

   "     "   27th,   "     Gaines' Mill.

   "     "   "    "     Savage Station.

   "     "   "    "     Allen's Farm and Peach Orchard.

   "     "   30th,   "     White Oak Swamp.

   "     July 1st,   "     Malvern Hill.

   "     Sept. 17th,   "     Antietam.

   "     Dec. 13th,   "     Fredericksburg.

1863.—May 3d,   "     Chancellorsville.

   "     July 3d,   "     Gettysburg, followed by Auburn and Bristow Station.

1864.—May 5th, battle of the Wilderness.

   "     "   8th,   "     Todd's Tavern.

   "     "   10th,   "     Po River.

   "     "   12th,   "     Spottsylvania.

   "     "   18th,   "     "     (No. 2.)

---

* The badge of the Irish Brigade was that of the First Division, Second Corps, the red trefoil or Shamrock.

1864.—May 25th, battle of the North Anna River.
   "     " 30th,     "     Tolapotomy Creek.
   "   June 3d,     "     Coal Harbor.
   "     " 16th,     "     Petersburg, followed by Yellow Tav-
                                  ern, Strawberry Plains, and Pe-
                                  tersburg (No. 2.)
1865.—April 25th, Skinner's Farm.

---

## BREVET MAJOR-GENERAL THOMAS FRANCIS MEAGHER.

IRELAND has given birth to many a gifted child of genius, whose great intellects were destined to enrich the literature of other lands.

The commercial ability, the military genius, the comprehensive statesmanship of the exiled children of the Gael have added to the renown and lustre of almost every country on the globe, whilst their "own loved island of sorrow" weeps as Niobe among the nations of the earth.

We are not going to investigate this strange anomaly now, but simply to give a short sketch of one who has run the outlaw's brief career, to wipe away her tears; and has since occupied a prominent position both in the civil and military history of his adopted country.

Thomas F. Meagher was born in the city of Waterford, in 1823. His father represented that borough in Parliament, and being in every sense a respectable and loyal burgher, wished to bring up his son in the same law-abiding faith. The better to do so, he placed him under the tuition of the venerable Jesuits of Clongowes and Stonyhurst. While the reverend fathers were trying to store his mind with religious maxims that might fit him for a cloister ; philosophy from the school of Plato, and strict submission to the laws of the ruling powers, because St. Paul says, "He that resisteth the power resisteth the ordinance of God ;" while receiving these lessons, nature and his own impassioned poetic mind were teaching him another—a more brilliant, a more generous, though a more dangerous one.

O'Connell had roused and swayed the heart of Ireland. Even the sedate Mr. Meagher, M. P., joined his school of repealers, and was rather flattered at the brilliant efforts of his son, who accompanied him to some of their banquets. O'Connell saw what a power so imaginative a mind, so well stored with historical lore, and so highly gifted with declamatory powers, would be to him ; so, through his influence with the father, the young man came prominently before the public, and became the most brilliant and fascinating repeal orator of the day.

He soon formed an acquaintance with O'Brien, Mitchel, Davis, Duffy, and others of the leading repealers. For some time a coldness was springing up between the adherents of the no-blood policy of O'Connell and the more ardent repealers, which soon split up into what was called the "Young Ireland Party." It is thought that the good sense of O'Connell would have made certain concessions, which would tend to consolidate the two factions, had not the sectional, mischievous spirit of his son John interfered.

The three glorious days of revolution in Paris fired the enthusiastic hearts of the Irish revolutionists. The French had been successful. Louis Philippe was hurled from the throne, and a democracy was springing up on the ruins of an empire. *Vox populi, vox Dei,* should be the motto of all nations; why not of Ireland, too?

Meagher was one of the deputation that went to Paris to congratulate the republic on its new-born liberty.

He came home and sowed the revolutionary seed broadcast. The gifted Davis was dead, Mitchel was in prison, and soon sentenced to penal servitude.

Death, exile, or prison threatened the revolutionary leaders of '48, and soon followed the upheaving of the weak against the strong, the oppressed against the oppressors, to be followed by the bitter fruits of the expatriation and death of the noblest of the country.

It was so in '98, yet the men of '98 would have been successful had they military leaders, and did they but know how to use the victories they had gained. The rum-shops of New Ross did more to suppress the rebellion than the army of England.

In '48 we again wanted military leaders. The men of '48 were as bright a galaxy of genius, eloquence, and poetry as Ireland, or any other country, ever produced. What could be nobler than the high-toned, defiant conduct of Smith O'Brien? He bearded the lion in his den, and told that august body, called the British Lords and Commons assembled, that poor oppressed Ireland should have her own, even with the sword. It was a bold declaration, coming from such a man and in such a place.

What could tend more to fire up a people who yearned for freedom than the bitter, caustic writings of Mitchel; the fiery, impassioned words of Meagher; the burning, defiant poems of Davis, Duffy, Speranza, Eva Barry, and a host of other poets, whose burning stanzas corroded the tyrant's chain, and fired the patriot's heart to dare the barricades?

The people were inflamed; the country swarmed with clubs; the government put that powerful engine, trial by jury—save the mark! —into operation; and then, in order to precipitate the movement, they suspended the *habeas corpus* act, compelling Smith O'Brien and his associates to appeal to the country before they had matured their plans, or, in fact, formed any plans at all.

These men, who shone so brilliantly with the patriot's tongue and poet's pen, were but mere children at the game of war. The peasantry rushed around Smith O'Brien in Tipperary, armed with every rude weapon they could grasp. He told them that he did not want to fight for the present, he only wanted to protect himself from arrest. This was in the month of July; a famine was raging through the country; the disheartened people returned to their homes to die of starvation, instead of falling on the battle-field as they desired, and the fiasco exploded at Farrinrory, in July, 1848.

The arrests and trials of O'Brien, Meagher, McManus, O'Donoghue, and several others followed.

The conspirators, as they were called, were all sentenced to be executed at Clonmel Jail, which sentence was subsequently commuted to penal servitude for life.

Meagher's address, when asked what he had to say that sentence of death should not be passed upon him, whether considered in its literary bearings, or as a calm manly exposition of his policy and the cause that influenced him to take up arms against the government of England, scarcely ranks second to Robert Emmet's death speech. There was nothing of the braggadocio, nothing of the straining after fame in his bold, manly speech, under the shadow of the gallows. He was sent to Australia, to undergo his penal servitude. Away in the wild bush he formed some agreeable acquaintances. He spent his time fishing and fowling, and visiting the respectable settlers within his prescribed limits. O'Brien and he often spent evenings together. Meagher, in some of his letters, gives quite graphic and entertaining sketches of his penal servitude,· which, in justice, we must say, was servitude only so far as it limited him to a certain locality, and to certain prescribed forms that merely curtailed his general liberty. We would like to dwell upon these wanderings by lake and wood, only that it would render our sketch too long for our limits. In the course of his rambles and visits he formed the acquaintance of an estimable young lady, daughter to a wealthy settler. Her companionship, for she was well-educated and accomplished, relieved the monotony of his sequestered life. This romantic friendship grew into love, and she became his wife. After the birth of their child,

Meagher, having formed his resolution of making his escape to America, had to leave her after him. She sailed for Ireland, and, accompanied by his father, she visited him in America; but her health being delicate, she had to return.

Much has been said and written about his escape from Australia, his enemies charging him with violating his parole, while his friends state the contrary. Meagher's own statement, confirmed by the testimony of John Mitchel and Smith O'Brien, who was remarkable for his strict observance of honor, should satisfy all parties that Meagher's conduct was strictly honorable all through.

He effected his escape to America in 1852, and on his arrival he was enthusiastically received and fêted.

He soon afterwards delivered a series of lectures throughout the North, making a tour also of the Southern States. His orations were brilliant and effective, but rather partaking of the florid; however, time has considerably curbed this declamatory style.

He was warmly received in the Southern States, and fêted everywhere he went. The appreciation of this kindness made him feel reluctant in subsequently taking up arms against such warm personal friends; but he felt that all friendship should be merged in the salvation of the Union. He travelled through Costa Rica, in the service of the government, and succeeded in establishing some very advantageous relations between these republics and the United States. His descriptions of this tour, published in Harper's, were very fine and brilliant.

After his arrival in New York from Australia, he devoted himself to the practice of the law, but found it rather dry and methodical for one of his ardent temperament.

In April, 1856, he started the " Irish News," which reached a large circulation, and was a very able journal, displaying great ability and honesty.

His career in America, until the breaking out of the war, was that of a successful literary man. As a writer, a lecturer, and a journalist he was eminently successful, and had he the same amount of indomitable perseverance as he had of talent, he might have won an enviable reputation either in the field of literature or politics.

His first wife having died at his father's in Waterford, he, after two years' widowerhood, married a Miss Townsend, daughter to a wealthy merchant of the Empire City. She has made him an excellent, loving wife. Possessing all the refinement and elegance of a highly cultivated lady, she partook of his camp-fare, and now is sharing his fortunes amidst the rough scenes of pioneer life on the

Pacific coast. At the breaking out of the war he was captain of a guard, called after him Meagher's Guards, which served with him at Bull Run.

The history of his services during the war being given in full in the body of the work, it is needless to recapitulate them. In 1864 he was reinstated in his command, and ordered to report to General Sherman in the South.

He did so, and was assigned to the command of a division formed of the invalids and returning veterans of Sherman's army. These were stationed at Chattanooga, Tennessee, when Hood was moving on Nashville, and Sherman had gone down to the sea. General Steedman, who commanded at Chattanooga, had to fall back towards Nashville, covering the line of railroad, leaving General Meagher in command at Chattanooga.

The railroad was cut, the battle of Nashville fought, Chattanooga was for several days cut off and threatened; but the admirable disposition made of the garrison, and the fortification of the outer line of works, deterred the enemy's attack.

Major-General Steedman highly complimented General Meagher in special orders and private letters for his able management of affairs.

The troops under General Meagher were ordered in 1865 to join Sherman's army in North Carolina, and were assigned to their different commands. This threw General Meagher out of command again, and the war soon coming to an end, he resigned. He was, however, brevetted major-general; and, by order of the President, went to Montana, where he now fills the position of acting governor of that Territory.

## BRIGADIER-GENERAL MICHAEL CORCORAN.

In times of popular excitement and revolutions men of power and energy are sure to rise to the surface. The people bow before the decisions of superior minds, and the latter soon mould them to their wills. Michael Corcoran was a man who forced his way upwards from the people. He was descended from an old stock, his family claiming direct relationship to the renowned Earl of Lucan—the bravest soldier of his day—through his great grandmother, who was fourth daughter of William Fitzgerald, of Cloonmore, in the county of Roscommon, and great grand-daughter of Sarsfield.

In 1746 she married Patrick McDonagh Thomas Corcoran. The father of the general was a half-pay officer, who had served in the

West Indies for several years. On his retirement he married Mary McDonagh.

Michael Corcoran was born on the 21st September, 1827, in Carrowkeel, county Sligo. After receiving as good an education as circumstances would admit, he joined the Irish constabulary force, when only nineteen, and remained in them three years, during which time he was stationed at Creislough, county Donegal. In August, 1849, he resigned and emigrated to America, where he at first had to undergo many of the hardships and vicissitudes which emigrants have too often to encounter in their early career in America. These young Corcoran soon overcame, owing to his directness of purpose and steadiness of action. After some time he entered the employment of Mr. John Heeney, of "Hibernian Hall," New York, whom he soon afterwards succeeded as proprietor. He subsequently held a position as clerk in the post-office.

General Corcoran's history commences with his military career, and may be dated from the time he joined the Sixty-ninth as private. His military passion and his previous knowledge of military tactics were of great advantage to him, and he soon rose to be orderly sergeant, next first lieutenant, and next captain, displaying all through the greatest ability and fitness for the different positions. During what was called the Quarantine War, on Staten Island, Captain Corcoran's services elicited the following tribute of merit from the Inspector-General:

"What I might say of Captain Corcoran, as to his military knowl. edge, would not add to his already known reputation as the best, if not the very best, officer of his rank in the First Division."

He was elected to fill the vacant colonelcy of his regiment, the Sixty-ninth, August 25th, 1859.

On the occasion of the visit of the Prince of Wales to New York, when flunkeys were in a craze to pay him honor, Colonel Corcoran refused to parade his regiment on the occasion.

He simply said that, as an Irishman, he could not consistently parade Irish-born citizens in honor of the son of a sovereign, under whose rule Ireland was left a desert and her best sons exiled or banished.

The subsequent action of England during the rebellion fully justified Colonel Corcoran in refusing to parade his men on such a sham display of mock royalty. Colonel Corcoran was court-martialled for disobedience of orders, but the inception of the war dissolved the court-martial, for one of the first regiments to volunteer for the seat of war was the gallant Sixty-ninth. Even while the court-martial was pending, Colonel Corcoran showed his disinterestedness and purity. While under arrest, some of the officers of the regiment thought that they should not turn out; but the colonel immediately published a letter, telling them not to take his position into account, but to stand by the flag of the Union and the sacred principles involved in its sustainment.

We need not here recapitulate the services of the gallant Sixty-ninth at Bull Run. General Corcoran, in reply to a presentation speech at the Astor House, speaking of Bull Run, said:

"I did not surrender until I found myself, after having successfully taken my regiment off the field, left with only seven men and surrounded by the enemy."

Elsewhere he said:

"The Sixty-ninth did not fear the rebel cavalry, and on their approach formed a hollow square, inside of which Generals Sherman and McDowell sought shelter and received it. The attack of cavalry was repulsed. Immediately afterwards a general stampede had taken place; ambulances and wagons came on like an avalanche, and in order to get his regiment out of the way he ordered them to the right. He was satisfied the men did not hear this order, as only Lieutenant Connelly and Captain McIvor and some seven or eight others followed him, the regiment being broken and carried along with the current. With these few men he held some of the rebel cavalry at bay, until remonstrated with by Captain McIvor and others, who said: 'For God's sake, colonel, surrender, and save the lives of these few brave men—there is no use in sacrificing them.'"

Colonel Corcoran and his brave companions were hurried off to Richmond prison. After being detained here for several months, and treated with unusual severity, he was transferred to Columbia, thence to Charleston, South Carolina.

When in Richmond, several officers were writing letters begging the interposition of the Government in their behalf. And also when he and several other officers were selected for execution, in retaliation for some privateersmen in the hands of the Federal authorities, Colonel Corcoran wrote a dignified, patriotic letter, saying, "that he wished the Government to act on its own conviction of just policy, and that if it were best for the cause that the privateersmen should be hung as pirates, he would cheerfully surrender his life, if the South chose to take it in retaliation."

His treatment was so unfair, that Schuyler Colfax, of Indiana, made the following motion in the House of Representatives, at Washington:

"Whereas, Michael Corcoran, who was taken prisoner at the battle-field of Manassas, has, after suffering other indignities, been confined, by the rebel authorities, in the cell of a convicted felon, therefore,

"Resolved, that the President of the United States be requested to similarly confine James M. Mason, late of Virginia, now in custody at Fort Warren, until Colonel Corcoran shall be treated as the United States have treated all prisoners taken by them on the battle-field."

Colonel Corcoran was detained thirteen months in Southern prisons before exchanged. He was finally released about the middle of August, 1862.

On his way home his reception in Washington, Baltimore, and Philadelphia, was one perfect ovation, perhaps never surpassed since the days of the immortal Washington.

In New York, the reception accorded him surpassed any similar display of modern times. All classes, without distinction, united with a heartiness, truly inspiring, to do honor to a man whose truly American patriotism had subjected him to such dangers and privations, and whose well-known love of Ireland had been the most prominent trait in his character. Corcoran's character was fully vindicated by subsequent events.

The bitter hostility of England towards the Republic, manifested in the actions of her politicians and the material aid given to the Confederacy, justified his refusal in turning out to honor the Prince of Wales, and showed the correctness of the Irish-American sentiment towards England.

At Jersey City the members of the Common Council, heads of departments, members of the press, and other distinguished citizens waited on him with congratulatory addresses. Common Councils, corporate bodies, and private individuals vied with one another in paying him respect.

Presentation swords and medals were given him. Civil appointments were offered him. All this pomp and parade did not turn his head. He steadily and persistently devoted himself to the grand object he had in view—namely, to raise a brigade to sustain the flag of his adopted country, and, *perhaps,* to raise a flag on the soil of his native land.

He was frank, heroic, and purely unselfish. The following noble expression, which occurs in one of his speeches at the time, fully shows the honesty of the man and the purity of his patriotism:

" Democrat as I am, I will grasp the hand of an Abolitionist, or a

Know-Nothing, who will stand shoulder to shoulder with me in this war."

With the full commission of a brigadier-general and power to raise a Legion, he set to work and embodied the Irish Legion, which was more generally called the "Corcoran Legion."

In a very short time he saw himself at the head of one of the finest commands that ever took the field. After a probationary stay at Camp Scott, Staten Island, they proceeded to Virginia, and were stationed at Suffolk.

Towards the close of January, 1863, the rebel general, Roger A. Pryor, crossed the Blackwater, with three regiments of infantry, fourteen pieces of artillery, and about one hundred cavalry.

General Corcoran had received orders from General Peck to advance from Suffolk on a reconnoissance, to observe Pryor's movements. A very sharp engagement followed at a place called the Deserted House, in which the Legion was eminently successful. This was the first fight in which the Legion participated, and the skill of the general, as well as the bravery of the men, were highly extolled by General Peck in his general orders.

The Legion spent the summer of 1863 guarding the forts and lines of communications, also in picketing the front around Fairfax and other points. This service required continual vigilance, and was a first-rate school to train the men for more active campaigning; besides, they had several brushes with Moseby and his men, also with rebel posts and pickets.

While stationed near Fairfax, General Corcoran resolved to celebrate the Christmas holidays of 1863 in splendid style, and had invited several guests for the occasion—among them General Meagher, who was spending a few days with him in camp. Immediately before Christmas he had ridden from his headquarters to the station with General Meagher, and on his return back had ridden the general's horse, a very spirited animal. He was somewhat in advance of his staff, and going rather hard at the time; suddenly he was seen to fall from the horse, and on his officers coming up they found him senseless, merely breathing. Whether he fell off in a fit or was killed by the fall is not known. He died in the course of the following night.

Thus died, in the prime of manhood, as brave a soldier and as sterling an Irishman as ever lived. He was a loss to America, for his name and reputation were talismanic to collect his countrymen to his standard. He was a loss to Ireland, for the dearest wish of his heart was to live to strike for her independence; and from his experience as a soldier, his wisdom as a general, and his prudence and foresight as a man, who knows what he would have accomplished had he lived ?

## BRIGADIER-GENERAL THOMAS SMYTH.

THE lives of some men are crowded with incidents from their boyhood. This is owing to the cause that they mingle much in the busy scenes and strifes of life.

Other men live on in the quiet routine, until stirring events call them into action. Few thought that the courteous, skilled mechanic possessed all the attributes of the hero ; and only for the civil war, Thomas Smyth would have lived unseen, unknown to all save his neighbors and those whom business relations brought him in contact with.

Thomas Smyth was born December 25, 1832, in Fermoy, county Cork, and emigrated to this country in 1854, then a young man of twenty-two years. He was always remarkable for his intelligence and application to study and business.

On his arrival in America he went to work for his uncle, who was engaged in the carriage business at Philadelphia. After four years at the trade in Philadelphia he removed to Wilmington, Delaware, and followed the same business as his uncle. He was then a young man of much promise. He had read much, and had well stored his mind with history, philosophy, and poetry. In literary circles and debating societies he took a prominent part. At the breaking out of the war his military ardor was stirred. He was fired with a desire of doing something for his adopted country, and he felt that he had the right stuff within him to make his mark, if he only got the chance. He at once raised a company of ardent young patriots like himself, and joined the Twenty-fourth Pennsylvania Volunteers as captain of company H. At the expiration of their term of service he returned to his home in Wilmington for a short time.

The first Delaware regiment of volunteers was being organized, and Captain Smyth was offered the majority.

The regiment was attached to the Third Brigade, Second Division, Second Army Corps.

It is needless to follow its history, for it is that of the gallant Second Corps, which was second to none in the army. Smyth's executive ability and coolness as an officer, and his romantic bravery in action, made him not only a favorite with his men, who almost idolized him, but also with his superior officers, who respected and admired him.

He rose rapidly to the colonelcy of the regiment, and also to the command of his brigade. His daring exploits and narrow escapes in battle were remarkable, and he at length began to fancy that he had a charmed life.

In March, 1864, he was appointed to the command of the Irish Brigade, with which he was a great favorite. He had a fine, portly, soldierly appearance, a pleasing, insinuating address, and always tried to correct evils in camp more by contrast and moral effect than by punishment. On this account his camps were always remarkable for their cleanliness, his men for their order, sobriety, and efficiency. While commanding the Irish Brigade he had so ingratiated himself with the troops that they actually wept when he left, and the officers presented him with an address.

About the end of May, Colonel Burnes, having been on recruiting duty for some time, returned to his command. He outranked Colonel Smyth, so the latter went back to his former command.

In September he was appointed Brigadier-General. He distinguished himself in the various engagements, and was killed near Farmville just two days before Lee's surrender. He was riding outside the picket-lines when shot through the face by a sharpshooter. At the time, he stood one of the first on the list for a major-generalship.

In appearance General Smyth had few superiors ; tall, of a muscular frame, with a native dignity and commanding grace about him, you could scarcely see a finer-looking man or a truer specimen of a soldier. His military history is a history of the campaigns in Virginia, for there were but few battles of importance in which he did not serve. With the coolness and judgment of the scientific officer he combined a bravery almost amounting to rashness. He generally rode in front of his own picket-lines, along the outer posts, to make sure that all was right. It was a general remark among the men— " Well, if General Smyth escapes he has a charmed life." General Smyth was in every sense a credit to his race and his country. Like Corcoran, he was thoroughly national, and joined every patriotic movement which had for its aim the liberation of Ireland. The greatest hope of his life was to strike a blow for her freedom, for, like most Irishmen, he felt the degradation of being a race without a country, and of winning renown on foreign battle-fields, while his countrymen at home were a starved, despised race. In him and General Corcoran, Ireland lost two of her noblest and purest patriots —England, two of her bitterest foes.

## BATTERY OF THE IRISH BRIGADE.

This is an arm of the service of which I have made but little mention in the body of my work, simply because the artillery, though raised specially for the brigade, was divided among the other batteries of the division.

CAPTAIN WILLIAM H. HOGAN, after an adventurous life and many hairbreadth escapes, arrived in New York with prizes he had captured on the James River while serving in the Union Coast Guard. He, while in charge of a gunboat, captured the schooner Topsie, with a cargo of tobacco, valued at thirty-eight thousand dollars. His services on the James River were of the greatest importance in preventing privateering between Baltimore and the rebel lines.

Captain Hogan was born in Nenagh, county Tipperary, Ireland, about the year 1820. He went to Dublin at an early age, and became connected with the press and with every popular movement that agitated the times. Being actively engaged in the '48 movement, he had to fly to New York, where he became engaged in the printing and newspaper business.

On his arrival in New York with his prize from the James River, he found that General Meagher was organizing the Irish Brigade, and soon got transferred from the Coast Guard to his command, and raised a battery of artillery. When the Brigade left Fort Schuyler, the artillery sections, under command of Captains Hogan and McMahon, the whole being under the command of Major O'Neil, were sent to Capitol Hill for instruction. After a few months Captain Hogan's command was sent to join the Brigade, then before Yorktown. It comprised one hundred and fifty-four men, one hundred and fifteen horses, and six ten-pound Parrott guns. By a special order of McClellan's this fine battery was divided into three sections and assigned to the other batteries in the division. Thenceforth it lost its identity as a part of the Irish Brigade. Major O'Neil and Captain Hogan soon after joined General Meagher's staff. The former was killed by a fall from his horse—the latter has survived all the vicissitudes of life in camp and in the field.

One of the officers of this battery was the brave CAPTAIN RORTY. He was attached to General Hancock's staff, and for his good conduct and gallantry was transferred to the command of a battery just previous to the battle of Gettysburg, where he was killed at the close of the engagement, after having smashed the rebel column which had advanced on his guns and on our lines.

MAJOR TOM O'NEIL was well known in Boston as a whole-souled and generous man, ever ready to help any one needing his assistance. He was born in Youghal, county Cork, Ireland, and when yet quite young joined the Fifteenth Hussars, in which corps he remained eight years, when he was discharged and came to this country in 1842, arriving in New York. There he remained until 1845, when he enlisted in the Third Dragoons, at the breaking out of the Mexican War.

He went to Mexico, and soon after his arrival there was detailed as orderly to General Pierce, retaining that position until the close of the war. He then came back to New York and was discharged, and soon after married. He then came to Boston, where he remained until November, 1861, when he was commissioned Major of the Tenth Regiment N. Y. Artillery, which was assigned as the Fifth Regiment of Meagher's Irish Brigade; and in this he remained until, as senior major, he was appointed on the staff. He died, November 28th, at the Military Hospital in Georgetown, from injuries received by his horse running away and throwing him.

## SKETCHES OF A FEW PROMINENT OFFICERS OF THE OLD SIXTY-NINTH.

J. P. McIVOR, born 1837, in Ireland; came to America in 1852; volunteered as a private in 1861, in the Sixty-ninth Regiment, N. Y. S. M., when said regiment offered its services to the government, April, 1861; was elected and commissioned as captain of Company I, April 23, 1861; was at the first battle of Bull Run, at which he was taken prisoner, with Colonel Corcoran, and so remained till August, 1862; assisted in raising and organizing the One Hundred and Sixtieth Regiment, N. Y. V., for Corcoran's Irish Legion; was mustered into the service with the last-named regiment as lieutenant-colonel, October 7, 1862; March 1st, 1863, was promoted to be colonel; served during the siege of Suffolk; assigned to the guarding of the railroad from Alexandria to Bull Run Bridge; May, 1864, joined the Army of the Potomac; assigned to the Second Army Corps; took part in all the engagements of said army from Spottsylvania Courthouse to the surrender of the insurgent army under General R. E. Lee, April, 1865; was commissioned brigadier-general by brevet, for " gallantry and highly meritorious services" during the campaign, in which he commanded Corcoran's Irish Legion, Second Brigade, Second Division, Second Army Corps.

LIEUTENANT EDMOND CONNOLLY, born March, 1825, in Ireland ; emigrated to this country, 1839 ; entered the company of Lancers attached to the Fourth Brigade, First Division of New York Militia, as a private ; was afterwards promoted to a lieutenantcy, which position he held when the rebellion broke out. The lancers were ordered to report to General, then Colonel Corcoran, of the Sixty-ninth N. Y. M., when said regiment volunteered its services to the government in April, 1861. Lieutenant Connolly was one among the three members of the company who reported ; he was assigned to Company A, afterwards to Company K ; partook in the battle of Bull Run, at which engagement he was taken prisoner, and so remained until April, 1862. His conduct in action was gallant, in prison dignified to his enemies, to his fellow-prisoners kind and generous. If he was not a hero he would not have been taken prisoner. In the retreat of his regiment from the battle-field of Bull Run, he was well in advance and in no danger ; but when he heard the command of his colonel to "rally on the colors," he obeyed the order.

JAMES B. KIRKER, a native of New York, for years in the Sixty-ninth, was captain of engineers, and served with it until after the battle of Bull Run. He subsequently joined the Corcoran Legion as quartermaster, in which capacity he rendered good service, and possessed the confidence and approval of General Corcoran. Captain Kirker rendered important services on the different committees formed to raise and equip the Irish regiments, as also to provide for their families.

In conjunction with the Union Fund Committee, he raised about forty thousand dollars, and rendered many more important services to the cause.

For the sketches of the Corcoran Legion, the writer is much indebted to the able letters of Brigade Surgeon John Dwyer, which have appeared in the Irish American.

*Names of Company Officers commanding the Sixty-ninth New York State Militia at Bull Run.*

James Kelly, captain Company H ; James Cavanagh, captain Company C ; Patrick Kelly, captain Company E ; Thomas Clarke, captain Company D ; John Breslin, captain Company F ; Wm. Butler, lieutenant Company I ; John Coonan, lieutenant Company I ;

Theodore Kelly, lieutenant Company A ; Wm. M. Giles, lieutenant Company B ; Ed. K. Butler, lieutenant Company K·; James Quinlan, captain engineers ; Daniel Strain, lieutenant Company A ; D. L. Sullivan, lieutenant Company A ; Thomas Leddy, lieutenant Company B ; Laurence Cahill, lieutenant Company B ; James Smith, lieutenant Company C ; Jasper M. Whitty, lieutenant Company C ; Richard Dalton, lieutenant Company D ; Michael O'Boyle, lieutenant Company D ; Wm. S. McManus, lieutenant Company E ; Patrick Duffy, lieutenant Company F ; John H. Nugent, lieutenant Company F ; Henry J. Mahon, lieutenant Company G ; Matthew Murphy, lieutenant Company G ; James Lowry, lieutenant Company H ; Francis Whelpy, lieutenant Company H ; Thomas M. Canton, lieutenant Company I ; Wm. Fogarty, lieutenant Company I ; Maurice W. Wall, lieutenant Company K.

*The following officers of the Papal Brigade distinguished themselves in the American War.*

CAPTAIN JOHN DILLON MULHALL, is a native of Boyle, county Roscommon. On the organization of the Papal Brigade he at once joined as lieutenant, and served at Spoleto, where he was captured. He was decorated with the order of St. Sebastian and the campaign medal. His restless spirit drove him to America, where he at once joined the Irish Brigade, and served with it from the battle of Chancellorsville to the fall of Richmond, and got wounded at Coal Harbor and Skinner's Farm.

COLONEL COPPINGER, Fifteenth New York Volunteers, is a native of Cork. He was wounded at Malvern Hill, and was appointed to a captaincy in the Fourteenth Regulars for his distinguished services.

COLONEL DAN KEILY, of the First Louisiana Cavalry, is from Waterford, and has also got a captaincy in the Regulars for distinguished services.

LIEUTENANT-COLONEL O'KEEFE, of the Second New York Cavalry, was from Cork, and nephew of the Right Rev. Dr. Delaney. He served on Phil. Sheridan's staff; was a dashing officer and fine young man. He was wounded at Winchester, and killed at the battle of Five Forks, April 7, 1864.

COLONEL MILES KEOGH, of Carlow, served as aid-de-camp to General Stoneman, and distinguished himself on many a hard-fought field. During Stoneman's celebrated raid around Atlanta, when surrounded by the rebels, Keogh rallied and charged while a man stood to him. Finding his general hemmed in, though Keogh might have effected his escape, he disdained to do so, but surrendered with him.

CAPTAIN LUTHER, of the One Hundred and Sixty-fifth New York, is a native of Clonmel, Tipperary. Captain Luther distinguished himself while serving with the Papal Brigade. Here, too, he has maintained his high reputation as a dashing, chivalric soldier. He served in several battles with credit and distinction, and, I am informed, died of disease contracted on the field.

LIEUTENANT WILLIAM CRONAN, of the Sixteenth New York, was also a brave, chivalric officer.

LIEUTENANT MICHAEL O'CONNELL, of the One Hundred and Fifty-fifth New York (Corcoran Legion), was a native of Kerry; chevalier of the Papal Army; fell bravely leading his company at the battle of Spottsylvania.

CAPTAIN WILLIAM STAFFORD, of Dublin. I have not learned his regiment or his services; but I have heard him spoken of as a brave soldier.

CAPTAIN CLOONEY, of Waterford—the bravest of the brave—was a good officer and a dashing, intrepid soldier. His career was short and brilliant. Had he lived he would have been an honor to his profession, and would have carved out for himself, with his sword, a distinguished future. He, amidst the foremost, fell at Antietam.

These are but a few names selected from that brilliant school of young heroes who fleshed their maiden swords in Italy. There were several others, too, but they have either escaped my research, or have fallen too early in the war to have attained any marked public distinction.

## SKETCHES OF THE OFFICERS OF THE SIXTY-NINTH NEW YORK VOLUNTEERS.

GENERAL ROBERT NUGENT, brevet-colonel and captain Thirteenth

Infantry, U. S. A., formerly major and lieutenant-colonel of the Sixty-ninth Militia, is a native of Kilkeel, county Down; was in all the battles of the Brigade, except Antietam, when he was absent, sick, until Fredericksburg, when he was wounded by a rifle ball in the groin, his pistol, which was shattered, saving his life; was acting assistant provost-marshal-general of New York for a considerable period, during which he administered a dangerous and important office with dignity and honor. He commanded the Brigade after General Meagher's resignation. Is a very dignified commander and an officer of high executive ability and undoubted gallantry.

LIEUTENANT-COLONEL JAMES KELLY, also captain Sixteenth Infantry, U S. A., is a native of Monaghan; was with the regiment up to the battle of Antietam, when he commanded and led the Sixty-ninth in their famous charge. Here he received two wounds in the face and shoulder.

On the consolidation of the regiment, June, 1863, he was ordered to join his regiment in the regular army, and was subsequently in command of the recruiting depot at Grand Rapids, Mich., from which post he was transferred to his old command as lieutenant-colonel. He then commanded the Brigade for a short period, at the end of which he rejoined his regular command, and served with renewed distinction and popularity under Sherman in his famous campaigns. No braver or more efficient officer could be found in the service.

LIEUTENANT-COLONEL JAMES E. MCGEE succeeded Colonel Kelly, and commanded two brigades of the First Division, Second Corps, for a considerable period during the most active preliminary movements of Grant's campaign, until he was honorably discharged after three years' service, and on account of wounds received at Petersburg, Va., June 16, 1864.

Colonel McGee was born in 1830, near the village of Cushendall, in the county of Antrim, Ireland; was educated at St. Peter's College. In 1847–48, sub-editor of the *Nation*, and secretary of a Confederate club. After the failure of the young Ireland movement he emigrated to the United States, and was for several years connected with the *Irish American* Press, and finally joined the volunteer service of the United States; commanded Company F, Sixty-ninth, until 1865, when, after reorganizing the regiment, he was commissioned lieutenant-colonel.

Colonel McGee was very popular in the army, on account of his agreeable, social, manly demeanor ; for gallantry and great executive ability and military tact, he had few superiors.

LIEUTENANT-COLONEL JAMES J. SMITH, for a long period adjutant of the " Old Sixty-ninth," entered into active service with that command in the early months of the rebellion ; was with the Brigade in that capacity in every engagement, except Fredericksburg, when he was absent, detailed on recruiting service. Colonel Smith was a fine executive officer, and remarkable for coolness, intrepidity, and almost excessive modesty. Promoted lieutenant-colonel, February 16th, 1865. He was a native of Monaghan.

MAJOR JAMES CAVANAGH, popularly known as " the little Major," is a native of Tipperary, and a gallant soldier. He was severely wounded at Fredericksburg, and was obliged to resign after that disastrous battle.

MAJOR JOHN GARRET comes next on the roster. He, I believe, was oorn in Ireland, served in the Mexican war, and then in the Fifteenth New York Volunteers, under J. McLeod Murphy, as captain of a company. He was wounded in the shoulder at Cold Harbor.

### *Medical Staff.*

SURGEON J. PASCAL SMITH, resigned from ill health.

ASSISTANT-SURGEON HURLEY was unhappily killed by a fall from his horse. He was a very able, popular officer, and universally regretted.

ASSISTANT-SURGEON REED, a gentlemanly medical practitioner of New York.

SURGEON WILLIAM O'MEAGHER, a native of Killenaule, county Tipperary. He first joined the gallant Thirty-seventh New York as surgeon, in which he distinguished himself by his coolness in action, his unwearied attention to his patients, and his affable, gentlemanly demeanor. His sketches of the services of that regiment were descriptive and truthful. He subsequently joined the Sixty-ninth New York Volunteers as surgeon, and became popular in the Brigade, both as a clever surgeon and polished gentleman.

The doctor was frequently under fire, and on three occasions a prisoner, but was immediately released. He was principally engaged as operator, brigade surgeon, or in charge of hospitals.

DR. JAMES PURCELL (whose father, Dr. Purcell, of Henry-street, New York—a native of Carrick-on-Suir, Tipperary—had to emigrate to this country on account of his connection with the '48 business), was born in Ireland, and after taking out his diploma, joined the Irish Brigade as assistant-surgeon, with which he served all through the war. He was a great favorite, and a young man of much promise in his profession.

ASSISTANT-SURGEON CROSBY, a native of New York State, was obliged to resign from ill health.

CHAPLAIN--THE REV. THOMAS WILLET, S. J., a native of Lower Canada ; a most zealous and indefatigable priest, universally respected.

QUARTERMASTER RICHARD MAYBURY, a native of Brooklyn, graduated from the ranks. An intelligent, energetic officer.

MAJOR RICHARD MORONY served in the First New York Volunteers during the Mexican war, then in the old Sixty-ninth ; next as first-lieutenant in the new Sixty-ninth ; promoted captain and finally major. He was a brave, active, and efficient officer ; witty, genial, and a universal favorite. Mustered out with the regiment. A native of New York State.

CAPTAIN B. S. O'NEILL left Ireland for the purpose of joining the Brigade, and very early distinguished himself by bravery and gentlemanly conduct ; was promoted from the ranks, step by step, until at times he commanded the regiment. He was killed in front of Petersburg, June 16th, 1864.

CAPTAIN R. H. MILLIKEN, born in Newburg, New York, of Irish parents, served in the Ninth New York Militia. A brave, prompt, and careful officer, always ready for duty. He was severely wounded at Cold Harbor, June 3, 1864, from which he recovered with a slight lameness.

LIEUTENANT WILLIAM O'DONOHUE entered the service as sergeant Company K (Meagher's Zouaves) ; taken prisoner with Corcoran at Bull Run ; escaped from Richmond, and enlisted with the Fourth United States Artillery ; rose to rank of lieutenant, and was killed at Chancellorsville.

CAPTAIN D. S. SHANLEY was formerly lieutenant in the Chicago Shields Guard, which, under the gallant Mulligan, took a distinguished part in the famous siege of Lexington. After being exchanged, he joined Gen. Meagher, as Captain in the Sixty-ninth, amongst whose officers he was beloved, and served in every hardfought battle in which the green flag was borne against the enemy. He was wounded at the battle of Malvern Hill, but had again taken command of his company before the evacuation of Harrison's Landing. He was a thoroughly brave young officer, of the most cheerful disposition and unblemished reputation, who would feel a stain deeper than a wound. He fell at Antietam, while bravely leading on his company. His remains were interred in the Catholic Cemetery at Frederick.

CAPTAIN FELIX DUFFY, commanding Company G, Sixty-ninth, was a brave and experienced officer, and had already served his adopted country in the Mexican war, receiving the strongest marks of approbation from his commanding officers. He was for many years connected with the First Division of New York State Militia, and for some time before the breaking out of the rebellion held the post of Captain of Co. G., Sixty-ninth Regiment N. Y. S. M., which corps he accompanied to the defence of the National Capitol in 1861. He was killed at Antietam.

LIEUT. JAS. E. BYRNE, a native of Clonmel, Co. Tipperary, was educated for the priesthood, emigrated and joined the Brigade, and bravely served until he fell at Cold Harbor.

LIEUTENANT R. A. KELLY was a native of Athy Co., Kildare, Ireland, and was a splendid specimen of manhood, being, though only twenty-one years of age, fully six feet three inches in height. A soldier, almost by instinct, he accompanied the Sixty-ninth Regiment, under Colonel Corcoran, to Virginia at the outbreak of the rebellion, and at the first battle of Bull Run was wounded in the right hand. When the Irish Brigade was commenced, he at once joined its ranks, and served with his regiment all through the desperate struggles in which it has borne so distinguished a part. No braver man has given his life for the cause of the Union, or no better soldier fell on the bloody plain of Antietam.

SECOND-LIEUTENANT LUKE BRENNAN, promoted from the ranks.

CAPTAIN WM. BENSON (Company E), resigned.

FIRST-LIEUTENANT CHARLES M. LUCKY

SECOND-LIEUTENANT PETER CONLON.

SECOND-LIEUTENANT MICHAEL J. BRENNAN, promoted from the ranks; received four wounds at Fredericksburg; resigned in consequence. In Veteran Reserve Corps.

SECOND-LIEUTENANT JOSEPH M. BURNS, a native of Scotland, of Irish descent, wounded at White Oak Swamp. Now an officer in the navy.

FIRST-LIEUTENANT PATRICK BUCKLEY, promoted from the ranks. Killed at Fredericksburg.

CAPTAIN FELIX DUFFY. In the Mexican war. Killed on the field at Antietam while acting as major.

FIRST-LIEUTENANT PATRICK J. KELLY. Killed on the field at Antietam.

SECOND-LIEUTENANT TERENCE DUFFY, resigned after the battle of Fredericksburg, from disability.

FIRST-LIEUTENANT PATRICK CALLAHAN, promoted from the ranks. Served twenty-three years in the U. S. regular army; wounded at Fredericksburg in four places. Now an officer in Veteran Reserve Corps.

SECOND-LIEUTENANT DAVID BURKE, promoted from the ranks of Captain M'Gee's company; wounded at Fredericksburg. Mustered out on the consolidation of regiment.

CAPTAIN JAMES LOWRY (Company H), resigned from ill health.

FIRST-LIEUTENANT PHILIP CARR, wounded at Malvern Hill. Resigned from disability.

CAPTAIN JOHN T. TOAL, wounded at Fredericksburg. Resigned in consequence. Was successively promoted to a first-lieutenantcy and captaincy for distinguished service.

FIRST-LIEUTENANT JOHN D. MULHALL, formerly a first-lieutenant in the Brigade of St. Patrick, in the Papal service. Distinguished himself in Lamoriciere's campaign against the French, and received the medal of St. Peter and two other decorations.

SECOND-LIEUTENANT PATRICK CARNEY, promoted from the ranks. Received nine wounds at the battle of Fredericksburg, from the effects of which he was obliged to resign. Now in the Veteran Reserve Corps.

CAPTAIN THOMAS SCANLAN, resigned from ill health.

FIRST-LIEUTENANT PATRICK MORRIS.

SECOND-LIEUTENANT JAMES COLLINS, promoted from the ranks of Captain M'Gee's company. Wounded at Fredericksburg.

CAPTAIN JAMES MCMAHON, formerly on General Meagher's and General Richardson's staffs, then Colonel of the One hundred and Sixty-fourth N. Y. Vols. Killed at Coal Harbor, June 5th, 1864.

FIRST-LIEUTENANT JOHN CONWAY, killed at Antietam.

SECOND-LIEUTENANT PETER KELLY, wounded at the first battle of Bull Run, taken prisoner, and escaped from Richmond ; resigned.

CAPTAIN LYNCH, a native of the town of Limerick, joined the Sixty-ninth as private, and soon rose to a captaincy. He was captured twice, and was a good and faithful officer. Color-bearer Henry Croker, who gallantly carried the colors of his regiment at Coal Harbor, belonged to his company.

CAPTAIN M. H. MURPHY, Co. A, also graduated from the ranks ; was severely wounded in front of Petersburg. A brave, intelligent, soldierly officer, and, I think, a native of Tipperary.

LIEUTENANT R. H. MURPHY, originally belonged to the Corcoran Legion, in which he served with credit until commissioned in the

Sixty-ninth. He was mortally wounded at Amelia Springs, and died subsequently in hospital.

CAPTAIN DAVID LYNCH, a thorough soldier and excellent officer, was promoted from the ranks, having served throughout the war. Was severely wounded at Fredericksburg, transferred to the Veteran Corps, but again returned to his old command at his own request; was taken prisoner at Reams' Station, exchanged, and then promoted to a captaincy.

CAPTAIN HARRY MCQUADE, graduated from the ranks; was severely wounded at Deep Bottom, taken prisoner at Reams' Station, exchanged, and then promoted to a captaincy.

LIEUTENANT JOHN NUGENT, served with Corcoran; re-enlisted in the new regiment, was promoted from the ranks for bravery and good conduct.

LIEUTENANT JOHN MEAGHER, entered the service August, 1862, promoted sergeant, then lieutenant. He was wounded severely on two or three occasions.

QUARTERMASTER DENIS SULLIVAN, a native of Halifax, N. S., of Irish parentage. Always with the regiment. Was instrumental in rallying the Twentieth N. Y. V. when panic-stricken at White Oak Swamp. Mustered out at expiration of term of service

CAPTAIN JAMES SAUNDERS (Company A), native of Cavan; in every action with his regiment except Chancellorsville. Mustered out on consolidation of service.

FIRST-LIEUTENANT ANDREW BIRMINGHAM, died of wounds received at Fredericksburg, December, 1862.

FIRST-LIEUTENANT THOMAS REYNOLDS, killed at Malvern Hill, July 1st, 1862.

CAPTAIN RICHARD A. KELLY, promoted from the ranks for distinguished bravery at Malvern Hill, having personally taken prisoner the Lieutenant-Colonel of the Tenth La. Vols., and two others. Mustered out on the consolidation of the regiment; afterwards commissioned as Captain of Company A, on the reorganization of regi ment, and died of wounds received at Spottsylvania, May, 1865, while a prisoner in the hands of the enemy.

CAPTAIN LEDDY (Company B), wounded dangerously at Malvern Hill and Fredericksburg. Now in Veteran Reserve Corps.

LIEUTENANT M. LEDDY, a brother of the above, was promoted from the ranks for bravery and long service. He was wounded on two or three occasions.

FIRST-LIEUTENANT LAURENCE CAHILL, wounded badly at Malvern Hill, and obliged to resign in consequence. Now in Veteran Reserve Corps.

JOHN J. GOSSON, Captain Company C, Sixty-ninth Regiment N. Y. S. M., and First A. D. C. Staff of General Meagher ; was with him in the above capacity in all the battles of the Irish Brigade. Son of J. Gosson, Esq., formerly of Swords, county Dublin. Entered the Austrian service through the influence of Daniel O'Connell, and served under his friend, General Count Nugent, as Lieutenant, in Syria, and subsequently, through the introduction of the Count, joined the Seventh Hussars of Austria (Prince Reuss' Hussars), a Hungarian regiment, commanded by Prince Frederick Lichtenstein.

SECOND-LIEUTENANT ROBERT LAFFAN, lost his arm at Antietam, September 17th, 1862. Promoted from Captain M'Gee's company for gallant service. Now in Veteran Reserve Corps.

CAPTAIN JASPER WHITTY (Company C), wounded at the first battle of Bull Run while with the Sixty-ninth N. Y. S. M. ; lost an eye at White Oak Swamp, and was wounded at Antietam. In consequence obliged to resign.

FIRST-LIEUTENANT (afterwards Captain) NAGLE (a descendant of the celebrated Edmund Burke, who was a cousin-german of his grandfather)—wounded seriously at Antietam, in the right shoulder. Now in Veteran Reserve Corps.

SECOND-LIEUTENANT CHARLES WILLIAMS, killed on the field at Antietam.

CAPTAIN MAURICE W. WALL, a native of Tipperary ; entered

the service in the old Sixty-ninth, Co. K ; was next commissioned in the Eighty-eighth. He was an excellent staff-officer, being equally brave, reliable, and intelligent.

CAPTAIN TIMOTHY L. SHANLEY, fought with Mulligan at Lexington, Mo. ; afterwards joined the Sixty-ninth with his company. Died in Frederick City, Md., October 2d, in consequence of wounds received at Antietam.

CAPTAIN JOHN H. DONOVAN, lost an eye at Malvern Hill, July 1st, 1862. Now Major in the Veteran Reserve Corps.

SECOND-LIEUTENANT MARTIN SCULLY, wounded at Fredericksburg, December 13th, 1862 ; also with Mulligan at Lexington.

CAPTAIN MURTHA MURPHY, Co. C, a native of gallant Wexford, graduated from the ranks of the old Sixty-ninth. I think he was in twenty-eight or thirty engagements ; was wounded only twice. His last achievement was the capture of thirteen rebels, including an officer, in front of Petersburg, by a little personal strategy worthy of note, for which he should have received the compliment of a general order, and at least a brevet appointment. But our gallant friend was too modest, and such acts were not very uncommon in the command.

CAPTAIN JOHN C. FOLEY. See Eighty-eighth N. Y.

CAPTAIN EDWARD F. O'CONNOR, a fine, intelligent young officer, who also sprang from the ranks through merit and bravery ; was wounded at Fredericksburg and Spottsylvania ; taken prisoner at Reams' Station ; exchanged, and then promoted captain Company F.

ADJUTANT DANIEL DOLAN, a native of Tipperary ; was originally hospital steward, in which position he showed unusual tact, discretion, and capacity ; but being ambitious he was promoted into the line, and then to the staff. In this position, for which he was very well fitted, he acquitted himself with distinction, and maintained the previous character of the regiment for order and discipline. He was in almost every engagement with the regiment.

LIEUTENANT JOHN NUGENT, graduated from the ranks of the old Sixty-ninth ; taken prisoner at Bull Run and released ; he then joined the new regiment; was wounded at the battle of Fredericksburg; participated in all the other battles of the Brigade up to the end of the war. A good, reliable officer.

LIEUTENANT JAMES MCCANN, promoted from the ranks. A steady, reliable officer.

LIEUTENANT OWEN MCNULTY, also from the ranks. A good disciplinarian.

LIEUTENANT PATRICK WARD, also from the ranks. A steady, well-conducted officer.

LIEUTENANT JAMES CONWAY, a good soldier and officer, promoted from the ranks.

LIEUTENANT GEORGE M. BELDING, a native of New York State, served in the Thirty-second New York Volunteers, then in the Sixth Cavalry, from which he was promoted to the Sixty-ninth, in which he was quite a favorite, by his gentlemanly conduct and rigid performance of duty.

LIEUTENANT TERENCE SCANLON, a graduate of the old Sixty-ninth; was wounded at the battle of Malvern Hill; taken prisoner and released; promoted from the ranks for good conduct, long and gallant services.

LIEUTENANT THOMAS MCGRATH was with the Brigade from its first organization; wounded at Gettysburg; taken prisoner at Reams' Station; released, and promoted for gallant services.

LIEUTENANT GEORGE NEVINS, promoted from the ranks. An intelligent, brave soldier.

LIEUTENANT ROBERT MCKINLEY, a native of Scotland; served three months in the Seventy-ninth New York, also in the First New York Cavalry; promoted from the ranks of the Sixty-ninth for bravery and good conduct; was taken prisoner before Petersburg.

LIEUTENANT WILLIAM HERBERT, also from the ranks; was in every battle with the regiment.

## SKETCHES OF THE OFFICERS OF THE EIGHTY-EIGHTH NEW YORK VOLUNTEERS.

COLONEL PATRICK KELLY, born in Galway, Ireland; joined the regiment in December, 1861, as lieutenant-colonel; was engaged at Fair Oaks, Antietam, Fredericksburg, Chancellorsville, Gettysburg, Bristoe Station, Mine Run, North Anna, Tolopotomy Creek, Cold Harbor, and was killed while commanding the Brigade at the battle of Petersburg, Va., June 16, 1864. Gentle, brave, and unassuming, no truer man nor braver officer fell during the war.

ADJUTANT JOHN R. YOUNG, born in King's County, Ireland; fought at Bull Run with the Sixty-ninth, and afterwards joined the Eighty-eighth; was in every battle up to Fredericksburg, where he was mortally wounded; his remains were not recovered. A truly noble man and officer.

CAPTAIN P. RYDER, Company B, continued with the regiment as captain till the battle of the Wilderness, May 5th, 1864, when he was killed while leading his company. A well-disciplined and distinguished officer.

FIRST-LIEUTENANT CHARLES M. GRAINGER, a native of County Cork, Ireland; went out as sergeant in Company B. On the death of Lieutenant Temple Emmet, August, 1862, was promoted to second-lieutenancy; was afterwards appointed first-lieutenant, on the resignation of Captain M. Cartan, November, 1862; was mustered out with the regiment, July, 1865.

SECOND-LIEUTENANT WILLIAM L. D. O'GRADY—son of Lieutenant-Colonel O'Grady, of the East Indian Army—went out as private in Company C; was promoted second-lieutenant for conspicuous bravery. Served with the regiment until March, 1864, when he resigned on surgeon's certificate of disability. Was a good officer and a courteous gentleman.

CAPTAIN J. W. BYRON, of Company E before consolidation, rejoined the regiment as adjutant—vice McClellan, killed at Gettysburg—November, 1863, and continued as such till June, 1864, when he was commissioned major. Was taken prisoner at the battle of Reams' Station, Virginia, August 25, 1864; was exchanged in February, 1865, and commissioned lieutenant-colonel, but was not mustered in. He was mustered out of service with the regiment, July, 1865. An active, intelligent officer.

QUARTERMASTER P. M. HAVERTY was placed on detached service immediately after the consolidation, on which he continued until mustered out of the service by order of the Secretary of War, December 15, 1864.

ADJUTANT WILLIAM McCLELLAN (an Irish-American)—native of New Jersey—was private of Company G ; promoted before the consolidation, at which he was appointed adjutant. He was killed at Gettysburg, July 2, 1863. He was a good executive officer and a brave soldier.

FRANCIS REYNOLDS, Fellow Royal College of Surgeons, Ireland, came out with the regiment as surgeon. He was a native of County Kilkenny, Ireland, and served on the British Medical Staff during the Crimean.War. As a professional man he had no superior in the Army of the Potomac, particularly in operative surgery. He was, during the time he remained in the West, one of the operating surgeons of the division ; was a most cultivated gentleman and a jovial companion. He remained with the regiment till August, 1863, when he was mustered out of service to accept a commission from the President as assistant-surgeon, U. S. V., which he retained till the organization of the First Corps by General Hancock, when he was appointed surgeon of the Second Regiment in that corps.

RICHARD POWELL, licentiate Royal College of Surgeons, Ireland, is a native of county Clare, Ireland. Came out with the regiment as assistant-surgeon ; continued as such until August, 1863, when he was appointed surgeon, Dr. Reynolds being mustered out. His three years' term of service having expired in November, 1864, he was mustered out. Dr. Powell was highly respected in the Brigade both for his professional skill and gentlemanly demeanor.

DENIS F. BURKE, born in Cork, served as captain, but commanded the regiment while Colonel Kelly was in command of the Brigade, until September, 1864. Was commissioned and mustered in as lieutenant-colonel, and was subsequently commissioned as colonel. Colonel Burke was a dashing soldier and an efficient officer. He was twice wounded.

CAPTAIN PATRICK F. CLOONEY was a native of Waterford, Ireland. He originally joined that gallant band of young Irish heroes, who, fired with military ardor and chivalric devotion to the head of the Catholic Church, went to Italy to fight for the Holy Father. Soon after his return home the war had broken out in America; and filled with the military spirit of his race and country, and the noble ambition of aspiring minds, he left the land of his birth, his endearments, and his love, to seek a soldier's fame, and perhaps acquire that teaching that would one day enable him to serve his own native land. He arrived at New York in July, 1861, and enlisted as a private in Company K, Sixty-ninth N. Y. S. M. He served with that regiment in the three months' campaign, and distinguished himself at Blackburn Ford and Bull Run. He subsequently raised a company for the Irish Brigade, and was commissioned captain in the Eighty-eighth, on the 2d October, 1861. He devoted himself with all the zeal of a good officer to his military duties, and never absented himself a single day from his command, until the day he was killed, on the 17th of September, 1862. He was present at all the battles on the Peninsula, where he nobly distinguished himself, winning the thanks of his general and brother officers on more than one occasion. On the battle-field of Antietam his commanding form could be seen remarkably conspicuous among his comrades. High above the din of battle, his rich, manly voice could be heard encouraging his men and inspiring them to action. To see him unflinchingly and fearlessly stand, like one of the heroes of Grecian lore, sword in hand, his green plume waving in the wind, whilst the leaden hail flew thick and fast around him, you would perceive a sublimity of person, appearance, and of action no pen can portray nor words express. After receiving a severe gunshot wound in the knee, he would not leave the field, though he was urged and entreated repeatedly by his men to do so. No; he still kept his place, until a rifle-bullet passed through his body, killing him instantly. The news of his death spread rapidly through the regiment, and many a manly, fearless heart, that never quailed before an enemy, trembled at the sad intelligence. He was buried where he fell, by those in whose hearts his memory shall be as green as the grass that grows above his grave. But he "rests in the bosom of his Father and his God." The rudely-carved and lettered cross of wood that marks his last resting-place, whereon is written "*He like a soldier fell*," speaks more unto the thinking mind than the grandest marble monument in Westminster.

CAPTAIN JOHN O'CONNELL JOYCE was a native of Fermoy, county Cork, where he was born about the year 1840, and emigrated with his family to this country in 1860. He obtained the position of sergeant in Meagher's Zouaves, and as such served in Bull Run. He joined the Eighty-eighth, Irish Brigade, as first-lieutenant, and served with distinction all through the Peninsular Campaign. He was promoted captain, vice O'Donoghoe, killed at Malvern Hill. Though much prostrated by camp-fever, he would not leave his command in time of action, and fell on the bloody field of Antietam, while gallantly heading his company.

CAPTAIN W. G. HART participated in the battles of Antietam and Fredericksburg, and served for some time on General Meagher's Staff.

CAPTAIN JAMES TURNER.—On the organization of the Brigade he served on General Meagher's staff, and was severely wounded at Antietam. He was detailed for duty in New York, and was subsequently commissioned as adjutant-general, U. S. A., and appointed to the Irish Brigade, where he again served with distinction, and was killed at the battle of the Wilderness, May, 1864. He was a brave soldier, an accomplished writer and scholar, and chronicled the services of the Brigade in the columns of the "Irish American," under the *nom de plume* of *Galloglass.* I have been much indebted to his graphic letters for valuable information.

FIRST-LIEUTENANT THOMAS BRIEN, from Troy, New York, went out as first-sergeant, Company F; promoted after the battle of Antietam, November, 1862; was severely wounded at the battle of Fredericksburg, Virginia, December 13, 1862; he rejoined the regiment before the consolidation, and was with it through the Gettysburg Campaign; he resigned in January, 1864.

SECOND-LIEUTENANT P. MCCABE was promoted from sergeant-major; was with the regiment up to May, 1864, when he was sent to the rear, sick; he was afterwards dismissed the service for over-staying his leave of absence.

REV. WILLIAM CORBY, native of the State of Michigan; joined the regiment in December, 1861; resigned in September, 1864. Distinguished himself by his zeal as a good priest, venturing in the midst of battle, in the discharge of his sacred duties.

24*

FIRST-LIEUTENANT THOMAS H. O'BRIEN, born in New York; promoted from the ranks; wounded at Fredericksburg; resigned in January, 1864.

SECOND-LIEUTENANT W. L. D. O'GRADY, native of East Indies; promoted from the ranks; resigned on surgeon's certificate of disability, March, 1864.

CAPTAIN JOHN SMITH, served until the close of the war; mustered out with the regiment, June 30, 1865.

FIRST-LIEUTENANT JAMES BYRNES, killed in action, June 3, 1865, at Cold Harbor, Virginia.

SECOND-LIEUTENANT JOHN SPARKS, died of wounds received in action at the Wilderness, Virginia, May 5, 1865.

CAPTAIN JOHN DESMOND, born in New York; served until close of the war; mustered out with regiment, June 30, 1865.

FIRST-LIEUTENANT GEORGE W. FORD, served till the end of the war; mustered out with the regiment, June 30, 1865; received from Congress a medal of honor for capturing a flag.

COLONEL HENRY M. BAKER, a native of Dublin; mustered out after Antietam.

MAJOR JAMES QUINLAN, native of Clonmel, commanded the Engineer Company of the Sixty-ninth N. Y. S. M. in the first Bull Run fight; joined the Eighty-eighth as major; commanded the regiment through the seven days' fight; was mustered out, on account of disability, after Fredericksburg.

LIEUTENANT THOMAS MURPHY joined the regiment on its organization; was in every battle up to Fredericksburg, where he was killed.

CAPTAIN JOHN J. BLAKE joined the regiment as second-lieutenant; was promoted first-lieutenant and captain; mustered out on consolidation of regiment; afterwards joined the Sixty-ninth as captain; was mortally wounded, May 12th, at Spottsylvania.

CAPTAIN JOHN MCCARTAN, resigned after Fredericksburg.

TEMPLE EMMET, a grandson of Thomas Addis Emmet, the eminent New York lawyer, and grand-nephew of Robert Emmet, the patriot martyr of 1803, joined the regiment as first-lieutenant ; was aid on General Meagher's staff at Fair Oaks and through the seven days' fight; died in New York, August, 1862, of fever contracted on the Peninsula.

RICHARD RIKER EMMET, a brother of the above, joined the regiment after his brother's death ; served on General Meagher's staff at Fredericksburg; died a short time after, of the same ailing as his brother.

CAPTAIN JOSEPH DONOHUE was acting-major in the seven days' fight ; was killed at Malvern Hill.

CAPTAIN P. K. HORGAN, a brave soldier, was with the regiment up to Fredericksburg, when he resigned.

LIEUTENANT WILLIAM MCMAHON O'BRIEN, county Clare, mustered out on consolidation of the regiment.

CAPTAIN WILLIAM J. NAGLE was mustered out on consolidation of regiment. Captain Nagle was a brave, efficient officer.

LIEUTENANT EDMUND NAGLE, a brother of the above, was mustered out on consolidation of regiment; afterwards killed in the Third New Jersey Cavalry at Winchester.

CAPTAIN MICHAEL EAGAN was with the regiment up to Chancellorsville, where he was severely wounded.

CAPTAIN MICHAEL GALLAGHER, was in every battle up to Chancellorsville ; on consolidation of regiment was mustered out ; joined as captain the Second New Jersey Cavalry, in which regiment he was killed, charging at the head of his company at Egypt Miss.

LIEUTENANT THOMAS MCCOY, promoted from the ranks ; was mustered out on consolidation of the regiment ; joined the Thirty-third New Jersey as captain ; served under Sherman to the end of the war.

CAPTAIN WILLIAM HORGAN, was promoted major after Antietam, and was killed December 13 1863, at Fredericksburg. A gallant and distinguished officer.

LIEUTENANT HACKETT resigned after the seven days' fight.

LIEUTENANT HACKETT, a brother of the above, was killed at Malvern Hill.

CAPTAIN MAXWELL O'SULLIVAN, died from injuries received by accidental burning of his tent, April 2d, 1862, near Alexandria.

LIEUTENANT CHARLES J. CLARKE was an officer of the United States Signal Service; was promoted captain on the death of Captain O'Sullivan; mustered out on consolidation of regiment.

LIEUTENANT P. O'CONNOR was dangerously wounded through the chest at Fair Oaks; subsequently an officer in the Veteran Reserve Corps.

CAPTAIN MAURICE W. WALL, mustered out on consolidation of regiment; joined the Sixty-ninth as captain on its veteran enlistment; served to the end of the war.

CAPTAIN JOHN C. FOLEY is a native of Tipperary, Ireland; he entered the Eighty-eighth as first lieutenant at the formation of the brigade, and served all through with his command until the mustering out of the brigade. He afterwards raised a company and joined the Sixty-ninth, and acted as assistant acting-adjutant-general; was wounded at Mine Run, and was finally mustered out of the regiment at the close of the war.

FIRST-LIEUTENANT ROBERT J. KELLY, born in Ireland; resignation accepted on surgeon's certificate of disability, September, 1864.

CAPTAIN RICHARD S. HARRISON rose from the ranks; served till the end of the war; mustered out with the regiment, June 30, 1865.

SECOND-LIEUTENANT JOHN W. CONKLIN, served until close of the war; mustered out with regiment.

ADJUTANT JAMES M. BIRMINGHAM, wounded at Fredericksburg and Reams' Station; mustered out with regiment.

SECOND LIEUTENANT JOHN SHEA; in all the battles from Fair Oaks to Petersburg, where he was wounded, June 15, 1865; mustered out with the regiment at the close of the war.

CAPTAIN JOSEPH HYLAND, native of Waterford; promoted from the ranks; wounded at Spottsylvania; mustered out with regiment.

SECOND-LIEUTENANT PATRICK J. HEALY, born in New York; served until the close of the war; mustered out with regiment.

SECOND-LIEUTENANT ROBERT J. O'DRISCOLL; killed in action at Petersburg, Va., October 29, 1864.

CAPTAIN W. J. O'CONNOR; a native of Fethard, county Tipperary; promoted from the ranks; wounded at Spottsylvania; served till the end of the war; mustered out with regiment; was a brave, efficient officer.

SECOND LIEUTENANT BENEDICT J. O'DRISCOLL; born in Nova Scotia; wounded at Petersburg; honorably discharged out of service by order of the Secretary of War, February, 1865.

SECOND LIEUTENANT THOMAS P. NUGENT; served until close of the war; mustered out with regiment.

SECOND LIEUTENANT FRANCIS KIERNAN; born in New York; was in all engagements from Fair Oaks to Sailor's Creek; mustered out with regiment.

FIRST LIEUTENANT TIMOTHY PLUNKETT; wounded at Gettysburg and Antietam; mustered out with regiment.

SURGEON JOHN T. STILLMAN, born in New York; served until close of the war; mustered out with regiment.

QUARTERMASTER RICHARD E. DOWDELL; served until close of the war; mustered out with regiment.

## SKETCH OF THE OFFICERS OF THE SIXTY-THIRD NEW YORK VOLUNTEERS.

COLONEL RICHARD ENRIGHT, a native of Kerry, Ireland, belonged to the regiment from its first organization. Was at first commissioned as major; resigned in the latter part of 1861.

COLONEL JOHN BURKE, a native of Ireland, succeeded Colonel Enright, having served in the Thirty-seventh New York Irish Rifles as lieutenant-colonel; resigned his commission as such, and was commissioned as colonel of the Sixty-third; a splendid tactician, who was the chief means of bringing the regiment to the high place it attained as a well-disciplined battalion.

COLONEL HENRY J. FOWLER, a native of this country, of English descent, was commissioned as lieutenant-colonel on the organization of the regiment; afterwards promoted to colonel; a brave officer; he was a favorite with the officers and men of the regiment for his soldierly and gentlemanly qualities; was wounded severely at the battle of Antietam by a rifle-ball, which caused a fracture of the arm at the elbow, from which he suffered much, thus rendering him incapable of performing his duties with the regiment, in active service.

COLONEL JOHN H. GLEESON, a native of Tipperary, served with distinction in the Papal Brigade in Italy; emigrated to this country in the early part of 1861; joined the Sixty-ninth New York State Militia as a private; participated in the first battle of Bull Run, and on the return of the Sixty-ninth, commenced organizing a company for the Sixty-third; commissioned and mustered as first-lieutenant, September, 1861; afterwards promoted to captain. In the spring of 1864 he was appointed captain in the Sixty-third; he was subsequently commissioned major, lieutenant-colonel, and colonel.

LIEUTENANT-COLONEL R. BENTLEY, a native of Albany, New York, was commissioned as major in the early part of 1862; afterwards promoted to lieutenant-colonel, which position he held until the battle of Cold Harbor, at which engagement he left the regiment on sick leave, and resigned a short time afterwards.

MAJOR JOSEPH O'NEILL, a native of Cork, Ireland, organized Com pany A, and left New York with the regiment as captain of said company; was wounded at the battle of Fredericksburg, December 12th, 1862, in the arm, from the effect of which he was totally incapable of performing his duty with the regiment; was transferred to the Veteran Reserve Corps.

CAPTAIN JOHN WARREN, a native of Cork, Ireland; organized Company B, and was commissioned and mustered as captain of it; served with the regiment until the battle of Antietam, when he was mustered out.

COLONEL JAMES D. BRADY, born in this country, of Irish parents; joined the regiment as adjutant early in 1862; afterwards promoted to captain; held the position of acting assistant-inspector-general of the Third Brigade, First Division, Second Corps; also as division and subsequently as acting inspector-general Second Corps; was wounded at the battle of Cold Harbor, December 13th, 1862; he came home to New York with the regiment which he commanded.

MAJOR THOMAS TOUHEY, a native of Clare, Ireland; commissioned as second-lieutenant, August, 1861; promoted to captain, October, 1862, and subsequently commissioned as major; served through almost all the engagements with the regiment up to the battle of the Wilderness, May 5th, 1864, when he was mortally wounded and died at home a short time after. A gallant, unassuming officer.

MAJOR LYNCH, a native of Ireland, died in Camp California, near Alexandria, Va., December, 1861.

SURGEON LAURENCE REYNOLDS, a native of Waterford, a highly educated and refined gentleman, and very experienced surgeon, a true Irish gentleman and patriot, served with honor as surgeon of the regiment from its first organization; although advanced in years is still young in vigor. He has written several beautiful and touching poems on his unfortunate native land, and is endowed with wit and humor to a great degree, also a remarkable memory. He was a distinguished Chartist in England, and was also amongst those of his countrymen who had to fly from Ireland in '48, his only crime being that he loved his country dearly.

LIEUTENANT AND ADJUTANT MILES M'DONALD, born in Albany,

of Irish parents; joined the regiment as a private in October, 1861; served with his regiment in every engagement; promoted to second-lieutenant, October, 1862; afterwards to first-lieutenant and adjutant; mortally wounded on the 16th of June, 1864, before Petersburg, and died the following morning.

CAPTAIN JOHN KAVANAGH, was born in Dublin about the year 1826, and was married there on the 11th June, 1847, to Miss Nannie Frances Byrne.

Though quite young he became an active member of the Irish Confederation, and was unanimously chosen president of the Fitzgerald Club, Dublin. He was a devoted, zealous patriot, and was ably sustained by the patriotic enthusiasm and deep affection of his devoted young wife. After the suspension of the *habeas corpus* act he followed the fortunes of Smith O'Brien in Tipperary, and was rather severely wounded in the leg at the Farrinrory *fiasco.* As soon as he was able to travel he made his way to Havre, and even while there the English authorities made numerous efforts to arrest him. He fled to America, where he arrived in the fall of 1848. Here he was soon joined by his lovely, faithful wife and child.

Captain Kavanagh was one of the principal organizers of the Thirty-seventh Regiment New York Volunteers. He was subsequently transferred to the command of Company I, Sixty-third Regiment, Irish Brigade, in conformity with his own desire to serve under his friend and fellow-exile, General Meagher. He was a most energetic and fearless officer. He fell at the head of his company, in the heat of action, in the great battle of Antietam, on the 17th of September. Captain Kavanagh had won for himself the enthusiastic devotion of a numerous circle of friends. He was comparatively a young man, less than thirty-seven years of age; of medium height; slender, but sinewy frame; fair complexion; and of prompt, decisive mental habits.

Had he lived, he would have carved out a bright career as a soldier, for few were so brave or thoroughly devoted to his profession, and few possessed nobler or more generous qualities.

He left after him, to mourn his loss, his devoted wife and seven children.

DOCTOR CHARLES SMART, a Scotchman by birth, and a licentiate of the College of Surgeons, Aberdeen, joined the Sixty-third as assistant surgeon; was afterwards promoted to be medical inspector of the corps. He underwent a very creditable examination for the regular service, in which he is at present serving. Dr. Smart was a refined scholar, a good surgeon, and a young man of the most amiable disposition, taking second place out of a large list of competitors. He also possessed very high qualifications as a poet, producing some pieces that might rate favorably with Burns.

CAPTAIN JOHN C. LYNCH, a native of Galway, Ireland, organized Company C, of which he was commissioned captain; served with his regiment until the battle of Chancellorsville, when he was killed while his regiment was lying on the ground under a heavy fire from the enemy's batteries; a solid shot struck him in the side, crushing the scabbard of his sword partly through his body, horribly mutilating him, from the effects of which he died immediately.

CAPTAIN TOBIN, served with the regiment until August, 1862.

CAPTAIN JAMES PRENDERGAST, a native of Limerick, organized and afterwards commissioned as captain of Company E; served until August, 1863, when he resigned his commission.

CAPTAIN MICHAEL O'SULLIVAN, a native of Dublin, organized and commissioned captain of Company E; served with distinction through the different battles until that of Antietam, when he was wounded in the knee by a rifle-ball; resigned and mustered out afterwards in consequence of his wounds.

CAPTAIN WALSHE, a native of Drogheda; served as an officer in the Papal Brigade; transferred to the Veteran Reserve Corps.

CAPTAIN BRANNIGAN, a native of Mayo; organized Company K, and mustered as captain; wounded at Antietam, after which he resigned.

CAPTAIN JOHN FLYNN, a native of Queen's County, went out as first-lieutenant; served through the campaigns of 1862 and '63, and was mustered out on consolidation of the regiment.

CAPTAIN JOHN SULLIVAN, a native of Albany, of Irish parentage; commissioned in October, 1861, as first-lieutenant; promoted to captain; mortally wounded at Fredericksburg, December 13, 1862, while the regiment was coming out of action. On passing through one of the streets a cannon ball came bounding along, striking him in the leg and breaking the bone, from the effects of which he died a few days after; a dashing, brave, and fearless soldier.

CAPTAIN CHARLES J. QUIRK, a native of Lismore, county Waterford, joined the regiment with Company K, October, 1861; served in every engagement until the consolidation of the regiment, June, 1863, when he was honorably mustered out; promoted from sergeant-major, October, 1862, to first-lieutenant, afterwards to captain.

CAPTAIN ALEXANDER WATTS, a native of Dublin; commissioned as first-lieutenant, Company C, and joined the regiment, October, 1863; served with distinction in all the engagements of 1861; promoted to captain, and had the honor of commanding the regiment for some time. A good officer. Mustered out the early part of 1865.

FIRST-LIEUTENANT AND QUARTERMASTER JAMES McCORMICK, commissioned as lieutenant; appointed subsequently quartermaster, which position he retained until he resigned.

CAPTAIN BOYLE, a native of Donegal, commissioned as captain of Company C, having organized it himself. Joined the regiment with his company in October, 1863. Killed at the battle of the Wilderness, May 5, 1864.

CAPTAIN MICHAEL KELLEHER, born in Brooklyn, of Irish parents, was commissioned as second-lieutenant of Company C, May, 1864; promoted to first-lieutenant and captain; wounded severely in the leg and hip on the 16th of June, 1864.

FIRST-LIEUTENANT AND ADJUTANT FREEMAN joined the regiment as a private in May, 1864; promoted a short time after to first-lieutenant and adjutant, which position he retained until the regiment was mustered out.

MAJOR JAMES McQUADE, a native of Utica, New York, of Irish parents, joined the Sixty-third regiment as a private, September, 1861; served through almost all the battles that his regiment was engaged in; also on the brigade staff as aid-de-camp to General Nugent. Promoted from first-sergeant to first-lieutenant, November, 1864; subsequently to captain, Company F, and finally commissioned as major. He was a great favorite with the officers and men of the regiment.

CAPTAIN WILLIAM FRANCIS HALLEY, a native of Clonmel, Tipperary, joined the Sixty-third Regiment on its first organization as a private, August, 1861; served on the brigade non-commissioned staff under General Meagher and Colonel T. Kelly, for over a year. Promoted from sergeant-major to second-lieutenant, November, 1864, and was placed in command of his Company C; also commanded Companies A, B, and F, of which latter company he was finally commissioned captain.

LIEUTENANT JOHN DILLON, a native of Dungarvan, county Waterford, joined the regiment as a private, and was mustered in with Company F, September, 1861; served as color-sergeant with distinction in many battles. Promoted for planting our flag on the enemy's works at Cold Harbor, January, 1865, to second-lieutenant; participated in all the engagements with his regiment; a brave soldier. Mustered out a short time before the regiment came home.

LIEUTENANT JOHN RYAN, a native of Tipperary; promoted from the ranks, and was through all the battles with his regiment until he was mustered out on consolidation.

CAPTAIN JOSEPH GLEASON, a native of Tipperary; commissioned second-lieutenant, February, 1864; served through the campaigns of '64 and '65.

CAPTAIN JOSEPH McDONOUGH, a native of Galway, went out with regiment as first-lieutenant; promoted to captain.

CAPTAIN DANIEL MAHER, a native of Albany, of Irish parents; joined the regiment in 1862; promoted from commissary-sergeant to first-lieutenant, and subsequently to captain.

LIEUTENANT PATRICK MAHER, a native of Tipperary, joined the regiment early in 1862; promoted to first-lieutenant; mustered out on consolidation of the regiment; afterwards joined the regiment and commissioned lieutenant; wounded on the 22d June, 1865, in the thigh, which caused the leg to be amputated; died from the effects of the wound.

CAPTAIN EDWARD O'CARROLL, a native of Tipperary; mustered into the regiment, October, 1861; promoted to second-lieutenant, and mustered out on consolidation of the regiment, June, 1863. Again joined the regiment as a private in 1864. Promoted to second-lieutenant and captain. Killed on the 3d May, 1865, before Petersburg, Va.

LIEUTENANT DANIEL KIERNAN, a native of Monaghan, joined the regiment, September, 1861, as a private; served through all the campaigns until June, 1861, when he was mustered out; promoted to second-lieutenant and also to first-lieutenant.

CAPTAIN CHARLES BENNETT joined the regiment early in 1862; served through almost all the different battles with the regiment; promoted from first-sergeant to second-lieutenant, January, 1865, and captain; mustered out with the regiment.

MAJOR W. H. TERWILLIGER joined the regiment, March, 1864; commanded the regiment for a short time, and passed through the entire campaigns of 1864 and '65.

CAPTAIN CHARLES TERWILLIGER entered the regiment about March; he served through the campaigns of 1864 and was promoted to major, 1865; was mustered out with the regiment.

LIEUTENANT LYDEN, a brave soldier and a good officer; killed at the battle of Antietam.

LIEUTENANT MCCONNELL, a native of Roscommon, Ireland; commanded as second lieutenant, October, 1862; killed at the battle of Antietam. A very brave, efficient officer.

LIEUTENANT CADWALADER SMYTH, a native of this country, of Irish parents; a brave, gallant young officer; killed at Antietam, 7th September, 1862.

LIEUTENANT PATRICK H. RIORDAN, a native of Meentogues, county Kerry. He joined the Sixty-third as a private in 1861; was wounded at Malvern Hill, and taken prisoner at Belle Isle. After his exchange he was promoted to a second lieutenancy. He was again wounded at Fredericksburg while in command of a company, in consequence of which he had to resign, April, 1862.

LIEUTENANT JOHN FITZGERALD, a native of Monaghan; joined the Sixty-third at the organization of the regiment; was soon after transferred to the Fourth New York Volunteers.

ADJUTANT HENRY M'CONNELL, was born in Mitchelstown, county Cork, Ireland; being intended for the medical profession, he received a liberal education. He was for some time connected with the Sixty-ninth New York State Militia. Upon the reorganization of the Sixty-third New York Volunteers he was promoted to a second-lieutenancy; he was distinguished for his gallantry, and participated in every engagement with the Brigade to Antietam, where he was killed.

At the organization of the regiment DAVID P. SHANAHAN was surgeon; MICHAEL G. GILLIGAN, assistant-surgeon; and PHILIP O'HANLON, Junior, quartermaster. I have not been supplied with materials to give a sketch of the above gentlemen.

LIEUTENANT JAMES MACKEY was son to Dr. Mackey, Buffalo. He joined the Sixty-third regiment, and was soon transferred to General Meagher's staff, and was mortally wounded at the battle of Antietam, while carrying orders from the general.

He was removed to the Hospital at Frederick, and was subsequently brought home by easy stages, by his father, who was anxiously attending him.

Though he had apparently rallied, he finally sank and died, on the 17th of October, just a month from the day he had received his wound. He was a brave young officer, and an intelligent, courteous young man, whose services were appreciated by his general, and whose amiable qualities made him a general favorite.

CAPTAIN DOMINICK CONNELLY was an able, efficient officer, and transferred to Invalid Corps on account of wounds received in action.

LIEUTENANT JOHN G. SELLERS, promoted from the ranks.

ADJUTANT P. GORMLEY, resigned on surgeon's certificate.

LIEUTENANT JOHN McCAFFREY, resigned from ill-health.

LIEUTENANT HURLEY, promoted from the rank of sergeant; discharged for physical disability.

LIEUTENANT EDWARD LEE was a brave, efficient officer; possessed considerable skill as an engineer.

LIEUTENANT MICHAEL GROGAN, wounded at Antietam.

LIEUTENANT TIMOTHY MURRAY.

LIEUTENANT CHARLES MCCARTHY, resigned from ill-health.

LIEUTENANT WILLIAM HIGGINS, resigned from ill-health.

LIEUTENANT LAURENCE DAIDY, promoted from sergeant.

LIEUTENANT JAMES GALLAGHER, promoted from sergeant.

CAPTAIN RICHARD P. MOORE, promoted from second-lieutenant, wounded at Fredericksburg.

CAPTAIN JOHN DWYER, promoted from sergeantcy, wounded at Antietam, was a brave, efficient, and intelligent officer.

JAMES H. ELLIOT, Assistant-surgeon, afterwards transferred.

LIEUTENANT WILLIAM F. MEEHAN, an excellent, efficient officer, resigned on surgeon's certificate.

LIEUTENANT LYNCH, wounded at Antietam, from the effects of which he died.

LIEUTENANTS WILLIAM TAYLOR and HART.

CAPTAIN THOMAS W. CARTWRIGHT, native of Kings County, was first adjutant of the regiment; wounded at Antietam; promoted to captain; resigned in 1863.

LIEUTENANT MATTHEW HART, native of Albany, Irish parents; enlisted as private in 1861; wounded at Fair Oaks; promoted to lieutenant, March, 1863; mustered out at consolidation.

LIEUTENANT PATRICK CHAMBERS, native of Mayo; enlisted

private in 1861; color-sergeant at first battle of Fredericksburg; promoted to lieutenant, and discharged in 1864 for disability.

LIEUTENANT WILLIAM DALY, native of Albany; of Irish parentage; enlisted in 1861; color-sergeant at Antietam, where he was wounded; promoted to lieutenant in December, 1862; mustered out by consolidation of regiment; enlisted again, served as private, and discharged for disability.

LIEUTENANT MICHAEL GROGAN, native of Tipperary, enlisted in 1861; promoted to sergeant; wounded at Antietam; promoted to lieutenant, and mustered out at consolidation; re-enlisted and attained rank of lieutenant; wounded again at Petersburg, and mustered out in consequence.

LIEUTENANT PATRICK J. O'CONNOR, promoted lieutenant from Quartermaster-sergeant, and mustered out by consolidation; native of Galway; enlisted in 1861.

CAPTAIN BRANNEGAN, discharged for ill-health.

CAPTAIN PATRICK JOSEPH CONDON, of Company G, Sixty-third Regiment, Irish Brigade, was born February 16th, 1831, at Craves, county Limerick, Ireland. At the outset of the American civil war he joined the Second Regiment N. Y. S. M., as private, but left it to aid in forming the Irish Brigade. He raised Company G, Sixty-third regiment, of which he was commissioned captain, September 24th, 1861. He served through the campaigns of 1861, '62, and '63, and was mustered out in June of the latter year. His devotedness to the cause of American liberty is second only to that of his native land.

LIEUTENANT JAMES M. SMART, a brave and efficient officer, killed in battle, May 12th, 1864.

LIEUTENANT D. P. ROOD.

CAPTAIN S. V. REEVES, promoted from first-lieutenant.

## A CONCISE HISTORY OF THE TWENTY-EIGHTH REGIMENT MASSACHUSETTS VOLUNTEER INFANTRY AND ITS LEADING OFFICERS.

The Twenty-eighth Massachusetts Volunteer Infantry, called into service by the President, September 24, 1861, organized at Boston, Massachusetts, October 8, 1861, and mustered into the United States service at Camp Cameron, Cambridge, Massachusetts, December 13, 1861, Colonel Monteith commanding, left Camp Cameron, January 11, 1862, and proceeded to Fort Columbus, New York harbor, where it remained till February 14, whence it embarked for Hilton Head, South Carolina, arriving there February 22, 1862. April 7, the regiment embarked on transports for Dawfusky Island. The right wing of the regiment, under Colonel Monteith, proceeded to Tybee Island, Georgia, May 12, where it remained till May 28, when it proceeded to Hilton Head. Placed in arrest May 20, Colonel Monteith did not again resume command of his regiment, and was discharged August 12, 1862, at Newport News, Virginia. The left wing embarked for Hilton Head, May 27, and on May 30 the whole regiment, Lieutenant-Colonel Moore commanding, left Hilton Head in transports for James Island, reaching there on the 1st of June.

### JAMES ISLAND.

The regiment skirmished June 1 and 2, losing five men wounded. June 16, in an unsuccessful assault upon Fort Johnson, on the upper part of the island, the regiment lost fourteen killed, fifty-two wounded, and four prisoners—aggregate seventy. Of this engagement, General H. W. Benham, U. S. A., in a letter to Governor Andrew, dated December 21, 1862, says * * "The major, G. W. Cartwright, and the most of the officers, with the great body of the regiment, behaved very handsomely through that affair, until they were recalled from the front by the order of General Stevens." July 6th, the regiment evacuated James Island, and returned to Hilton Head. July 16th, proceeded in transports to Newport News, Virginia, landing there July 18th. The same day the regimental band was mustered out of service. On the 20th the regiment was assigned to General Burnside's Corps. Lieutenant-Colonel Moore resigned July 25th.

### SECOND BULL RUN.

August 3d, Major Cartwright commanding, the regiment left Newport News, Virginia, and landed at Aquia Creek August 6th, proceeding the same day to Fredericksburg, where it went into camp. August 12th, left Fredericksburg to join General Pope, at Culpepper. The regiment was engaged in the campaigns of the Rapidan and Rappahannock, arriving at Centreville on the 28th of August. The regiment was ordered to the support of a battery, August 29th, remaining in that position all day. On the 30th of August, about two P. M., the regiment was ordered into the woods, and was exposed to a heavy fire of artillery and musketry. Falling back, under orders, at the end of three-quarters of an hour, it supported a battery until night, exposed to a heavy fire from the enemy's batteries. Eighteen men were killed, one hundred and nine wounded, and eight missing in this engagement, in which Major Cartwright was wounded.

### CHANTILLY.

On the afternoon of September 1st the regiment marched to Chantilly, where it engaged the enemy heavily and with success, losing fifteen killed, seventy-nine wounded, and five missing. The next day marched to Alexandria and through Washington.

### SOUTH MOUNTAIN.

Leaving Meridian Hill, September 7th, the regiment entered upon the Maryland campaign. On the 14th the regiment, at Turner's Gap, South Mountain, supported a battery during the day, and being on picket at night, was exposed to a heavy fire of musketry, losing six men wounded.

### ANTIETAM.

On the 17th day of September, the regiment was engaged at Antietam Creek. At eleven A. M. the regiment advanced, under fire from the enemy's batteries, till sheltered by a hill on the opposite bank of the creek. It crossed the creek, ascended the hill under a murderous fire, driving the enemy before it, till ordered back by the general commanding. Casualties, twelve killed and thirty-six wounded. On the 18th skirmished with the enemy.

During the fall the regiment remained with the Army of the Potomac, under Generals McClellan and Burnside. Colonel Richard Byrnes assumed command of the regiment October 18th, at Nolan's Ferry. On the 23d of November the regiment was transferred from the Ninth to the Second Corps, and was assigned to the Irish Brigade, of General Hancock's division.

### FREDERICKSBURG.

December 11th, the regiment broke camp at Falmouth, and cross-

49

ing the Rappahannock near Fredericksburg, took part in the gallant charge of General Hancock's division upon the enemy's works, December 13th, losing one hundred and fifty-seven killed, wounded, and missing. On the night of the 15th recrossed the river and returned to Falmouth, where it was still encamped December 31st.

The strength, present and absent, on that day was seven hundred and twenty, officers and men. During the year one hundred and nineteen recruits joined the regiment, ninety enlisted men were discharged, eighty-six deserted, and one hundred and thirty-seven died. Nine deserters were apprehended. Nineteen officers resigned, and seven died. Seventy-five men were killed in action, and twenty-seven died of their wounds. Total number of killed, wounded, and missing, for the year, five hundred and twenty.

### CHANCELLORSVILLE.

After the arduous campaigns of the year the regiment remained in camp till April 28th, when it moved with General Hancock's division to Chancellorsville, participating in that action and suffering a loss of twenty-six, killed, wounded, and missing. May 3d, the regiment assisted in hauling to the rear the guns of the Fifth Maine Battery by hand. May 5th, the regiment left the battle-field at night, and crossing the Rapidan at daybreak of the 6th, arrived in camp the same day.

### GETTYSBURG.

After the battle of Chancellorsville the regiment remained in camp and was exercised in drill till the 13th day of June, when it marched to the banks of the Rappahannock. The next day it marched to Stafford Courthouse. With the Second Corps it passed the remainder of the month in long and arduous marches, till it reached the battle-field of Gettysburg, Pennsylvania, early A. M. of the 2d of July. In the afternoon the Twenty-eighth Regiment, with the Brigade, was ordered to advance, and engaged the enemy at Little Round Top, driving them before it for a long distance, till after a long and obstinate engagement it was flanked both right and left, and compelled to retire with the Brigade precipitately, by order of the Brigade commander. One hundred and seven officers and enlisted men were killed, wounded, and missing, out of two hundred and twenty-four, on this day. The 3d of July, the regiment threw up breastworks on Cemetery Hill, and assisted in repelling the fierce onsets of the enemy. Although exposed to the tremendous cannonading of the enemy during the fight, but one man was wounded, owing to the felicitous nature of the ground.

On the 7th the regiment left the battle-field and marched to Taney-town, Maryland; the 8th, to near Frederick; the 9th, through Crampton's Gap, South Mountain; the 10th, to Jones's Cross Roads; the 14th, to Falling Waters; the 15th, to opposite Harper's Ferry; the 16th, to Pleasant Valley, Maryland; the 18th, through Harper's Ferry, Virginia, crossing the Potomac; 19th, to near Snicker's Gap; 20th, to Bloomfield; 22d, to Ashby's Gap; 23d, into Manassas Gap; 24th, to Markham; 25th, to White Plains; 26th, to Warrenton Junction; 30th, to Elk Run; 31st to Morrisville, Virginia, where it encamped during the month of August.

August 31st the regiment marched to U. S. Ford, supporting cavalry, returning to camp September 4th. September 12th, left Morrisville, and marched to Rappahannock Station; 13th, to Culpepper; 15th, to Slaughter Mountain; 17th, to Rapidan Station, where the regiment remained engaged in arduous picket duty, till October 6th, when it left the front for Culpepper, Auburn Hill, and Bristow Station. October 12th, marched and countermarched till October 14th, when the regiment was vigorously shelled while at rest on Auburn Hill. The regiment retreated to Bristow Station, with the division, skirmishing a part of the journey, losing one killed, two wounded, and three missing, till it arrived at Bristow Station, where it assisted materially in repelling the onsets of the enemy. Marched to Bull Run that night, remaining there till the 19th, when the regiment marched, reaching Auburn the next day. To near Warrenton on the 23d. The regiment crossed the Rappahannock at Kelly's Ford on the 7th day of November, and on the 8th went into camp on Shackleford's Farm. There the regiment remained till November 26th, when it crossed the Rapidan at Germania Ford, the army moving to Mine Run, Virginia.

## MINE RUN.

November 29th, near Robinson's Tavern, the left touching the plankroad, as skirmishers, Colonel Byrnes commanding, the regiment gallantly charged, driving the enemy's skirmishers from their pits back upon their works in the rear, losing nine men, wounded. December 1st, recrossed the river and returned to camp. December 5th, to Stevensburg, Virginia, near which town the regiment rested in substantial winter-quarters, constructed of logs.

The strength, present and absent, of the regiment, December 31st, 1863, was twenty-five commissioned officers and four hundred and seventy-seven enlisted men.

During the year one hundred and ninety-seven recruites, etc., joined the regiment; two hundred and forty-one enlisted men were discharged or transferred; one hundred and thirty-two deserted; fourteen died, and twenty-eight were killed in action. Thirty-nine deserters were apprehended; twenty-nine officers resigned. The aggregate killed, wounded, and missing, as far as reported, was one hundred and fifty-one.

## THE WILDERNESS.

The regiment remained quietly in winter-quarters, until May 3d, 1864, the monotony of camp-life disturbed only by a reconnoissance to the Rapidan River, February 6th, in which the Twenty-eighth took part. The regiment was becoming stronger, day by day, by the arrival of recruits.

On the 3d of May its aggregate strength was twenty-six commissioned officers, and seven hundred and five enlisted men; of these, four hundred and ninety-five officers and men were present with the regiment, and eighteen officers and four hundred and thirty-two men were for duty.

On this day the Twenty-eighth Massachusetts Volunteers broke camp at Stevensburg, Virginia, at 10 P. M., and marching all night, crossed the Rapidan River, at Ely's Ford, May 4th. During the early part of the day of May 5th the regiment acted as flankers to the Brigade, till the enemy was found, when several companies were sent out as skirmishers. Late in the afternoon most of the companies were collected together, and the regiment advanced in line into the woods, in the Wilderness, and engaged the enemy. Lieutenant-Colonel Cartwright, commanding, ordered the regiment to lie down, and in that mode awaited the driving in of our skirmishers. The battle soon opened. Veterans fought with the dash of recruits, recruits with the steadiness of veterans, and repulsed the oft-repeated charges of the enemy with heavy loss, strewing the ground in their front with files of dead and wounded. They fought steadily all the afternoon, until being out of ammunition, they were relieved by the One Hundred and Sixteenth Pennsylvania Volunteers, and retired. Here the gallant Captain McIntyre was fatally hit, while endeavoring to assist a wounded skirmisher inside of our line. Captain C. V. Smith was mortally wounded; Lieutenant-Colonel Cartwright also receiving a severe and painful wound in the left shoulder. The regiment was complimented by the brigade and division commanders for the gallant and successful manner in which they repulsed every attempt to break our line of battle.

On the 6th and 7th of May the regiment skirmished all day, losing a few men. The total loss in the Wilderness was two commissioned officers killed, and three wounded; fourteen enlisted men were killed, eighty-two wounded, and eighteen missing. Aggregate, one hundred and nineteen. To Todd's Tavern, May 8; the regiment and brigade advanced against the enemy late in the afternoon, but being flanked, retired in good order, without loss, to the intrenchment.

## Po River.

May 9, crossed the Po River. The next day the regiment was subjected to a heavy artillery fire; threw up breastworks the next day; during these operations the loss was four killed, five wounded, and two missing.

## Spottsylvania.

On the night of the 11th of May, Major Lawler commanding, the regiment left its works near the banks of the Po, leaving out a hundred men on picket, and passing through the Sixth Corps camp with the division, massed in a field in front of the enemy's works at Spottsylvania. At daylight, May 12th, charged the enemy's works with fixed bayonets, and uncapped pieces in column of division, closed in mass, and assisted in the capture of many guns, colors, and prisoners. Ten enlisted men were killed, one commissioned officer and forty-six enlisted men wounded and missing; aggregate, sixty-two, in the memorable charge of Hancock's invincible corps.

May 14th a part of the regiment was on the picket-line, where two guns between the lines were drawn out. One man was killed and one wounded.

## Spottsylvania—Second.

May 17, at night formed in column behind our works, and at daylight charged enemy's intrenchments, Major Lawler commanding the regiment, and Colonel Byrnes the brigade. Took the first line of works and held it for six hours, when the regiment was withdrawn in perfect order by the direction of General Barlow. The major and two captains were killed; three captains and one lieutenant wounded; nine enlisted men were killed, and twenty-six wounded; aggregate, 42.

May 20, at night, and May 21, marched to Millford Station; May 23, to the North Anna River; crossed that river on the 24th; May 27, recrossed the river, and May 29 reached Tolapotomy Creek, where the regiment remained till June 1st, losing

49*

men daily on picket. One killed and twelve wounded during these operations.

## COLD HARBOR.

June 1, a most severe march to Cold Harbor, reaching there the next day. At daybreak, June 3, Lieutenant A. B. West commanding the regiment, charged in line, advancing steadily over two ranges of hills, under a very heavy fire of musketry and artillery from the rebel position, on a third range. Enfiladed both right and left the Brigade was ordered back by the Brigade commander, after holding its advanced position for some hours. Colonel Byrnes commanding the Brigade, and Lieutenant West commanding the regiment, and eight enlisted men were killed; two commissioned officers, and thirty-five enlisted men were wounded; total, 47. Remained at Cold Harbor in works, exposed to the enemy's fire till June 12, losing one man killed and two wounded, when the regiment at night left its works for James River, which river was reached the next day.

## PETERSBURG.

June 14, at night crossed the James River on the transport Massachusetts. Remained near the bank of the river till two P. M. of the fifteenth, when the regiment made a forced march to Petersburg, reaching there at the end of eleven hours. Late in the afternoon of June 16, Lieutenant John B. Noyes commanding the regiment, charged in line, and took one line of the enemy's works, but pressed still further till brought to a stand-still on the slope of a hill, by the determined resistance of the enemy, who in vain assailed the advanced position of our troops; relieved at midnight, having sustained a loss of three killed, fourteen wounded and two missing. June 17, supported the gallant charge of the Ninth Corps. June 18, again charged the enemy, driving them from several pits without loss.

June 20th, the regiment was transferred from the Second to the First Brigade of the First Division, Second Corps; marched at night in the direction of the Weldon Railroad. The regiment acted as flankers during the day, and at night was sent out on picket.

## FIGHT OF JUNE 22D, BEFORE PETERSBURG.

Withdrawn from the picket-line at noon of the 22d, the regiment with the Brigade moved to the right, to the assistance of the Second Brigade, which was hard pressed, when the whole brigade was double-quicked back to its former position, and the Twenty-eighth Massachusetts Volunteers deployed as skirmishers on the right, and connecting with the Sixth Corps. By vigorously holding their ground and rapid firing the rebels were compelled to move towards the right, which was unprotected by skirmishers. They then charged, yelling; but meeting an unlooked-for obstacle in a strong line of works, were hurled back howling. The regiment was highly complimented on the spot by Generals Barlow and Miles for its splendid conduct. But two officers and one hundred enlisted men were in the engagement. Of these one was killed, nine wounded, and two missing.

The regiment remained in camp in reserve till the 9th day of July, when it relieved the pickets of the Fifth Corps, and so remained till sent out to support General Gregg's cavalry on the Jerusalem Plankroad on the 12th of July; the next day marched to the rear of the Eighteenth Corps and went into camp.

## Deep Bottom.

July 26, Captain James Fleming commanding the regiment, broke camp before Petersburg, about three P. M., and marched to Deep Bottom, arriving there about two A. M. of the 27th. The march was very hurried and exhausting. Shortly after daybreak the regiment was deployed as skirmishers, occupying the right of the line of the First Brigade, the One Hundred and Eighty-third Pennsylvania being in the centre, and the Fifth New Hampshire on the left.

While the One Hundred and Eighty-third Pennsylvania and Fifth New Hampshire were engaging the enemy in front, the Twenty-eighth succeeded in getting in on the enemy's left flank, and by a well-directed fire along their works, caused them to retire in confusion, leaving in our possession four twenty-pounder Parrott guns, with caissons and ammunition. Several prisoners also were captured, among them one commanding officer. The following is official :

" Headquarters First Brigade, First Division, Second Corps.

" Captain Fleming commanded the Twenty-eighth Regiment Massachusetts Volunteers, under my charge on the 27th inst., and to his gallantry was due, in great measure, the success of the assault, which resulted in the capture of four guns and a number of prisoners.

" Jas. C. Lynch,
" Colonel commanding Brigade."

" HEADQUARTERS FIRST DIVISION, SECOND CORPS.

"The Twenty-eighth Massachusetts Volunteers were the first to strike the enemy's lines on the 27th, when the First Brigade drove a brigade of rebels from their works, capturing four twenty-pounder rifled pieces and several prisoners.

"NELSON A. MILES,

"Brigadier-General Volunteers."

At dark of the 29th the regiment, with the corps, marched back to Petersburg, arriving there before daybreak, and during the day lay in rear of the Ninth Corps. Casualties during the period two enlisted men killed and two wounded.

## DEEP BOTTOM NO. 2.

Remained in camp till the 12th day of August, when the regiment, Captain Fleming commanding, marched to City Point. The next day at noon the regiment took transportation for Deep Bottom, arriving there Sunday at daybreak. The regiment made a demonstration upon a rebel battery during the forenoon, suffered a loss of one commissioned officer and three enlisted men killed and eleven enlisted men wounded. Early on the 16th the regiment with the Brigade moved out to the Charles City Cross-Roads, supporting General Gregg's Cavalry. The regiment advanced as skirmishers on the right of the road, and engaged the enemy. After a stubborn and well-contested resistance against superior forces, the regiment was obliged to fall back upon the Brigade, losing heavily in killed, wounded, and missing. After dark of the 20th the regiment, with the corps, marched back to before Petersburg, reaching there at eight A. M. of the 21st, whence it marched to the Gurley House, near the Weldon Railroad, during the afternoon. Losses during this period seven enlisted men wounded, twenty-two missing in action. On the 22d the regiment marched to

## REAMS' STATION

and to the Perkins House, and commenced destroying the railroad towards Reams' Station ; continued destroying the railroad on the 23d and 24th, tearing up the road and burning rails to beyond Mrs. Smart's house. During portions of these days the regiment was on picket. Returned to Reams' Station on the evening of the 24th, occupied the works to the right of the station, the left of the regiment resting near the railroad. On the 25th the regiment participated in the well-contested engagement at Reams' Station. The regiment fought gallantly, and were the last to leave the works and among the first to reoccupy them. The casualties were, one enlisted man killed, two commissioned officers and seven enlisted men wounded, and twenty-four enlisted men missing in action. After dark the regiment, with the division, fell back to the vicinity of Williams' Farm, where it remained till the 27th, when it returned to its old camping-ground near Petersburg.

On the 6th September broke camp and marched to the Williams' House—the Brigade marched the day before—where the regiment was busily engaged in constructing the works connected with the Ninth Corps, till the 8th inst., when the regiment marched to the Jones House and encamped. September 16th, the regiment, with the Brigade, went out to support the cavalry, which had gone in search of stolen cattle. Returned to camp on the 17th.

September 24th, relieved a portion of the Tenth Corps in the front line of works. Relieved on the 29th. October 1st marched to the left. On the 2d to battery No. 4, to garrison the work and change it to a fort. Remained there till the 4th of October, when the regiment marched to the front, to guard the front line of works. Relieved October 9th, and on the 14th detailed to guard battery No. 9, where the regiment is at present stationed. Late casualties, one killed and three wounded.

During the months of April and May the men were engaged in planting batteries upon the islands surrounding Fort Pulaski, working chiefly at night, under the guns of the fort, up to their middle in water; and such was the secrecy of their movements, that it was not until the steamboat from Savannah, carrying supplies to the fort, was brought to by a thirty-pound shot from the masked battery erected on Jones' Island, that the enemy were made aware that the "Faugh-a-Ballaghs" (as the Twenty-eighth were called) had been working with such effect under the most disheartening circumstances. The island upon which this battery was erected is a small one, situated in the Savannah River, composed of marshy ground, so soft that a man could not stand upon it without danger of sinking out of sight. One of the Twenty-eighth was missed one night, and never heard of after; it was supposed that, in groping in the dark, he had missed his footing and sank through the mire until he was drowned or suffocated; yet upon such ground was a formidable battery erected, by night, by laying a platform of plank and long timbers, and then hauling the heavy guns by hand from the flat-boats. One of the guns slipped from the planks laid from the boat to the platform, and instantly sank out of sight through the mud. This work was performed chiefly under the supervision of Colonel Beard, late of the Forty-eighth N. Y. Vols., who deserves the utmost credit for the untiring energy and perseverance he displayed, and the splendid success of his apparently vain undertaking.

On the 20th of December, 1864, the term of service of the regiment having expired, Colonel Cartwright, commanding, received orders to proceed to Boston with the remnant of his gallant regiment, consisting of *twenty-one* enlisted men, he being the only officer of the original organization whose name still appeared on the muster-roll.

The aggregate number joined for duty since the organization was about 1,703 ; the list of killed, wounded, and missing in action reach 1,133—a fearfully heavy proportion. During the Wilderness campaign alone the Twenty-eighth lost eight commanding officers killed, and twelve wounded, and four hundred and eight enlisted men. But one officer escaped unhurt during this fearful campaign. Who shall say, in view of this record of the devotion of Irishmen to the cause of freedom in this their adopted country, that they are not entitled to the sympathy, aid, and support of this nation, in the endeavor to free their own beloved, down-trodden land ?

The officers and men whose term of service had not expired were consolidated into a battalion under the command of Major James Fleming, and remained with the Brigade until the close of hostilities, when, with the Brigade, they were mustered out.

Among the officers of this regiment were many who deserve more than a passing notice.

COLONEL RICHARD BYRNES, its commander, during the greater part of 1863 and '64, was an officer of the regular army, having served about fifteen years, and was promoted from the ranks for gallant and meritorious services. Brave almost to rashness, he always led his men, who knew no fear under his eye ; a strict disciplinarian, just to each and all in the exercise of his authority, he commanded the respect and esteem of those under him, and to his efforts is mainly due the high reputation for steadiness and discipline which the Twenty-eighth enjoyed. During the winter and spring of 1864 he was engaged in recruiting, but the moment the campaign opened hastened to join his command. On his arrival he assumed command of the Brigade, and at the battle of Cold Harbor, June 3d, he was fatally wounded. He lived long enough to be conveyed to Washington, where his wife (being apprised by telegraph) was permitted the sad privilege, denied to so many during the war, of ministering to his wants and receiving his last words. His remains were brought to Jersey City, where he resided, and buried with military honors.

COLONEL GEORGE W. CARTWRIGHT, who succeeded the lamented Byrnes, was born in Dublin, Ireland. His family came to this country when he was a child, and have since resided in New York and vicinity. He entered the service on the 19th of April, 1861, as a private in the Twelfth N. Y. S. M., Colonel Daniel Butterfield, under whose strict discipline he soon became one of the best soldiers in the command, and was promoted three times during the short campaign of the regiment, being mustered out at expiration of three months' term of service, as second-sergeant of Company A. A few days after being mustered out, having recruited the requisite number of men, he was mustered in for three years in the Twelfth N. Y. Vols., Colonel Weeks, as lieutenant. While serving in this capacity, he was invited to accept the position of adjutant of the Twenty-eighth Massachusetts Vols., then forming in Boston as the second Irish regiment from that State, the Ninth being the first. Though a perfect stranger in Massachusetts, the offer was too flattering to decline, and resigning his commission in the Twelfth he entered the Twenty-eighth, and by his military knowledge and well-known energy of character rendered good service in organizing the command, and establishing the discipline necessary to success. As major, he commanded the regiment during the latter part of the battle of James Island, S. C., June 16th, 1862, and received the favorable notice of the general commanding for his conduct under very trying circumstances. He was in command during the memorable Pope campaign of 1862, and the fatigue and privations endured, with wounds received at second Bull Run, nearly cost him his life. Recovering, against the opinion of medical men, he rejoined his command, and shared in all their hardships and glories until December 20th, 1864, when mustered out by reason of expiration of term of service. His father, Captain Thomas W. Cartwright, served with distinction in the Sixty-third, and his brother, Captain Thomas W. Cartwright, Jun., was killed at Malvern Hill.

LIEUTENANT-COLONEL JEREMIAH W. COVENEY joined the regiment as Lieutenant of Company A, at its organization, and won his subsequent promotions by gallant and meritorious conduct in the field. He was a fine officer in all respects. While serving on the staff of General Miles, in the Wilderness campaign, he received a severe wound, which it was feared would prove fatal, and incapacitate him from further service. Colonel Coveney took a very active part in the late Fenian movement on Canada.

MAJOR ANDREW J. LAWLER, who was killed in the fight at Spottsylvania, May 18, was a fine type of the Irish soldier—brave, frank, impressive, and generous. He was beloved by all; possessed of an ardent, hopeful temperament which no hardship, however severe, could dampen, he was the life of a bivouac; while his rollicking humor and endless jokes often shortened the weary march, until the "irrepressible major" of the Twenty-eighth and his ambling pony, were as well known throughout the division as the general commanding. Severely wounded at James' Island, S. C., 1862, he remained a prisoner in Charleston for a long time; on his return he was made major of the regiment, and while thus serving and in command of his regiment he fell, fighting nobly for the land of his adoption, and in a few short minutes all that remained of the gay, gallant, whole-souled Lawler was clay.

MAJOR JAMES FLEMING.—This officer entered the Twenty-eighth as a private in Company B, and won his promotion to his subsequent rank by merit and bravery. Small in stature, very quiet and unassuming in his deportment, distrustful of his own powers, it was only when under fire that he was seen to advantage. Cool and brave, he was quick to seize any advantage the enemy might leave open. He was wounded at Fredericksburg, and seriously in the Wilderness campaign; at Deep Bottom, July 27, 1864, the Twenty-eighth under his command charged, and captured a four-gun battery of parrot pieces. Of his conduct at that time the general commanding division took special notice, and he was complimented in General Orders for gallantry. He remained in the field until the close of hostilities.

CAPTAIN JAMES MAGNER.—This officer resigned a position on the staff of General Hunter, to accept a commission in the Irish Twenty-eighth; of fine personal appearance, a splendid rider and swordsman, he could have enjoyed a life of comparative ease as a staff officer, but his ambition was to be a regimental officer or commander, and well did he deserve the fulfilment of his hopes. But, just as the chances of war had placed him in command, the fatal bullet cut short his thirst for a glorious career, and with sword in hand, cheering on his men to the charge, on the 18th of May, 1864, he fell dead at Spottsylvania, far from home and family (he resided in Minnesota).

The bivouac in summer, or social circle in winter quarters, keenly missed the manly form of Magner, and the voice that had so often interested us with jokes of Irish life at home, and thrilling adventures of Indian warfare in the far West, in which he was an active participant, was stilled in death.

DOCTOR PETER EMMET HUBON,—born in Ireland; practising before the war in Warrenton, Massachussetts. A highly educated and skilful surgeon, much endeared to the Brigade by his amiable disposition and social qualities. Mustered out with the regiment.

ASSISTANT-SURGEON BARRINGTON.—Mustered out with the regiment.

## SKETCH OF THE OFFICERS AND SERVICES OF THE ONE HUNDRED AND SIXTEENTH PENNSYLVANIA VOLUNTEERS, IRISH BRIGADE.

The One Hundred and Sixteenth Pennsylvania Regiment left Philadelphia for the seat of war September 3d, 1862, and arrived at Fairfax, Virginia, on the 20th, where it joined General Seigel's command, and remained with him until the 6th of October, when it started towards Harper's Ferry, which it reached on the 9th, and was then placed in the Irish Brigade.

The Second Corps was ordered out on a reconnoissance towards Charlestown, this place being about eight miles back of Harper's Ferry. It was on this reconnoissance that the One Hundred and Sixteenth could form the first idea of a skirmish or battle. Marched across the Shenandoah River, around and across Loudon Heights, down through Loudon Valley towards Worcester; on reaching Snickersville found some of the enemy's cavalry on picket duty, which were driven away after a short skirmish; on the next day marched again, and reached Warrenton on the 9th of November. Here they were encamped for a few days, and then led towards Fredericksburg, arriving near Falmouth on the 17th of November.

The regiment participated in the bloody battle of Fredericksburg, and distinguished itself by its coolness and bravery during that fearful ordeal through which the Brigade passed. Among its officers wounded were Colonel D. Heenan and Major G. H. Bardwell.

The regiment was then left in command of Lieutenant-Colonel St. Clair Mulholland, who led it bravely and nobly to the very front, and whilst gallantly performing his duties, he fell wounded, and left it without any field-officers. Amongst other officers wounded were

50

Lieutenant Williams, in command of Company C ; Garrett Nowlan ; Captain J. O. O'Neill, who was so badly wounded that he had to leave the service ; Robert Montgomery met his death while gallantly performing his duties ; Color-Sergeant William Tyrrel, being wounded in six different places, was for his gallantry promoted to second-lieutenant Company C.

The loss in the One Hundred and Sixteenth Regiment on this day was as follows : Two officers killed, ten officers wounded, eighteen men killed, fifty-two men wounded, seventeen men missing.

On Sunday the Brigade crossed into the city again and remained there until the evening of the 15th, when it recrossed the river and proceeded to camp.

On 26th of January, 1863, the One Hundred and Sixteenth was consolidated into a battalion of four companies, commanded by Major St. Clair A. Mulholland.

The company officers retained were as follows : William A. Peet, captain Company A ; William M. Hobart, first-lieutenant ; Louis J. Sacriste, second-lieutenant. John Teed, captain Company C ; S. G. Willaur, first-lieutenant ; J. B. Parker, second-lieutenant. J. McNamara, captain Company B ; Francis F. Quinlan, first-lieutenant ; Robert T. McGuire, second-lieutenant. J. O. O'Neill, captain Company D ; Garrett Nowlan, first-lieutenant ; Henry D. Price, second-lieutenant.

A great many changes were subsequently made with the officers, owing to resignations, discharges, etc. Remained here in camp in winter-quarters, passing away the time in drilling, reviews, and inspections, etc., until the 27th of April, when the brigade once more broke camp and marched up the river, leaving a part of the Sixty-third at Banks' Ford for picket duty, while the rest marched to United States Ford, where they were stationed to hold that post.

They participated in the battle of Chancellorsville, as the accompanying official reports and documents will show. We must state, though, that the saving of the Fifth Maine Battery was not solely confined to the One Hundred and Sixteenth, for volunteers from the other regiments participated in the noble deed.

HEADQUARTERS ONE HUNDRED AND SIXTEENTH REGIMENT
PENNSYLVANIA VOLUNTEERS, IRISH BRIGADE,
CAMP NEAR FALMOUTH, VIRGINIA, May 7, 1863.

CAPTAIN M. W. WALL, A. A. A. GENERAL, IRISH BRIGADE :

SIR—In accordance with Paragraph 742, Article 36, Army Regulations, I have the honor to submit the following report of the part taken by my regiment in the action near Scott's Mills, Virginia, May 3d, 4th, and 5th, 1863, to your consideration.

After sundown, on the evening of May 1st, I marched my command, in obedience to orders received, from U. S. Ford, where we were then stationed, to a point near Scott's Mills, Va., and took up a position indicated to me by Brig.-Gen. Meagher, commanding the Irish Brigade, with orders to hold the position. I at once established my regiment in line facing the enemy, and then threw out a sufficient number of pickets to cover the front and flanks of my command. I then caused my men to stack arms, and ordered them to remain near their arms during the night, in order that we might be prepared to repel any attack of the enemy.

Every thing remained quiet during the night in the vicinity of my command, although heavy firing was heard on our left until late in the evening. On the morning of May 2d my regiment still remained in the same position. Heavy firing was heard all day, consisting chiefly of artillery, intermixed with volleys of musketry ; but the principal attack of the evening commenced about four o'clock P. M. From this hour until long after dark the fire was incessant, never stopping for a moment, and seeming to be about one and a half miles distant. At the commencement of the action I caused my men to take arms, and shortly afterwards (by order of Gen. Meagher) changed front to the rear on first company, and took up a position along the edge of a wood, with orders to give the enemy a flanking fire should they make their appearance on the road. No enemy appearing, and the firing having ceased, we once more stacked arms, and awaited with anxious hearts for the coming morrow.

On the morning of May 3d the firing again began. My regiment was under arms at an early hour, and calmly awaited the moment when the Irish Brigade would once more be ordered to the front, to add new laurels to its already historic name, and new lustre to its already time-worn and honored flags.

Shortly after nine o'clock A. M. the order came. I immediately called in my pickets ; with my regiment on the left of the Brigade, marched by the right flank up the main road towards the scene of action. Passing many brigades and divisions in line of battle, we soon came in sight of the enemy, who appeared on our right. The Brigade, marching by the right flank, here countermarched, in order to avoid inversion. Brig.-Gen. Meagher now formed line, the left resting on the edge of a wood. During the time the Brigade was forming line of battle the shells fell among us in great quantities, killing and wounding many in the several regiments of the Brigade.

Shortly after the line was formed the Fifth Maine Battery, commanded by Captain Leppene, came dashing up the road and took a position in an open field on the left of the Brigade and of my regiment, and opened fire on the enemy's infantry, dense masses of which were plainly visible. The battery had hardly got in position ere two or three batteries of the enemy's guns opened on them with fearful effect, killing and wounding the men and horses with great rapidity. In about an hour from the time the battery had commenced firing, every gun, with the exception of one, had been silenced, and but two men remained with their guns.

At this moment Major Scott, of General Hancock's staff, dashed up to me, and ordered me to take enough men of my command and remove the deserted guns to the rear, as they were in great danger of being captured by the enemy. I immediately instructed my men what to do, and led them towards the guns in question. We took three guns off the field, and I dispatched a sufficient number of men with each to haul it up the road, and to the rear. Some men of the One-Hundred and Fortieth Pennsylvania Vols. removed one off the field, and had taken it some distance up the road, when, for want of enough force, they had to stop. I at once sent some of my men to their assistance, and the gun was got off in safety. After passing to the rear some distance I found that one of my lieutenants, Sacriste, of Co. D, had taken off another gun, entirely unknown to me, and had it then in his possession—thus making, in all, four guns taken off the field by my command.

In removing, I found it necessary to order some of my men to lay down their muskets, as it was impossible to work at their guns with them in their hands. Seventy-three of the men did so. After I saved the guns, I ordered some of my men who remained to gather up as many of the muskets as they could carry, and bring them along; but the close proximity of the enemy rendered it impossible to save them. Captain Nowlan, who was one of those that went back for the muskets, reports that the enemy was within a few yards of where the muskets were lying, and that it would be impossible to save them without having the men taken prisoners by the enemy. I took the four guns about three miles to the rear, and turned them, along with the one taken by the One-Hundred and Fortieth Pennsylvania Vols., over to Lieutenant Wilson, of Gen. Hancock's staff. In removing the guns I was greatly assisted by Lieutenant Wilson, of the One Hundred and Forty-eighth Pennsylvania Vols., now of Gen. Hancock's staff. This officer acted with great bravery, and personally assisted me in removing the guns.

During the action Lieutenant Whitford, of Gen. Meagher's staff, called on me for twenty-five men, for the purpose of throwing out skirmishers in front of the Brigade. I detailed twenty-five men from Company C, who reported to A. A. A. General at once.

The following named men of the Sixty-ninth and Sixty-third N. Y. came gallantly on the field and assisted in the removal of the guns. Sergeant James Dwyer, Sergeant John Murray, Sergeant John Coghlen, and Captain John Harney, of the Sixty-third N. Y.; Sergeant Thomas Neelan, privates William Lennox, Martin Morgan, James Quigley and James Sheehan, Sixty-ninth N. Y. The name of the man who remained with his gun when all others had left was James H. Lebrookes; this man is worthy of all praise.

I would be doing injustice to the regiment I have the honor to command were I to close my report without mentioning the cool and gallant manner in which the regiment behaved under fire. In regard to my officers, I cannot say too much in their praise. Captains Teed and Nowlan vied with each other in their gallant behavior.

Lieutenants Sacriste, Roeder, McKnight, and Halpin, all acted in a manner that challenges our admiration. The services of our regimental adjutant, T. A. Dorwart, were invaluable. He acted in his usual manner, brave to a fault.

The casualties were one man killed; one officer slightly wounded; eighteen men wounded, and four men missing. Respectfully submitted,

ST. CLAIR MULHOLLAND,

Maj. com'ing One Hundred and Sixteenth
Pa. Vols., Irish Brigade.

HEADQUARTERS HANCOCK'S DIVISION,
May 7, 1863.

MAJOR—The major-general commanding the division directs me to express to you his gratification at the manner in which you performed your duty as Field-Officer of the Day for the division, on the 3d and 6th inst., at Chancellorsville.

The general was especially pleased with your action in reference to extinguishing the fire in front of the picket-line. He had ordered the fire to be put out several times, but the order was not carried into effect till you were placed in command of the pickets. I am, sir, very respectfully, your obedient servant,

(Signed)    W. G. MITCHELL, A. D. C. & A. A. A. G.

50*

(OFFICIAL.)

HEADQUARTERS IRISH BRIGADE,
May 8th, 1863.

MAURICE W. WALL, Capt. & A. A. A. G., to Major St. Clair Mulholland, commanding Battalion One Hundred and Sixteenth Pa. Vols.,—through Brigadier-General Meagher, commanding 2d Brigade 1st Division :

HEADQUARTERS IRISH BRIGADE,
FALMOUTH, VA., May, '63.

The Brig.-Gen. commanding directs me to add his own expression of gratification to that of the Major-General commanding division, in his letter of commendation to you for your conduct on the 3d and 6th, at the battle of Chancellorsville.

I have the honor to remain, your obedient servant,

MAURICE W. WALL, Capt. & A. A. A. G.
To Major Mulholland, One Hundred and Sixteenth Pa. Vols.

COLONEL DENNIS HEENAN, wounded at the battle of Fredericksburg, and honorably discharged the service, January 26th, 1863. Was formerly in the English service, and for many years held the position of lieutenant-colonel of the Second Brigade, Pennsylvania Militia. Colonel Heenan recruited a regiment of Militia in Philadelphia, in honor of Thomas Francis Meagher. The company was called the Meagher Guards. Born in Tipperary, Ireland, aged 42.

LIEUTENANT-COLONEL ST. CLAIR A. MULHOLLAND went out with the regiment, and commanded at the battle of Fredericksburg, where he was wounded in the early part of the day. The regiment being consolidated into a battalion of four companies, Lieutenant-Colonel Mulholland was mustered out as lieutenant-colonel, and mustered in as major. Commanded the battalion at the battle of Chancellorsville, May 3d and 4th, 1863, and received a letter of commendation from Major-General Hancock, indorsed by General Meagher, for his conduct during the fight. Born in Lisburn, county Antrim, Ireland ; aged 28. He was subsequently brevetted brigadier-general.

MAJOR GEORGE H. BARDWELL went out as major of the regiment. Fought gallantly at the battle of Fredericksburg, and received a severe wound in the left hand, which rendered it useless for life. Was honorably discharged February 24th, 1863, on account of disability. Born in Pennsylvania ; aged 32 years.

CAPTAIN LAWRENCE KELLY fought well at the battle of Fredericksburg; honorably discharged January 26th, 1863, the regiment being consolidated into a battalion. Born in Ireland.

CAPTAIN JOHN TEED was formerly connected with the regular service; behaved gallantly during the battle of Chancellorsville; born in State of New York; aged 47.

CAPTAIN JOHN O'NEILL fought gallantly at the battle of Springfield, Miss., under General Lyon. Was greatly distinguished for his splendid conduct at the battle of Fredericksburg, and received a frightful wound, and was in consequence honorably discharged. Born in Ireland; aged 30 years.

CAPTAIN FRANCIS T. QUINLAN commanded Company H at the battle of Fredericksburg, and fought well; was honorably discharged on account of physical disability. Born in Ireland; aged 28 years.

CAPTAIN SENECA G. WILLAUR went out with the regiment as first-lieutenant, and was promoted to captain for gallant conduct at the battle of Fredericksburg, at which place he received a shell wound. Participated in the battle of Chancellorsville. Born in Pennsylvania; aged 30 years.

CAPTAIN GARRETT ST. PATRICK NOWLEN went out with the regiment as second-lieutenant, and was promoted to captain for gallant conduct at the battle of Fredericksburg, where he was severely wounded. Again distinguished himself at Chancellorsville. Born in Philadelphia, of Irish parents; aged 29 years.

ADJUTANT J. ROBINSON MILES fought at Fredericksburg, and was slightly wounded; since then was honorably discharged on account of physical disability. Born in Philadelphia; aged 30 years.

CHAPLAIN REV. EDWARD McKEE, distinguished for his gentleness in camp and bravery in battle, attending to his duties under fire. Born in Ireland; aged 35 years.

FIRST-LIEUTENANT GEORGE M. BOOK—promoted from the ranks for good conduct, and was honorably discharged.

FIRST-LIEUTENANT JOSEPH H. G. MILES distinguished himself for gallant conduct at Fredericksburg; aged 29 years.

FIRST-LIEUTENANT HENRY D. PRICE went out with the regiment as second-lieutenant; promoted for his bravery at the battle of Fredericksburg.

FIRST-LIEUTENANT RICHARD WADE fought well at Fredericksburg, and was at that time second-lieutenant of Company H; went out with the regiment as sergeant; aged 28 years.

FIRST-LIEUTENANT J. LOUIS SACRISTE was distinguished for his gallantry at the battle of Chancellorsville, May 3d, 4th, and 5th, 1863. Born in Philadelphia, of French and Irish parents; aged 24 years.

SECOND-LIEUTENANT ROBERT MONTGOMERY, killed in the battle of Fredericksburg, where he fought gallantly, and commanded Company J during the action; was an excellent man, a good officer, and a pleasant companion.

SECOND-LIEUTENANT CHRIS. FOLTZ, killed at the battle of Fredericksburg, where he fought gallantly, in command of Company H; an excellent man and a good officer; aged 35 years.

SECOND-LIEUTENANT WILLIAM H. TYRRELL came out with the regiment as color-sergeant; promoted for his excellent and gallant conduct at the battle of Fredericksburg, where he kept the colors flying until he was shot six times. Born in Ireland; aged 26 years.

SECOND-LIEUTENANT WM. H. BILLINGHAUS went out with the regiment as sergeant; promoted for gallant conduct in battle, December 13th, 1863.

FIRST-LIEUTENANT GEORGE ROEDER went out with the regiment as private, and rose to first-lieutenant by his military ability and good conduct; participated in the battles of Fredericksburg and Chancellorsville; aged 28 years; was for many years in the regular service.

SECOND-LIEUTENANT McKNIGHT was promoted from the ranks for good conduct; fought well and acted bravely.

SECOND-LIEUTENANT GEORGE HALPIN was promoted for his good conduct and bravery in the battles of Fredericksburg and Chancellorsville; served in the English army, and was severely wounded in the leg at the siege of Delhi, and afterwards in the side, in the same campaign.

## ORIGINAL STRENGTH OF THE THREE OLD REGIMENTS OF THE BRIGADE, WITH OFFICIAL LIST OF CASUALTIES.*

This does not include the losses at Bristow Station, and other minor engagements, nor the losses from sickness and other causes.

| | | |
|---|---:|---|
| Sixty-ninth New York Volunteers | 950 | men |
| Recruits received at Camp California, Va., winter of '61 and '62 | 61 | " |
| Recruits received in the Peninsula, 1862 | 13 | " |
| "        "        in Maryland, September 12th, 1862 | 95 | " |
| "        "        "        "        19th,        " | 50 | " |
| Total | 1,069 | |

| | | |
|---|---:|---|
| Sixty-third New York Volunteers | 750 | men |
| Recruits received April, 1862, at Camp California, Va., | 100 | " |
| "        "        September, in Maryland | 50 | " |
| Total | 900 | |

| | | |
|---|---:|---|
| Eighty-eighth New York Volunteers | 800 | men |
| Recruits at Camp California to winter of '61 and '62 | 150 | " |
| At other times | 25 | " |
| Total | 975 | |
| Grand Total | 2,944 | |

### CASUALTIES.

#### GAINES' HILL, June 27th, 1862.

| | |
|---|---:|
| Sixty-ninth.—5 enlisted men missing | 5 |
| Sixty-third.—1 enlisted man wounded and 5 missing | 6 |
| Eighty-eighth.—None. | |
| | 11 |

---

* This report has been taken from official documents, in the hands of Colonel James E McGee, who, I am happy to learn, is preparing for publication a history of the Irish regiments and organizations that have served in the American war.

D. P. C.

ALLEN'S FARM, SAVAGE STATION, NELSON'S FARM, AND MALVERN HILL, June 29th and 30th, and July 1st, 1862.

Sixty-ninth.—1 officer killed, 7 wounded, 19 enlisted men killed, 120 wounded, and 56 missing........................ 203

Sixty-third.—1 officer killed, 1 missing, 18 enlisted men wounded, and 50 missing............................. 70

Eighty-eighth.—2 officers killed, 2 wounded, 6 enlisted men killed, 57 wounded, and 50 missing................... 127

Total......................................... 400

### ANTIETAM.

Sixty-ninth.—4 officers killed, 6 wounded, 40 enlisted men killed, 151 wounded................................ 201

Sixty-third.—5 officers killed, 6 wounded, 31 enlisted men killed, 158 wounded................................ 200

Eighty-eighth.—2 officers killed, 2 wounded, 26 enlisted men killed, 75 wounded................................ 105

Total......................................... 506

### FREDERICKSBURG, VA., December 13th, 1862.

Sixty-ninth.—2 officers killed, 14 wounded, 112 enlisted men killed, wounded, and missing....................... 128

Sixty-third.—1 officer killed, 6 wounded, 1 enlisted man killed, 32 wounded, 4 missing ...................... 44

Eighty-eighth.—4 officers killed, 8 wounded, 14 enlisted men killed, 88 wounded, and 10 missing................... 124

Total......................................... 296

### CHANCELLORSVILLE, VA., May, 1863.

Sixty-ninth.—2 officers wounded, 3 enlisted men killed, 5 wounded........................................ 10

Sixty-third.—1 officer killed, 2 wounded, and 3 enlisted men wounded........................................ 6

Eighty-eighth.—4 officers wounded, 3 enlisted men killed, 18 wounded, and 23 missing.......................... 48

Total......................................... 64

## GETTYSBURG.

Sixty-ninth.—1 officer wounded, 5 enlisted men killed, 13
  wounded, 6 missing.................................... 25
Sixty-third.—1 officer wounded, 5 enlisted men killed, 9
  wounded, and 1 officer missing, and 7 men ............. 25
Eighty-eighth.—1 officer killed, 1 wounded, 7 enlisted men
  killed, and 16 wounded............................... 25
                                                        ——
    Total........................................... 75

Grand total, killed, wounded, and missing............. 1,352

# INDEX